EXPRESSIONISM IN THE CINEMA

Traditions in World Cinema

General Editors
Linda Badley (Middle Tennessee State University)
R. Barton Palmer (Clemson University)

Founding Editor
Steven Jay Schneider (New York University)

Titles in the series include:
Traditions in World Cinema
by Linda Badley, R. Barton Palmer and Steven Jay Schneider (eds.)
Japanese Horror Cinema
by Jay McRoy (ed.)
New Punk Cinema
by Nicholas Rombes (ed.)
African Filmmaking
by Roy Armes
Palestinian Cinema
by Nurith Gertz and George Khleifi
Czech and Slovak Cinema
by Peter Hames
The New Neapolitan Cinema
by Alex Marlow-Mann
American Smart Cinema
by Claire Perkins
The International Film Musical
by Corey Creekmur and Linda Mokdad (eds.)
Italian Neorealist Cinema
by Torunn Haaland

Magic Realist Cinema in East Central Europe
by Aga Skrodzka
Italian Post-Neorealist Cinema
by Luca Barattoni
Spanish Horror Film
by Antonio Lázaro-Reboll
Post-beur Cinema
by Will Higbee
New Taiwanese Cinema in Focus
by Flannery Wilson
International Noir
by Homer B. Pettey and R. Barton Palmer (eds.)
Films on Ice
by Scott MacKenzie and Anna Westerståhl Stenport (eds.)
Nordic Genre Film
by Tommy Gustafsson and Pietari Kääpä (eds.)
Contemporary Japanese Cinema Since Hana-Bi
by Adam Bingham
Chinese Martial Arts Cinema 2nd edn.
by Stephen Teo
Expressionism in the Cinema
by Olaf Brill and Gary D. Rhodes (eds.)

www.edinburghuniversitypress.com

EXPRESSIONISM IN THE CINEMA

Edited by Olaf Brill and Gary D. Rhodes

EDINBURGH
University Press

Edinburgh University Press is one of the leading university presses in the UK. We publish academic books and journals in our selected subject areas across the humanities and social sciences, combining cutting-edge scholarship with high editorial and production values to produce academic works of lasting importance. For more information visit our website: www.edinburghuniversitypress.com

© editorial matter and organization Olaf Brill and Gary D. Rhodes, 2016
© the chapters their several authors, 2016

Edinburgh University Press Ltd
The Tun—Holyrood Road
12 (2f) Jackson's Entry
Edinburgh EH8 8PJ

Typeset in 10/12.5 pt Sabon by
Servis Filmsetting Ltd, Stockport, Cheshire

A CIP record for this book is available from the British Library

ISBN 978 1 4744 0325 2 (hardback)
ISBN 978 1 4744 0326 9 (webready PDF)
ISBN 978 1 4744 1119 6 (epub)

The right of the contributors to be identified as authors of this work has been asserted in accordance with the Copyright, Designs and Patents Act 1988 and the Copyright and Related Rights Regulations 2003 (SI No. 2498).

Published with the friendly support of the Friedrich-Wilhelm-Murnau-Stiftung, Wiesbaden.

MURNAU STIFTUNG

CONTENTS

List of Illustrations — vii
List of Contributors — xi
Traditions in World Cinema — xv

Introduction — 1

PART I. EXPRESSIONISM IN GERMAN CINEMA

1. Expressionist Cinema—Style and Design in Film History — 15
   Thomas Elsaesser

2. Of Nerves and Men: Postwar Delusion and Robert Reinert's *Nerven* — 41
   Steve Choe

3. Franjo Ledić: A Forgotten Pioneer of German Expressionism — 67
   Daniel Rafaelić

4. Expressionist Film and Gender: *Genuine, A Tale of a Vampire* (1920) — 77
   Mirjam Kappes

5. "The Secrets of Nature and Its Unifying Principles": *Nosferatu* (1922) and Jakob von Uexküll on *Umwelt* — 93
   Steve Choe

CONTENTS

6. *Raskolnikow* (1923): Russian Literature as Impetus for German
   Expressionism 117
   John T. Soister

PART II. EXPRESSIONISM IN GLOBAL CINEMA

7. The Austrian Connection: The Frame Story and Insanity in Paul
   Czinner's *Inferno* (1919) and Fritz Freisler's
   The Mandarin (1918) 133
   Olaf Brill

8. "The Reawakening of French Cinema": Expression and
   Innovation in Abel Gance's *J'accuse (1919)* 145
   Paul Cuff

9. Here Among the Dead: *The Phantom Carriage* (1921) and the
   Cinema of the Occulted Taboo 169
   Robert Guffey

10. *Drakula halála* (1921): The Cinema's First Dracula 190
    Gary D. Rhodes

11. *Le Brasier ardent* (1923): Ivan Mosjoukine's *clin d'œil*
    to German Expressionism 220
    Bernard McCarron

12. Nietzsche's Fingerprints on *The Hands of Orlac* (1924) 235
    Phillip Sipiora

13. "True, Nervous": American Expressionist Cinema and the
    Destabilized Male 248
    Robert Singer

14. *Dos monjes* (1934) and the Tortured Search for Truth 266
    David J. Hogan

15. Maya Deren in Person in Expressionism 287
    Graeme Harper

    Index of Names 303
    Index of Film Titles 309

ILLUSTRATIONS

Frontispiece	Fern Andra and Hans Heinrich von Twardowski in a publicity still for *Genuine*	xviii
I.1	Werner Krauß as the title character in *Das Cabinet des Dr. Caligari/The Cabinet of Dr. Caligari*	1
I.2	Trade advertisement for *Das Haus zum Mond*	3
I.3	Frame from Watson and Webber's Expressionist version of *The Fall of the House of Usher*	9
I.4	Frame from *The Life and Death of 9413: A Hollywood Extra*	9
1.1	Werner Krauß in a publicity still for *Das Cabinet des Dr. Caligari/The Cabinet of Dr. Caligari*	17
1.2	Werner Krauß in a publicity still for *Das Cabinet des Dr. Caligari/The Cabinet of Dr. Caligari*	23
1.3	Hans Heinrich von Twardowski, Lil Dagover, and Friedrich Fehér in a publicity still for *Das Cabinet des Dr. Caligari/The Cabinet of Dr. Caligari*	28
1.4	Hans Heinrich von Twardowski and Erna Morena in a publicity still for Karlheinz Martin's *Von morgens bis Mitternacht/From Morning to Midnight*	31
1.5	Werner Krauß as Jack the Ripper in a publicity still for Paul Leni's *Das Wachsfigurenkabinett/Waxworks*	34
2.1	German trade advertisement for Robert Reinert's *Nerven*	46
2.2	A frame from *Nerven*	47

2.3	A frame from *Nerven*	47
2.4	A frame from *Nerven*	49
2.5	A frame from *Nerven*	58
2.6	A frame from *Nerven*	58
2.7	A frame from *Nerven*	60
3.1	Franjo Ledić	66
3.2	Franjo Ledić	67
3.3	German Film program brochure *Illustrierter Film-Kurier*	68
3.4	German trade advertisement, published in *Der Kinematograph*	70
3.5	Croatian trade advertisement	71
3.6	German trade advertisement	73
3.7	Book cover, Berlin, 1920	75
4.1	German film poster, artwork by Josef Fenneker	78
4.2	Fern Andra in a publicity still for *Genuine*	80
4.3	Fern Andra and Ernst Gronau in a publicity still for *Genuine*	81
4.4	Hans Heinrich von Twardowski, Ernst Gronau, and Fern Andra in a publicity still for *Genuine*	82
4.5	Hans Heinrich von Twardowski and Fern Andra in a publicity still for *Genuine*	85
4.6	Hans Heinrich von Twardowski and Fern Andra in a publicity still for *Genuine*	88
5.1	A frame from *Nosferatu*	94
5.2	A frame from *Nosferatu*	96
5.3	A frame from *Nosferatu*	97
5.4	A frame from *Nosferatu*	98
5.5	A frame from *Nosferatu*	99
5.6	A frame from *Nosferatu*	103
5.7	A frame from *Nosferatu*	109
5.8	A frame from *Nosferatu*	113
6.1	Publicity still for Robert Wiene's *Raskolnikow*	119
6.2	Publicity still for Robert Wiene's *Raskolnikow*	124
6.3	Autographed postcard of Grigori Chmara in *Raskolnikow*	127
7.1	Franz Herterich and Grete Lundt in a publicity still for *Inferno*	135
7.2	German trade advertisement, published in *Der Film*	137
7.3	Vienna Insane Asylum in *The Mandarin*	138
7.4	Harry Walden and Carl Goetz in *The Mandarin*	139
7.5	Harry Walden in *The Mandarin*	140
7.6	Harry Walden in *The Mandarin*	142
8.1	Romuald Joubé as Jean Diaz	146
8.2	Séverin-Mars as François Laurin	152
8.3	Jean Diaz stands guard over the dead, who await their resurrection	157

9.1	Victor Sjöström's innovative use of double exposure dramatically brings to life the legend that lies at the heart of *The Phantom Carriage*	182
9.2	At midnight on New Year's Eve, David Holm (Victor Sjöström) comes face to face with Death's Driver (Tore Svennberg)	186
10.1	Paul Askonas and Margit Lux in *Drakula halála*	193
10.2	Paul Askonas in *Drakula halála*	196
10.3	Paul Askonas in *Drakula halála*	201
10.4	Károly Lajthay in *Vorrei morir*	206
10.5	Actor Carl Goetz, aka Karl Götz	210
10.6	Actress Magda Sonja, who likely played one of Drakula's brides	214
10.7	The cover of Lajos Pánczél's novella adaption of *Drakula halála*	218
11.1	Ivan Mosjoukine	220
11.2 and 11.3	The Expressionist Gaze: Elle and Z's intimacy, as depicted in the nightmare sequence at the beginning of *Le Brazier ardent*	223
11.4	Dark desires exposed: in Elle's nightmare, a wealthy man is solicited on the seedy backstreets of Paris	226
11.5	"The husband" gains admission to "The Seekers Club"	228
11.6	"The husband" faces a panel of psychologists in the committee room	228
11.7	The dance contest begins: Elle looks on as Z begins playing the piano	231
11.8	Licentious female dancers affected by the dance contest	232
12.1	Orlac's furrowed brow reveals his new identity	236
12.2	Pure evil	237
12.3	Orlac grasps his fate but struggles to understand why	239
12.4	Orlac holds his identity in his hands	240
12.5	The eyes are a window to the soul	242
12.6	Orlac has insight into his transformed nature	243
12.7	Grotesquerie in the service of evil	245
13.1	*The Telltale Heart*; the insane man	253
13.2	*The Wrong Man*; Manny is questioned by the police	256
13.3	*Shadows and Fog*; Kleinman is questioned	258
13.4	Edvard Munch, *Ashes*	260
13.5	Ernst Ludwig Kirchner, *Nollendorfplatz*	261
14.1	The disturbed composer Javier (Carlos Villatoro) longs so fiercely for love that his reality shifts, and assumes a sinister aspect	272
14.2	Javier secretly watches his beloved Ana (Magda Haller), who appears to give her heart to Javier's rival, Juan (Victor Urruchúa)	275

ILLUSTRATIONS

14.3	Driven to despair and, possibly, madness, Javier retreats to the monastery's organ	279
15.1	The play of light and shadow	288
15.2	Dreams in a dreamscape	291
15.3	The hooded figure	293
15.4	Maya Deren	295
15.5	Attention to emotional states	297
15.6	Symbolic objects	300

CONTRIBUTORS

Olaf Brill works as a freelance writer and editor for film institutes, museums and festivals, including the German Film Institute—DIF, Frankfurt, the Filmmuseum Berlin, and CineGraph, Hamburg. For seven years, he has edited the festival catalogues for *cinefest* International Festival of German Film Heritage. Brill received a PhD from Bremen University for a thesis on *The Cabinet of Dr. Caligari*. His elementary book *Der Caligari-Komplex* was published in German in 2012. He also writes for science fiction magazines and comic books.

Steve Choe is Associate Professor of Film Studies at San Francisco State University. He is the author of *Afterlives: Allegories of Film and Mortality in Early Weimar Germany* (2014). He researches and teaches courses on German cinema, South Korean cinema, and topics in film theory, philosophy, and phenomenology.

Paul Cuff is an Associate Fellow within the Department of Film and Television Studies at the University of Warwick, England. The main focus of his research has been silent cinema and, in particular, the work of the French filmmaker Abel Gance. His work has been published in *Film History*, *La Furia Umana*, and *Studies in French Cinema*. Cuff's first monograph, *A Revolution for the Screen: Abel Gance's "Napoléon"*, was published in June 2015.

Thomas Elsaesser is Professor Emeritus at the Department of Media and Culture of the University of Amsterdam and, since 2013, Visiting Professor at Columbia University. He has authored, edited and co-edited some twenty volumes on early cinema, film theory, European cinema, Hollywood, new media and installation art. His most recent books are *German Cinema—Terror and Trauma: Cultural Memory Since 1945* (2013) and (with Malte Hagener) *Film Theory—An Introduction through the Senses* (2nd edition, 2015). He is currently completing a book on *European Cinema and Continental Thought*.

Robert Guffey is a lecturer in the Department of English at California State University, Long Beach. His most recent book is a journalistic memoir entitled *Chameleo* (2015). He is also the author of a collection of novellas entitled *Spies and Saucers* (2014). His first book of nonfiction, *Cryptoscatology: Conspiracy Theory as Art Form*, was published in 2012. He has written stories and articles for numerous magazines and anthologies, among them *After Shocks*, *Catastrophia*, *The Chiron Review*, *The Los Angeles Review of Books*, *The Mailer Review*, *The New York Review of Science Fiction*, *Pearl*, *Phantom Drift*, *Postscripts*, *The Third Alternative*, and *Video Watchdog Magazine*. "Here Among the Dead," Guffey's contribution to this anthology, will be included in his forthcoming book entitled *Hollywood Haunts the World: An Investigation into the Cinema of Occulted Taboos*.

Graeme Harper is Dean of the Honors College at Oakland University, Michigan. He was formerly a Research Professor at the University of Texas Medical Branch, Galveston, and Paschal P. Vacca Distinguished Professor of Liberal Arts at the University of Montevallo, Alabama. Prior to that he was foundation director of the National Institute for Excellence in the Creative Industries (NIECI) at the University of Wales, Bangor. His previous works include *Film Landscapes: Cinema, Environment and Visual Culture* (2013), with Jonathan Rayner, and *The Unsilvered Screen: Surrealism in Cinema* (2007), with Rob Stone. He is co-editor of the journals *Studies in European Cinema* and the *Journal of European Popular Culture*. A fiction writer, he also writes on the practice and critical understanding of creative writing.

David J. Hogan began his professional life as a magazine writer, while in college in 1973. He became a Los Angeles-based film journalist and, later, an editor and executive in Chicago book publishing, specializing in film, general nineteenth- and twentieth-century history, military aviation, World War II, and vintage automobiles. He has worked with notables that include Walter Cronkite, Myrlie Evers-Williams, Herman Spertus, Tom Hayden, Sen. Daniel K. Inouye, Maureen O'Hara, and John S. D. Eisenhower. As a film historian and author, Hogan is engaged by the aesthetics and cultural significances of just about everything shot in black and white, particularly vintage horror and science fiction, thrillers, comic shorts, and film noir. His first book about genre film was published in 1980; he is currently at work on his eighth. His essays have appeared in numerous multi-author books, including titles devoted to Edgar Ulmer, Joseph H. Lewis, and neglected B-movies. Hogan has three grown-up children and lives with his wife Kim in Arlington Heights, Illinois.

Mirjam Kappes is a PhD candidate in Media and Cultural studies at the a.r.t.e.s. Graduate School for the Humanities in Cologne. Her research interests include digital media and nostalgia, transmedia storytelling, visual discourses in urban space, and media aesthetics with a focus on photography and film. Prior to her graduate studies, Mirjam has worked in journalism, public relations and communications; she regularly writes for *Kultur-Port*, a German art and culture magazine, and *MEDIENwissenschaft: Rezensionen*, a reviews journal on media science publications. She became interested in expressionist cinema while working for CineGraph, a Hamburg-based institute for historical film research.

Bernard McCarron holds a PhD in Film Studies from The Queen's University of Belfast. He has written extensively on the influence of Alfred Hitchcock's films on the contemporary visual arts. His main research interests include the afterlife of cinema and its legacy in the digital age. He is the author of the forthcoming book *The Paradigm Case: The Cinema of Hitchcock and the Contemporary Visual Arts* (2015).

Daniel Rafaelić is an independent film historian from Zagreb, Croatia. While an employee of Croatian Cinematheque he was Head of the Film Restoration and Preservation Department. He has edited several books and special DVD releases, and has published papers in numerous journals. In 2005, he directed the documentary *The Other Side of Welles* about the life of Orson Welles and his legacy in Croatia. In 2013, he published the book *Kinematografija u NDH: Filmmaking in the Independent State of Croatia, 1941–1945*. Currently, he teaches film in the departments of History, Archaeology and Psychology in the Zagreb Faculty of Humanities. His forthcoming book *Cinema of the Sun*, which interrogates the subject of Ancient Egypt in the cinema, will be published in 2016.

Gary D. Rhodes, PhD, currently serves as Postgraduate Director for Film Studies at The Queen's University in Belfast, Northern Ireland. He is the author of *Lugosi* (1997), *White Zombie: Anatomy of a Horror Film* (2002), and *The Perils of Moviegoing in America* (2012), as well as the editor of such anthologies as *Edgar G. Ulmer: Detour on Poverty Row* (2008) and *The Films of Joseph H. Lewis* (2012). Rhodes is also the writer-director of such documentary films as *Lugosi: Hollywood's Dracula* (1997) and *Banned* *in Oklahoma* (2004). Currently, he is at work on a history of the American horror film to 1915 and a biography of William Fox.

Robert Singer is a Professor of English at Kingsborough, CUNY, and Professor of Liberal Studies at the CUNY Graduate Center, where he also served as Deputy Executive Director of the program. He received a PhD from New York University in Comparative Literature. He co-edited *Zola and Film* (2005) and *The Brooklyn Film* (2003), and he also co-authored *The History of Brooklyn's Three Major Performing Arts Institutions* (2003). He is currently working on a book on naturalism and film interrelations. He has also written articles on the Faust myth for the Mellen Series in Comparative Literature, the Rodopi Perspectives in Modern Literature, and the *Centennial Review*, as well as articles on film studies for *Film/Literature Quarterly*, *Griffithiana*, *Dedalus*, *Act 4*, *Teaching English in the Two Year College*, and *Postscript*.

Phillip Sipiora is Professor of English and Film Studies at the University of South Florida. He is the author or editor of five books and has published approximately three dozen scholarly essays. He has lectured nationally and internationally on twentieth-century literature and film and was founding editor of *The Mailer Review*. Sipiora has published essays on the films of Billy Wilder, Stanley Kubrick, Edgar Ulmer, and Joseph H. Lewis, and is editor of the forthcoming volume *The Films of Ida Lupino* (Edinburgh University Press).

John T. Soister, who recently retired from teaching English, Spanish, and Latin to mostly uninterested young Americans, currently enjoys putting his feet up. He intends to keep writing about old films until ordered to stop. With his wife Nancy, he is planning on traveling, sponging off his adult progeny, volunteering at animal shelters, and working with folks more elderly than he. He is the author of the following books: *Of Gods and Monsters* (1998), *Claude Rains: A Comprehensive Illustrated Reference* (1999), *Conrad Veidt On Screen* (2002), *Up from the Vault* (2004). He is also co-author of *American Silent Horror, Science Fiction and Fantasy Feature Films 1913–1929* (2012) and *Many Selves: The Horror and Fantasy Films of Paul Wegener* (2012). Together with frequent collaborator Henry Nicolella, he is working on yet another invaluable collection of essays on vintage genre motion pictures.

TRADITIONS IN WORLD CINEMA

General editors: **Linda Badley and R. Barton Palmer**
Founding editor: **Steven Jay Schneider**

Traditions in World Cinema is a series of textbooks and monographs devoted to the analysis of currently popular and previously underexamined or undervalued film movements from around the globe. Also intended for general interest readers, the textbooks in this series offer undergraduate- and graduate-level film students accessible and comprehensive introductions to diverse traditions in world cinema. The monographs open up for advanced academic study more specialized groups of films, including those that require theoretically-oriented approaches. Both textbooks and monographs provide thorough examinations of the industrial, cultural, and socio-historical conditions of production and reception.

The flagship textbook for the series includes chapters by noted scholars on traditions of acknowledged importance (the French New Wave, German Expressionism), recent and emergent traditions (New Iranian, post-Cinema Novo), and those whose rightful claim to recognition has yet to be established (the Israeli persecution film, global found footage cinema). Other volumes concentrate on individual national, regional or global cinema traditions. As the introductory chapter to each volume makes clear, the films under discussion form a coherent group on the basis of substantive and relatively transparent, if not always obvious, commonalities. These commonalities may be formal, stylistic or thematic, and the groupings may, although they need not, be popularly identified as genres, cycles or movements (Japanese horror, Chinese martial arts cinema, Italian Neorealism). Indeed, in cases in which a group of films is not already commonly identified as a tradition, one purpose of the volume is to establish its claim to importance and make it visible (East Central European Magical Realist cinema, Palestinian cinema).

Textbooks and monographs include:

- An introduction that clarifies the rationale for the grouping of films under examination
- A concise history of the regional, national, or transnational cinema in question
- A summary of previous published work on the tradition
- Contextual analysis of industrial, cultural and socio-historical conditions of production and reception
- Textual analysis of specific and notable films, with clear and judicious application of relevant film theoretical approaches
- Bibliograph(ies)/filmograph(ies)

Monographs may additionally include:

- Discussion of the dynamics of cross-cultural exchange in light of current research and thinking about cultural imperialism and globalization, as well as issues of regional/national cinema or political/aesthetic movements (such as new waves, postmodernism, or identity politics)
- Interview(s) with key filmmakers working within the tradition.

For our friends, George Chastain and Henry Nicolella

—O.B. and G.R.

Fern Andra and Hans Heinrich von Twardowski in a publicity still for Robert Wiene's *Genuine* (1920). *(Source: German Film Institute—DIF, Frankfurt)*

INTRODUCTION

Figure I.1 Werner Krauß as the title character in Robert Wiene's *Das Cabinet des Dr. Caligari/The Cabinet of Dr. Caligari* (1920). *(Courtesy of Friedrich-Wilhelm-Murnau-Stiftung, Wiesbaden; source: German Film Institute—DIF, Frankfurt)*

INTRODUCTION

The history of Expressionism in the cinema is marked not only by those films that embraced the German art movements of the early twentieth century, most famously *The Cabinet of Dr. Caligari* (Robert Wiene, 1920), but also by those who have sought to study, define, and explain the subject area, resulting in an extended conversation that may have obfuscated as much as it has clarified.

Despite commentary from such notable figures as Béla Balázs and Kasimir Edschmid, two figures have towered above the others in terms of their lasting influence. In *From Caligari to Hitler: A Psychological History of the German Film* (Princeton University Press, 1947), Siegfried Kracauer attempted to explain Weimar-era German cinema not for its own sake, but rather to increase "knowledge of pre-Hitler Germany in a specific way." He adds, "the films of a nation reflect its mentality in a more direct way than other artistic media for two reasons," the first being that they are collaborative works and the second that they target the "multitude."[1]

Of the Weimar period, meaning November 1918 to January 1933, he added: "The German soul, haunted by the alternative images of tyrannic rule and instinct-governed chaos, threatened by doom on either side, tossed about in gloomy space like the phantom ship in *Nosferatu* [F. W. Murnau, 1922]."[2] For Kracauer, Expressionism in the cinema was German, and it anticipated the rise of Nazism.

And then there was Lotte Eisner, who also sought to connect Expressionism and film culture with political culture, albeit in a manner quite different from Kracauer. In her landmark text *The Haunted Screen* of 1952 (English edition 1969), she complains: "the word 'Expressionist' is commonly applied to every German film of the so-called 'classical' period," meaning Weimar cinema produced between 1918 and 1933.[3] And yet, *The Haunted Screen* nevertheless constructs an expansive category for Expressionism, one in which Fritz Lang, F. W. Murnau, and many others operated. Eisner's approach draws not only upon Expressionism, but also German Romanticism and the theater of Max Reinhardt in an effort to understand key works of Weimar cinema from an art-historical perspective. As for Kracauer, the foundation of her discussion is national cinema.

As Thomas Elsaesser observes in *Weimar Cinema and After: Germany's Historical Imaginary*, "Kracauer and Eisner have become part of this film history, have become themselves Caligari-like and Cassandra-like figures, at least as long as the history of Nazism 'haunts' the history of modern Germany."[4] Put another way, the views of Kracauer and Eisner—particularly as recorded in those two books—have become a part of the story of German Expressionism, and of the historical imaginary that comprehends it. And to them much credit should go, not merely for problematizing the meaning of Expressionism, but for bringing much important attention to the films they discussed.

While elusive, the label "Expressionism" retains much power to fascinate and engage viewers. The advertising slogan "You Must Become Caligari!" haunts us even in the twenty-first century, though precisely what that phrase might mean continues to be a source of debate. Elsaesser notes:

> No single stylistic label could hope to cover the many innovative ideas about film décor, the distinctive *mise-en-scene* of light and shadow, or the technical advances in cinematography usually attributed to Weimar filmmakers. And yet, in retrospect, a unity imposed itself on the films, their subjects and stories.[5]
>
> [. . .] It seems that, starting with *The Cabinet of Dr. Caligari*, the films usually indexed as Weimar cinema have one thing in common: they are invariably constructed as picture puzzles. Consistently if not systematically, they refuse to be "tied down" to a single meaning.[6]

The pieces of those puzzles are many, and some remain missing, whether in the form of lost films like *Das Haus zum Mond* (1921) or in films which survive, but which have not been critically examined.

Figure I.2 Trade advertisement for Karlheinz Martin's lost Expressionist film *Das Haus zum Mond* (1921), published in *Der Kinematograph* (1920).

INTRODUCTION

At a minimum, one can and perhaps should talk about Expressionism in the cinema, rather than an Expressionist cinema, by which we mean that the cinema in Germany or elsewhere has rarely presented an unadulterated Expressionist aesthetic. After all, *Caligari*—the quintessential Expressionist film—actually features very little of the lighting stimmung that marks much of the visual aesthetic commonly understood to be Expressionist. Here one might also invoke the "Jack the Ripper" segment of Paul Leni's *Waxworks* (1924), though it prompted even Eisner in *The Haunted Screen* to refer to its "purely decorative" use of Expressionism; such an analysis is in addition to the fact that it is a segment within an anthology, and the other two stories feature little of the aesthetic hallmarks of Expressionism.[7]

Nevertheless, many films do make use of Expressionism, even as they also draw upon other aesthetic traditions and ideologies. Indeed, this very fact has provided an anchor story of film history, one that tells the tale of *Caligari*'s heirs. German Expressionism came to life onscreen in the Weimar era, or at least during the first few years of it, and then, as if a cinematic ghost, it reappeared in the Hollywood horror films of the 1930s, in part owing to non-German filmmakers intentionally drawing upon *Caligari*, such as James Whale with *Frankenstein* (1931) and Robert Florey with *Murders in the Rue Morgue* (1932). Other versions of the same story might begin even earlier, citing such Hollywood films as Paul Leni's *The Cat and the Canary* (1927). At any rate, the third act of the story is Hollywood film noir, influenced by the aforementioned eras and created in some cases by German *émigrés*, those persons like Fritz Lang, Robert Siodmak, and Edgar G. Ulmer who had relocated to America, often owing to the rise of Nazism.

If there is a fourth act in this version of events, it takes place later in the twentieth century. For example, Elsaesser describes renewed interest among filmmakers in deploying Expressionist motifs in the cinema of neo-noir, science fiction, and horror. Here he is likely thinking of such Hollywood films as *L.A. Confidential* (1997), *Blade Runner* (1982), and *Dark City* (1998). To be sure, it would be difficult to argue that *The Crow* (1994) is an Expressionist film, but it would be equally difficult to deny that Expressionism influenced its *mise-en-scène*. Here again is Expressionism in the cinema, rather than an Expressionist cinema.

In academic treatment of Expressionism in the cinema, a deliverance was needed from the paradigmatic works of Kracauer and Eisner. Their versions of film history had been repeated for many years and seemed to be the final word on the subject, even though many things stated there were inaccurate, viewed only in the light of the authors' respective theories, or even downright wrong. Starting in the 1980s, a movement labeled by Thomas Elsaesser "New Film History" sought to explore new sources and ultimately find new theories to explain film history, regarding complex factors such as technology, sociology, economy, and many others. Elsaesser noted in 1986:

> To do film history today, one has to become an economic historian, a legal expert, a sociologist, an architectural historian, know about censorship and fiscal policy, read trade papers and fan magazines, even study Lloyds Lists of ships sunk during World War One to calculate how much of the film footage exported to Europe actually reached its destination.[8]

Our view of film history has changed, because more and better sources have become available over the last few decades. Restoration projects have been conducted on many "forgotten" films which were unavailable before, or even believed to be lost. In recent years, many pictures have been restored which were practically unknown before, and therefore not taken into account by film historians, including the *Caligari* successor *Genuine* (Robert Wiene, 1920) and, even more importantly, the *Caligari* predecessors *Nerven* (1919) and *The Mandarin* (1918). Much new information has been discovered about classic films which was not considered by Kracauer and Eisner, such as the finding of an original *Caligari* script in the 1970s, and the unraveling of the *Caligari* production history in Olaf's book *Der Caligari-Komplex* (German edition 2012, not yet available in English).

To the extent that the present anthology attempts to engage with the history of Expressionism and the cinema, it does not only seek to resolve ongoing debates about the precise parameters of the art movement and how they manifest in particular films (though certain chapters do broach that necessarily unavoidable controversy). By contrast, this collection has two other goals. One of these is to follow Elsaesser's call for further serious study in this area. Elsaesser wrote:

> My hope is that Weimar films, now that they have been embraced by today's popular culture, can once more become objects of "serious" study, and besides being appropriated, can also be appreciated: maybe even giving rise to a new "kino-debate."[9]

Popular culture needs to continue to discuss Weimar cinema along with what have, at least at times, been understood as Expressionist films. Important restorations have continued, most famously of *Metropolis* in 2010, which incorporated footage rediscovered in Argentina, and even *Caligari* in 2014, based on the newly-found camera negative. Works like John Soister's popular-audience biographies *Conrad Veidt On Screen: A Comprehensive Illustrated Filmography* (McFarland, 2002) and *Many Selves: The Horror and Fantasy Films of Paul Wegener* (BearManor Media, 2012, coauthored with Henry Nicollela) have been published.[10]

However, the restorations of films like Robert Wiene's *Genuine* have provoked relatively little discussion in scholarly circles. Certainly this is not to suggest that major interventions in the area ceased after the publication of Elsaesser's monograph. Most notably, Camden House published the collection *Expressionist Film: New Perspectives* in 2003; Tony Kaes took a different look at Weimar cinema as "shell shock cinema" in 2009; and, in a huge exhibition organized via cooperation between the German Film Institute and Mathildenhöhe Darmstadt, an institute for research on German art and culture from around 1900 onwards, Expressionism was viewed as "Total Artwork."[11] Those books have added importantly to the body of knowledge about key German films, including avant-garde cinema of the Weimar period.

Nevertheless, the editors of this volume perceive the need for continued discussion in this area, in particular as it seems that academics currently working in Film Studies, particularly those publishing in the English language, are not concentrating on Weimar cinema. Indeed, one of the editors was recently (and quite confidently) told by a notable colleague that the subject of German Expressionism was "dead." Such a comment is clearly debatable, but it is true that English-language publications in the area have been few. It is further true that German Studies seems to be in decline in the academy, particularly in English-speaking countries.

Arising from these concerns, Part I of this volume focuses on German films that have often been read as Expressionist, or at least as featuring Expressionist motifs, and also expands the discussion by considering films that have been largely overlooked in previous scholarship. Here is one of the two key reasons that the present volume has been compiled: to shed light on German films that have been hiding in the dark.

Part I begins with Thomas Elsaesser's "Expressionist Cinema—Style and Design in Film History," which undertakes an interrogation of what he refers to as an "ambiguously coded" film movement that arrived in Germany with "high culture credentials" and "extreme stylization in décor" born out of "penury and necessity." In his view, "Expressionism chose to enlist the cinema not in issues of realism, not even in the quest for 'truth,' but in the search for enduringly equivocal, fundamentally sceptical, and transparently ironic modes of representation."

Steve Choe's "Of Nerves and Men: Postwar Delusion in Robert Reinert's *Nerven*" builds on the foundation provided by Elsaesser and proceeds to examine a specific film, one that has hitherto received little attention. Choe rightly provides a psychoanalytic reading of the paranoid delusions depicted in the film, specifically around its character Roloff, whose internalized trauma is "expressed through irrational imagery" that "allegorize[s] the wounds of war."

From there, Daniel Rafaelić examines Franjo Ledić's little-known film *Angelo, das Mysterium des Schlosses* (1919). Here the issues involve questions both of transnational cinema—insofar as Ledić was a Croatian director working in Berlin—and of lost cinema, as no copy of this pivotal yet forgotten film is known to survive.

As already noted, a dearth of scholarly work exists on Robert Wiene's *Genuine, A Tale of a Vampire*. Mirjam Kappes intervenes in this area by applying gender studies to the "dramatic social changes in the post-war Weimar society, especially the erosion of traditional male and female roles." Here Wiene creates primary narrative danger for the male lead not in the form of a male rival, but instead from an "empowered, dangerous woman who pulls all the strings."

Revisiting a key work in this area, Steve Choe illuminates Murnau's *Nosferatu* (1922) by reading the sequence in which vampires are depicted as corresponding with spiders, polyps, and flesh-eating plants. As Choe notes, the sequence recalls science films of the era, but he also argues that the cinematic image does not merely document reality, but is continuous with the flux of life. For Choe, the surface of the film screen is composed as an expressionist surface, whereby figure and ground, interior and exterior interact with one another.

John Soister concludes Part I by engaging with Robert Wiene's *Raskolnikow* (1923) in a manner familiar to those who know his biographies of Veidt and Wegener. Soister's popular style attempts to narrativize a film plot that adapts Dostoevsky's novel *Crime and Punishment* (1866) into abbreviated form, one suited for "Expressionistic interpretation, what with its dealing with madness and sundry other forms of askew behavior." As with Rafaelić's work on *Angelo*, Soister's on *Raskolnikow* reiterates the important point that non-German source material played a role in what are often regarded as examples of German Expressionist cinema.

Part II of the book seeks to augment the narrative of "From German Expressionism to Hollywood Horror and Film Noir" by liberating the discussion of Expressionism from the confines of German studies, Weimar cinema, and mainstream American movies. Here a number of scholars collectively attempt to redefine our understanding of the Expressionist aesthetic by exploring particular film texts made prior to and shortly after *Caligari* in countries *other* than Germany and in paradigms other than Hollywood.

Olaf Brill initiates this section with his discussion of two Austrian films produced shortly before *The Cabinet of Dr. Caligari*: Paul Czinner's lost, supposedly "expressionistic" *Inferno* (1919) and, especially, Fritz Freisler's recently restored *The Mandarin* (1918), which anticipates some of *Caligari*'s key motifs. With his intimate knowledge of *Caligari*'s production history, Brill raises the question of whether *The Mandarin* could even have had an influence on the *Caligari* shooting script.

Paul Cuff's "The Reawakening of French Cinema" extends the discussion geographically further from Germany by offering a detailed textual and contextual study of Abel Gance's epic war drama *J'accuse* (1919). For Cuff, *J'accuse* is a product not merely of commercial and artistic ambition, but also of the "competing influences of Romanticism and Modernism, Expressionism and Impressionism."

For Robert Guffey, Victor Sjöström's Swedish film *The Phantom Carriage* (1921) bears the influence of the transgressive metaphysics of Theosophy, particularly in its challenge to the Judeo-Christian ethos as regards what awaits humans after death. The esoteric subtext informs a film that is, as Guffey maintains, a "strange and elegant mixture of realism and expressionism, Christianity and hermeticism, complexity and simplicity."

While Murnau's *Nosferatu* constituted the first screen adaptation of Stoker's 1897 novel *Dracula*, Gary D. Rhodes' "*Drakula halála* (1921): The Cinema's First Dracula" reveals that the novel had inspired an earlier film, one directed by Károly Lajthay in Hungary in 1921. As with Rafaelić's work on Ledić, Rhodes explores a lost film through other primary sources that do survive. Such materials make it apparent that Lajthay's film bore the narrative influence of *Caligari*, as well as—even if in a small measure—its *mise-en-scène* as well.

Bernard McCarron helps concretize the volume's emphasis on the influence of German Expressionism in other national cinemas, particularly insofar as it presented a *mise-en-scène* that also drew upon other artistic and cinematic traditions and movements. Working along lines similar to Cuff and Guffey, McCarron brings much-needed attention to Ivan Mosjoukine's *Le Brasier ardent* (1923), the product of a Russian actor/director working in France.

Philip Sipiora provides a speculative inquiry into the "fragments of Nietzschean gesture, sensibility, and sensitivity" connected to Expressionism in general and Robert Wiene's Austrian film *The Hands of Orlac* (1924) in particular. Sipiora thus discovers a tragic spirit embedded in the film, one that can be decoded by an understanding of Nietzsche's exploration of irrationality and horror. As with *Genuine*, restorations of *Orlac* are readily available, but have not thus far elicited extended discussion from scholars.

While gender issues have provided the source of discussion in terms of Weimar cinema, similar concerns in American Expressionist films of the 1920s have been largely ignored. Robert Singer seeks to redress that fact in his chapter on the destabilized male in such films as Charles Klein's *The Telltale Heart* (1927) and Melville Webber and James Watson's *The Fall of the House of Usher* (1928). As with Soister's *Raskolnikow*, Singer's chapter provides insight into the use of non-German narrative source material (in this case Poe) as a vehicle for Expressionist cinema.

Continuing this volume's effort to reclaim not only lost films, but those which have been undeservedly ignored, David J. Hogan leads us into the expressionist landscape of Juan Bustillo Oro's *Dos monjes* (*Two Monks*,

INTRODUCTION

Figure I.3 Frame from James Sibley Watson and Melville Webber's Expressionist version of *The Fall of the House of Usher* (1928).

Figure I.4 Frame from Robert Florey's Expressionist film *The Life and Death of 9413: A Hollywood Extra* (1928).

1934). As he reveals, the film is a key example of the cross-continental influence of Weimar cinema, one that "ruminates on the differences between art and reality, and the misleading and potentially disastrous collisions of reality and perception."

As Graeme Harper notes in his "Maya Deren in Person in Expressionism," critical explorations of the subject area under review can "produce profound ambiguities," an result that he sees as a natural outcome given Expressionism's individual contexts. His inquiry into the work of Maya Deren leads him to suggest that we "need to look more closely at the ways in which around the mid-twentieth century what was once called 'the old world' of Europe and the 'new world' of North America came jointly to define the debate in film authorship as a sort of victory over the relationship between the self and others—to see how this influenced the ways in which filmic expressionism was perceived and perhaps even prevented an understanding and observation of its continuing influence." Harper's insights into Deren are crucial, as are the questions he poses about Expressionist cinema.

Whether focused on pre-dawn urban streets, full of signifying shadows and two-legged wildlife, or in the boudoir of eccentric dreams, many films have drawn upon the simultaneously complicated, diffuse, and shifting perceptions of Expressionism. It is our sincere hope that this collection re-inscribes the theoretical, critical, and historical range of Expressionist cinema by investigating both well-known and largely forgotten films, produced not only in Germany, but across the globe, thus expanding a conversation that should continue. We must become, and remain, Caligari.

Notes

1. Siegfried Kracauer, *From Caligari to Hitler: A Psychological History of the German Film* (Princeton, NJ: Princeton University Press, 1947), p. 5.
2. Ibid. p. 107.
3. Lotte H. Eisner, *The Haunted Screen: Expressionism in the German Cinema and the Influence of Max Reinhardt* (trans. Roger Graeves) (Berkeley, CA: University of California Press, 1969 [1952]), p. 39.
4. Thomas Elsaesser, *Weimar Cinema and After: Germany's Historical Imaginary* (London: Routledge, 2000), p. 36.
5. Ibid. p. 3.
6. Ibid. p. 4.
7. Eisner, *The Haunted Screen*, p. 125.
8. Thomas Elsaesser, "The New Film History," *Sight and Sound*, No. 55, Autumn 1986, p. 248.
9. Elsaesser, *Weimar Cinema and After*, p. 14.
10. John Soister, *Conrad Veidt On Screen: A Comprehensive Illustrated Filmography* (Jefferson, NC: McFarland, 2002); John Soister and Henry Nicolella, *Many Selves: The Horror and Fantasy Films of Paul Wegener* (Duncan, OK: BearManor Media, 2012).

11. Dietrich Scheunemann (ed.), *Expressionist Film: New Perspectives* (Rochester, NY: Camden House, 2003); Anton Kaes, *Shell Shock Cinema: Weimar Culture and the Wounds of War* (Princeton, NJ: Princeton University Press, 2009); Claudia Dillmann and Ralf Beil (eds.), *The Total Artwork in Expressionism: Art, Film, Literature, Theater, Dance, and Architecture* 1905–25 (Ostfildern: Hatje Cantz 2010).

PART I

EXPRESSIONISM IN GERMAN CINEMA

1. EXPRESSIONIST CINEMA—
STYLE AND DESIGN IN FILM HISTORY

Thomas Elsaesser

GERMAN EXPRESSIONISM—EVERYONE'S FAVORITE NIGHTMARE?

The German cinema of the Weimar period, usually regarded as one of the "golden ages" of world cinema, stays in the spotlight until the emergence of Soviet montage cinema in the mid- and late 1920s, by which time it competes, under the heading of *Neue Sachlichkeit*, with the gritty realism of Erich von Stroheim, Ralph Ince, Joseph von Sternberg and King Vidor. The German films from the first half of the decade, of which the best-known is still Robert Wiene's *The Cabinet of Dr. Caligari* (1920), are often labeled "German Expressionism," borrowing the name from an avant-garde movement in literature, drama, painting and sculpture, and associated with such artists' groups as *Der Blaue Reiter*, *Der Sturm* and *Die Brücke*, which peaked around 1912, and whose creative energies were largely spent by the end of World War I.

The reasons for labeling some of the more internationally successful films of the Weimar period "Expressionist" were complex and are still contested.[1] What undoubtedly played a role were efforts to associate the provenance "German" with something more elevated and artistic than Prussian militarism and the horrors of a brutal war of recent memory. Such efforts may even have originated in France, Germany's arch-enemy in those days, where *Caligari* was enthusiastically received among Paris intellectuals and praised more warmly than, for instance, in Berlin.[2] There, audiences had the choice among a wide array of indigenous genre films, such as social melodrama and detective films, comedies and "star vehicles" (Asta Nielsen and Harry Piel, Henny Porten and

Harry Liedtke). None of these could be considered "Expressionist," and besides the Asta Nielsen films, most had little international resonance. Thus, the label "Expressionist" treats as representative of the German cinema of the period quite a small sample of films, favoring a handful of exceptional productions at the expense of what was the mainstay of a rapidly expanding and consolidating film industry, centered on the Ufa studio and its network of theaters.[3] On the other hand, Expressionist cinema did connote a niche product for export, pioneering what would later be called "art cinema" or "auteur cinema," so that the films tend to be identified either with their directors' enigmatic or flamboyant personalities, or with the other creative individuals making up the teams. Best-known are Fritz Lang, G. W. Pabst, F. W. Murnau, Paul Wegener, their scriptwriters Carl Mayer and Thea von Harbou, their cameramen Guido Seeber, Karl Freund, Eugen Schüfftan and Fritz Arno Wagner, and their set designers Fritz Kettelhut, Walter Reimann, Hermann Warm and Walter Röhrig. By contrast, Joe May, Richard Oswald, Max Mack, Ludwig Berger, Reinhold Schünzel and countless other equally popular and successful directors did not benefit from the quality label "Expressionist," and—until recently—had as a consequence largely been forgotten.[4] However, in view of this demotion of mainstream films as the measure of a national cinema, in favor of art- and auteur cinema, it is surprising how many of the films that are now part of the canon and have entered movie mythology carry titillating and sensationalist titles: apart from *The Cabinet of Dr. Caligari*, there is *Dr. Mabuse the Gambler, From Morning to Midnight, Alraune, Nerves, Destiny, The Golem, Phantom, The Street, Backstairs, Waxworks, Warning Shadows, Metropolis, Nosferatu, The Hands of Orlac, Pandora's Box, Joyless Street, Secrets of a Soul*.

Either popular taste did have its part to play, or another story was being told as well: while signaling "film as art" and demonstrating the unexpected flowering of creative talent in a defeated nation, Expressionist film also suggested the sudden, brief frisson of a never-to-be-forgotten glimpse into the abyss. But what sort of abyss—of unconscious urges, of the German soul, of war and trauma, of inflation and social unrest, of the cinema's own "uncanny"? Why this interest in the dark side of human nature and the demons of fevered imaginations? How seriously did audiences take these films? Trying to answer why these films should have been so morbid, fantastic, full of foreboding and horror has kept the multi-faceted but also occasionally murky debate over the definition, origin and reach of Expressionist cinema alive over the decades—a debate kicked off thanks to two well-known books, Siegfried Kracauer's *From Caligari to Hitler*[5] and Lotte Eisner's *The Haunted Screen*,[6] authors for whom mad doctors, cruel tyrants, rapists, vampires, magicians, golems and robots, or German Romanticism, Caspar David Friedrich, stimmung, chiaroscuro lighting and painted sets occupy center stage.

EXPRESSIONIST CINEMA—STYLE AND DESIGN IN FILM HISTORY

Figure 1.1 Werner Krauß in a publicity still for Robert Wiene's *Das Cabinet des Dr. Caligari/The Cabinet of Dr. Caligari* (1920). (*Courtesy of Friedrich-Wilhelm-Murnau-Stiftung, Wiesbaden; source: German Film Institute—DIF, Frankfurt*)

The larger-than-life, dark, demonic, twisted, haunted and tormented protagonists have firmed up the impression that the German cinema is inward-looking and psychological rather than action-oriented, that its stories and settings belong to the fantastic rather than realist pole of filmmaking. As a case study of a film movement, a period style, or a national cinema, or, more broadly, as an example of the relation between cinema and society, German Expressionist film has been a favorite in textbooks,[7] film style surveys,[8] books about the sociology of cinema,[9] and distinct chapters in film histories or as part of "world cinema."[10] In popular movie memory, on the other hand, it is not the directors who have entered the afterlife of myth, but the films; and in the films, not the convoluted stories but the often-eponymous heroes or villains: mad Dr. Caligari; mastermind Dr. Mabuse; Ivan the Terrible or Jack the Ripper from *Waxworks*; lean, weary Death from *Destiny/Der müde Tod*; the legendary *Golem*; Attila and Hagen from *The Nibelungen*; *The Student of Prague* and his murderous double; the mad scientist Rotwang and the robot Maria from *Metropolis*; *Orlac* of the severed hands; *Nosferatu*, the German

Dracula; Haghi the super-spy of *Spione*; the diabolical Mephisto of *Faust*; the insinuatingly smooth *Tartuffe*; and the creepily pitiable child-murderer in *M*. Its (male) actors, too, have stayed in the mind: Conrad Veidt, Emil Jannings, Rudolf Klein-Rogge, Max Schreck, Werner Krauß, Peter Lorre. Titles and heroes come from *grand guignol* or the fairground (a frequent setting, as Kracauer also noted), and the villains resemble the bogey-men of children's fairy tales and folk-legend, precisely the regions of the popular imagination and mass entertainment that Expressionist films are said to have helped the cinema leave behind. There is thus a certain irony or duplicity at work, where "Expressionist" is meant to connote art and high culture, while generously helping itself to the attractions and thrills that have popular appeal and sensationalist associations. This dual legacy may well be one additional reason why the debate about Expressionism in cinema has continued well past the period of the 1920s, and well beyond Germany, since it alludes to a tension between artistic aspiration and universal appeal that is inherent in the cinema itself.

More specifically, what in the films is identified with "Expressionism" is the stylization of the sets and the acting,[11] "Gothic" stories and perverse eroticism, angular exteriors, claustrophobic interiors, and above all, that uncanny feeling of not quite knowing what is going on, a lack of causal logic, and stories with twists and turns that double up on themselves. Only much later—after World War II—did the association of nightmare visions and depth psychology give credibility to conjectures about the society that had given birth to these monsters of the screen: the foreshadowing of ideological turmoil to come, or testimony to the troubled political reality of post-World War I German society, only became self-evidently true in retrospect, through a factoring in of the lost World War of 1918, the rise of Nazism at the end of the decade, and another lost war twelve years later.[12] A less apocalyptic but no less retrospective interpretation has preferred the term "Weimar cinema," to "Expressionist film," signaling the cinema's affinity with the complex and still fascinating phenomenon of "Weimar culture,"[13] lasting from 1918 to 1933.

The two standard works on the subject reflect further differences of perspective. *The Haunted Screen* and *From Caligari to Hitler* appeared almost simultaneously, but largely independently from each other, shortly after World War II, and in response to the disclosure of the horrors of the Holocaust. Significantly, the books were published, respectively, in France and the USA, rather than in Germany, where their publishing history is a chapter all by itself.[14] Each is the work of a Jewish exile who in the 1920s wrote as a professional film critic or journalist, and each in its distinct way is a profoundly personal attempt to grasp through the cinema something of the tragedy that had befallen the country and the culture its author had loved and even over-identified with. Hence also the vehemence of their ambiguity about this cinema, reflected in the appropriately lurid and brilliantly suggestive titles they chose for their books. As with the films they so prominently featured, the sensationalist slant has paid off in terms of recognition value, but it has also given their interpretations a certain mirror-illusion of intuitive truth, making one at times forget that this perspectival alignment is one that imposes itself only with hindsight: in this instance, the view of two outsiders looking in, and of insiders looking back, as much in sorrow and pain as in anger.

While *The Haunted Screen* is the work of an art historian, trying to account for the prevalence of the fantastic in the themes of the German cinema, as well as for the pervasive elements of stylization, by demonstrating the persisting legacy of the Gothic and Romanticism in German art and culture, Kracauer's title is itself an interpretation. *From Caligari to Hitler* boldly suggests that the madmen, tyrant-figures, supermen and charlatans populating the German screens from the end of World War I onwards are the ancestors and prototypes of that singular madman, charlatan and tyrant who took Germany, Europe and finally most of the rest of the world into another disastrous war. It is true that there have been many general and particular objections to *From Caligari to Hitler* and *The Haunted Screen*.[15] However, despite the fact that Kracauer's methodology as well as Eisner's assumptions are questionable and open to criticism,[16] the central message of these books has imposed itself with singular self-evidence: in Kracauer, the claim for a demonstrable relation between postwar trauma, social unrest, Weimar cinema and Nazi ideology; in Eisner, the demonstrable relation between German Romanticism, Expressionist art, Weimar cinema and Nazi ideology.

Thus, "Expressionist film" and "Weimar cinema" continue to signal ready-made identities, slanted, respectively, toward the artists who produced the films and the society that consumed them—two halves of a whole that spells German national cinema. The self-evidence of this identity suggests that the two books are based on imaginary constructs, each naming an entity only retrospectively given coherence, when seen from this particular vantage point that implies certain explanatory schemas, and excludes others. Their interpretative sweep of Germany's national trauma across its cinema bears the marks of their authors' personal trauma. One only needs to remind oneself of the fact that Eisner worked in Paris and Kracauer in New York to realize that they addressed themselves (or had reason to believe they addressed themselves) to a doubting, hostile and suspicious audience (of non-German readers), with whom they were trying to make (em)phatic contact, by accommodating in each case French and US sensibilities about Germany's disastrous twentieth century. As exiles, they both served their host countries well, mediating between their respective national predilections or prejudices and a West Germany trying to face up to its responsibilities as the legal successor of the "Third Reich." At the same time, on a more personal level, both exiles also enjoyed patronage, and their books can be understood as addressing their benefactors—Eisner was working for Henri Langlois of the Cinémathèque française, and Kracauer wanted to express his gratitude to Iris Barry of the MoMA and the Institute of Social Research, as well as offering his services to the US Government. In other words, and again only with hindsight, one can discern in these influential texts certain kinds of mirror relations at work right from the start, providing ample occasion for imaginary recognition/miscognition effects, which in turn favored perspectives on their subject that necessarily repressed other, equally film-historical approaches and film-aesthetic evaluations, or at any rate made these others more difficult to articulate.[17]

For instance, the notion of "expressionist film" was initially introduced by Rudolf Kurtz, a well-known art critic and the first theorist of 1920s German cinema. Kurtz refers himself to the art historian Wilhelm Worringer and his notions of abstraction and empathy. Favoring musical and architectural analogies, he aligns this cinema with post-1918 constructivist tendencies in art and design, rather than drawing political parallels.[18] An exception is his remark about *Caligari*, which in 1926 he misremembers as follows:

> Like a fever dream, having its premiere in wild days, surrounded by dark streets, across which echo commands shouted by republican paramilitary units; elsewhere, the piercing voices of street corner orators, and in the background, the centre of town plunged into total darkness, occupied by radical insurgents, machine-gun rattle, soldiers forming human chains, [falling] roof-supports and hand-grenades.[19]

It is as if Kurtz had added to *Caligari*'s framing narrative yet another frame, locating the film's opening week in the cinemas during the street battles of the November Days of 1918, but forgetting that *Caligari* was only shot less than a year later, in September–October 1919.[20] But with his recollection of war and revolutionary unrest, Kurtz anticipates the controversies that broke out between Hans Janowitz, one of the screenwriters, Carl Mayer, the other screenwriter, and Robert Wiene, the director, about the political "message" of the film.[21] While Janowitz was able to pass his version of the story to Kracauer, and Warm gave his recollections to Lotte Eisner, Erich Pommer, the producer, made sure that, in the guise of a tribute to Mayer, he, too, was on the record.[22] The longer one looks at *Caligari*, it seems, the more its historical protagonists and purported authors become part of the plot, engaged in a complicated series of exchanges and reversals.[23]

As indicated, German film producers after 1918 were confronted with significant obstacles if they wanted to export films. Many countries in Europe operated a boycott of German goods, creating the need either to find a protected niche or to market such products under a label which an international audience was likely to associate positively with a provenance from Germany. "Expressionism," already in circulation before the war, connoting revolt against the established order, was elevated enough as high culture, and thus helped mitigate the then current (and wholly negative) association of "German" with the Kaiser, the "Beast of Berlin." Here the function of "Expressionism" was to establish a historical imaginary: a mirror-style in which could be reversed out the negative image one thinks or knows that the Other has of oneself. Acting, reacting or counter-acting accordingly, *Caligari* mobilizes Germany's cultural patrimony (Romanticism) and avant-garde credibility (Expressionism) in the medium of high art as self-promotion in another medium (the cinema), for the purposes of (national or commercial) prestige.[24] But inside this cross-cultural mirror-construction which was *Caligari*, foreign audiences could, if they so wished, "recognize" the evil, mad doctor, thus confirming the negative image of the German "beast" of their own country's war propaganda, which the positive associations of the high art style did not disavow or displace, but merely placed in an infinitely reversible frame, by allegorizing it in the nested narrative of the flashback prologue, which forever vacillates between two interpretations: the story of a mild-mannered doctor and his mad (or simulating) patient, or that of a sane patient, criminally imprisoned by a malevolent hypnotist.

In Germany itself, the situation was reversed once more: the reviews of *Caligari* published by Willy Haas, Rudolf Arnheim and Kurt Tucholsky after the film's Berlin opening speak of imposture and bluff, of phoney effects and an attempt to hoodwink the public.[25] One critic commented on the commercial interests that were quick to spot and exploit a trend:

> In the shop-windows, one is greeted by [expressionist] book-covers, all beating the same resounding gong. On fairgrounds and in bars, zigzag flames. In arts-and-craft displays, convulsive tremors. Shop-window signs, weekly journals and printed matter mail-drops are jiggling and cannot keep steady.[26]

But after its unexpectedly triumphant success abroad, opinion began to change—with audiences and critics drenching the nation's damaged pride in the sunshine of the film's foreign acclaim. As a quality label, "Expressionism" is in this case not altogether far from the epithet that Dr. Mabuse in Fritz Lang's film of that title applies to it, when he says "Expressionism—it's just a game." The lack of conviction, after the first surprise had worn off, that critics complained about in the self-consciously stylized Expressionist films following *Caligari*, such as *Alraune*, *Raskolnikow* and *From Morning to Midnight*, seems to bear out the suspicion of someone passing off as gold what is merely gilded: a calculated, but perhaps too transparent put-on, pastiching itself, even before Ernst Lubitsch hilariously parodied all such stylizations in *The Mountain Cat*. Pommer was equally sanguine and pragmatic about his reasons for promoting Expressionist films:

> The German film industry made "stylized films" to make money. Let me explain. At the end of World War One the Hollywood industry moved towards world supremacy ... We tried something new; the Expressionist or stylized films. This was possible because Germany had an overflow of good artists and writers, a strong literary tradition, and a great tradition of theatre.[27]

Kracauer's and Eisner's seminal interventions dating from the end of World War II thus continue an already existing debate and yet mark a decisive break. Kracauer's book, especially, recasts in negative terms and flatly contradicts the positive reputation that the German cinema enjoyed from around 1920/1 until the early 1930s all over Western Europe, Russia and the USA as a model of aesthetically innovative and often enough also politically progressive filmmaking. It began with French enthusiasm for "Caligarisme" (Delluc),[28] which was shared in the Soviet Union (Eisenstein published admiring articles on German cinema).[29] German cinema had a unique reputation in the USA after the success of Lubitsch's *Passion*; it was a model cinema for the Dutch Filmliga,[30] and in Britain, it inspired the London Film Society movement and the journal *Close-up*, whose writers championed G. W. Pabst especially as a political progressive.[31] By way of "influence," the German cinema had a formative role for Luis Buñuel, discovering his calling after seeing films by Lang (*Destiny/Der müde Tod*),[32] and for Alfred Hitchcock, also impressed by Lang (*Dr. Mabuse*), Leni (*Waxworks*) and Dupont (*Variety*) and even going to Berlin in order to watch Murnau on the set of *The Last Laugh*, as well as working as set-designer and assistant director on *The Blackguard* for Ufa in Neubabelsberg in 1924/5 and directing *The Pleasure Garden* and *The Mountain Eagle* for Emelka in Munich in 1925/6.[33] The articles written about the German cinema during the 1920s are legion, yet none of them discovers "demonic" traits, "haunted" characters or "proto-fascist" tendencies in the films or the filmmakers. Some typical examples, such as *The Cabinet of Dr. Caligari*,[34] *Nosferatu*,[35] and *Destiny*,[36] were considered key works of avant-garde cinema, while others, equally typical, such as *Madame Dubarry*, *The Last Laugh*, or *Joyless Street*, had an appreciable influence on fixing norms of mainstream narrative cinema, and not only in Europe.

That this estimation changed after World War II is all too understandable, in the wake of international demands for accountability and explanations: how could it have come to Nazism, the exiling and extermination of Jews, both supported by a majority of the population? The cinema fell under suspicion not least because of the role films had had in the Nazi propaganda machine. For the subsequent two decades, almost all major studies of both Weimar and Nazi cinema were written by exiled Germans or non-Germans, a fact that honors their authors. Besides economic or ideological accounts of the takeover of the film industry after 1933, studies of Weimar cinema also generated other explanatory models, almost all of them binary. The style and genre paradigm fell into the two categories fantasy and realist; the art-historical periodization knew two phases, Expressionism and *Neue Sachlichkeit*; the aesthetic judgments divided into avant-garde and "kitsch;" and the political tendencies were assessed under either "nationalist" (i.e. reactionary) or "international" (progressive). German film history became a series of oppositional discourses, mirroring structures of embattled or ideological terms, even when the labels were subsequently taken apart.

Hence the difficulty of writing about the films without falling into such categories: their symmetry seems to repress something, and therefore the choice between Expressionist *film* and Weimar *cinema* is not an arbitrary one. The terms cannot be simply "deconstructed," nor can either label lay claim to any

Figure 1.2 Werner Krauß (left) in a publicity still for *Das Cabinet des Dr. Caligari/ The Cabinet of Dr. Caligari* (1920). (*Courtesy of Friedrich-Wilhelm-Murnau-Stiftung, Wiesbaden; source: German Film Institute—DIF, Frankfurt*)

obvious historical truth, other than the likelihood that they, too, represent different kinds of "imaginaries," which hide as much as they reveal. Thus, in order to understand why these films still—once more—fascinate spectators everywhere, one has to recognize that these labels and their imaginaries now belong to the films, are part and parcel of their identity for cinema history. Even if the assumption that films "reflect" their society directly has become increasingly untenable, the imaginaries attached to a national cinema ensure that the films remain implicated in the construction of these identities. But this "implicated in" might in the 1920s have been a "testing" or "trying out" of what identities fit or resonate, alerting one not only to the mirror-relations just mentioned, but also to the processes of self-fashioning through the eyes of significant others, and the habitual gestures and stereotypes across which communities speak to each other—or fail to do so. These dynamics are, again, typical of the cinema in general, as a cultural practice with demographic (class, gender) and ethnographic (nation, race) resonances, which help to make the label "expressionist" (now understood as the cinematic "imaginary" of mutual mirroring and an exchange of recognition–miscognition) a floating signifier that can transfer from one national cinema to another and become a feature of very different genres, from horror to film noir, from fantasy to science fiction.

The Haunted Screen: Image and Influence

Lotte Eisner concentrates on the stylistic continuities of a number of motifs, mostly literary and from the fine arts, as they persist, transform themselves and mutate through more than a hundred years of German aesthetics, philosophy and popular sensibility. She is persuasive on the many kinds of intertextuality existing between film, theater and painting, as she traces the extraordinarily resilient legacy of German Romanticism from the 1820s to the 1920s, with its predilection for extreme states of feeling, the sublime in nature, torn and divided personalities and a ready penchant for grotesque humor or morbid fantasies. The cinema of the 1920s seems to her the culmination of a long development of the "demonic" (which originally meant also a spiritual urge toward transcendence) in the German character, exacerbated by the lost war, and testifying to a nation inclined at times of crisis or defeat to turn irrational, choleric and manic-depressive.

However, when one looks more closely, one sees that Eisner's main protagonist determining this cinema's aesthetic sensibility is not the purported "national character," but specific individuals. Besides her favorite directors, Fritz Lang and F. W. Murnau, much of her book focuses on the charismatic personality of Max Reinhardt, whose stagecraft dominated the lighting design and *mise-en-scène* of the period, but who was also the Godfather-Caligari in another sense, since almost the entire personnel of the German screen trained with him or owed to him their artistic breakthrough.[37]

Eisner's central (art-) historical category is "influence": her study details how specific artists influenced film style, documenting the many links from nineteenth-century paintings to 1920s set design, decor, and the use of (chiaroscuro, or Rembrandt-) lighting in the key films of the "Expressionist" mode. The fact that paintings by Caspar David Friedrich are quite evidently the inspiration for certain compositions in Fritz Lang's *Destiny*, or that the importance of lesser painters like August Böcklin and Hans Thoma for film design and iconography had not been fully appreciated, can be credited as among her major insights. Her sensitivity toward the mutations that the Romantic heritage underwent as it entered the cinema makes *The Haunted Screen* still an important source book. As more films became viewable again, this aspect of Eisner's work has been extended to include the popular image culture of Germany at the turn of the century, indicating the migration of motifs and the permeability of the arts in relation to each other.[38] Eisner's eye for the multimedia space that the German cinema inhabited with the theater, architecture and the visual arts give such a range to her argument that it makes one almost forget and forgive its central weaknesses: in order to describe the dynamics of this "new romanticism," the term "influence" fails as an explanatory concept: appropriation, opportunist adaptation, or performative pastiche might be more suitable descriptions. Her appeal to the idea of the *Gesamtkunstwerk* does not convince either, nor does "Expressionism" seem the best name for the pressures of stylization, special effects and spectacle at work in the films meant to impress an international public, such as the blockbusters made by Lang (*Metropolis*, *Spies*, *Woman on the Moon*) and Murnau (*The Last Laugh*, *Faust*, *Tartuffe*) for Erich Pommer as part of the Parufamet Agreement.

Not surprisingly, there are other ways of analyzing the stylistic elements and peculiarities of the so-called Expressionist films. Barry Salt, for instance, has challenged both Kracauer and Eisner. In his essay "From Caligari to Who?" he points out, among other things, that the particular lighting which Eisner traces to German cinema and especially to the influence of Max Reinhardt can be found much earlier in American films; he demonstrates that of the films generally listed as "Expressionist," only very few show actual features of expressionist style; and he also avers that any ideological reading of the films is so selective as to remain unconvincing.[39] In another important essay, Salt goes on the counter-offensive and persuasively shows to what extent German set design and film architecture were influenced by the theater, tracing very precisely the various productions—and not exclusively by Reinhardt—which stood as models for the style of specific films.[40]

By studying more closely the career of a set-designer-turned-director such as Paul Leni, one gets a good sense of the professional exchanges that took place in Berlin between the various crafts and trades concerned with the graphic arts (such as newspaper cartoons), the stage, cabaret performance and poster art, allowing a professional like Leni to move with ease between different kinds of assignments and tasks, including directing.[41] Leni's career also shows just how eclectic and opportunist, how tongue-in-cheek, iconoclastic and sarcastic, the visual arts scene and film world were in the early 1920s, as German cinema tried to build up a domestic market share (against Hollywood) and an international industry (to penetrate Eastern and Southern Europe). Many of the film architects, costume makers and set designers were just as likely to frequent Dadaist circles and cabarets in their spare time, while during the day dressing the most sumptuous sets of orientalist follies or art-deco elegance, which once more suggests that the concept of "influence" as understood in art history for the anxious or rebellious relation of artists to their predecessors or rivalries among the members of the same generation does not apply in the cinema, where styles are, strictly speaking, not so much an expression of an individual signature or "will to style" as they are the special effects, the means for achieving a mood, an atmosphere, or for suggesting a period feel that can trigger period connotations or evoke nostalgic reminiscences. A particular style may also serve as a convenient visual shorthand to tie together disparate elements of story, character and setting, as in the different but thematically related stories that make up films like *Destiny* or *Waxworks*.

Along such lines, Kristin Thompson has inscribed Expressionist style in a more materially and historically grounded film poetics, insofar as she does not only demonstrate how complexly determined the choice of style actually was, or how "Expressionism" was first launched as a label for *The Cabinet of Dr. Caligari*, in order then to be deployed much more calculatedly as a marketing ploy, albeit ultimately without lasting success. She is also able to offer a set of formal criteria which, while having little to do with Expressionism as we know it from literature, theater or painting, make a good deal of sense within the framework sketched in Rudolf Kurtz's study of "Expressionist cinema," as well as within certain choices that Ufa producer Erich Pommer made, in order to launch German films as a nationally specific cinema within an international competitive situation.[42] Thompson implicitly confirms that the attempt to create for this cinema a rationale, or account for a perceived stylistic coherence, risks becoming trapped in a tautology: that of a style as the self-expression of an epoch, and of an epoch as defined by its style.

Both Salt and Thompson arrive, by different routes, at the conclusion that not only "Expressionism" but also the very conception of style in its art-historical sense is not applicable to this cinema. Most banally, the reasons for this are pragmatic when one recalls some of the material constraints Pommer was confronted with immediately after the war, which apparently necessitated the "Expressionist" stylization in *Caligari* as a consequence of economic conditions and the lack of technical infrastructure.[43] Lotte Eisner has a similar explanation for Max Reinhardt's innovative styles of symbolic and dramatic lighting, arguing that war shortages obliged him to use *ersatz* materials for his sets, whose shabbiness had to be disguised with light.[44] Yet even if these stories are partly apocryphal, and invented after the fact as a diversionary or mythologizing manoeuvre, there remain other important considerations: for instance, Pommer's awareness, after the success of *Caligari* in Paris, of the potential of the term "Expressionism" to become what can only be called a "brand-name."

Expressionism in the technical sense, as Salt has argued, is applied consistently in very few of the films commonly traded under this name.[45] When one views them with an art-historical interest, what are striking are the many self-conscious references to other known styles, or the more or less subtle forms of stylization: Weimar cinema, examined across all its genres, presents an eclectic mixture of *Heimatkunst*, orientalism and ornamentalism *à la mode*, from chinoiserie and Egyptian art to African or Aztec colonial spoils, *Jugendstil* furnishings and Expressionist paintings, art deco interiors and even Bauhaus easy chairs, as in the later films of Pabst. These stylistic idioms are borrowed from the stage (in Leni's *Waxworks*, for instance), taken from children's book illustration (in the case of Lang's *Die Nibelungen*), or look like they come from home-furnishing catalogues and ladies' journals advertisements (as in Pabst's *Pandora's Box*). In less well-known films, like military comedies or costume dramas, the styles allude to postcards (*Feldpostkarten*),[46] newspaper comics, illustrations in popular magazines, tourist brochures and other commercial art—just as in any other national cinema, including the eclecticism of Hollywood.

So why this persistence of the term "Expressionism," not just as a technical term for some of the films of the early 1920s, but as a generic term for most of the art cinema of Weimar? Why did it spread beyond Germany, echoing down film history across the periods and the genres, turning up in the description of Universal horror films of the 1930s and film noir of the 1940s, until it became, according to the *Monthly Film Bulletin*, "such a general description for any stylistic departure from strict naturalism as to be virtually meaningless"?[47] The anonymous writer adds, however: "perhaps Expressionism was the first movement which allowed the cinema broadly to formulate certain ideas about itself."[48]

The Constructivist Turn: From Style to Design

Paradoxically, it is this suggestion of Expressionist cinema's persistent reflexivity about the cinema's conditions of possibility not only at crisis moments, as in Germany after the war, but at any given point in time, when

Figure 1.3   Hans Heinrich von Twardowski, Lil Dagover, and Friedrich Fehér in a publicity still for *Das Cabinet des Dr. Caligari/The Cabinet of Dr. Caligari* (1920). (*Courtesy of Friedrich-Wilhelm-Murnau-Stiftung, Wiesbaden; source: German Film Institute—DIF, Frankfurt*)

the cinema itself undergoes technological changes, that supplies one answer as to why Expressionism has emerged as among the most enduring stylistic labels in film history. For instance, Siegfried Kracauer's argument in *From Caligari to Hitler* provides, above all, the categories for a reception study of Weimar cinema. Concerned with identifying a period mentality, Kracauer is indifferent to the art-historical notion of a self-defined movement or group style, nor does he give much space to the idea of an avant-garde, be it aesthetic or technical, working in a popular medium. His ability to grasp the films of the Weimar period as a super-text, and this super-text as a social text, so to speak, is one of the strengths of his approach.[49] It contrasts with Eisner's work, for whom influence, intertextuality and the celebration of artistic "genius" are central, while neglecting reception. Quite apart from the fact that—looked at as a whole—the many different styles and genres of Weimar cinema responded to different audiences, both foreign and domestic, might it be possible to think of Expressionism not as a style at all, but as an idiom that adapts itself to the respective conditions of production *and* reception—one, that is, that interposes itself, interprets or mediates between industry, its products and the expectations of specific segments of consumers? The name for such a pragmatic concept of style is "design," signifying aesthetic and material parameters, as well as economic and technical priorities. Design would seem to fit several features of the distinctiveness of Expressionism in Weimar cinema so far discussed, including its strategic uses as a possible label for a product (i.e. German culture) that needed rebranding.

For instance, once one scratches the art-historical idealism of her mode of creativity, Eisner actually discusses very intelligently the Weimar cinema's technical excellence and craftsman-like proficiency. The feats of German film technology and technique were, after all, the features most admired among film industry professionals internationally in the 1920s and regularly commented on by critics well into the 1930s. Virtuosity and the pursuit of excellence were proudly shown off in the camera work (from the special effects of Guido Seeber in the 1910s to the "unchained camera" of Karl Freund and the lighting of Fritz Arno Wagner in the 1920s). No contemporary review of any major film misses out on praising design, set construction and special effects, the areas where Robert Herlth, Herman Warm, Erich Kettelhut or Eugen Schüfftan made their reputation. But directors, too, were often known for their hands-on technical knowledge: Fritz Lang, for instance, was feared for his technical expertise, perfectionism and seemingly inexhaustible patience when it came to trying out new special effects. Pabst was equally versed in state-of-the art film equipment. In fact, even the most "spiritual" of Weimar directors, F. W. Murnau was something of a film technology freak, as were E. A. Dupont, who began as a screenwriter, and Paul Leni, who throughout his career doubled as a set designer.

This high level of proficiency in film technique and film design, combined with the formation of teams,[50] suggests that filmmakers, cameramen and art directors were not concerned about questions of individual talent as much as they were engaged in a process of unifying different elements, citing or recycling aesthetic styles as set-pieces, according to story, situation and demand. Insofar as particular styles were "made to measure," by functionally retooling and adapting recognizable idioms to serve purposes defined by other agendas, "Expressionism" in film, too, falls under this verdict of a "borrowed" idiom, though one where, for the reasons discussed above, the sense of a style that could convey externally and through formal elements the reality of subjective states, hidden motives and inner turmoil was among the most sought-after effects.

There is a documented case for this reversal of outer form and inner content in the art cinema (*Autorenfilm*) of the 1910s, that is, when technical experimentation was looking for appropriate subject matter, rather than a certain subject matter requiring adequate technology to realize itself. Early in 1913

Paul Wegener approached Guido Seeber because he had seen astounding trick photography in a French film, where through double exposure the same actor seemed to play cards with himself. To reproduce this special effect in a more dramatic context, the two decided that they needed suitable story material.[51] They contacted Hanns Heinz Ewers, who wrote for them a romantic tale, a collage of standard Gothic motifs involving lost shadows, Faustian pacts and *doppelgängers*, just what Seeber needed for best displaying the special effects he was planning, and for Wegener to astonish the world by playing opposite himself as his evil twin. In this sense, *The Student of Prague* can be considered the first Expressionist film, even though its style bears little resemblance to the angular sets and starkly stylized interiors of *Caligari*, which it predates by seven years. Nor is it because *The Student of Prague* has the literary motif of the double that it deserves its vanguard role, but because it embodies a principle behind "German Expressionist film" in general, whose identity is stylistic only insofar as story and style are interdependent, because driven by exigencies of technique and the state-of-the-art of film technology, not the other way round. Once the underlying dynamics of technological change in the film industry and the productive force of the art cinema offensive from 1913 onwards are factored in, "Expressionist cinema" can perhaps be better understood as the German variant of constructivism, concerned with giving technologically produced art and artifacts a wholly different space—literally and discursively—from that traditionally occupied by paintings, literature and even the theater. Expressionism signals the emancipation of cinema from the other arts, the testing of its own powers, and is to this extent the forerunner of what Hitchcock would call "pure cinema." The difference would be that Expressionist cinema engages and challenges the bourgeois arts on their own grounds, rather than (like the popular cinematic genres of comedy or the detective film) by simply developing an alternative public space.

Expressionism would then be the name of a toolbox or Lego set[52] of style features, whose functions do not coincide with art-historical connotations at all. Rather, the attribute "Expressionist" would connote a set of "effects," capable of disguising itself—when necessary—as a "cause," impersonating the aesthetic revolt, the political unrest, or character-specific psychological turmoil, for the purpose of authenticating the protean and adaptable medium which is film. It is in this sense that, through Expressionism, the cinema formulates something about itself, namely its technical capacity to simulate both authenticity and autonomy. In other words, expressionism is the moment of cinema expressing itself, performing itself—which is one of the clues as to why it can periodically return, as it has done in the 1940s as film noir, in the 1970s as neo-noir, and now again with the change to digital cinema, once more self-consciously displaying the prowess of the cinema's expressive means.

Figure 1.4 Hans Heinrich von Twardowski and Erna Morena in a publicity still for Karlheinz Martin's *Von morgens bis Mitternacht/From Morning to Midnight* (1920). (*Source: German Film Institute—DIF, Frankfurt*)

EXPRESSIONISM AFTER WEIMAR

To return briefly to Kracauer's main thesis: if, from the vantage point of 1945, he can detect proto-fascist tendencies in Weimar cinema, which casts Expressionism as the symptom of irrationality and aberrant or decadent psychologies (a charge reminiscent of the so-called "expressionism" debate in literature, which pitted the "expressionists" Bert Brecht and Ernst Bloch against the "realist" Georg Lukács),[53] my argument would be different. Any affinities with Nazism are to be found not so much in the supposed allegories of leader-figures and demonic seducers distilled by Kracauer and Eisner, but because the Nazi entertainment industry, in crucial respects, took over the design version of artistic style, but in its kitsch or pastiche simulations, tailoring them to the new rulers' chief ideological requirement on the home front: to appropriate national history by inventing for itself a "tradition," a retroactive legitimation and a pedigree. The principle of disguise and make-believe became Joseph

Goebbels' political principle par excellence, and life and politics took a cynical lesson from art, as Kracauer (and Walter Benjamin) had woefully noted. Thus, Nazism as a regime of both spectacle and camouflage had an uncanny capacity for "inheriting" its different political predecessors and indeed even its ideological enemies, such as the socialists and communists. In this respect, Nazi culture was a kind of mimicry of modernity *and* of tradition, but also a sort of dress rehearsal for some of the attitudes and values of modern consumer culture. As a society of the spectacle, it energetically used cinema and the visual media for propaganda purposes: purposes which before, during and after the Hitler regime continued to be practiced as "advertising" and "marketing." Borrowed from the arts and the avant-garde and transferred to the cinema and popular culture, Expressionist cinema risked becoming no more than a brilliant move of marketing and branding—the flipside of its ability to celebrate the cinema itself through the versatility of its techniques and the virtuosity of its professionals.

Some of the émigrés who had to flee Germany after 1933 did in fact think, upon arrival in California, that out of the frying pan they had landed right in the fire. With a certain shock of recognition, for instance, T. W. Adorno and Max Horkheimer realized that the commercial culture they encountered in the USA recalled nothing more vividly than the "administered culture" they had fled,[54] especially in the way the popular arts under both capitalism and Nazism had—as it seemed to them, cynically—appropriated and raided art history as fancy dress, with the entertainment industry busy producing seductive simulacra of every style and every ideology, treating these styles—but also the pleasures and values they connoted—as design features of commodities. This shock of recognition may well have armed the Weimar exiles, and reminded them of their need not to drop their guard too much, but instead to maintain their own camouflage and mimicry. On the other hand, "Expressionism" in this sense had also equipped many of the émigré filmmakers to fit right in, in Hollywood, and to demonstrate their proficiency in thinking "cinema" even before they could think in English.

The result was one of Weimar cinema's most enduring legacies. As is well-known, it is the German exile community in Hollywood, these "strangers in paradise," that is credited with having found their most existential but also professional self-representation in a quintessentially American film genre which is also held to be quintessentially "Expressionist." I am referring, of course, to film noir, a genre that did not become one until after the fact, and a style that perhaps refuses and resists definition as stubbornly as the great Weimar classics. Elsewhere, I have tried to present a more skeptical but also multi-layered genealogy of the German "influence" on film noir, arguing that these émigrés have had, in the 1930s at least, an equally strong contribution to make to (musical) comedy, and in the 1940s and 1950s, to melodrama, thus somewhat complicating the (retroactive) "fit" between personal fate, political persecution and a cinematic genre.[55] And yet, nothing seems to speak more vividly to movie audiences today than "noir"—in all its shades.

The ease with which certain aspects and elements of Expressionism were able to travel and migrate to other periods, genres and filmmaking countries thus testifies to the success of creating a brand. But the high recognition value and mobility of Expressionism also suggest that it might have been "skin deep," or put more sharply, that its essence was to act as either a surface sheen or a design feature. This might explain the revival of Expressionism in the popular arts since the 1980s, and especially during what came to be known as postmodernism. What was rediscovered both in the films themselves and the stylistic peculiarities was neither German Romanticism nor political proto-fascism, but a zest and energy that spoke of youthful vitality and a bodily engagement with expressive gesture and performative panache. When high-profile rock artists such as Mick Jagger, David Bowie or Freddie Mercury, or superstars like Madonna, borrowed or stole from *Caligari*, *Metropolis* and *Pandora's Box* for their music videos, was this the "pop-appropriation" of a rather heavy legacy—"Weimar-lite," so to speak—or did it indicate another kind of affinity—the freedom to "reinvent" oneself as someone else in yet another medium of make-believe?[56] These stylized films of another era have been given legitimacy, or rather street-credibility, by the very epitome of commercialized popular culture, the music business: selectively adopted and suitably sampled, Expressionist cinema became a collection of "film clips with attitude."

What exactly was the appeal, where was the moment of recognition? A first guess is that it is the energy and the body language, the androgyny, gender ambiguity and bisexuality of German cinema, which make it instantly familiar to today's popular culture. But perhaps it is also a certain knowingness—the pastiche elements already present in the 1920s, the reverse of all that angst and trauma—now called postmodern irony, with which we have no difficulty in entering into a dialogue: the "devil" with whom, to quote Mick Jagger, we have a great deal of "sympathy." As the opening night of *Nosferatu* indicated, Expressionist cinema had a serious sense of self-parody: even its tragic moments are not without tongue-in-cheek, a sign of a culture coming out of catastrophe, but dancing at the edge of a precipice.[57] However, the contemporary recognition-effect may also be fueled by a media culture of "excess" and "precipice"—especially where these moments beyond-the-limits are associated with technology, automatons, the borderline between body and machine, when the cyborgs and avatars of today are second cousins to the somnambulists and hypnotists of Weimar. In other words: the secret affinities are also with ecstatic bodies and psychic prosthetics, with techno-mutants and the post-human.

Figure 1.5 Werner Krauß as Jack the Ripper in a publicity still for Paul Leni's *Das Wachsfigurenkabinett/Waxworks* (1924). (*Source: German Film Institute—DIF, Frankfurt*)

The Legacy

And so to sum up and to conclude: Expressionist cinema, although introduced as a quality brand (connoting the good Germany of Romantic poets, avant-garde artists and deep thinkers, as opposed to the bad Germany of a warmongering Kaiser, mustard gas and territorial-imperial ambitions) was ambiguously coded right from the start. Coming with high culture credentials (from the fine arts and promoted as an authors' cinema), the films, with their lurid titles, hinted at sensationalism and fairground attractions, but were also born out of penury and necessity. Extreme stylization in decor was only one aspect: it could go hand in hand with more conventional narratives, so that even *The Cabinet of Dr. Caligari* relies on the formula of a detective film, with a psycho-pathological twist.[58] On the other hand, the frame-tales and nested narratives of so many Weimar films are recognizable precursors of what today we know as mind-game or puzzle films, such as *The Sixth Sense*, *Fight Club* or *Inception*.[59] If, rather, the most enduring legacy of German Expressionism is said to be the lighting, I argue that it is the open display and performativity of film technology, sometimes in the service of aberrant psychological states in the protagonists, but sometimes also for the sheer pleasure of spectacle and showing off, as in the special effects of Fritz Lang's *Metropolis*, or F. W. Murnau's *Faust* and *Nosferatu*.

At the time, there is little evidence, from the critical reception either in Germany or abroad, that audiences or commentators at the time noted any of the political implications drawn retrospectively by Siegfried Kracauer, although the inherent ambivalences, stylizations and suspended plot resolutions of so many films made it easy to project meanings after the fact, when the need for explanation became more urgent, as it did after 1945. The same ambiguities and open-endedness also made it easier for the differently described idioms of Expressionism to move and migrate, irrespective of whether those who traveled with Expressionism were immigrants, refugees and exiles, or found in Expressionism a palette or toolbox that allowed them to celebrate the cinema and their stylistic bravura or technical prowess.

This is also the reason why the reference to "influence" (inaugurated by Lotte Eisner's *Haunted Screen*, but perpetuated by many film historians since)[60] is misleading and misplaced. Better to speak of appropriation and borrowing, of migration and transfer, in order to avoid spurious genealogies and do justice to the mutability and adaptability of an idiom I described as transferable design features rather than the manifestation of a "will-to-style."

With respect to Expressionism as a feature of Weimar cinema, it was the Kracauer of the 1920s (rather than of 1947) who came closest to seizing the moment of its historical truth, when arguing that the competing claims of both high modernism and popular culture are better served by a cult(ure) of distraction than a mass medium promoting its exceptions as art.[61] On the other hand, Eisner was also right. Expressionism has triumphed in the cinema, though not as a period style or as the signature style of singularly gifted directors, but as the historical imaginary of filmic representation as such, today perhaps rather too complacently distrusted as to any truth claims it might put forward, having decided to make stylization, simulation and fantasy the default value of motion picture reality. Yet the challenge of Weimar cinema was precisely this: in its very first masterpiece—*The Cabinet of Dr. Caligari*—Expressionism chose to enlist the cinema not in issues of realism, not even in the quest for "truth," but in the search for enduringly equivocal, fundamentally skeptical, and transparently ironic modes of representation. This is Expressionism's live legacy, worth once more to be investigated, but also celebrated, as filmmakers are navigating the still uncharted waters of the cinema's post-photographic future.

NOTES

1. Among the abundant literature on German Expressionism as an art movement and a film style, see Richard Murphy, *Theorizing the Avant-Garde: Modernism, Expressionism, and the Problem of Postmodernity* (Cambridge: Cambridge University Press, 1999), and Dietrich Scheunemann (ed.), *Expressionist Film: New Perspectives* (New York: Camden House, 2003).
2. Kristin Thompson, "Dr. Caligari at the Folies-Bergère: or, The Successes of an Early Avant-Garde Film," in Michael Budd (ed.), *The Cabinet of Dr. Caligari: Texts, Contexts, Histories* (New Brunswick, NJ: Rutgers University Press, 1990), pp. 121–69.
3. For more on Ufa, see Klaus Kreimeier, *The Ufa Story: A History of Germany's Greatest Film Company, 1918–1945* (trans. Robert and Rita Kimber) (New York: Hill & Wang, 1996) and my "German Cinema 1986–1929," in Geoffrey Nowell-Smith (ed.), *Oxford World History of Cinema* (Oxford: Oxford University Press, 1996), pp. 136–51.
4. According to a leading trade journal, the top ten directors of 1927, ranked by popularity, were: Richard Eichberg, Fritz Lang, Richard Oswald, Friedrich Zelnick, Joe May, Gerhard Lamprecht, Arnold Fanck, Franz Osten, Georg Jacoby, Holger Madsen (*Filmbühne*, No. 8, 1927, p. 5).
5. Siegfried Kracauer, *From Caligari to Hitler* (Princeton, NJ: Princeton University Press, 1947).
6. Lotte H. Eisner, *The Haunted Screen: Expressionism in the German Cinema and the Influence of Max Reinhardt* (trans. Roger Graeves) (Berkeley, CA: University of California Press, 1969 [1952]).
7. Examples of such textbook accounts are: David Bordwell and Kristin Thompson, *Film Art* (New York: McGraw-Hill, multiple editions since 1979), David Cook, *A History of Narrative Film* (New York: Norton, multiple editions since 1980).
8. See Eric Rhode, *A History of Cinema* (London: Penguin, 1976).
9. George A. Huaco, *Towards A Sociology of Cinema* (New York: Basic Books, 1965), pp. 27–91; Andrew Tudor, *Image and Influence* (London: Allen & Unwin, 1974), pp. 55–77; see also Paul Monaco, *Ribbons of Time: Cinema and Society* (New York: Elsevier, 1976) and Ian Jarvie, *Towards a Sociology of Cinema* (London: Routledge, 1970).
10. See Douglas Gomery and Robert C. Allen, *Film History: Theory and Practice* (New York: Knopf, 1985) and J. P. Telotte, "German Expressionism: a Cinematic/Cultural Problem," in Linda Badley, R. Barton Palmer and Steven Jay Schneider (eds.), *Traditions in World Cinema* (New Brunswick, NJ: Rutgers University Press, 2006), pp. 15–29.
11. Especially the question of what was appropriate film acting was vividly discussed at the time. See Herbert Ihering, "Der Schauspieler im Film" (1920), in Herbert Ihering, *Von Reinhardt bis Brecht. Vier Jahrzehnte Theater und Film*, Vol. I

(Berlin: Aufbau Verlag, 1958), pp. 378–414; and Julius Bab, *Schauspieler und Schauspielkunst* (Berlin, 1926). For further discussions, see Dennis Calandra, "The Nature of Expressionist Performance," *Theatre Quarterly*, 21 (Spring 1976), pp. 45–53 and Barry Salt, *Film Style and Technology: History and Analysis* (London: Starword, 1983), p. 198.
12. "Homunculus walked about in the flesh. Self-appointed Caligaris hypnotized innumerable Cesares into murder. Raving Mabuses committed fantastic crimes with impunity, and mad Ivans devised unheard-of tortures. Along with this unholy procession, many motifs known from the screen turned into actual events" (Kracauer, *From Caligari to Hitler*, p. 272).
13. The books on Weimar culture fill a small library. For a long time, the standard works were John Willett, *Art and Politics in the Weimar Period: The New Sobriety, 1917–1933* (New York: Pantheon, 1978), Walter Laqueur, *Weimar—A Cultural History* (New York: Putnam, 1974) and Peter Gay, *Weimar Culture: The Outsider as Insider* (Westport, CT: Greenwood, 1981). In all three books, Weimar culture is a cluster of contradictory representations and mirror relations, formed around the names Marlene Dietrich, Martin Heidegger, Bert Brecht, Berlin in the 1920s and Christopher Isherwood's Sally Bowles. For first-hand documents, see also Anton Kaes, Martin Jay and Edward Dimendberg (eds.), *The Weimar Republic Sourcebook* (Berkeley, CA: University of California Press, 1995).
14. For Kracauer, see Karsten Witte, preface to *Von Caligari zu Hitler* (Frankfurt: Suhrkamp, 1978), pp. 7–14.
15. Critical evaluations of Kracauer can be found in all the studies listed. For an early critique see John Tulloch, "Genetic Structuralism and the Cinema," *The Australian Journal of Screen Theory*, 1 (1976), pp. 3–50. For a discussion of the initial critical response to *From Caligari to Hitler*, not only in Germany, see Karsten Witte, postface to *Von Caligari zu Hitler*, pp. 605–15.
16. Among the most trenchant critiques, each from a very different vantage point, see Barry Salt, "From Caligari to Who?," *Sight and Sound*, Spring 1979, pp. 119–23; Noel Carroll, "Dr. Caligari and Dr. Kracauer," *Millennium Film Journal* 2, Spring–Summer 1978, pp. 77–85; and Martin Sopocy, "Re-examining Kracauer's *From Caligari to Hitler*," *Griffithiana* (October 1991), pp. 40–2.
17. Neither Kracauer nor Eisner mentions Ernst Lubitsch's *The Mountain Cat* (1921), a parody of Expressionist decor and sets, which become mere props and obstacles in a slapstick comedy. Such a counter-example indicates a more playful (or cynical) relation to Expressionist style and decor than the symptomatic interpretations as a reflection of the national character would seem to allow.
18. Rudolf Kurtz, *Expressionismus und Film* (Berlin: Verlag der Lichtbildbühne, 1926; facsimile reprints: Zurich: Verlag Hans Rohr, 1965; Zurich: Chronos 2007), p. 61.
19. Ibid. p. 46.
20. Dating according to Olaf Brill, *Der Caligari-Komplex* (Munich: Belleville, 2012), pp. 196–212.
21. Janowitz's story, endorsed by Kracauer, is that he and Carl Mayer had fought against the producer, Erich Pommer, who demanded a narrative frame. Their original story was a polemic against the tyranny of authority, while framing the narrative resulted in an affirmation of authority, the opposite of the writers' intentions. Yet this version of events has been largely discredited by Gero Gandert's acquisition, on behalf of the Stiftung Deutsche Kinemathek Berlin, of an early version of the screenplay from the estate of Werner Krauß, the actor playing Dr. Caligari. It transpires that the script had always opened with a prologue leading into a flashback. This prologue "neutralized" the supposedly revolutionary message even more effectively than the framing tale of the film as it was eventually made, because

the frame leaves the "message" ambiguous and open-ended, thus reinstating the menace. For a summary of the debate, see Budd, *The Cabinet of Dr. Caligari*, pp. 28–9; see also Brill, *Caligari-Komplex*, pp. 159–62 and 247–51.
22. Erich Pommer, "Carl Mayer's Debut," in *The Cabinet of Dr Caligari* (Classic Film Scripts, New York: Simon & Schuster, 1972), pp. 27–9. For a discussion of the contract between Mayer, Janowitz and Decla, see Jürgen Kasten, "Die Verträge des Dr Caligari," in M. Schaudig (ed.), *Positionen deutscher Filmgeschichte* (Munich: diskurs film, 1996), pp. 75–90, which also discusses the subsequent history of the screenplay, the rights, litigations, and the attempted and actual remakes of *Dr Caligari*.
23. On Robert Wiene, see Uli Jung and Walter Schatzberg, *Robert Wiene, der Caligari Regisseur* (Berlin: Henschel, 1996), pp. 60–81, and also Mike Budd, "The Moments of *Caligari*," pp. 32–6 for another account of the question of rights and remakes.
24. Erich Pommer: "At first Caligari was a big box-office flop ... so I forced Caligari through a poster and publicity campaign. We had posters all over Berlin, with Conrad Veidt and the words 'You must see Caligari', 'Have you seen Caligari' etc." Cited in George A. Huaco, *The Sociology of Film Art* (New York: Basic Books, 1965), p. 34. This, in fact, repeats an advertising campaign from 1913, around the Max Mack film *Wo ist Coletti?*. See Michael Wedel, *Max Mack, Showman im Glashaus* (Berlin: Freunde der Deutschen Kinemathek, 1998). Most commentators mention the advertising campaign but with the slogan "Du mußt Caligari werden" (You have to become Caligari). A historical context for such advertising is given in Michael Cowan, "Advertising, Rhythm, and the Filmic Avant-Garde in Weimar: Guido Seeber and Julius Pinschewer's Kipho Film," *October*, 131, Winter 2010, pp. 23–50.
25. After watching *Caligari*, the well-known writer Kurt Tucholsky asked sarcastically, where, in these crooked houses, would one find such sharp clothes and starched stiff collars as the male characters are sporting? *Die Weltbühne*, No. 11, 11 March 1920, p. 347; another critic, Herbert Ihering, worried about the female lead's sturdy iron bedstead, arguing that the film lacks the courage of its convictions, dithering too much between popular appeal and high-brow affectation, "Ein expressionistischer Film," *Berliner Börsen Courier*, No. 101, 29 February 1920, p. 8. Rudolf Arnheim, writing after a revival in 1925, comments on how old-fashioned it felt: "Dr. Caligari redivivus," *Das Stachelschwein*, No. 19, October 1925, p. 47.
26. Max Osborn, "Die Lage des Expressionismus," *Vossische Zeitung*, 8 November 1920, cited in Leonardo Quaresima, "Der Expressionismus als Filmgattung," in Uli Jung and Walter Schatzberg, *Filmkultur zur Zeit der Weimarer Republik* (Munich: Saur, 1992), p. 175.
27. Pommer, quoted in Ursula Hardt, *From Caligari to California: Erich Pommer's Life in the International Film Wars* (Oxford: Berghahn, 1996), p. 48.
28. Louis Delluc, "Le Cabinet du Docteur Caligari," *Cinéma*, 44, 10 March 1922. For an extended discussion of *Caligari* in France, see Kristin Thompson, "Dr. Caligari at the Folies-Bergère."
29. See Yuri Tsivian, "Caligari in Rußland," in Oksana Bulgakowa (ed.), *Die ungewöhnlichen Abenteuer des Dr. Mabuse im Land der Bolschwiki* (Berlin: Freunde der deutschen Kinemathek, 1995), pp. 169–76.
30. German cinema's supporters in the Netherlands were—apart from Joris Ivens—L. J. Jordaan, Mannus Franken and Menno ter Braak. See Ansje van Beusekom, *Film als Kunst: reacties op een nieuw medium in Nederland, 1895–1940* (Amsterdam: Vrije Universiteit, 1998), pp. 134–230.
31. Bryher, "G. W. Pabst: A Survey," in *Close Up*, December 1927; John Moore,

"Pabst, Dovjenko: A Comparison," in *Close Up*, September 1932; Paul Rotha, "Pabst, Pudovkin, and the Producers," in *Sight and Sound*, Summer 1933. Rotha was also one of the first film historians to canonize Expressionist cinema as a distinctly "national" (i.e. German) film style. His *The Film Till Now* (London: Cape, 1930) served as a model for several generations of historical surveys.

32. Luis Buñuel, *My Last Breath* (London: Cape, 1984), p. 88.
33. Those films were shot as co-productions with British company Gainsborough Pictures, London. Michael Balcon, Hitchcock's producer, had a special agreement with Ufa, as a consequence of which Oscar Werndorff and Alfred Junge, two young German art directors, came to London and began very successful careers. See Tim Bergfelder, "Rooms with a view" in Jörg Schöning (ed.), *London Calling* (Munich: text + kritik, 1993), pp. 55–68. On Hitchcock and Expressionism, see also Sid Gottlieb, "Early Hitchcock: the German Influence," *Hitchcock Annual* (1999), pp. 100–30.
34. See Standish D. Lawder, *The Cubist Cinema* (New York: New York University Press, 1975), pp. 96–7.
35. See the monumental work by Michel Bouvier and Jean Louis Leutrat, *Nosferatu* (Paris: Gallimard, 1981).
36. Noël Burch and Jorge Dana, "Propositions," *Afterimage*, No. 5, Spring 1974, pp. 44–66 and Noël Burch, "Notes on Fritz Lang's first *Mabuse*," *Cine-tracts*, Vol. 4, No. 1, Spring 1981.
37. On Max Reinhardt's influence on Weimar cinema, see Jo Leslie Collier, *From Wagner to Murnau* (Ann Arbor, MI: UMI Research Press, 1988), pp. 77–104.
38. Heide Schönemann's *Fritz Lang, Filmbilder, Vorbilder* (1992) details the echoes from art, painting and architecture in the films of Lang, explicitly setting out to continue and complement the work of Lotte Eisner. Besides Eisner, she mentions Rune Waldekranz, Jurek Mikuz and Frieda Grafe, who have all worked on the origins and recurrence of visual motifs in Lang's films. On Lang's *Siegfried*, see also Sabine Hake, "Architectural Hi/stories: Fritz Lang and *The Nibelungs*," *Wide Angle*, Vol. 12, No. 3, July 1990, pp. 38–57, and Angelika BreitmoserBock, *Bild, Filmbild, Schlüsselbild* (Munich: diskurs film, 1993).
39. Barry Salt, "From Caligari to Who?," *Sight and Sound*, Spring 1979, pp. 119–23.
40. Barry Salt, "From German Stage to German Screen," in Paolo Cherchi Usai and Lorenzo Codelli (eds.), *Prima di Caligari/Before Caligari* (Pordenone: Biblioteca dell'Immagine, 1990), pp. 402–22.
41. Hans-Michael Bock (ed.), *Paul Leni* (Frankfurt: Deutsches Filmmuseum, 1985).
42. See also Kristin Thompson, "Expressionistic Mise-en-scène," in her *Eisenstein's Ivan the Terrible* (Princeton, NJ: Princeton University Press, 1981), p. 173.
43. Pommer claimed that the painted shadows in *Caligari* were said to be due to power shortages, and that the company nearly went bankrupt during the period of shooting. See Ursula Hardt, *From Caligari to California: Erich Pommer's Life in the International Film Wars* (Oxford: Berghahn, 1996), pp. 48–50.
44. Eisner, *The Haunted Screen*, p. 48.
45. Lotte Eisner herself backtracked a few years later, and restricted Expressionism to only three films: *The Cabinet of Dr. Caligari, From Morning to Midnight* and *Alraune*. See her "Der Einfluß des expressionistischen Stils auf die Ausstattung der deutschen Filme der zwanziger Jahre," in *Paris–Berlin: 1900–1933* (Munich: Prestel, 1979), p. 270, and "stile und Gattungen des Films," in Lotte H. Eisner and Heinz Friedrich (eds.), *Das Fischer Lexikon. Film. Rundfunk. Fernsehen* (Frankfurt: Fischer, 1958), p. 264.
46. Both Fritz Lang and Carl Mayer for a time earned their living as young men in the postcard trade (Kracauer, *From Caligari to Hitler*, p. 62).

47. Anon., "Aspects of Expressionism (3) It Lives Again," *Monthly Film Bulletin*, August 1979 (backpage).
48. Ibid.
49. The term "super-text" I adapt from Nick Browne, "The Political Economy of the Television (Super) Text," in Nick Browne (ed.) *American Television* (Langhorne, PA: Harwood, 1994), pp. 69–80.
50. Eisner's detailed accounts of who worked with whom shows a fairly close-knit community, whether its members actually worked for and trained with Max Reinhardt or not. But see also Kreimeier, *The Ufa Story* on the Ufa producer-director teams.
51. See Paul Wegener, "Die künstlerischen Möglichkeiten des Films" (1916), in Kai Möller (ed.), *Paul Wegener: Sein Leben und seine Rollen. Ein Buch von ihm und über ihn* (Hamburg: Rowohlt, 1954), pp. 110–11.
52. See Robert Herlth, "Zur Technik der Filmarchitektur," in his *Filmarchitektur* (Munich: Deutsches Institut für Film und Fernsehen, 1965), p. 60.
53. The key texts of the Expressionism debate can be found in Ronald Taylor (ed.), *Aesthetics and Politics: Radical Thinkers* (New York: Verso, 1980).
54. Theodor W. Adorno and Max Horkheimer, "The Culture Industry: Enlightenment as Mass Deception," in their *Dialectic of Enlightenment* (trans. Edmund Jephcott) (Stanford, CA: Stanford University Press, 2002), pp. 94–136.
55. Thomas Elsaesser, "A German Ancestry to Film Noir?—Film History and its Imaginary," in *Iris (Paris)*, No. 21, Spring 1996, pp. 129–44.
56. Among the music videos referencing *The Cabinet of Dr. Caligari* are Rob Zombie's "Living Dead Girl," Rainbow's "Can't Let You Go" and Red Hot Chili Peppers' "Otherside."
57. *Nosferatu* (1922, F. W. Murnau) premiered in Berlin with a high-society ball and had as "prologue" a modern dance performance. After the screening, "the guests quickly turned the 'symphony of horror' into a delightful symphony of merriment." *Film-Kurier*, No. 52, 6 March 1922.
58. For an extensive historical re-assessment of *Caligari*, see my "Dr Caligari's Family: Expressionism, Frame Tales, and Master Narratives" in my *Weimar Cinema and After* (New York: Routledge, 2000), pp. 61–105. Since then, there has been a "remake" by David Lee Fischer (2005) which uses the original sets, but digitally replaces the original characters with contemporary actors and a digital restoration of the original, by the Murnau Foundation (2014), with brilliant image quality and luminous tints, successfully revived at festivals all over the world.
59. See the essays in Warren Buckland (ed.), *Puzzle Films—Complex Storytelling in Contemporary Cinema* (Oxford: Wiley-Blackwell, 2009).
60. Paul Cooke neatly sums up this tendency: "Numerous critics have suggested that the psychological despair of Weimar identified by Kracauer was transposed neatly to the bleak world of 1940s and 1950s film noir and the society in crisis to be found in the American films of Lang, Billy Wilder, Robert Siodmak and others. Moreover, it is an influence which has rubbed off on a variety of subsequent filmmakers, from Orson Welles and Alfred Hitchcock to Ridley Scott and Tim Burton. In the work of these later film-makers, critics generally view this German avant-garde movement as a kind of inherited style that casts its shadow over the production design they adopt in their work." Paul Cooke, "From Caligari to Edward Scissorhands: The Continuing Meta-Cinematic Journey of German Expressionism," in Paul Cooke (ed.), *World Cinema's Dialogue with Hollywood* (Houndmills: Palgrave Macmillan, 2007), p. 18. I am assuming that "transposed neatly," "rubbed off," "casts its shadow" are terms meant to be taken ironically.
61. See, for instance, the essays collected in Siegfried Kracauer, *The Mass Ornament—Weimar Essays* (Cambridge, MA: Harvard University Press, 1995).

2. OF NERVES AND MEN: POSTWAR DELUSION AND ROBERT REINERT'S *NERVEN*

Steve Choe

Robert Reinert's frenetic film *Nerven*[1] was conceived as World War I ended and revolutions broke out throughout Germany in November 1918. Spearheaded in large part by Karl Liebknecht, Rosa Luxemburg, and the communist Spartacist League, the uprisings consisted of exploited workers, unwilling sailors, pacifist soldiers, and other war-weary Germans who sought to overthrow the Kaiser's military regime. They dismantled the monarchy and paved the way for watershed political developments to take place throughout the empire, including the founding of the socialist *Räterepublik* in Munich. For a few months it seemed a socialist state would be implemented. On November 7, over sixty thousand workers and soldiers assembled in the *Theresienwiese* for the one-year anniversary of the Russian Revolution. They forced the abdication of the Bavarian King and, filled with revolutionary zeal the following day, declared the new Soviet Republic, the "*Freistaat Bayern*."

The socialist aims of the revolution would ultimately not be realized. However, its democratic goals would inform specific articles of the Weimar constitution, drafted in early 1919. Germany's first attempt at a republican form of government represented a definitive break from the assumptions of the old Wilhelmine order. Its founding document, however, was hastily drafted and too ambitious, as its many provisions permitted massive compromises between the political extremes. And in what would become one of its most fatal flaws, Article 48, the so-called *Notverordnung* clause, expanded the power of the Chancellor to suspend civil liberties under certain "states of emergency." One week after Lenin sent a message of greeting to the Bavarian Soviet Republic in early May 1919,[2] the Freikorps and other soldiers still loyal to the German Army stormed Munich and defeated the Socialists in a series of intense street fights. When the Weimar constitution was signed and implemented in August of that year, Munich became a hotbed for extreme right-wing politics, mobilizing those who felt betrayed by the government and who demanded a return to the nationalist Fatherland. One of these movements would manifest itself in Hitler's beer hall putsch in 1923.

The crowd scenes in the first two acts of *Nerven* were filmed on location in the summer of 1919 in Munich. Recalling the violent changes of power in this politically volatile city, they re-enact the political chaos that had taken place over the past year. According to film scholar Jan-Christopher Horak:

> The film is, in fact, Reinert's conservative interpretation of the civil war that raged in Germany after the fall of the Imperial German government, just as *Homunculus* had been a conservative interpretation of the connection between World War I and the rise of the Social International.[3]

Horak expands on this reading in an essay written for the 2008 *Filmmuseum München* DVD release, placing *Nerven* in context with *The Decline of the West* (1918–22), Oswald Spengler's two-volume work of pessimistic *Kulturkritik* contemporaneous with Reinert's film. Horak argues that *Nerven* depicts a "Caesarist" individual in the character of Teacher Johannes, an authoritarian personality who will ostensibly unify the nation following the decline of Western civilization. In the midst of massive political and economic upheaval, this image of sovereign authority would have powerfully resonated with Germany's postwar audiences.

Anton Kaes seems to concur with Horak's characterization in his treatment of Reinert's film. In *Shell Shock Cinema* Kaes argues that Weimar films, including *Nerven*, must be read through the experience of trauma that pervaded all culture following the war. He writes:

> Seen from this angle, war and revolution were symptoms of a larger malaise: a collective neurasthenia in response to belated but frenzied modernization and urbanization. The discourse on nerves also allowed the filmmaker to create a nexus between the battlefield and the home front.[4]

While it does not show explicit scenes of military combat, *Nerven* depicts the profound effects of war on the nerves of those who were survivors of it: uncontrollable shakes, stutters, tremors, and delusions of sight and hearing. "Reinert's film dramatizes the extent to which the toxic effects of war and defeat have infected an entire culture."[5] Barbara Hales' essay "Unsettling

Nerves: Investigating War Trauma in Robert Reinert's *Nerven* (1919)" extends this reading and contextualizes *Nerven* within postwar understandings of male hysteria and the war malingerer:[6] "In contrast to the neurasthenic, who has the will but not the stamina, the hysteric possesses a faulty genetic make-up, resulting in the rejection of the will to fight."[7] At a time when war neurosis was not understood, traumatized soldiers were vilified for claiming unhealthy nerves and for refusing to reenter combat. Shell-shocked veterans were belittled for requesting pensions and psychiatric treatment for their ailments, and thus perceived as burdens on the struggling postwar state. Hales shows that the vilification of the war-neurotic is indicative of a larger denial, "of Germany's overall inability to accept defeat."[8] The paranoiac delusions that are depicted throughout the film may be explained by this disavowal, for the highly volatile, Expressionist imagery depicted in Reinert's film seems to manifest internalized, psychic wounds resulting from the experience of mechanized warfare.

In the following, I will work with the notion that war trauma and male hysteria go hand in hand in Weimar cultural representation; however, I would like to provide a more focused analysis of *Nerven* by analyzing the depictions of paranoid delusion that compulsively return throughout the film. These delusions originate in the character of Roloff, who experiences an unexpected event akin to shell shock and later begins to hallucinate irrational imagery (constructed through image superimposition and other in-camera special effects) as a consequence. These visual disturbances allegorize the aftereffects of war, psychic injuries left unmourned that were also often misunderstood, undiagnosed, and vilified by the Weimar medical community.[9] In this chapter, I will describe their etiology by drawing from psychoanalytic texts written by Sigmund Freud and Karl Abraham, not in order to discover the truth of Roloff's psychic suffering, but to show how Expressionist delusion puts a line of thinking about the postwar self into motion.

Nerves and Nervousness

In the late nineteenth century, the "nerves" were the generally accepted locus for what George M. Beard in 1869 called "neuroasthenia," or nervous exhaustion. The *Handbuch der Neurasthenie*, published in 1893, begins with a bibliographic chapter that lists hundreds of titles in German, English, and French published since Beard defined the expression. It concretized emerging scientific developments that linked psychology, physiology, and philosophy, while manifesting Nietzsche's critique of idealist metaphysics as a condition of life. The physiologist Ludimar Hermann makes a finer distinction in his text *Allgemeine Nervenphysiologie* (1879), and argues that the nerves, controlled by a rational will, mark the essential difference between animals and plants.

So crucial are the nerves in allowing organs to communicate with each other that "a defect of a part of the central nervous system results a corresponding failure of the nerve and animal muscles on which they are dependent."[10] Such failures were often attributed to the travails of modern life. The bustle of nineteenth-century urbanization and the mental stresses concomitant with the human animal's adaptation to new technologies, such as the telegraph, telephone, and the cinema, wore on healthy nerves. Modern civilization and progress strained the mind and body. In order to counteract the deleterious effects of modern living, one was often advised to return to nature and take up physical exercise so that the body might be "toughened up" and returned to health. Nervousness was often thought to be feminine and hysterical, in contrast to the spiritual strength associated with masculine vigor. In his extensive study, *Cult of the Will*, Michael Cowan correspondingly shows how late nineteenth- and early twentieth-century discourses of the will were mobilized to tame bodily and spiritual nervousness. Tic, spasms, paralysis and other signs of nervous ailment attest to the weakness of the internal will and its inability to rein in the nerves. "More than any other," writes Cowan, "the nervous subject appeared to be determined from the outside in and, correspondingly, unable to impose his subjectivity from the inside out."[11]

Between 1900 and 1913 a journal series, *Grenzfragen des Nerven- und Seelenlebens*, repeatedly referenced the discourse of nerves for understanding experiences of modernity that lie at the edge of established science: somnambulism, hypnosis, and the relationship between neurosis and creativity. In the second volume, the neurologist Heinrich Obersteiner makes the connection between nerves and nervous exhaustion (*Nervenanspannung*) explicit: "Commonly all purely functional symptoms or groups of symptoms on the part of the nervous systems belong to a range of psychic symptoms, when they are manifest outward like for example in the case of hysterical paralysis."[12] Obersteiner later identifies the pineal body as the "soul-organ of Descartes," isolating this endocrine gland, located between the two hemispheres of the brain, as the seat of Cartesian epistemology. Mind and body congeal in the nerves; idealist philosophy finds its genesis in the body's physiology.

When put through the trials of modern warfare, the nerves undergo unprecedented agitation. In his 1915 text *The War and the Nerves*, the neuropathologist Alois Alzheimer reiterates assumptions about healthy nerves and discusses what happens to men when they go off to war:

> When we take a close look at the relationship between the war and the nerves, we think less of nerves in the narrow sense, those white strands that run from the brain and spinal cord through the body to the sense organs, the skin, the muscles, and joints, in order that sensations may be carried to the brain or impulses of the will to the muscles. Rather, it refers

to the nervous central organ, particularly the brain, the organ of our soul, where thinking, feeling and human action originates.[13]

Alzheimer, who had already been recognized for identifying the symptoms of late-onset dementia now referred to as "Alzheimer's disease," reiterates the importance of the network of nerves while figuring the soul, not simply a metaphysical category, but as concretely localized in the brain. He emphasizes the relationship of the nerves to the mettle of the German people in wartime, isolating this organ, commonly associated with cogitation, as the seat of courage: "Where we speak of tough nerves, a brave heart, or cold blood, we are really talking about the accomplishments of the brain."[14] The constitution of the strong warrior is directly linked for Alzheimer to the efficient and proper functioning of the nervous system. In his wartime text he draws attention to the traumas experienced by soldiers,

> those who found themselves in the immediate vicinity of a grenade and were severely wounded by an exploding shell. Because of this violent terror, some have lost their ability to speak or hear and became deaf and silent, experiencing paralysis in both legs or in one-half of their body, having cramps, or entered into a dazed state, a traumatic, foggy condition of consciousness, in which the sick do not know their orientation in place and time, are confused, and often express experiences of terror or something to that effect.[15]

Despite his call for the hardening of the nerves in wartime, Alzheimer acknowledges their harrowing, life-changing effect on the human soul. The war has dulled the "prudence, calm, and clarity of the faculty of judgment,"[16] he writes. He also acknowledges those on the home front who must suffer and sacrifice by caring for the traumatized fathers, brothers, and uncles returned from the battlefield.[17] For Alzheimer, the war put the future of the German family at risk.

This cultural context provides the backdrop for Reinert's *Nerven*, whose imagery seems to draw from contemporaneous discourses about the nerves. The film's opening scenes depict watershed moments that will give rise to the production of traumatic delusions later in the film. Act 1 begins with the prominent industrialist Roloff (Eduard von Winterstein) and his wife Elisabeth (Lia Borré) celebrating the 500th anniversary of The House of Roloff. Marja (Erna Morena), his sister, is to be married to the aristocratic Richard (Rio Ellbon), the Count of Colonna. Marja admires Teacher Johannes (Paul Bender), whom she has known since her student days. In the opening scene, Roloff stands before a mass gathering and announces that his machines and tools will allow him and his followers to conquer the earth, making them "masters of the world."

Figure 2.1 German trade advertisement for Robert Reinert's *Nerven* (1919).

At the very moment Roloff announces his megalomaniac plans for world domination, and as his mesmerized listeners raise their fists in victory, the film suddenly cuts to Roloff's factories exploding into flames while their smokestacks collapse. Foreshadowing scenes of the malfunctioning Moloch in Fritz Lang's *Metropolis*, the "exploding machine" in *Nerves* soon "destroys the newly opened factory," sending Roloff's followers to pandemonium.

Amid the mounting state of emergency, Teacher Johannes makes an appear-

Figure 2.2 A frame from *Nerven*.

Figure 2.3 A frame from *Nerven*.

ance before the people and, to calm their desperate confusion, begins speaking of the devastation reaped by war and of the nation's collective trauma. "The peoples are mourning on bloody battlefields," he declares, while calling for the end of the "greed for power which marched across the earth like some hideous beast." Cutting back to Roloff, the agitated industrialist convalesces at home, incapacitated with a serious case of the nerves. "I used to have nerves of steel, but since then," he remarks to his wife Elisabeth, "I keep seeing the ghosts of the dead rising to wreak their terrible revenge on us, and especially on me."

Intercut with his words are two short shots that express his inner turmoil: one reiterates the imagery of his exploding factories and another showing a young man holding a large sword and standing over corpses on a battlefield. The latter riterates its corresponding shot from the prologue, featuring dead bodies strewn under a gnarled tree, perhaps referencing corpses on a battlefield. However, here the shot is more ominous, symbolizing two catastrophes: one that has already taken place and one that soon will.

While riots take place in the streets, Marja challenges their nervous gardener, who has secretly loved her since they were childhood friends, to action. "Down there people are fighting for their lives and you're running around love struck, you coward!" Her denunciation inflames him. "I am no coward," he protests to his mother and father. Agitated, he grabs an ax, enters a busy intersection of his town, and chops down the first man who accosts him. The humiliated gardener is then quickly apprehended by armed citizens, stood against a wall, and shot. Meanwhile, people on the streets march and engage in firefights, as factions vie to gain control following the social and political chaos unleashed by Roloff's exploding factories.

So that she may prepare for the coming political utopia, Marja calls off her arranged marriage to Richard, rejecting bourgeois social affiliations. This bond would have maintained the longstanding reputation of Roloff and his lineage. Marja confesses that she does not love the count. Instead, she is driven by a passionate desire for a new societal order, one that will interrupt old habits and do away with traditional social relations. Her brother Roloff, shocked by her decision to call off the wedding, asks, "For God's sake, what's the matter with you?" He desperately urges Marja to speak, violently shaking her shoulders and pleading with her. Overcome with shame, she is unable to explain why Johannes "possesses" her while Richard does not. Her continuing intransigence exacerbates Roloff's "overwrought nerves" (*überreizten Nerven*) and incites his delusional imagination. The film cuts to a brief hallucination, belonging to Roloff, of Teacher Johannes forcing himself onto Marja. Like the repeated memories of his exploding factories, the hallucination appears in a moment of extreme anxiety. In the brief cutaway scene, Johannes aggressively grabs Marja and, overcoming her resistance, kisses her. When the film cuts back, Roloff has already convinced himself that his sister was the victim of sexual assault. "I swore I saw it . . .," he gravely remarks.

His fantasy is later used as evidence in the courtroom sequence, proof that eventually indicts Johannes as an adulterer. That the industrialist is fully aware of the political opportunity revealed by Marja's imagined violation is revealed in a scene between him and the District Attorney. This is the moment, Roloff states, when we may "eliminate our most powerful enemy." Such sentiment

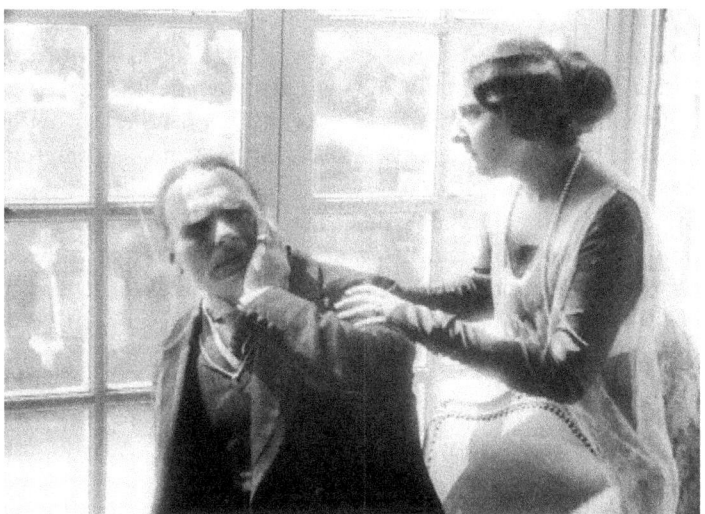

Figure 2.4 A frame from *Nerven*.

would have resonated with Munich audiences, who had witnessed the politics of revenge in the rapid exchange of power in 1918 and 1919, and watched how political lines that separated the Spartacist League, the SPD, and the nationalistic right had become increasingly contentious and militarized.

Roloff's delusion is shown two more times in *Nerves*, like a repetition compulsion, each constituting key moments in its plot. With each reiteration, Roloff begins to question whether the memory actually took place. He is unable to purge his traumatic memories, while his desperate self-scrutinizing only further escalates his nervous suffering. Meanwhile, as the film unfolds, his delusions become increasingly bizarre and extreme. Portrayed through in-camera special effects, Roloff sees himself wandering through a distorted forest, then drifting through an angry crowd of people, and later choking his wife. While the discourse of the nerves and nervousness describes his agitated condition, Roloff's mounting anxiety and hallucination, particularly the sexual content of his vision of Marja's assault, seem to gesture toward another mode of explanation that was quickly gaining currency after the war: the science of psychoanalysis. It is this discourse that will allow us to clearly see how and why Roloff continues to hallucinate in a massive effort to shore up his traumatized self.

Freud's 1908 essay "'Civilized' Sexual Morality and Modern Nervousness" shifts the analytical concerns regarding neurasthenia away from the nerves to the area of psychic life. The essay responds directly to Christian von Ehrenfels' paper "*Sexualethik*," published in *Grenzfragen des Nerven- und*

Seelenlebens, and quotes at length passages on the nerves by Wilhelm Heinrich Erb, Otto Ludwig Binswanger, and the sexologist Richard von Kraft-Ebbig. While commenting on contemporaneous tracts on neurasthenia written by these and other researchers, Freud moves away from "the less definite forms of 'nervousness'" and "considers the actual forms of nervous disease."[18] The psychoanalyst argues that neurotic disorder may be linked to the interdictions imposed by modern sexual ethics, and that the actual origins of what is called neurasthenia may be traced back to "the undue suppression of the sexual life in civilized peoples (or classes) as a result of the 'civilized' sexual morality which prevails among them."[19] Freud thus shifts from the organic-mechanistic terminology of neurasthenia to the psychoanalytic vocabulary of neurosis and the politics of civilized sexuality.

Still, Freud acknowledges the crucial link between neurosis and the stresses of modernity, albeit a negative one, by asserting that neurosis remains a type of sexual expression that defies societal prohibition. Neurosis is a flight from psychic conflict into disease when the libido cannot find its normal path to satisfaction in modern life. In short, neurosis in psychoanalysis is the symptomatic expression of illicit wishes repressed by society. This interpretation of sexual desire allowed Freud to consider cases of nervousness beyond the discourse of the nerves, beyond their excitability and exhaustibility, theorized by writers such as Obersteiner and Alzheimer, and to reconsider symptoms such as melancholy and anxiety. If *Nerves* is an allegory about war trauma, a psychoanalytic consideration of damaged nerves allows us to assess its psychic etiology.

Freud's colleague Karl Abraham was afforded the opportunity to observe the symptoms of war trauma directly during his service to the Fatherland as the chief physician of the Berlin Grunewald military hospital. Donning an official uniform, sword, and heavy boots, he received injured soldiers and treated their physical and mental wounds.[20] In January 1915, Abraham wrote to Freud describing his observation of nervous symptoms already familiar to him:

> I have seen a number of traumatic neuroses, well known to us from peacetime, in a typical form. They were all men who had had accidents at the front, such as being run over; they had not been wounded. I have also seen several severe cases of hysteria in men knocked unconscious by explosions. They mostly have aphasia-abasia and hysterical attacks.[21]

Two months later, in early March, he was relocated to Allenstein in East Prussia in order to continue his work with traumatized soldiers. There he observed signs of male hysteria corresponding to archetypes of the prewar "impotent male." This correspondence between prewar and postwar subject formations quickly confirmed for Abraham that the symptoms of war trauma should be diagnosed as stemming from some unknown, unconscious sexual irregularity.

Abraham's experience with returned soldiers thus convinced him that psychoanalysis could serve as a viable curative method. His analysis of neurosis, and its link to sexual repression, suggested therapeutic solutions other than those resolved by Fritz Kaufmann's electrotherapy, the most popular method of dealing with war trauma at the time. "Kaufmannization" combined verbal suggestion with five minutes of high-voltage electrical current, in order to "reset" the nerves back to health. In a lecture presented at the 1918 Symposium of the Fifth International Psycho-analytical Congress in Budapest, a conference significant for reconvening colleagues under the banner of psychoanalysis, Abraham attests to the superiority of the psychoanalytic method over "'active' curative procedures,"[22] such as shock therapy. He also rebuffs popular skepticism surrounding the illegitimacy of the mentally disturbed soldier, rejecting the charge that traumatized veterans assert their victimization so that they may avoid returning to the Front or win a pension. Instead, Abraham explains that their neurosis should be described as "the impulse to a regressive alteration which endeavours to reach narcissism."[23]

Indeed, the patients he treated during wartime displayed symptoms similar to those exhibited by Roloff in *Nerven*. In Abraham's Budapest lecture he recounts a case involving a patient, who before the war had demonstrated neurotic tendencies and "behaved like a terrified little child" after standing in the proximity of a mine explosion. His portrayal uncannily corresponds to Roloff's terrified response to his exploding factories. The psychoanalyst writes that "For many weeks he could only reply to all questions about his trouble with the two words, 'mine bombs.' He had therefore gone back to the mode of expression of a child hardly two years old."[24] Many neurotics, despite their propensity toward thoughts of death and bouts of depression, Abraham goes on to explain, maintain their relatively healthy demeanor only by believing in a narcissistic fantasy of immortality. However, the effect of an explosion, a severe physical wound, or other extreme experience quickly extinguishes this belief, and "the narcissistic security gives way to a feeling of powerlessness and the neurosis sets in."[25] The film scholar Philipp Stiasny, in his reading of Reinert's film, seems to corroborate this when he writes: "The collapse of his aged factories through an unexpected explosion, the experience of shock, followed by unrest, is a powerful metaphor for Germany's defeat in the war and the collapse of the empire."[26] Stiasny makes a comparison between Roloff and Kaiser Wilhelm II, in that while the industrialist fled into madness after his factories exploded, the Kaiser fled to Holland after military defeat.

In a handful of cases, the psychic trauma of the returned soldier gives rise to the formation of delusions. These cases shed greater light on the specific role of sexuality in the etiology of war trauma while illuminating the primacy of sexuality in psychic life in general. Delusions point to a libidinal undecidability, Abraham writes, concomitant precisely with the symptoms of shell shock:

> In the cases I have seen the delusions are partly of jealousy, partly of homosexual persecution by comrades. I might mention the paranoid illness of a soldier which broke out when he, after long service in the field, went home on furlough and turned out to be impotent with his wife. A very transparent symbolism and other signs pointed with certainty to the significance of homosexual components as the fundamental cause of the delusion.[27]

The soldier's peacetime narcissism comes into conflict with homosexual desires that had found an outlet in the community of male soldiers during the war. On the battlefield, soldiers must be prepared to give themselves over completely to their military unit and identify with the Fatherland. Through the homosocial bond of the unit, the ego is forced to renounce all individual narcissistic privileges and transfer his libido onto the group. Following the return to peacetime, the exclusive relations with men that were constitutive of the military unit come into intense conflict with the soldier's heterosexual relations with women:

> The narcissism breaks out. The capability of the transference of the sexual hunger (libido) dies away as well as the capacity of self-sacrifice in favour of the community. On the contrary, we now have a patient before us who himself needs care and consideration on the part of others, who in a typically narcissistic manner is in constant anxiety about his life and health. The obtrusiveness of the symptoms (tremors, arrack, etc.) is also narcissistic. Many of the patients show themselves complete female-passive in the surrender to their suffering. In their symptoms they are experiencing anew the situation which had caused the neurosis to break out, and soliciting the sympathy of other people.[28]

Delusions, according to Abraham, occur as the wartime libido attempts to reconnect with the external world. They arise through the conflict that comes about when homosexual tendencies associated with wartime are forcibly redirected toward normative, heterosexual aims in peacetime.

In Reinert's *Nerven*, the industrialist Roloff hallucinates the assault of his sister Marja by Teacher Johannes. The explosion of his factories precipitates these delusions. This key narrative element repeats the trauma of war and the subsequent formation of paranoiac delusions by soldiers returning from the Front. If we interpret this explosion as being allegorical of the exploding shells experienced in the trenches, then Roloff's unreal visions could be said to correspond to the delusions concocted by the traumatized soldier. And if we follow the logic set out by Abraham in his 1918 paper, we can see how Roloff's hallucinations may be connected to his regression to a narcissistic state, and to his behaving like a "terrified little child." Yet if this regression represents a retreat from the world, it is not clear why Roloff mistakes his inner delusions as external reality while simultaneously claiming to recognize the differences between them. As an intertitle from *Nerven* indicates, the paranoid industrialist keeps hallucinating and "seeing the ghosts of the dead rising to wreak their terrible revenge on us, and especially on me." It remains unclear why these visions must remain conspiratorial and even persecutory in nature. I would like to explore this further by delving deeper into the psychoanalytic theory around trauma and delusion elaborated at the time, returning to Freud's prewar writing on the nerves and paranoia. The following digression will, I hope, allow us to understand the narcissistic subjectivity that lies at the heart of postwar delusional fantasy. This etiology, in turn, deeply informs the Expressionist aesthetics of Reinert's film.

Freud articulated his theory of paranoia in 1911, in his reading of Daniel Paul Schreber's 1903 chronicle, *Memoirs of a Neurotic (Denkwürdigkeiten eines Nervenkranken)*. In these memoirs, the judge Schreber relates a number of significant disappointments in his life that led up to his mental collapse. In the 1884 Reichstag elections Schreber ran as a candidate of the National Liberal Party and humiliatingly lost to the socialist Bruno Geiser. His defeat resulted in a mild nervous breakdown and a six-month stay at the psychiatric hospital in Leipzig under the care of Paul Emil Flechsig. Following his treatment, and adding to his despair, Schreber's wife suffered a series of miscarriages. However, it was following his nomination in 1893 to the position of the presiding judge, or *Senatspräsident*, in the Supreme Court of Appeals that he began to experience severe symptoms of anxiety, sleeplessness, and hallucination. Schreber's memoirs recount details of his collapse, megalomania, fantasies of becoming a woman, delusions of persecution, and finally his paranoiac communion with the Sun and God.

Appropriating contemporary neurasthenic discourses, Schreber asserts that the human soul is constituted in and through the nerves of the body, "extraordinarily delicate structures—comparable to the finest filaments," and that "the total mental life of a human being rests on his/her excitability by external impressions."[29] The nerves bring impulses to their destination so that the body can perform their directed tasks. In contrast, God is without body, is nothing but nerves, and strangely, "they have in particular the faculty of transforming themselves into all things of the created world; in this capacity they are called rays; and herein lies the essence of divine creation."[30] Contact between man and God can only happen after death, when the dead corpse may avail itself to the divine gaze. The paranoid judge believes that his purpose on Earth is to prepare for his adjudication before God. The "nerves of morally depraved men are blackened; morally pure men have white nerves; the higher a man's moral standard in life, the more his nerves become completely white or pure, an intrinsic property of God's nerves."[31]

This understanding may be traced back Schreber's therapist Flechsig, whose research on the brain and phrenology, drawing extensively on nerve theory, localized mental functions such as the signaling of hunger and the perception of external objects in the cerebral cortex. In his 1896 lecture "*Gehirn und Seele*," Flechsig specifies their role in connecting the body to the soul:

> The nerves, which allow the representation of sensuous impulses in consciousness, enter into the brain cortex and the centers of sensation—and probably the sphere of bodily feeling—and run along nerve passages which present the judgments and excitations of the outside world together with the body's needs in the form of longings to consciousness. Both alike stimulate, from the activity of these sensitive points, on one side the apparatuses for physical movement and on the other the mental centers—this touches also on the problem of the expressivity of the eyes, in which countless nuances of feeling reflect themselves.[32]

Flechsig's explanation connects the brain with *Geist* and also with the expressivity of the eyes as organs dense with nerves and nerve activity. Both Flechsig and Schreber's accounts recall the first intertitle of Reinert's film, that asserts the nerves to be the "mysterious avenues of the soul," "messengers of highest desire and deepest suffering," and even the "soul itself." All operate from the nineteenth-century premise that the self exists only insofar as it may be reduced to a network of nerve fibers and thus cannot be localized in a single organ.

In Freud's reading of Schreber's memoirs, the linguistic signifiers that constitute his corpus avail themselves not to God, but to the hermeneutics of psychoanalysis. In his analysis, he proposes first that Schreber's persecutory God is indeed Dr Flechsig. This person is someone who at one point had been a particularly respected figure and is now considered hated and feared:[33]

> It appears that the person to whom the delusion ascribes so much power and influence, in whose hands all the threats of the conspiracy converge, is either, if he is definitely named, identical with someone who played an equally important part in the patient's emotional life before his illness, or else is easily recognizable as a substitute for him.[34]

Through another hermeneutic substitution, Freud writes that Schreber had discovered in Flechsig a substitute for his father, Moritz Schreber. The father Schreber had published, among a number of other books, *Ärztliche Zimmergymnastik* in 1855, an instructional text for children detailing exercises and child-rearing techniques for proper health and hygiene. If, Freud concludes, all intimate relationships are characterized by a fundamental ambivalence,[35] Schreber's emphasis on Flechsig as a feared figure coexists with the judge's homosexual attachment to the neuropathologist. "The intensity of the emotion," Freud continues, "is projected outwards in the shape of an external power, while its quality is changed into the opposite. The person who is now hated and feared as a persecutor was at one time loved and honoured."[36] When Schreber's libido had retracted from the external world onto himself, it led to a struggle between the narcissistic and homosexual impulses that had been revived in connection with his increasing dependence on Flechsig. Throughout his memoirs Schreber writes that Flechsig had repeatedly attempted to commit "soul-murder" upon him and regarded the physician as the one true enemy, over against which he had placed the almighty God. This juxtaposition suggested to Freud that Flechsig was figured as the person to whom Schreber had become erotically attached, becoming in turn his eternal persecutor as a result of his struggle with these unconscious homosexual impulses.[37]

Freud schematically works through the ways in which the paranoiac unconscious struggles against the proposition "I (a man) love him." He articulates this as a series of disavowals, not unlike those he articulates in his 1919 essay on the etiology of masochism, "A Child Is Being Beaten." With respect to the paranoiac, Freud recounts: "I do not love him—I hate him"; "I do not love him—I love her, because she loves me"; "It is not I who love the man—she loves him." Finally, in the last movement of this series of renunciations, the paranoiac performs the final claim that enacts an extreme form of regression: "I do not love at all—I do not love any one." This is the most significant substitution. Here the ego performatively renounces love yet unconsciously diverts the libido back onto the self, causing the self to retreat into a shell. For Freud this narcissistic movement, the performative disavowal of love, originates the delusions of the paranoiac.

In order to explain how this comes to be, Freud begins by observing that the statement, 'I do not love at all' places the ego in a passive relationship to the external world. What has been rejected and made unacceptable, namely the homoeroticism of the first proposition, is shifted to a perception emerging outside the ego. This shift is essentially part of a series of reaction-formations that attempt to expunge what is thought to be foreign to the paranoiac self. "An internal perception is suppressed," Freud writes, "and, instead, its content, after undergoing a certain degree of distortion, enters consciousness in the form of an external perception."[38] This helps us to understand Schreber's apocalyptic delusions and his forebodings of a forthcoming catastrophe. In the following, Freud explains that such delusions are not simply the result of a series of distortions that deflect what is undesired from the self, but are attempts to rebuild the world:

> And the paranoiac builds it up again, not more splendid, it is true, but at least so that he can once more live in it. He builds it up by the work of his delusions. *The delusion-formation, which we take to be a pathological product, is in reality an attempt at recovery, a process of reconstruction.* Such a reconstruction after the catastrophe is more or less successful, but never wholly so; in Schreber's words, there has been a "profound internal change" in the world. But the man has recaptured a relation, and often a very intense one, to the people and things in the world, although the relation may be a hostile one now, where formerly it was sympathetic and affectionate.[39]

Delusion is an attempt to reconnect with the world, after it has already been decathected, and is the result of an aporia that moves between negation and projection. As a massive psychic effort of homophobic repression, this "profound internal change" is brought about by the withdrawal of libidinal cathexes from entities external to the self. Delusions are thus the phantasms of an ego that has regressed to a narcissistic state and cannot abide by the homosexual components of this regression.[40]

As Reinert's film continues, Roloff's mental state becomes increasingly unstable. On the basis of the testimony of his hallucination, the sexual criminal Johannes is sentenced in court to six years' hard labor. And yet, far from fulfilling his death wish against his political enemy, Roloff begins to feel guilty for having been responsible for Johannes's indictment. In Act 4 of *Nerven*, he protests, "I saw it. After all, I swore that I did," and violently shakes Marja, demanding the truth. In order to reassure himself, he reiterates that he swore under oath that he saw it and yet asks, "Am I a fool, or a criminal?" Seriously questioning the truth content of what he perceived, he says to his wife Elisabeth, "We must keep it a secret, Marja has to remain silent. I took an oath . . .!" At this moment he comes to a watershed realization: "I have committed perjury. I am the most vile of all creatures." Finally giving in to the untruth of his delusions, Roloff also acknowledges his culpability for putting an innocent man in prison.

Roloff consults a nerve specialist and asks for his advice. Leading him through his psychiatric ward, the doctor explains that while his patients may look healthy, they are actually seriously ill, for they suffer because of "the progression of civilization [*Zivilisation*], the struggle for existence, anxiety and the terrors of war, the sins of the parents . . ." This list of what has gone wrong in modernity would certainly have resonated with cynical film audiences in the early Weimar period, who sought explanations for their own nervous illnesses.

Nervous Cinema

To the neurologist's list may be added the specific effects of the cinema on the nerves. In one of his first published essays from 1924, the film theorist Sergei Eisenstein explains that the aim of the modern cinema is to influence the audience "through a series of calculated pressures on its psyche."[41] It provokes this response in the spectator through radical montage which juxtaposes and accumulates image fragments in order to shock the spectator into a position of critical distance. Eisenstein calls this the "montage of attractions," a highly political approach toward film production whereby the spatial and temporal non-linearity of montage is purposefully heightened, so as to in effect assault the viewer with its brute, mechanical force. Roloff's delusions, made up of montages of unreal visions as well as accumulations of space through filmic superimposition, seem to allegorize this cinema of attractions[42] and its potentially traumatizing effects on the viewer. Reinert's film depicts this montage of attractions to a highly sensitive, postwar audience in early Weimar Germany, reproducing the delusions resultant from the trauma of the war through cinematic means.

This montage of attractions is played out in an account by the writer Josefa Halbinger, conveyed by her daughter Carlamaria Heim. Halbinger writes:

> It must have been 1921, when a film called *Nerven* played in Munich, and something extraordinary happened. The film was—in my opinion at the time—very good. However there were some people who saw the film and were delivered to a *Nervenklinik*. Afterwards the film was banned.[43]

Halbinger told her friend Bettl not to see the film. Curious and perhaps even a little defiant, Bettl promptly went to see it. The modern shocks offered up by *Nerven* apparently had a profound effect on her. One night after the screening she woke up and ran out in the street screaming, "I'm dying! I'm dying! Now I'm dying!"[44] Bettl began to insist that her mother be sent to the *Nervenklinik*, convinced that she was the one who was mentally disturbed. Halbinger finally persuaded Bettl to admit herself to the clinic, where she stayed for four months.

Originating in the delusions of Roloff, *Nerves* disturbs the psyche of the spectator through film's own medium-specific means. Montage, delusion, the depiction of hysteria and uncontrollable nervousness: these were all quite effective in unsettling Halbinger's friend. Yet her mental state is mirrored in Roloff's own interior instability. Both are reflected once more in the unsettled and highly agitated psyches that lived in the Republic immediately following the war. The cinema puts into motion this delusional, traumatized thinking through its characters, form, and aesthetics.

Figure 2.5 A frame from *Nerven*.

Figure 2.6 A frame from *Nerven*.

An intertitle from Act 4 unambiguously keys the spectator to Roloff's hallucinatory logic, and it presents the spectator with a single word: "Paranoia" (*Verfolgungswahn*). The word seems to describe the spectator's own disturbed state at this late moment in the film. It appears after Johannes had been released from prison and before a series of images that depict Roloff's paranoid delusions. Their extent seems to know no end.

Roloff walks in a stupor through his large mansion, and he asks himself where he is.

His familiar surroundings are made strange as the floor reflects the walls of the building in pools of water, while his image and then his double appear through superimposition. In the most extended of these delusions, Roloff accompanies Johannes' ghost into his house and an intertitle appears that reiterates his culpability: "Roloff, you have killed me!" They continue to walk and then encounter the doubled body of Johannes, lying dead on a funeral bier. Roloff's wife Elisabeth is there, mourning his death. "No one ever went to heaven the way he did!" The film then cuts to a strange occult scene of Johannes in robes, climbing the steps of a small neoclassical temple. Open hands wave and reach toward it from below the screen. Overwhelmed by these delusions, Roloff runs to the actual Elisabeth with his hands over his ears and exclaims, "I am no murderer: he killed himself!" She is shocked and they revisit the spot where Roloff had seen Johannes' dead body. The bier has disappeared. He desperately asks himself if he is "really that ill," while his wife stares incredulously at her delusional husband.

In Roloff's visions, Teacher Johannes is both loved and hated. At the moment of his death, the paranoid industrialist experiences guilt for having murdered Johannes, his primal father-substitute. Roloff's dream of controlling the world was shattered by the explosion of his factories, bringing about a profound internal change, like that claimed by Daniel Paul Schreber. The trauma of the catastrophic explosion, following this psychoanalytic logic, forced a regression to an infantile narcissistic state. It is Roloff's struggles in reestablishing connections with the external world, and his fundamentally ambivalent attitude toward Johannes, that give rise to his particular delusions. That such a profound change has taken place may be attested to by Roloff's increasingly delusional state, for he finally exclaims, "My own nerves mirror the nerves of the world. And the world's nerves are ill!" His megalomania is now complete. The collapse has taken place "inside" the paranoiac as well as "outside" in the world.[45]

In the final pages of his case study, Freud links Schreber's "rays of God" to the projection of his internal collapse. The rays of God, he writes,

> which are made up of a condensation of the sun's rays, of nerve-fibers [Nervenfasern], and of spermatozoa, are in reality nothing else than a concrete representation and external projection of libidinal cathexes; and they thus lend his delusions a striking similarity with our theory.[46]

If Schreber's interpretation of God as "nothing but nerves" may be read in this manner, the delusions made manifest in Nerves may be historically read in a similar way. For the techniques, special effects, and juxtapositions specific to the aesthetics of the cinema that depict Roloff's paranoid hallucinations are strikingly similar to those described by Freud and Abraham in their theory of postwar trauma and delusion.

This historical correspondence, moreover, reveals an ontological possibility that belongs to the film medium. The filmstrip, like the nerves that connect Schreber to his God, connect a series of expressionistic images that depict "internal" psychic tensions and anxieties that arise in response to a past catastrophe. They return what has been repressed in the form of cinematic hallucinations. A statement by Roloff, articulated moments before his death, corroborates this: "These dreadful images, which the nerves doctors call illusions, are back again." Though he ostensibly speaks about his own delusions, with which he attempted to recoup his postwar self, his words seem to reflect on the nature of the film medium itself and its capacity to rebuild a collapsing world through image and montage. These dreadful images in turn express the desperation, paranoia, and sense of apocalypse pervasive in postwar Weimar culture.

Dead Nerves

"What kind of world," asks Henri Bergson prophetically in his 1915 treatise *The Meaning of the War*, "would it be if this mechanism should seize the human race entire, and if the peoples, instead of raising themselves to a richer and more harmonious diversity, as *persons* may do, were to fall into the uniformity of *things*?"[47] In this short text, Bergson argues that Prussian milita-

Figure 2.7 A frame from *Nerven*.

rism and German industry have culminated in the aggression of the war. He isolates Bismarck, "a genius, I admit, but an evil genius," and his handling of Germany's unification in 1871 as key for understanding the mobilization of science and technology toward the mechanization of the soul:

> Industry was free to develop in all directions; but, from the first, war was the end in view. In enormous factories, such as the world had never seen, tens of thousands of workmen toiled in casting great guns, while by their side, in workshops and laboratories, every invention which the disinterested genius of neighboring peoples had been able to achieve was immediately captured, bent from its intended use, and converted into an engine of war.[48]

The invocation of factories and building up of industry seem prescient with respect to Roloff's dreams of conquering the earth with his machines. Armed with mechanized matter, the German body, propped up with healthy nerves, will ostensibly become "masters of the world." Bergson asks, however:

> What would happen, in short, if the moral effort of humanity should turn in its tracks at the moment of attaining its goal, and if some diabolical contrivance should cause it to produce the mechanization of spirit instead of the spiritualization of matter?[49]

It is this dream that traumatically fails for Roloff. Yet the cinema is particularly relevant for its capacity to animate inert matter and for objectively recording pro-filmic events so that they may be represented to a spectator at a later time. The cinema inspires the belief that the dead may be revived and the narcissistic dream of immortality may be fulfilled. Granting the dead a celluloidal afterlife, the cinema reassures the traumatized that death may be staved off once more. In this spirit, Bergson sardonically concludes:

> That the powers of death might be matched against life in one supreme combat, destiny had gathered them all at a single point. And behold how death was conquered; how humanity was saved by material suffering from the moral downfall which would have been its end; while the peoples, joyful in their desolation, raised on high the song of deliverance from the depths of ruin and grief![50]

NOTES

1. *Nerven*, DVD, directed by Robert Reinert, 1919, Munich: Edition Filmmuseum, 2008. All reference to the film will be derived from this DVD release.
2. Vladimir Ilyich Lenin, *Collected Works Vol. 29* (trans. George Hanna) (Moscow: Progress Publishers, 1972), pp. 325–6.

3. Jan-Christopher Horak, "Robert Reinert: Film as Metaphor," *Griffithiana*, Vol. 60/61, 1997, pp. 181–9, quoted p. 185.
4. Anton Kaes, *Shell Shock Cinema: Weimar Culture and the Wounds of War* (Princeton, NJ: Princeton University Press, 2009), p. 43.
5. Ibid.
6. Paul Lerner, *Hysterical Men: War, Psychiatry, and the Politics of Trauma in Germany, 1890–1930* (Ithaca, NY: Cornell University Press, 2003).
7. Barbara Hales, "Unsettling Nerves: Investigating War Trauma in Robert Reinert's *Nerven* (1919)," in Christian Rogowski (ed.), *The Many Faces of Weimar Cinema: Rediscovering Germany's Filmic Legacy* (Rochester, NY: Camden House, 2010), pp. 31–47, quoted p. 35.
8. Ibid. p. 44.
9. Andreas Killen, *Berlin Electropolis: Shock, Nerves, and German Modernity* (Berkeley, CA: University of California Press, 2006).
10. Ludimar Hermann, *Handbuch der Physiologie: Erster Theil, Allgemeine Nervenphysiologie* (Leipzig: F. C. W. Fogel, 1879), p. 135. For a brief history of the relationship between the body and nervous impulses, see "Nerves and Electricity" in Christoph Asendorf, *Batteries of Life* (trans. Don Reneau) (Berkeley, CA: University of California Press, 1993), pp. 153–77. Hermann would utilize Edison's phonograph to conduct research in the human voice and phonetics.
11. Michael Cowan, *Cult of the Will: Nervousness and German Modernity* (University Park: Pennsylvania State Press, 2008), p. 8.
12. Heinrich Obersteiner, *Functionelle und Organische Nerven-Krankheiten* (Wiesbaden: J. F. Bergmann, 1900), p. 80.
13. Alois Alzheimer, *Der Krieg und die Nerven* (Breslau: Preuss & Jünger, 1915), p. 3.
14. Ibid.
15. Ibid. p. 17.
16. Ibid. p. 4.
17. Alzheimer's eighteen-year-old son, Hans, had volunteered to go to the Front, a gesture that had greatly pleased the father. After he died of heart failure in December 1915, shortly after *Der Krieg und die Nerven* was published, one wonders if he would have perhaps rethought his militancy at the Great War's beginning. See Konrad Maurer and Ulrike Maurer, *Alzheimer: The Life of a Physician and the Career of a Disease* (trans. Neil Levi and Alistair Burns) (New York: Columbia University Press, 2003). See particularly the section "Psychiatry in a Time of War" in Chapter 6.
18. Sigmund Freud, "'Civilized' Sexuality and Modern Nervousness," in Philip Rieff (ed.), *Sexuality and the Psychology of Love* (New York: Touchstone, 1997), pp. 10–30, quoted p. 14.
19. Ibid.
20. In a letter to Freud dated April 26, 1915, Abraham relates how his daughter and son had responded to his leaving. He notes that while his daughter was delighted with his uniform, the boy had taken the matter "in a very different way in accordance with his sex and age." While Abraham had paced around the house with heavy boots, the boy began to imitate the "length, rhythm, and heaviness" of every step he took. See Hilda C. Abraham and Ernst L. Freud, *A Psychoanalytic Dialogue: The Letters of Sigmund Freud and Karl Abraham* (New York: Basic Books, 1965), pp. 219–20.
21. Abraham and Freud, *A Psychoanalytic Dialogue*, p. 210.
22. Karl Abraham, *Psycho-Analysis and the War Neurosis* (Vienna: International Psycho-Analytical Press, 1921), p. 28.
23. Ibid. p. 23.

24. Abraham, *Psycho-Analysis and the War Neurosis*, p. 26.
25. Ibid.
26. Philipp Stiasny, *Das Kino und der Krieg: Deutschland 1914–1929* (Munich: text + kritik, 2009), p. 202.
27. Abraham, *Psycho-Analysis and the War Neurosis*, p. 27.
28. Ibid. p. 25.
29. Daniel Paul Schreber, *Memoirs of My Nervous Illness* (trans. Ida Macalpine and Richard A. Hunter) (Cambridge, MA: Harvard University Press, 1988), p. 45.
30. Ibid. p. 46.
31. Ibid. p. 49.
32. Paul Flechsig, *Gehirn und Seele* (Leipzig: Veit & Co., 1896), p. 30.
33. This emotional ambivalence constitutes, moreover, the figure of the uncanny, the harbinger of death who is the spokesperson for the return of the repressed.
34. Sigmund Freud, "Psychoanalytic Notes Upon an Autobiographical Account of a Case of Paranoia (Dementia Paranoides)," in Philip Rieff (ed.), *Three Case Histories* (New York: Collier, 1996), pp. 83–160, quoted p. 116.
35. See for example Freud's account of the "Rat Man," from 1909, a case which attests to the bisexuality of human subjects with respect to a single, desired object. Sigmund Freud, "Notes Upon a Case of Obsessional Neurosis," in Philip Rieff (ed.), *Three Case Histories*.
36. Freud, "Psychoanalytic Notes," p. 116.
37. Strangely, the persecutory nature of delusion reflects the politics of war and psychoanalysis within the scientific community at the time. In a letter dated September 9, 1914, Freud wrote to Karl Abraham that he had all but given up hope for a rapid end to military conflict, yet was nevertheless encouraged by Germany's recent progress. On that day the *Septemberprogramm*, which detailed Germany's aims for the war and declared its desire to secure space for the Reich on both eastern and western fronts, was signed by the Chancellor. "The chief virtue," Freud writes, "will be endurance" (Abraham and Freud, *A Psychoanalytic Dialogue*, p. 9). He jokes that Ernest Jones, their British counterpart, is now "of course our 'enemy,'" seemingly incredulous at the changed geopolitical situation since war broke out in July 1914. He ends the letter by pointing to a recently published paper that reiterates his awareness of the status of psychoanalysis within the scientific community: "A paper from the Flechsig clinic in Alzheimer's journal shows the beginning of a changed attitude to psycho-analysis even in Germany." (p. 195) Flechsig is course that named in the Schreber case. "Alzheimer's journal" was most certainly the *Zeitschrift für die gesamte Neurologie und Psychiatrie*, which published important papers on psychiatry and physiology between 1910 and 1945. The paper to which Freud refers in this statement is unfortunately not identified.
38. Freud, "Psychoanalytic Notes," p. 142.
39. Ibid. p. 147.
40. When Abraham spoke of the delusions of war neurotics in 1918, he was certainly thinking of Freud's analysis of the psychotic Dr Schreber, but he had already articulated the basic etiology of paranoia in his 1908 essay "The Psycho-sexual Differences Between Hysteria and Dementia Praecox." Describing how the libido has turned away from external objects and toward the ego, he writes: "The mental patient transfers on to himself alone as his only sexual object the whole of the libido which the healthy person turns upon all living and inanimate objects in his environment, and accordingly his sexual over-estimation is directed towards himself alone and assumes enormous dimensions. For he is his whole world. The origin of megalomania in dementia praecox is thus a reflected or auto-erotic sexual over-estimation—an over-estimation which is turned back on to the ego. Delusions

of persecution and megalomania are therefore closely connected with each other." Abraham's formulations may be read as anticipating Freud's: "I do not love at all—I do not love any one." (Karl Abraham, "The Psycho-sexual Differences Between Hysteria and Dementia Praecox," in *Selected Papers of Karl Abraham*, trans. Douglas Bryan and Alix Strachey) (New York: Basic Books, 1960), p. 75.) In a letter from March 1911, Freud acknowledges that Abraham's essay "contains almost all the essential view put forward in the present study of the case of Schreber."

41. Sergei Eisenstein, "The Montage of Film Attractions," in Richard Taylor (ed.), *The Eisenstein Reader* (London: BFI, 1998), p. 35.
42. Here, of course, I am referencing Tom Gunning's 1986 essay "The Cinema of Attraction: Early Film, Its Spectator and the Avant-Garde," published in Thomas Elsaesser and Adam Barker (eds.), *Early Cinema—Space, Frame, Narrative*. London: BFI 1990, pp. 56–62.
43. Carlamaria Heim, *Josefa Halbinger, Jahrgang 1900: Lebensgeschichte eines Münchner Arbeitkindes, nach Todbandaufzeichnungen zusammengestellt und niedergeschrieben* (Munich: Obalski & Astor, 1982), p. 46.
44. Ibid.
45. Eric Santner, in his study *My Own Private Germany* (Princeton, NJ: Princeton University Press, 1996), argues that the crises experienced by Schreber "were largely the same crises of modernity for which the Nazis would elaborate their own series of radical and ostensibly 'final' solutions." (xi) Santner notes that his project is not to show how Schreber's crises prefigured Nazi delusions about the other, but that the sick judge resisted the temptations of totalitarianism. *My Own Private Germany* shows that the interpellation of Schreber into a position of power generated concomitant anxieties of social space and proximity, anxieties which point to the failure of performative utterances to articulate a clear understanding of the self. "We cross of the threshold of modernity when the attenuation of these performatively effectuated social bonds becomes chronic, when they are no longer capable of seizing the subject in his or her self-understanding." (xxi)
46. Freud, "Psychoanalytic Notes," p. 154.
47. Henri Bergson, *The Meaning of the War: Life & Matter in Conflict* (New York: Macmillan, 1915), p. 35.
48. Ibid. pp. 24–5.
49. Ibid. pp. 35–6.
50. Ibid. pp. 38–9.

3. FRANJO LEDIĆ: A FORGOTTEN PIONEER OF GERMAN EXPRESSIONISM

Daniel Rafaelić

When we speak of the history of Croatian film, the subject of Expressionism is rarely mentioned. In fact, many believe that nothing that is visually exciting and inspiring about the global world of film expressionism made any impact on Croatian production. As it had merely been at an early stage in the 1910s and 1920s, this was not possible. Escape into mysticism, interest in the subconscious, poverty and destitution: these are only some of the most typical expressionist elements in film. Some say Croatian cinematography has never possessed the *mise-en-scène* associated with them. But perhaps it has.

While contemplating the pioneers of film in Croatia and elsewhere, it is impossible not to mention the versatile Franjo Ledić (Derventa, 1892–Zagreb, 1981). Early in the second decade of the twentieth century he ventured to Berlin, where he joined a throng of young German filmmakers in 1912. We find out from his records[1] that Ledić first worked as an extra, and then as a make-up artist, props manager, set designer, and assistant cameraman. He named Oskar Messter as his employer, the pioneer of German film who is credited with the invention of the Maltese Cross. While working in Messter's studios, Ledić started to collaborate with Ernst Lubitsch and his muse Pola Negri. Ledić stated that a bond between the three of them had been inevitable, primarily because of their common Slavic origin. Ledić continued his work for the *Messter-Woche* newsreel. After the outbreak of World War I, the German film industry ground to a halt, but at the end of the war Franjo Ledić—at the invitation of Ernst Lubitsch—joined the Projektions-AG "Union" (known also as PAGU) company as an assistant. He remembered working on the highly

Figure 3.1 Franjo Ledić.

Figure 3.2 Franjo Ledić.

successful Lubitsch films featuring Negri, such as *Carmen* (1918) and *Madame Dubarry* (1919), as well as on Negri's film *Mania, Die Geschichte einer Zigarettenarbeiterin* (1918), directed by Eugen Illés.

At roughly the same time, Ledić began working as a short film director. In 1918, he made *U borbi sa suncem* ("Fighting the Sun"), in four acts, *Klub samoubojica* ('suicide Club"), and *Propast svijeta* ("The End of the World"), in two acts. His first big success came while working for the Omnia film company, for whom he directed the historical drama *Cornelie Aredt* (not screened in Berlin until the spring of 1919, because of postwar unrest). The main role in the film went to Lina Salten, also the star of Ledić's first feature-length film, *Angelo, Misterij Zmajgrada* ("Angelo, the Mystery of Dragontown"), which was shot in Berlin in 1919, and screened for audiences in the same month in 1920 as *The Cabinet of Dr. Caligari* premiered.

Figure 3.3   German Film program brochure *Illustrierter Film-Kurier*. (*Courtesy of Verlag für Filmschriften, Christian Unucka, Hebertshausen*)

In August 1919, the *Film-Kurier* (Germany's most important daily film journal) and *Zentralblatt für die Filmindustrie* (the guild associations newspaper) devoted considerable space to the presentation of the "Orientalist" Franjo Ledić (whom they called "*ein Türke*," "a Turk"), who had founded the Ocean film company with the intention of increasing the export of German films to the East, as well as to shoot German films in diverse parts of the Balkans.[2] The stylized company logo—a filmstrip on a big wave—conspicuously presented the cinematic foreigner (*Ausländer*) to the German film industry. Indeed, it was not long before Franjo Ledić, realizing the paramount importance of film advertising, began a lavish campaign for his first production company film, the mysterious *Angelo, das Mysterium des Schlosses*. All relevant German film publications observed this film closely. In addition to the aforementioned, there were *Der Film, Der Kinematograph, Der Filmhandel, Lichtbild-Bühne* and *Illustrierte Film-Woche*.[3] They are also the most valuable source for understanding the circumstances of the origin and plot of the film. We see that Ledić worked on the film for two years, according to his own words adapting his Croatian novel of the same name, which was first published in German after the film's premiere in the Buch-Film-Verlag series. (A copy of the novel survives in Berlin in the German National Library.) Ledić expected the film to be a success in theaters, so he spared no expense on advertising. The ads represent the grandeur of Ledić's exaggeration, for which he would be famous later across the Kingdom of Yugoslavia. Even two months *before* the premiere, in November 1919, Ledić began advertising *Angelo* as a major success—a silent film in six acts, luxuriously grand, suspenseful, without competition, a film that would be the center of talk in every circle, and which would most surely bring huge earnings to movie theater owners. The ads claimed: "The great *Angelo* will earn as much money as there is sand in the sea." In a further exaggeration, Ledić informed the newspapers that he had already sold the film to the USA, where it would soon be screened.

Ledić kept the film synopsis secret for another month, publishing only text-based ads that highlighted the words *mystery, castle, mystique, the middle ages*, and *death* in accordance with society's escapist interests in the occult, which was in fashion at the time (a logical outcome of Germany's defeat in World War I and the inflation that followed). Ledić then, in mid-December, released entire cast and crew listings.[4] It was revealed that the main female part had gone to breakthrough actress Lina Salten, while others were members of distinguished German stage companies (each individual had his/her home theater specified). However, a new piece of information emerged among all the data. It revealed that Franjo Ledić was the screenwriter as well as artistic and technical production manager (a powerful producer, in today's terms), but that the film was directed (the *Spielleitung*) by Robert Leffler. Whether this shows Ledić was not adept at direction and/or was unwilling to do the entire work on a film by himself remains unclear. At any rate, he hired the famous supporting actor Leffler, who occasionally worked as a director. Leffler certainly did not make history with this film, as he did with his excellent supporting roles as a butler and as a chauffeur in F. W. Murnau's masterpieces (*The Haunted Castle*, 1921, *Burning Soil*, 1922, *The Expulsion*, 1923).

Immediately after celebrating New Year 1920, the Ocean-film company announced that *Angelo, das Mysterium des Schlosses* was ready to be premiered. Meanwhile, the editorial board of *Film-Kurier* had decided to regularly publish a supplement to its regular issue—the famous *Illustrierter Film-Kurier*, a small program brochure with all the relevant information on given film releases, including a detailed plot. (To this day, the *Illustrierter Film-Kurier* has remained an unsurpassed source for the study of German film history, offering information on German and foreign films which were screened in German theaters up until 1944.)

Figure 3.4   German trade advertisement, published in *Der Kinematograph* (1920).

Figure 3.5 Croatian trade advertisement.

Here was a real opportunity for Franjo Ledić, so the next issue of the *Illustrierter Film-Kurier* was dedicated to his film *Angelo, das Mysterium des Schlosses*. The film plot was retold act by act, followed by (now lost) frame shots. It needs to be said how the Yugoslav Film Archive in Belgrade purchased a few preserved film sequences from Ledić in the 1960s, the content of which it has still not been possible to reconstruct. These are now stored at the Croatian Film Archive in Zagreb. As a result, we can finally thoroughly understand what kind of film this was.

Angelo's plot follows Nelly, a banker's daughter, who—along with her father and his secretary—arrives at her new home, Castle Dragontown. It quickly becomes apparent that a supernatural force is haunting the castle. The old castellan then conveys the story of the Dragontown's mystic past.

Centuries earlier, the castle had been a monastery designed to give shelter to various knights. One of them, named Dragon, hid there from his enemies and spent his time working on a miraculous painting of Angelo. However, the castle soon came under siege and was eventually devastated. After their heavy defeat, the knights returned to the castle and attempted to rebuild it.

Nelly enjoys her life at her new home. Once, while sledding in the snow, she discovers a frozen man with a strange talisman around his neck. That night, a strange force causes Nelly to sleepwalk. The next morning, Nelly is missing, as are the secretary and the painting of Angelo. The worried banker turns to an alchemist named Alliver for help. Alliver comes equipped with a radio-telephone. With the help of his servant Bob, Alliver solves the mystery of Dragontown. It turns out that, during the night, the banker's secretary stole the talisman from the frozen man. With it, he stumbles upon centuries-old treasure of knight-monks. The secretary's greed is punished when he falls through the trap door and lands on spikes that kill him. An old parchment makes clear that the frozen guest is the real heir to the castle. He marries Nelly and they live happily ever after.

It is obvious that the film's plot abounds with expressionistic themes. Mysterious past, knights, hidden treasure, strange psychic phenomena, sleepwalking and exoticism are all intertwined in *Angelo*. According to Ledić's own statements, the film provoked much discussion at the time. Ledić describes his novel (upon which his film is based) as a bestseller. In addition, when we examine imagery from the film itself—claustrophobic sets of the castle, historical flashbacks, and the specially designed title cards—it is evident that *Angelo* bears the aesthetic hallmarks of expressionistic cinema.

The film premiere was set for February 13, 1920, at the Berlin cinema *Schauburg-Lichtspiele*, located in the Potsdamer Platz. A press screening had been held ten days before. This was during the so-called *"zensurfreie Zeit"* (era without censorship), in which films were censored by the local police authorities. A couple of months later, in May 1920, with the passage of the *Reichslichtspielgesetz* (film censorship law), Germany introduced national censorship. From that point, the *Filmprüfstellen* (Boards of Film Censors) approved every film intended for German theaters and issued so-called "censorship cards," which gave details about the film, from the main information to entire transcripts of title cards (for silent films), or partial or whole film dialogues (for sound films). All the technical data relating to the film were recorded there as well. It is interesting that the original censorship card for *Angelo* has been preserved, but not from 1920, the original premiere date when films were censored by police authorities, but rather from 1921 when the *Reichslichtspielgesetz* was in effect. The censorship card, also an invaluable source for film historians, tells us that the film's overall length was 1923 meters (70 mins). There, a year after its premiere, the film was called *Schreckensnacht auf Schloss Drachenegg* (*A Horrible Night at Castle Dragontown*). The reason for the title change is unknown.

At the time (much like today), the success of a film was measured in two ways: by the number of viewers (tickets sold), and by the response accorded by film critics. Despite an extensive search, no data on box-office receipts could

Figure 3.6   German trade advertisement.

be found. The reviews are a different matter. Three very different reviews of *Angelo* have been located. Interestingly, by the beginning of February 1920, German papers reported less and less on *Angelo*, while advertising became scarce, and later disappeared.

The film critics were divided, to say the least. On February 5, 1920, the *Film-Kurier* reported that, among other things,

> something mystical had loomed over the film itself, before it was splashed with premiere lights. One thing is being said, and another imagined. Meanwhile, Franjo Ledić, the author of the film and CEO of Ocean-Film Industrie, makes bombastic commercials (*Bombenreklame*) ... This is a half-detective, half-fantasy film, full of suspense at every turn. The film's logic could have been more explicable to the audience, a result that could have been achieved by adding more title cards. Here

we should commend the fact that the title cards were placed in an even and tasteful manner, which speaks volumes of the strength of the film plot. In addition to this, the title cards were made with artistic taste. The story is multi-faceted and powerful. Something is always happening. The events remain mysterious until the end. But then the resolution turns out to be something entirely different than what the audience imagined. In this work, the acting recedes into the background. The events carry the constructed [acted] personalities. Not the other way around. A rare case indeed. Commendation for the plot. Suspense, mystery ... Something for a wider audience. Franjo Ledić spared no expense for the necessary exterior shots. Everything has been arranged wonderfully, the decoration elements are enthralling ... The director Leffler proved to be perfect for this piece. The mass scenes were particularly exciting. Good direction, without a doubt. As already mentioned, the acting took a backseat. But when such an excellent cast, like Ernst Dernburg (Angelo), Lina Salten (Nelly), Aenderly Lebius (Devoir), Sybill Morell (Doritt) and Kurt Mierendorf (Sekretär) collaborate, it is a great pleasure to watch the piece. Especially high praise for cameraman Hermann Schadock who created the fairytale scenes by magic.

On February 9, 1920, the magazine *Der Film* highlighted that

an opinion on Lina Salten will be formed when she is given more film time in the future. The same goes for Ozean-Filmindustrie and their first attempt to create a path for themselves with this film. Praise for the beautiful nature shots, original title cards, and clear, effect-ridden scenes.

But response other than praise was also given to *Angelo*, as testified by the review published on February 2, 1920 in the Düsseldorf *Der Kinematograph*:

A nice idea, reflecting a strong film plot, coming from the screenplay essentially ... The whole story wanders off into such a mystery in the end, that the plot itself remains mysterious to the viewer. Lovely snow-covered landscapes are interrupted partly by medieval, and partly by modern interior shots. Magnificent shots of the castle also frame the film plot. The title cards, which appear in medieval and futuristic frames, are new and original. The actors, especially Aenderly Lebius, Lina Salten and Ernst Dernburg, try hard to justify the somewhat unclear, highly mysterious or overly suggestive plot. The acting gestures are unaesthetically abrupt. They all seem to jump around at a heightened pace like puppets. True, we live in hectic times, but such frighteningly fast, unnatural movements should have been announced earlier. Even the old knight-robber

Figure 3.7   Book cover, Berlin, 1920.

is in an awful hurry. The direction of grouped mass scenes leaves many things unfulfilled. The colorful tinted film shots seem useless at times; the overly bright coloring gives the scenes an unnatural feeling. The premiere of this narratively substantial and—with the help of a few fortunate scenes—embellished piece of work, will occur on the 13th of this month at Schauburg at Potsdamer Platz.

This gives us the information that the film was tinted, which further underlines the fact that Ledić invested much money in it. Whether his investment was repaid at the Berlin box office is not known. The timing of the film could not have been better, however; the interest in such topics was at its peak. It comes as no surprise, then, that Ledić sold *Angelo* to numerous countries (USA, Czech Republic, Italy, and others) and earned, by his own admission, large sums of money as a result. His career then took him to Italy, where he received offers to direct a few films. Displeased, he returned to Zagreb in 1925.

There Ledić began one of the most unusual film careers in the history of Croatian cinema. He founded a new company—Ocean film (distinguished from the German one largely by its location)—and set out to conquer the local film industry. Unambiguously calling himself "the first Yugoslav film director," he engaged himself in promoting public awareness of the film medium. He concentrated, first, on the importance of a studio for shooting films. He bought land on Horvaćanska Street and erected an impressive edifice there, calling it the "Yugoslav Hollywood." After the construction was finished, he began shooting the film which made him famous: *Ciganska krv—Dobrotvorka Balkana* (*Gypsy Blood: The Balkan Benefactor*), a tale of love, lust, murder and pursuit set in the Sava tents. The special significance of his film work was in his publishing the first book on Croatian film: *Film—kako se može postati filmski glumac i glumica Što o filmu mora znati svaki kandidat i kandidatkinja* (*Film—How To Become a Film Actor/Actress, What Every Candidate Needs to Know About Film*), in which he was cited as the author by use of the term *Dervenčanin* ("Derventa resident"). Only a year later, in 1926, he started the film magazine *Narodna filmska umjetnost* (*National Film Arts*), where, alongside poems dedicated to himself (!), he published details from his film shoots. All these activities, however, go beyond the scope of the present text. Franjo Ledić did not miss the opportunity to screen *Angelo* in his homeland, of course. The premiere was held in May 1921, as evidenced by the local censorship card published on May 2, 1921. In any case, Franjo Ledić's *Angelo* was the first local attempt at expressionism by a native filmmaker. Fortunately, the film's surviving 38 seconds only hint as to what exactly this film, which preceded the release of *The Cabinet of Dr. Caligari* by an entire month, was about.

Notes

1. Franjo Ledić, *Spomen-knjiga 1892–70–1962 godišnjice rodenja Franje Ledića* (Zagreb: Dervenčanina, 1962).
2. nn, "Filme für den Orient," *Zentralblatt für die Filmindustrie*, No. 4, 1919, p. 14.
3. *Illustrierte Film-Woche*, Nos. 5–7, 31 January 1920, p. 24; *Der Kinematograph*, No. 674, 3 December 1919; *Der Film*, No. 48, 30 November 1919.
4. *Der Film*, No. 50, 14 December 1919, p. 124.

4. EXPRESSIONIST FILM AND GENDER: GENUINE, A TALE OF A VAMPIRE (1920)

Mirjam Kappes

Genuine is the second expressionist film by the director Robert Wiene, produced right after the success of *The Cabinet of Dr. Caligari* in the same year, 1920. It stars Fern Andra as a blood-sucking slave girl and Hans Heinrich von Twardowski as a stripling who falls for her, another hapless young man with a terrible fate.

The male subject in crisis, a key motif of Weimar cinema that Wiene had already explored in *Caligari*, is deployed again in *Genuine* as plot-developing element—but now with a renewed emphasis on the female counterpart. While Caligari's Jane (Lil Dagover), though the main focus of the male protagonists' desires, was a passive "damsel in distress," Andra's *Genuine* is one of those dangerous femmes fatales who filled Weimar cinema screens in the decade to follow. Being a victim of cruel sect rituals, Genuine has lost all ability to feel empathy or mercy. She uses her talent for manipulation and seduction to escape slavery—and to take bloody revenge on all men for what has been done to her.

Even though *Genuine* was not a commercial success, it is still a valuable subject for research since it touches on dramatic social changes in postwar Weimar society, especially the erosion of traditional male and female roles. By undermining the male character as a weak, powerless and disoriented figure who is helpless in the face of a wicked woman's alluring sexuality, the film presents to us a distinctive narrative scenario in which the danger does not primarily come from a male rival but from an empowered, dangerous woman who pulls all the strings.

Figure 4.1 German film poster, artwork by Josef Fenneker. (*Source: German Film Institute—DIF, Frankfurt*)

Genuine: A Fantastic Story Full of Dark Secrets

An innocent girl in the clutches of a mysterious sect that forces her to participate in its bloody rituals before she escapes, ending up in the arms of slave traders who then resell her to an eccentric lord living in a secluded, closely-guarded house where she is again held captive—when Genuine, the lead protagonist of Robert Wiene's film of the same title, is first introduced to viewers, she is displayed as a victim, helpless in the hands of her male masters, abused and exploited. But any pity or compassion one might feel for the unfortunate girl is quickly choked off, for Genuine transforms herself into a merciless, bloodthirsty femme fatale who uses her erotic beauty and intimate art of seduction to drive men to insanity—and death. She not only frees herself from the "golden cage" that the old Lord Melos[1] has built for her beneath his extravagant property, a huge subterranean chamber full of exotic plants with an ornate glass roof, similar to an extravagant greenhouse. She also seduces Florian, the young, gullible barber's nephew who has been sent to the house in place of his uncle to give Lord Melos his daily shave. Since Lord Melos had so far refused to set Genuine free, the blood-thirsty girl manipulates Florian into killing him, and, intoxicated with love for the mysterious priestess, he obeys. But Genuine is still not satisfied. As proof of his love, she demands that Florian takes his own life. The stripling, however, fails to complete the gruesome task, and through fortunate circumstances he manages to escape. Genuine, now in control of Lord Melos's property and his black servant, is nonetheless still consumed with an insatiable thirst for blood.

From victim to vamp: *Genuine*, the second expressionist film of Robert Wiene (after his previous success *The Cabinet of Dr. Caligari*), is not only a grim horror story of wicked manslaughter, enriched with narrative elements of dark magic, supernatural powers and mysterious exoticism. It is also the story of Genuine's cruel emancipation of her male oppressors, a story in which her insane obsession with killing, her constant demand for blood sacrifices and her clever use of her erotic charms seem to give her endless power over her admirers—until she falls in love herself. Percy, the grandson of Lord Melos, pays a visit to the residence, unaware that Genuine is responsible for his grandfather's death. He quickly falls under her spell, doomed to be her next victim. But after having demanded Percy's death, Genuine realizes she has fallen in love with the handsome visitor, and with the help of Percy's friend Curzon[2] the couple are united. As soon as Genuine gives in to Percy, she is cured of her savage blood lust, her demons are tamed, and her irrepressible ferocity is domesticated. When she confesses her love, her flaunted eroticism and wild desire to kill are retransformed into a civilized form of love, a "socially acceptable sexuality."[3] But, in being freed from her mania, Genuine also relinquishes her power over men. A lynch mob of infuriated townsmen sets out to kill her, but Genuine

Figure 4.2 Fern Andra (center) in a publicity still for *Genuine* (1920). (*Source: German Film Institute—DIF, Frankfurt*)

falls victim to the vengeful Florian, who cannot stand to see her with another man.

Mysterious murders, magic spells, and two men competing for the same woman: it seems obvious that *Genuine* shares some striking resemblances with its famous predecessor. In trying to repeat the success of *The Cabinet of Dr. Caligari*, the Decla-Bioscop film company not only reassembled former cast and crew members, including director Robert Wiene, screenwriter Carl Mayer, cinematographer Willy Hameister and actor Hans Heinz von Twardowski. *Genuine* also follows *Caligari* in adopting distinctive features of its narrative form and pictorial realization. Both films tell grim fairy tales in which dark human desires and fears are explored through fantastic elements and psychological motifs. Both share a similar narrative structure. The main action is embedded in a frame story in which the male character reflects back on his prior tragic experiences. *Genuine* is also clearly inspired by the cinematic visual style of *Caligari* in terms of decor and light: ambient chiaroscuro, dark corridors, claustrophobic rooms, winding staircases, distorting angles and painted cardboard sets create a nightmarish, uncanny atmosphere. The

Figure 4.3 Fern Andra (front) and Ernst Gronau (right) in a publicity still for *Genuine* (1920). (*Source: German Film Institute—DIF, Frankfurt*)

renowned Expressionist artist César Klein designed *Genuine*'s film sets and was responsible for the opulent painted decor with its ornamental patterns. Both his participation and that of the famous actress Fern Andra in the role of Genuine drew further attention to the film before its release.[4] But despite all these efforts, *Genuine*'s erotic horror story, seasoned with an extra pinch of exoticism (the oriental sect, the slave market, the tropical underground grotto and the magic ring that controls Lord Melos's black servant), did not prove to be a recipe for success. The film received at best mixed responses. To only name a few, *Film-Kurier*[5] critic L. K. Frederik called *Genuine* a "textbook example for how fantastic reality can be created" and applauded the "brilliant photographic work" of Willy Hameister, but found the plot to be inconsequential, lacking in "psychological coherence."[6] Similarly, reviewers were thrilled by the performance of Hans Heinz von Twardowski as the bewitched barber's apprentice Florian,[7] but Fern Andra attracted more attention for her physical allure and revealing costumes than for her acting skills.[8] Despite the mixed reviews following the 1920s film's premiere,[9] *Genuine* turned out to be a commercial failure. It might have been the verdict of film critic Rudolf Kurtz—who was also editor-in-chief of the highly influential film journal *Lichtbild-Bühne*—that set the tone for the general negative reception of the Wiene production. Kurtz labeled the history of German Expressionist film a "history of a series of repetitions" whose "beginnings have never been surpassed."[10] On *Genuine*, he wrote:

> The success of the Caligari film encouraged the birth of Genuine. What first had been an attempt here was now supposed to become true there . . . Genuine is an expressionistic film because expressionism was a success. But instead of being a method of composition, in a way it became the content of the film. Expressionistic film died from this paradoxical discrepancy. Genuine was official proof that these films were not working commercially. Their time was over.[11]

Moreover, well-known contemporaries like Lotte Eisner[12] and Siegfried Kracauer[13] affirmed Kurtz's opinion and thus contributed to the (retrospective)

Figure 4.4   Hans Heinrich von Twardowski, Ernst Gronau, and Fern Andra in a publicity still for *Genuine* (1920). (*Source: German Film Institute—DIF, Frankfurt*)

dismissal of *Genuine*. This may also be the reason why the film has so far been neglected by most film scholars. Still, from today's perspective *Genuine* proves to be a valuable source for studying gender conceptions in Expressionist film and how these might point to the erosion of male and female identity in postwar Weimar society.

THE EROSION OF MALE AND FEMALE ROLES IN WEIMAR CULTURE

Looking back at German history, we find that the early 1900s are usually referred to as years of crisis.[14] Following World War I and the Treaty of Versailles, the defeated country's economy was burdened with immense war reparation payments and additionally suffered hyperinflation which resulted in a crippled financial system, mass unemployment, and rapidly declining living standards. The Weimar Republic that had emerged from the 1918 revolution tried to establish a democratic regime with a new constitution, but was faced with political turmoil from the start as opposing extremist parties, separatist movements and a series of uprisings threatened the young Republic. The ongoing economic and political insecurities were accompanied by profound social, cultural and demographic transformations, since young men and women left the provinces to come to the cities in search of work, which contributed to the replacement of prewar agricultural structures with an industrialized, rationalized and technologized economy.[15] Even though these developments induced a relatively stable, affluent period between 1924 and 1929 in which considerable economic recovery was achieved by rapid industrialization and modernization while consumerism and mass culture also began to flourish,[16] the following economic depression and increasing political polarization led to the ultimate demise of the Weimar Republic in 1933.[17]

The economic, political and social struggles the Weimar Republic had to face left their mark on society, often described in terms of a profound sense of insecurity and anxiety over societal change, an underlying feeling of disorientation and alienation in facing the fundamental transformations of the present.[18] Richard W. McCormick speaks of a crisis of subject identity caused by the "shock of modernity," that in particular put a strain on traditional conceptions of male and female roles: "A key element in this identity crisis was gender."[19] With millions of men dead and those returning broken in body and spirit, the traumatic experience of the war, and the humiliation of defeat, deeply unsettled (self-)perceptions of male gender identity.[20] "Not only had German men been stripped of their role as provider and father, but wartime conditions and the defeat had called into question their status as soldiers and protectors of home and fatherland."[21] In contrast, the changing social and cultural role of women in the Weimar Republic can best be described as ambivalent.[22] On the one hand, the new Republic gave women the right to vote and to run for office, and they were urgently needed in the workforce to replace those killed and wounded in the war. Paid employment and constitutional equality became essential aspects in the formation of a new, modern female identity, giving women the opportunity to follow their own ambitions and interests and to actively participate in social and cultural life. In the so-called "golden twenties," the idea of the "New Woman" emerged, an emancipated, autonomous, financially and socially independent woman with equal access to education and politics and free in her choice of partner.[23] On the other hand, traditionalist movements promoted the re-establishment of traditional gender hierarchies by advocating that women return to their traditional roles of mother and wife. In summary, the social position of women in the Weimar Republic oscillated between privilege and discrimination, between emancipation and subordination.[24]

The changing notions of male and female roles were extensively debated in Weimar culture, and found their way into literature, art, theater, and film. In this context, the medium of cinema is particularly interesting because whilst it was celebrated as a new form of mass entertainment culture, it was also dismissed as "low" art (in contradistinction to "high," bourgeois culture).[25] It might have been the denigration of cinema that allowed Expressionist film to articulate the darker psychological and sexual anxieties of men and enabled it to explore the idea of female emancipation. With regard to the analysis of *Genuine*, one can subscribe to the statement of Anton Kaes, who said that

> every film can be an intersection and transfer point for different discourses that were relevant at a certain time ... the fictional film plays a role for the discourses he "works through" precisely because it has the freedom to present solutions for the addressed problems that are not possible in reality or would be dismissed as criminal, deviant, illogical, or fairytale-like ... Even uncritical entertainment films thus often have a compensatory, unintended critical function: they show something that is missing in life outside of cinema, something that cannot happen "in reality". A study of the cinematic fictions at a specific point in time allows a glimpse into the secret history of collective wishes, fears, hopes and dreams.[26]

As Kaes's statement indicates, the sphere of fiction and the realm of the fantastic can be considered as the domains in which Expressionist film[27] was able to address the erosion of traditional social gender positions. Moreover, the variety of ways in which the figures of Expressionist film dramatize these changes served as a general matrix for expressing the collective experience of crisis under the impact of modernity.[28]

Figure 4.5 Hans Heinrich von Twardowski and Fern Andra in a publicity still for *Genuine* (1920). (*Source: German Film Institute—DIF, Frankfurt*)

Genuine: The Story of a Woman's Emancipation?

It may come as a surprise that issues concerning prescribed gender roles and identities were openly addressed in Weimar culture,[29] and the success of Expressionist film may indicate the relevance of these discourses in Weimar society. The German cinema at the turn of the century slowly lets go of the heroic, invincible male protagonist and turns to the figure of an insecure, vulnerable, flawed or failed man who is mostly determined by fate and has little to no control over his—usually increasingly worrying—situation. It is also striking that Expressionist film does not necessarily depict women as delicate, fragile creatures who hope to be saved, but instead offers a variety of female characters, as Jürgen Kasten elaborates:

> Female lead protagonists of expressionist films represented, each in their way, a popular established type of woman: Lil Dagover the desirable but reserved bourgeois woman, Fern Andra the libidinal vamp, Leontine Kühnberg the damsel in distress, Marija Leiko a melodramatically loving maid, Maria Kryschanowskaja the devoutly religious woman chastened by sorrow.[30]

If one accepts Kasten's analysis, it becomes apparent that these types of women can be arranged at different levels according to the "dependence" or "independence" of their film's male protagonists. It is important to notice that none of the female characters is entirely detached from their male counterparts or is unrestrictedly able to act on her own behalf, as some researchers have suggested. But there is indeed the admitted possibility of a power shift between male and female roles. This point is emphasized by Richard Murphy, who carefully articulates how in Weimar cinema the "weakened position of the male is often contrasted with a situation of apparently enhanced social mobility for the female."[31] He stresses that while the motif of the male subject in crisis is prominently featured in Weimar cinema whereas upward mobility is usually reserved for female characters, the rise of the latter is often linked "either to a chance encounter with a wealthy patron, or alternatively . . . to crime or prostitution."[32] He goes on to say that, as a consequence, the idea of female emancipation or empowerment can only be acted out within the realm of fantasy, and even though the ascendancy of women over men is clearly labeled "bizarre," "insane," "unnatural" or "perverse" in the film's narrative, the idea nevertheless achieves a degree of representation, even if it may be in disguise.[33]

Considering these findings, *Genuine* in many ways proves a valuable resource to take a closer look at the cinematic representation of male and female roles in Expressionist film. As was mentioned at the beginning of this chapter, Genuine's character evolves, from a helpless and abused victim to a bloodthirsty vamp, and then back to her former, innocent and pure self. Like Jane, played by Lil Dagover in *The Cabinet of Dr Caligari*, Genuine is the object of men's desire, but in contrast to the former the slave girl seizes power over men by using her talent for seduction and manipulation. But is this truly a story of a woman's emancipation?

Following the storyline, it might be helpful to consider the power struggles between male and female figures. In the main narrative, Genuine first sees herself captured by a strange religious sect with whom she experiences the "horror of cruelty," as told by the intertitle. Notably, she is introduced to the viewer as the tribe's priestess, suggesting that the sect members pay tribute to her. The visual narrative, however, tells a different story. The helpless girl is kept hanging like a puppet on strings and can barely move. As priestess, Genuine is forced to participate in the occultist, gory rituals of the sect, by which her blood thirst is awakened.

During a war with an enemy tribe, Genuine is taken away and ends up on a slave market, where she is sold to Lord Melos. The old eccentric ignores the warning of the slave trader ('she is beautiful but they corrupted her. She is now fierce and savage") and takes her to his secluded house. Genuine becomes the admired, but nevertheless captured and jealously guarded woman in Lord Melos's house, imprisoned in a tropical underground terrarium (which is probably intended to imitate Genuine's exotic natural habitat). The former slave girl now lives in luxury, fitted out in extravagant costumes lavishly decorated with feathers and veils. It is important to notice that Genuine is already infected with her insane thirst for blood as she shows signs of a feral and unrestrained nature, but at this point she is still submissive to Lord Melos. The old man refuses to release Genuine from her luxurious golden cage, but in doing so he is portrayed as a protective and caring parental figure: "No, my angel, no, my beauty, up there is life with its ugliness. Here, everything smiles at you. Only here can you be completely happy." Genuine, for her part, is not (yet) fully consumed by her demonic desires: she does not ask for her release to go on a murderous rampage, but instead wishes to "be free, to enjoy being young and falling in love."

The dynamics change when Florian, the young barber's nephew, enters the house to fill in for his uncle in giving Lord Melos his daily shave. The lean and sensitive young man becomes the first victim of Genuine, who has just escaped from her subterranean chambers. When she sees Florian with the sharp shaving blade, she snaps—maybe having a flashback—and demands her master's blood. Florian, mesmerized by her beauty, obeys and kills the sleeping Lord. At this point, Genuine has gained control over the film's male characters. Her owner is dead, the remorseful Florian is in her hands, and, with Lord Melos's magic ring, she has also gained control over his black servant. To illustrate this power shift, the film uses an established gesture of male defeat: with a sly smile, Genuine caresses the shivering Florian, who helplessly rests his head in her lap and on her bosom.[34] Still, Genuine's power is not unlimited: when she orders Florian to kill himself, he cannot accede to her demand, and even the black servant temporarily seems to be able to resist the ring's power and refrains from killing the young stripling. Instead, he forces Florian to leave the premises and brings Genuine his own blood in an act of self-sacrifice that is not further explained in the narrative. But Genuine rejects the servant's blood, suddenly again in control of herself. Her perilous mania seems to revive and abate in an uncontrollable manner. It is awakened again when Lord Melos's grandson Percy arrives and charms her with his compliments and expensive gifts. Among his presents is a sumptuous dagger, which again unleashes Genuine's inner demons. Percy's fate seems to be sealed, and his death is anticipated by the audience when Genuine flaunts her body in front of Percy and but also playfully wraps a net around his neck. But his friend Curzon comes to his aid, preventing the suicide and feigning Percy's death. Confronted with the stern and reprimanding demeanor of Curzon (who seems to be immune to her charms), Genuine realizes she has truly fallen in love with Percy and, seized with remorse, she is cured of her obsessions. The couple's happiness, however, is short-lived. Agitated by the barber's accusations of witchcraft, a mob of enraged townsmen invades the property to kill the femme fatale, but she has

Figure 4.6 Hans Heinrich von Twardowski (standing) and Fern Andra (lying) in a publicity still for *Genuine* (1920). (*Source: German Film Institute—DIF, Frankfurt*)

already been murdered by the madly jealous Florian. In the frame story, Percy is mourning Genuine, whose painting is his only memento of her.

Notably, Genuine is not quite the "vampire" as the film's English title indicates.[35] She neither subdues men by physical force nor actually kills them herself, but uses her erotic charms and beauty to seduce them. Also, she does not suck blood from her victims, and even though she demands blood sacrifices she only drinks the blood when she is forced to do so by the sect members, while later rejecting the offering. At best, Genuine is responsible for one murder, the killing of old Lord Melos, who held her captive in his house—and maybe for her own death, which she provoked by manipulating the young Florian. The barber's nephew is gullible and callow—"Florian's first experience with life," reads the intertitle when he enters the house—an easy target in the furtive glance of Genuine. At first glance Genuine seems to be a wicked creature, but the film narrative repeatedly offers a different interpretation by illustrating her underlying true, good and pure nature, that is simply submerged by the psychological trauma of the horrors she experienced as the sect's priestess. The trigger for her mania is clearly depicted in the film: first, it is the sharp shaving blade, and second, the dagger. The blame for her depravity is distinctly allocated to the tribe, as the slave trader's statement emphasizes:

"they corrupted her." Her innocence is, however, underlined by her youthful wish to "fall in love," her refusal of the servant's blood, and her final surrender in the arms of Percy. Also, it is remarkable that Genuine never has full control of the situation: Florian fails to commit suicide, the servant disobeys her order to kill Florian, Percy is saved by his friend Curzon, and Genuine is easily fooled into believing that her lover is dead. When she finally gives in and confesses her love for Percy, she is freed from her demonic powers, but is murdered by the man she drove into madness (otherwise, she would have been killed by an angry mob).

Still, in contrast to *Caligari*, Genuine is displayed as a particularly strong female character who for the greater part of the film takes action and does not bend to anyone's will. She gains power through her alluring sexuality, which charms Melos, Florian and Percy alike. The exotic underground chamber is her realm, metaphorically pointing to her untamed sexual nature, a place of unbridled eroticism and savage lusts where she brings her victims even after she has already freed herself from her master.[36] Lord Melos is the authoritarian figure who was able to restrain Genuine's destructive sexuality, but failed as soon as Genuine managed to escape and entered the above-ground, civilized world where her tantalizing and cunning vigors are set free, until Percy, a rational and self-controlled man, enters as a second authoritarian force and redraws the boundary between decent behavior and savage nature. Genuine is briefly re-established as a member of civilized society, but ultimately she is sentenced to death for her former crimes. The bourgeois order is only reinstalled when she falls victim to the man she had previously bewitched.[37]

Conclusion

From vampire to vamp: *Genuine* certainly falls into the category of Expressionist films which depict male anxieties about women and allegorically cast these insecurities into the form of a feminized "monster," a seductive, powerful and threatening woman beyond control who is both desired and feared.[38] The vamps of Weimar cinema are ambiguous. Their seductive appeals are usually associated with immorality, depravity and perverseness that need to be expelled from bourgeois society, but they also have appeal as autonomous, independent, strong women of emancipated sexuality who know exactly how to use their appearance and charm to get what they want.[39] It is striking that these types of women entered the cinema when German society experienced rapid modernization toward a consumer-oriented, mass entertainment culture that challenged traditional conceptions about male and female identities. By openly thematizing these concerns, expressionist film became an important part of discourses about a growing female liberation and its interpretation as "decadence" or "degeneracy."[40]

Notes

1. In the American print used by Jung/Schatzberg for their analysis, Lord Melos is called "Milo" and Percy's friend Curzon is called "Henry." Uli Jung and Walter Schatzberg, *Beyond Caligari: The Films of Robert Wiene* (Oxford/New York: Berghahn, 1999).
2. Ibid.
3. Ibid. p. 85.
4. Rudolf Kurtz, *Expressionismus und Film* (Berlin: Verlag der Lichtbild-Bühne, 1926), p. 70.
5. *Film-Kurier* and *Lichtbild-Bühne* (LBB) were two of the most prominent and influential early German film journals, famous for their reviews.
6. L. K. Frederik, "Genuine," *Film-Kurier*, Vol. 2, No. 196, 3 September 1920, p. 1. All film reviews mentioned here are my own translations from German. Note that some of the articles were published only with the author's initials.
7. L. K. Frederik praised the performance of Hans Heinz von Twardowsky as "extraordinary" (ibid.); Fritz Olimsky asserted that "also to be mentioned is Hans Heinz v. Twardowski whose wraithlike face believably portrayed the oversensitive barber's apprentice" (*Berliner Börsen-Zeitung*, 5 September 1920, quoted from *Film und Presse* [Berlin], 11 September 1920, Vol. 1, No. 9, p. 222); and G. P. (Georg Popper) wrote enthusiastically: "But Hans Heinz von Twardowsky surpassed everything. His performance: simply fantastic. It is unlikely he will be outperformed" (*Hamburger Theaterzeitung*, 17 September 1920, Vol. 2, No. 37, p. 18) [my translations].
8. "The actress of Genuine, Fern Andra, was too concerned with outer appearances" (E. K., *8 Uhr-Abendblatt*, 3 September 1920, quoted from *Film und Presse*, p. 221); "With Fern Andra an exceptionally beautiful and even mimically expressive actress was engaged who is given the opportunity to wear 36 bizarre costumes in 6 acts: being the prima donna that she is, she is playing her voluptuously, ferociously, tenderly, always conscious that the whole event is only there to show how goodlooking Fern Andra is" (tz, *Berliner Börsen-Zeitung*, 5 September 1920, quoted from *Film und Presse*, p. 222); "The female vampire of this magic world is Fern Andra. While conceding that she firmly intends to free herself from cliché, she does not succeed in grasping the demonic essence of the role" (ct, *Vossische Zeitung* [Berlin], 4 September 1920 (early edition), p. 4); "There are plenty of occasions [in the film] where she [Fern Andra] can show her charms, and she makes extensive use of them. Her acting as Genuine is humanised, maybe too humanised, maybe not feral enough. The bestiality and urging of blood frenzy is not conveyed as trenchantly as it might have been intended. Of course she prevails: She always looks beautiful. If that is enough for tragedy?" (Frederik, *Film-Kurier*, p. 1). My translations.
9. Jung and Schatzberg, *Beyond Caligari*, p. 79. The authors also emphasize that most of the negative reviews the film received are "second-hand opinions . . . which have never been revised, primarily because hardly any prints of the film have been available to film" (ibid. p. 78).
10. Kurtz, *Expressionismus und Film*, p. 62.
11. Ibid. pp. 70, 73.
12. In her famous book *The Haunted Screen*, Eisner wrote a scathing review of *Genuine* in which she assessed the film as a failed attempt of director Wiene to "establish Caligarism in his film *Genuine*." She found the painted sets of the "otherwise interesting artist Cesar Klein" to be too "muddled and overloaded" so that the "naturalistic actors just vanished into it" and criticized the "body-wriggling"

of Fern Andra, "a pretty woman but a mediocre actress." Lotte H. Eisner, *The Haunted Screen: Expressionism in the German Cinema and the Influence of Max Reinhardt* (trans. Roger Graeves), 2nd edn (Berkeley, CA: University of California Press, 2008 [1952]), p. 27.
13. Siegfried Kracauer briefly mentions *Genuine* in his book *From Caligari to Hitler*. Similarly to fellow critic Eisner (ibid.), he sees *Genuine* as a (half-hearted) attempt to reproduce the commercial success of its predecessor by noting that Wiene meant "to strike while the iron was hot." He elaborates: "This fantasy, in which an exuberant décor competes with a far-fetched, bizarre story, is of importance only in that it marks a turning point thematically ... The narrative shows [screenwriter] Mayer's interest shifting from the tyrant to the instinct theme." Siegfried Kracauer, *From Caligari to Hitler. A Psychological History of the German Film* (Princeton, NJ: Princeton University Press 1966 [1947]), p. 96.
14. Colin Storer, *A Short History of the Weimar Republic* (London: I. B. Tauris, 2013), p. 27; Eric D. Weitz, *Weimar Germany: Promise and Tragedy* (Princeton, NJ: Princeton University Press, 2007), p. 129; Kathleen Canning, *Gender History in Practice: Historical Perspectives on Bodies, Class, and Citizenship* (Ithaca, NY [et al.]: Cornell University Press, 2006), p. 212; Ruth Henig, *The Weimar Republic. 1919–1933* (London: Routledge, 1998), p. xii.
15. Katie Sutton, *The Masculine Woman in Weimar Germany* [Monographs in German history, Vol. 32] (New York [et al.]: Berghahn, 2013), pp. 3–4.
16. It should be noted that modernism, capitalist consumerism and the emerging mass culture were highly debated in Weimar culture and strongly opposed by traditionalist and anti-modernist movements. David C. Durst, *Weimar Modernism: Philosophy, Politics, and Culture in Germany, 1918–1933* (Lanham, MD [et al.]: Lexington, 2004); Eberhard Kolb, *The Weimar Republic* (London/New York: Routledge, 2001 [1988]), p. 84.
17. Richard W. McCormick, *Gender and Sexuality in Weimar Modernity. Film, Literature and "New Objectivity"* (New York: Palgrave, 2001), p. 3.
18. Peter Gay points out that the so-called "golden twenties" in Weimar culture were characterized by "exuberant creativity and experimentation, but much of it was anxiety, fear, a rising sense of doom." Peter Gay, *Weimar Culture: The Outsider as Insider* (New York [et al.]: Norton, 2001), p. xiv. A critical discussion about the notion of "consciousness of crisis" can be found in Kathleen Canning's introduction to the book *Weimar Subjects/Weimar Publics. Rethinking the Political Culture of Germany in the 1920s* (ed. Kathleen Canning/Kerstin Barndt/Kristin McGuire) (New York [et al.]: Berghahn, 2010), pp. 1–28.
19. McCormick, *Gender and Sexuality in Weimar Modernity*, p. 3.
20. Sutton, *The Masculine Woman in Weimar Germany*, pp. 3–4; Ingrid Sharp, "Gender Relations in Weimar Berlin," in Christiane Schönfeld (ed.), *Practicing Modernity: Female Creativity in the Weimar Republic* (Würzburg: Königshausen & Neumann, 2006), pp. 1–13, see pp. 6–7.
21. Birthe Kundrus, "The First World War and the Construction of Gender Relations in the Weimar Republic," in Karen Hagemann and Stefanie Schüler-Springorum (eds.), *Home/Front. The Military, War and Gender in Twentieth Century Germany* (Oxford/New York: Berg, 2003), pp. 159–80, see p. 159.
22. Andreas Wirsching, *Die Weimarer Republik: Politik und Gesellschaft* (Munich: Oldenbourg Wissenschaftsverlag, 2000), p. 94.
23. Gesa Kessemeier, *Sportlich, sachlich, männlich. Das Bild der "Neuen Frau" in den Zwanziger Jahren. Zur Konstruktion geschlechtsspezifischer Körperbilder in der Mode der Jahre 1920 bis 1929* (Dortmund: Ed. Ebersbach, 2000), p. 25; Sutton, *The Masculine Woman in Weimar Germany*, p. 6.

24. Wirsching, *Die Weimarer Republik: Politik und Gesellschaft*, p. 95. McCormick writes in *Gender and Sexuality in Weimar Modernity*, p. 4: "the blurring of traditionally gendered roles and behavior ... is precisely what is most emancipatory about Weimar culture ... although [it] was by no means an indication that power relations had become all that enlightened and egalitarian."
25. McCormick, *Gender and Sexuality in Weimar Modernity*, p. 3.
26. Anton Kaes, "Filmgeschichte als Kulturgeschichte: Reflexionen zum Kino der Weimarer Republik," in Uli Jung and Walter Schatzberg (eds.), *Filmkultur zur Zeit der Weimarer Republik* (Munich [et al.]: Saur, 1992), pp. 54–64, see p. 57 [my translation].
27. For a critical discussion on the term "Expressionist film" see Richard Murphy, "Modernist Film and Gender: Expressionism and the Fantastic in Karl Grune's *The Street*," in Frank Krause (ed.), *Expressionism and Gender/Expressionismus und Geschlecht* (Göttingen: V&R unipress, 2010), pp. 83–98, see p. 83.
28. Ibid. p. 86.
29. McCormick, *Gender and Sexuality in Weimar Modernity*, p. 6.
30. Jürgen Kasten, *Der expressionistische Film: Abgefilmtes Theater oder avantgardistisches Erzählkino? Eine stil-, produktions- und rezeptionsgeschichtliche Untersuchung* [Film- und fernsehwissenschaftliche Arbeiten] (Münster: MAkS Publikationen, 1990), p. 161 [my translation].
31. Murphy, "Modernist Film and Gender," p. 85.
32. Ibid. p. 86.
33. Ibid. pp. 86–7. Similarly, Kaes observes the expressionist filmmaker's fascination with the Other, which, however, is ultimately always interpreted as an "irrational attack on the existing order," often associated with criminality and madness. Kaes, "Filmgeschichte als Kulturgeschichte," p. 61 [my translation].
34. In *From Caligari to Hitler*, Siegfried Kracauer pays particular attention to this "gesture of capitulation." He associates it with male figures who have "never attained maturity" and therefore have an "instinctive reluctance to attempt emancipation." See Kracauer, *From Caligari to Hitler*, p. 99.
35. The original German title is *Genuine, Die Tragödie eines seltsamen Hauses* (Genuine, The Tragedy of a Strange House).
36. Jung and Schatzberg, *Beyond Caligari*, p. 83.
37. Ibid. 85
38. McCormick, *Gender and Sexuality in Weimar Modernity*, pp. 25, 30.
39. This ambivalence is mirrored in the bourgeois attitude to magic: "Desirous of something for nothing, one yet fears the magic that effects this miracle, for it demonstrates the existence of forces beyond the ken of commonsense philosophy." Paul Coates, *The Gorgon's Gaze. German Cinema, Expressionism, and the Image of Horror* (Cambridge [et al.]: Cambridge University Press, 1991), p. 29.
40 McCormick, *Gender and Sexuality in Weimar Modernity*, p. 169.

5. "THE SECRETS OF NATURE AND ITS UNIFYING PRINCIPLES": *NOSFERATU* (1922) AND JAKOB VON UEXKÜLL ON *UMWELT*

Steve Choe

Act 3 of F. W. Murnau's 1922 vampire film, *Nosferatu, eine Symphonie des Grauens*,[1] opens with the ill-fated Hutter (played by Gustav von Wangenheim) lying in a hospital bed. The real-estate agent has already completed his business with Count Orlok (Max Schreck) and made his departure from Orlok's Transylvanian castle, nestled in the Carpathian mountains. Meanwhile, Hutter's wife Ellen (Greta Schröter) remains in Wisborg, a small, fictionally-named port town, awaiting his safe return. During his stay with Orlok, Hutter was plagued by visions of the undead while asleep, of inanimate things becoming animate, and horrifying vampires lying in coffins. Frightened, he escaped Orlok's abode, but fell from a high window and was knocked unconscious.

As he lies recovering in the beginning of Act 3 of the film, a doctor remarks to a nurse: "He was brought to the hospital yesterday by farmers. They say he had fallen. He still has a fever . . ." As the film cuts back to Hutter, he begins to stir, evidently struggling with his nightmares. Suddenly, in a daze, he sits up and slowly stretches out his arm, pointing to the lower right of the film frame. Bewilderment and panic fill his face. The nurse attempts to calm him, but the hapless Hutter is possessed by a strange, unseen force that inspires him to utter a single word: "Coffins . . ." Following this great effort he falls back and returns to unconsciousness. An intertitle signals that, at this precise moment, other developments were taking place far away: "Nosferatu was coming. Danger was on its way to Wisborg. Professor Bulwer, a Paracelsian, who was investigating the secrets of nature and its unifying principles, told me

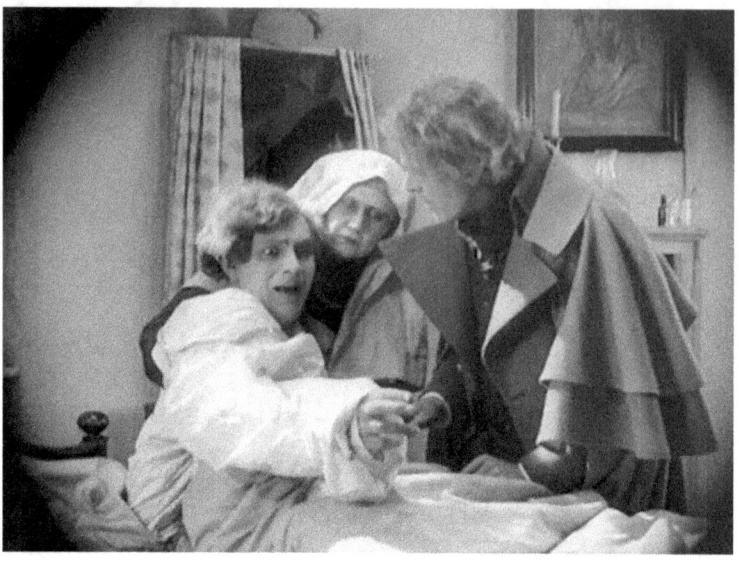

Figure 5.1 A frame from *Nosferatu*. (*Courtesy of Friedrich-Wilhelm-Murnau-Stiftung, Wiesbaden*)

about it: Caskets filled with dirt were loaded onto the double-masted schooner, Empusa."

As if to instigate the cut to the intertitle, Hutter's strange exclamation is followed by a sequence that depicts Nosferatu drawing near to his home and wife. Murnau juxtaposes shots of this allegorical figure of death traveling to Wisborg, depicted by a single coffin carried over water on a raft, with other images showing several coffins unloaded from a ship onto the Wisborg docks. Time and place in this sequence are unified through crosscuts. In her reading of *Nosferatu* in *Celluloid Vampires: Life After Death in the Modern World*, the media scholar Stacey Abbott argues that the crosscutting that takes place here and in other passages in the film allegorize the modern, technologically mediated conceptions of time and space: "The film uses its ability to edit and juxtapose shots together to embody the modern collapse of time, space, and communication, and to suggest the uncanny quality of the culture of simultaneous and interconnected experience brought about by modernity."[2] The capacity for montage is showcased in these shots, the cinema's unique ability to be a ubiquitous witness to any place and any time.[3] Abbott draws a number of striking parallels between *Nosferatu* and the film medium, noting that the vampiric condition may be compared to the uncanny ontology of the moving image itself. It is an ontology "made up of still images, ghostly shadows of the dead that are reanimated through technological means."[4] By embalming the ghosts of the past and bringing them to life on the film screen, Orlok self-consciously allegorizes the life-enabling capacities of the cinematic technology and underscores its peculiar non-organic form of life.[5]

Such parallels may be corroborated historically by recalling early Weimar arguments around the artistic status of the cinema, arguments which the film scholar Anton Kaes has called the *"Kino-Debatte."*[6] Many writers in these debates claim that the cinematic image not only represents life, but is itself a form of life, whose vital essence is based on embodiment, eloquent gesture and movement. In a short essay from 1922 by Arnold Zweig called "Theses on the Theoretical Foundation of Film," the ontology of the cinema is intimately linked to the themes of life and lifelessness, echoing some of the uncanny themes raised by Abbott and others: "The attraction that radiates from objects in film is that of seeing something inanimate become animate. Film is based entirely upon the free unfolding of the living." For Zweig, the cinema bestows on silent, inanimate objects an auratic "attraction," and as through this the objects acquire a kind of speech, speaking through the non-linguistic language of pure gesture. Partly in order to legitimize the emergent technology as a viable form of art, and partly to protect the native industry from the threat of the American product, proponents of cinema in the early Weimar context repeatedly identified its essence as inextricably linked to animation and the resurrection of the dead.

Such links call for deeper inquiry into the relationship between *Nosferatu* and the "living," cinematic technology. In this chapter I would like to place one scene from the film in dialogue with key passages from two texts produced in 1920 by the zoologist Jakob von Uexküll. Adopting von Uexküll's special definition of *"Umwelt"* ("environment" or, more literally, "surrounding-world"), I will show how *Nosferatu* specifies a fluid, chiasmatic relationship between film and environment, as well as classifications of the organic and inorganic. If Murnau's film allegorizes possibilities specific to the cinematic technology (and by co-extension technological modernity in general), Uexküll's contemporaneous text allows us to see how the allegorical life of the cinema relates to its surrounding world, and in so doing characterizes this aspect of Expressionist cinema as an uncanny form of non-human life. Specifically, we shall see how the cinema and its environment are based on the biopolitics of lived life, discourses inspired by Professor Bulwer, the "Paracelsian,"[7] and his inquiries into "the secrets of nature and its unifying principles."

Vampiric Correspondences

Hutter's exclamation, "Coffins . . .," motivates the cut to Galaz, a town near Orlok's castle, where wooden coffins are inspected before being loaded onto the ship. We are informed that these are "six crates of dirt for experimental purposes." One of them, filled almost to the top with soil, is pried open and overturned. As dirt falls onto the wooden deck, numerous rats also spill out and dart away, their place of hiding having been abruptly exposed. A large rodent bites the foot of an inspector and he shakes it off, seemingly mindless to danger of disease. Murnau cuts to the next intertitle: "I should note that in those days Professor Bulwer was teaching his students about the dreadful methods of carnivorous plants. One viewed with horror the mysterious workings of nature." Bulwer is shown in his seminar room in Wisborg, surrounded by curious pupils.

He gestures for them to gather round, directing their attention toward a small wooden box of soil sitting on his desk. The film cuts to a close-up of a fly crawling around a carnivorous plant. As the small insect lingers around its menacing leaves, the fly suddenly triggers the small hairs on its lobes and snaps the trap shut, becoming haplessly ensnared within its blades. The fly struggles to break free, but the trap slowly and relentlessly tightens its grasp. *Nosferatu* cuts to a close-up of Bulwer's face and he remarks with a sly look, "Like a vampire—no?" Then at this very moment, the film crosscuts once more, transitioning with the intertitle, "As the predator Nosferatu approached, it seems that the estate agent, Knock, had already begun to fall under his spell."

With this edit, the film brings shots of disease-infested coffins and Bulwer's

Figure 5.2 A frame from *Nosferatu*. (*Courtesy of Friedrich-Wilhelm-Murnau-Stiftung, Wiesbaden*)

Figure 5.3 A frame from *Nosferatu*. (*Courtesy of Friedrich-Wilhelm-Murnau-Stiftung, Wiesbaden*)

sinister botanical demonstration in correspondence with a shot of Knock's increasing agitation, the one instigating the other. Knock has been admitted to a psychiatric asylum. "The patient admitted yesterday has gone stark raving mad," a guard remarks.

Sitting in his cell, Knock laughs crazily and swats at the air for flies, nervously putting them into his mouth. He bizarrely becomes the Venus flytrap of Bulwer's experiment. The crazed man then excitedly repeats, without apparent reason, "Blood is life! Blood is life!" He leaps from his unkempt bed and motions toward an unseen fly hovering somewhere in his room, becoming increasingly agitated and volatile. Suddenly, he assaults the psychiatrist who stands before him and violently attempts to strangle the doctor. The guard rushes to pull Knock off and forcibly drags him back to bed.

The film then cuts back to Bulwer's classroom. The professor peers very intently and with great curiosity at the earth collected in his small box. He motions for his students to gather around even more closely, remarking, "And this one here . . ."

In order not to miss yet another instance of vampirism and the universal struggle between life and death, he gestures toward an elongated "polyp with tentacles . . ." In extreme close-up, it is suspended in dark water as one might observe under a microscope, illuminated such that its body is nearly "transparent . . . almost ethereal . . ." Bulwer speaks descriptively, almost elliptically, while small groups of words alternate with images that correspond

Figure 5.4 A frame from *Nosferatu*. (*Courtesy of Friedrich-Wilhelm-Murnau-Stiftung, Wiesbaden*)

to them. The organism almost takes on the appearance of a letter on a page, a provocation perhaps that the image itself be read as a living signifier. A more miniscule, perhaps more primitive life-form suddenly enters the frame and begins to flit around the polyp. After a few moments the diminutive creature becomes entangled in the larger organism's tentacles, and as it struggles to break free, the slender, finger-like members of its predator pull its prey toward its ostensible mouth. "Little more than a phantom . . .," Bulwer continues as he raises his pointer and turns his head obliquely toward his increasingly intrigued students.[8]

Nosferatu then cuts back to Knock in his small room, subdued by the psychiatric guard positioned behind him. The real-estate agent looks up and points toward one of the corners of the room: "spiders . . .!" he suddenly exclaims. Murnau shows us a close-up of a spider, shot in exactly the same manner as the polyp, phantom-like against a dark background. A web attached to the walls of the holding room suspends the arachnid. It is in the process of spinning a net around a small fly—apparently the one that Knock had earlier sought. Its spidery legs seem to visually echo the polyp's tentacles or perhaps even Nosferatu's own sinewy, grasping fingers. The film cuts back to a medium-shot of Knock and his subjugator, who proceeds to bind him with rope. The curious psychiatrist apprehensively approaches the now absolutely irrational man and rubs his chin, pondering his patient's erratic behavior once more.

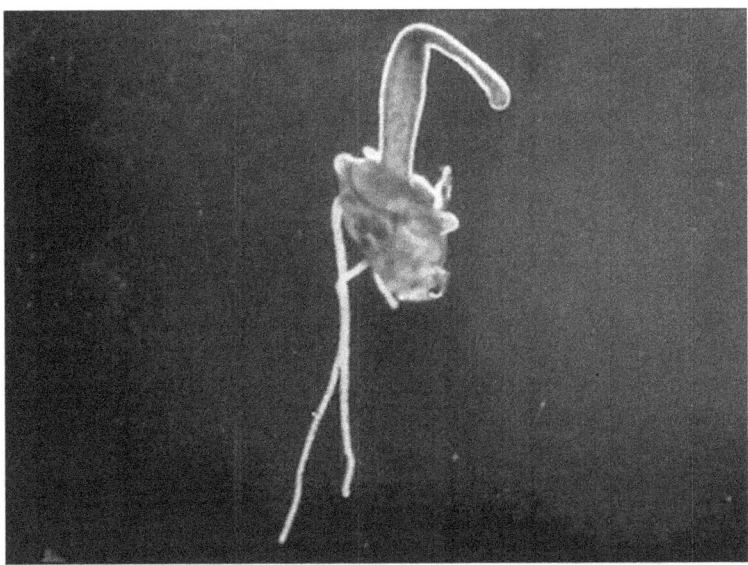

Figure 5.5 A frame from *Nosferatu*. (*Courtesy of Friedrich-Wilhelm-Murnau-Stiftung, Wiesbaden*)

Unholy earth, spiders, vampires, carnivorous plants, a microscopic polyp, the real-estate agent Knock, and spectral phantoms—what was Bulwer, who was investigating the secrets of nature and its unifying principles, proposing in these ominous demonstrations? What can we glean from this montage of life and death, connected by crosscuts and sinister correspondences? What is it that unifies these beings? Indeed, these juxtapositions, as Abbott argues, may be linked to conceptions of time in modernity, specifically notions of simultaneity and of vulgar clock time. Yet there seem to be other existential correspondences at work here, other border crossings, neither operating on the level of the diegesis nor following a strict logic of mechanistic causality. The extreme close-up of the polyp, for example, and Bulwer's pedagogical tone, may be read as a nod toward the contemporaneous *Kulturfilm*, serving to underscore the pedagogical uses to which images of microscopic organisms were put. These images underscore the clash between documentary truth and the film's fictional diegesis. A tiny organism, a carnivorous plant, and a highly unstable human being all become, as Bulwer notes, vampiric, each patterned on Orlok's own characterization as an undead, blood-sucking monster. In contrast to other well-known Expressionist films such as Robert Wiene's *The Cabinet of Dr. Caligari* (1920), Paul Wegener's *Golem: How He Came Into the World* (1920), or Fritz Lang's *Metropolis* (1927), *Nosferatu* was not shot exclusively in a studio, but combined built settings with outdoor, on-location shots. If, as a number of scholars have argued,[9] Nosferatu's undead body reflexively allegorizes the ontology of the cinema image, what do we make of such correspondences across indoor and outdoor settings, documentary and fiction, and strange, secret correlations across diverse forms of animate life? What might the worldly organism reveal to us about the relationship between the cinematic organism and its environment?

Mother Nature's Son

Uexküll's early work *Theoretical Biology* (1920) presents us with a highly original response to such questions. Seemingly heedless of the teleologically-oriented Darwinisms dominant at the time, Uexküll eschews explanations of Nature that reduce its complex actions to a series of mechanistic or chemical processes. He avoids ascribing an idealized aim to the development of a particular species and is opposed to explanations of living phenomena anchored in evolution's ostensible cunning of reason. Uexküll remains skeptical about thinking of life as having an all-encompassing telos, one that confirms the "survival of the fittest." Thus like Heidegger, he is extremely critical of attributing a metaphysics to lived life.

In contrast to these grand theories about the creative evolution of life, Uexküll's approach is empirical in the most immediate sense. For him, the biologist's primary task is to observe a particular organism, to notice its behavior and development within the particular environment that is proper to its form of existence. The scientific observer should pay close attention to the unseen, vital forces that animate and give purpose to its movements. These forces provide clues as to how the living entity perceives its environment, and demonstrate a relationship that expresses interlocking, and therefore necessary, parts within a functioning whole.

Uexküll thus abstains from drawing observations that implicate an antagonistic relationship between life and world. Instead of beginning with an "unfit" organism that must struggle to adapt to a hostile environment, an organism that must progressively develop coping mechanisms so that it can survive, Uexküll writes that every living being can "only be itself," and that within a specific environment it is already "perfect" (*vollkommen*). He adopts the term "congruity" (*Einpassung*) to describe the relationship between the living organism and its surroundings. There is no "more" or "less" as regards congruity. If all organisms are perfectly congruous with their surrounding world, there is no such thing as gradual attainment of perfection; the perfection of congruity exists everywhere from the very beginning.[10] Affirming what Darwin might have identified as the organism's "incongruence," Uexküll argues that the specific capacities of the organism—its abilities, limits, and physiological features—are already fit, or "perfect" for the environment in which it finds itself embedded. The living organism is already congruent with its natural habitat insofar as it already possesses the means for perceiving its surrounding world, possessing also the physiological means for conducting its own activity so that it may live. For Uexküll there are no accidental mutations in the organism that will make it more or less fit for its environment.

When an organism is placed in an environment that is foreign to it, such an environment does not allow the organism to realize its potentiality of being given the possibilities that are made readily available to its particular form of life-activity. "The external world," Uexküll writes,

> offers to the organism a certain number of properties separated in space and in time, from which to select, and therewith the possibility of making a poorer or a richer surrounding-world. But the external world itself takes no part in the selection, which has to be made by the organism without external assistance.[11]

Key in this passage is that the external world remains radically other to the organism. It does not exert a dialectical logic on the organism's development, constituting the conditions through which certain encounters turn out to be favorable or unfavorable to it. Rather, the world can only offer the means for making survival possible at all. It is up to the living being to exploit all such means for its material subsistence and express itself by realizing what it must become, given the specific environment in which it finds itself situated.[12]

As such, every organism embodies a specific relationship to its environment that cannot be schematically understood by a scientific, predetermining intelligence. The complex life of the organism must be considered within its context and not in isolation from it. The study of life cannot be observed apart from its *Umwelt*, proper or improper though it may be. The scientist thus allows for radically other ways of being, other ways of living and perceiving the world, beyond those belonging to the human observer. The result of these confrontations with otherness always exceeds scientific, rational forms of comprehension, for the perceptual capacities of the fly or the spider and their corresponding reactions cannot be understood through mechanistic description alone. The polyp does not "see" the amoeba like the human being, nor does the spider listen in a capacity similar to the human ear, or the carnivorous plant taste its prey in the manner we know taste.

In this, physiological difference constitutes ontological difference. For Uexküll, because of the infinite variety in which an organism may dwell in a specific *Umwelt*, there is no predetermined, universal law of life that every living entity adheres to; rather, he argues, each living being is a law unto itself.[13] The blue jay that returns to the back patio, as if to remember, or the dog which accompanies the professor on her walk—both possess morphological differences that constitute their capacity for life as different from that of the human being. As far as these other species are concerned, they do not perceive their respective worlds with the spatial and temporal coordinates devised by modern human consciousness. The carnivorous plant can only perceive the flicking of one of three sensitive hairs on its leaf. Triggered once, the plant awakens and becomes alert, sensing perhaps the strong wind or the raindrop that fell on its lobe. Triggered twice in succession, the leaf blades quickly snap shut, in order to trap its living prey for slow digestion. But the vampiric plant does not perceive its prey as the hapless fly sees it, for the physiological capacities of each organism distinguish one as mutually exclusive of the other. Each has its own capacities for being, for perceiving the world, each its own *Umwelt*. Indeed, the plant is never sure whether what remains trapped within its jaws is actually living prey or a drop of rain—it only can sense the flicking of its sensitive hairs. Yet for Uexküll both the plant and its prey coexist as if intimate partners in a grand symphony of vital life, unknowing participants choreographed by unseen fluctuations, organic individual parts perfectly congruent with their organic and inorganic surroundings.

Moreover, for Uexküll, the fly that is trapped in the spider's web is not simply a "fly." Rather, it is the prey-for-the-spider, structuring and giving meaning to the spider's activity, as it rushes toward its prey to spin another web around it. The ontology of life in *Theoretical Biology* is constituted by the organism's purposive activity and movement within a surrounding world. As the living organism receives stimuli from the environment, its gestures are made meaningful at the moment it carries out its specific functions, functions that in turn express its being. Such functions should not be understood as having a pre-conceived telos, for Uexküll is adamant in arguing that life's significance can only be constituted *ad hoc*, as it were. In other words, the meaning of life is constituted in the process of living life and as life creatively conceives a direction for itself:

> It is only the knowledge of the rule of action pertaining to its "function" that arranges the parts into the whole. If we do not know the function, which establishes fixed relations, we cannot know the design, and we do not recognize the significance of the implement. Accordingly, instead of the plan expressed by an implement, we may speak of its "functionality."[14]

A prison wall gains particular significance for the spider in its possibility of spider-being: it becomes an "implement" that functions as a surface that will anchor its web. Only in performing its web-spinning capacity does this form of life become a "spider."

Objects in its surrounding world become meaningful for a particular organism not as abstracted concepts, but as concrete means for life-activity. And

Figure 5.6   A frame from *Nosferatu*. (*Courtesy of Friedrich-Wilhelm-Murnau-Stiftung, Wiesbaden*)

from the perspective of the human prisoner, the same wall embodies an altogether different function, for it encloses the space in which he is incarcerated. Uexküll underscores these ontological differences with a short anecdote:

> When a boy collects "skipping-stones," which he wants to send dancing across the surface of a lake, there arises out of the general implement "stone" (whose function in general is to be thrown) a particular implement, the properties of which group themselves round the special function of "skipping." The skipping-stone is hard, flat, circular and of a certain weight. These are the properties required for this special function; the other properties it possesses, over and above these,—such as colour, smell, taste and resonance,—are "inessential," and are not determined by the function. It follows from this that, by the much misused word "nature" of an implement, we always mean its function.[15]

Depending on the particular form of life, its morphology, its peculiar capacities, and the environment, objects take on different meanings, meanings intimately related to its intended function for the specific organism. For the young boy standing at the edge of a lake, flat stones are not simply "stones," but become stones-for-skipping. The "stoniness" of the stone comes to the fore when it enters into relation with the boy's throwing arm and the surface of water.

Uexküll seems to imply that representational concepts, the domain of contemplative man, are constituted as something like an afterthought, after such implements have been recollected and subsequently codified in their functionality. There are no predetermined, phenomenological essences, only entities-for-life; no fixed categories like "stone" or "cinema," only a stone-for-the-boy or a cinema-for-the-biologist, a cinema-for-the-cinephile; no mere "beings," only being-for. Such hyphenated formulations indicate that life has direction, though this direction may be merely virtual in relation to the actuality of being, and it reveals how the surrounding environment is already present to life. It is precisely for this reason that life cannot be pursued outside the particular environment in which it is embedded. It is inextricably linked to the interactions the living organism has with other beings, through which vital life fulfills its specific functions. Ontology, Uexküll's *Theoretical Biology* seems to suggest, follows from the potentialities enabled by the interface of the organism with its *Umwelt*.

The montage sequence from Act 3 of *Nosferatu* allegorizes this interface, underscoring the existential conditions that constitute lived life in nature. Structured as a series of crosscuts, on the one hand the montage heightens the spectator's tension by constantly switching back and forth between places, as if not to settle on a singular space and time. On the other, the crosscuts provide a means to unify each of these discrete places, to show that vampire-functions can be found in all forms of life—in microscopic polyps, flesh-eating plants, and nervous real-estate agents. Each of these organisms carries physiological characteristics that make vampiric existence possible. Orlok's grasping fingers may be compared to the grasping tentacles of the tiny polyp. The poisonous bite of the Nosferatu is like the bite of the spider. Furthermore, the fang-like mouth of the horrifying fly-trap is akin to the sharp teeth of the vampire, constituting a specific mode of existence that remains radically other to the life of the human being.

These are the movements of cinematic vitality that thread their way through Murnau's film. Crosscuts suture such movements together by exploiting the formal, functional possibilities aligned with the art of film. The film scholar Judith Mayne, in her essay on Murnau's film, notes that the affinities between Bulwer and Knock, as well as between Nosferatu and Nina, "elude the written commentary of the narrator."[16] *Nosferatu* exploits the crosscut to show how the cinematic apparatus can be at multiple places at the same time, suturing various creatures into the body of the cinema. Like the living organism whose environment allows it to realize its specific potential for being, the cinema is charged with expressing its specific formal capacity: raw footage brought together through cutting and montage, to constitute the duration of the inorganic life of the cinema.

What makes Uexküll's approach toward life so useful is his insistence on the gestural possibilities of the living being as constitutive of life itself. Animals are not defined simply as entities, but as first and foremost being-toward-something, and at times on the way to becoming something else. Uexküll is keenly aware of how the scientist's approach toward life may limit proper representation of the organism as a mortal being that lives in time. The biologist should remain wary of the use of concepts that cannot respect life's most fundamental being as constant development, activity, becoming and change. Notably, it is the moving image that for Uexküll possesses the means necessary for expressing this creative evolution. When he describes the phenomenon of early protoplasmic development, it is not the representational word that best signals this becoming, but an altogether new medium. He writes:

> If, by the help of the cinematograph, we fix the bridge-formation that arises in this way, we get a picture of a changing tissue, the pattern of which remains the same at every repetition. A skilled musician could then read from the pattern what the melody had been that was played outside.[17]

In *Nosferatu*, the cinema relates to its surrounding world in its ability to describe the miracles of gesture and movement as occurring simultaneously within the cosmos. Unholy earth, spiders, vampires, carnivorous plants, a microscopic polyp, the real-estate agent Knock, spectral phantoms, and the cinema: all are unified in their will toward life. Cinema and the natural world, cinema on location as it were, thus function in parallel motion, for in film's very ability to depict change as inextricably linked to duration, both life and cinema are defined, and unified, as activity within the world.

Yet, as Nosferatu's own undead, allegorical figure indicates, life has something to do with death. Murnau's film moves us beyond the scope of Uexküll's *Theoretical Biology*, and emphasizes life's final aim, or its ultimate "function." In *Nosferatu*, each of these vampiric organisms shows how life at every moment is also a movement toward the end of life, toward mortality and inanimacy, or living-toward-death. If it is the nature of the vampire to consume the other, as it is allegorized in the carnivorous plant, or the spider, or Bulwer's polyp, it remains necessary so that the Nosferatu can find permanent rest. Nosferatu must consume the blood of another so that he himself may find his path toward death. From the perspective of the healthy human being, this thought is perhaps a horrifying prospect. Yet if understood from the perspective of "nature and its unifying principles," and also from the perspective that binds it together with the life of the cinema, the montage sequence reveals cinema's invisible death drive, by grimly depicting the cycles of life and death that make the animate world possible at all. For the human spectator, these shots horrify not only because they remind the living spectator of the inevitable conclusion to life, but also because they reveal this existential fact as underpinning all forms of life in the cosmos. The mortal human subject becomes radically decentered, becoming one participant in an infinite conversation of life, moving and gesturing in synchronous activity. "We can also think of this coming into being and then dying away," Uexküll writes elsewhere in his text, "as though it took place cinematographically; then we participate in the rhythm, and so get the right impression of the species as a rhythmical sequence of acts."[18] The movement of the image inevitably attests to the decay of life. As *Nosferatu* unfolds, so does the progression of life toward death.

Uexküll adopts musical metaphors, such as the reference to the "skilled musician," to describe this unseen evolution. In fact, throughout *Theoretical Biology* one of the most fruitful running themes is that between the direction an organism takes up in its efforts to pursue a specific function, life's conformity with plan, and a musical melody, whose materiality in time similarly remains invisible. The vital will toward life develops, he writes,

> like a melody, which controls the sequence of sound and the rhythm in accordance with law, but becomes apparent only as it becomes operative, and then takes on the tone-colour which the properties of the particular instruments impose on it.[19]

Indeed, this development is freely composed, without telos, and cannot be reduced to mechanistic or chemical processes. "It is just as impossible," Uexküll continues,

> for a melody to derive its law from the relationship of the notes (even if the related notes should mutually attract one another) as for the building-sequence of an organism to be deduced from the chemical affinity of the germinal elements (i.e. from the peg and socket joints, together with the polar tension).[20]

The subtitle of Murnau's film is *A Symphony of Horror* (*eine Symphonie des Grauens*). At first this subtitle may seem a bit odd, since music plays absolutely no role in the narrative development of the film. Yet the musical metaphor may provide us with another means by which nature and cinema are unified in *Nosferatu*. For Uexküll, a symphony is defined as the simultaneous sounding of life melodies:

> By "melody" we understand the orderly sounding of the musical notes one *after* the other; by symphony, their sounding *together* ... In glancing at objects, we drew a comparison between certain regularly recurring series of direction-signs and melodies; we might describe as the sym-

phonic theory of looking the rules that are revealed when all the optical local signs are consonant.[21]

The symphony is the simultaneity of living beings, expressed in *Nosferatu* through a series of images bound through a series of crosscuts. Each of these forms of life has a specific direction, particular in their paths but universal in their final goal. For as the coffins full of diseased rats make their arrival in Wisborg, this also introduces the possibility of death into the consciousness of human life. Bulwer's experiments make palpable the cruel inter-species struggle for life and death in the natural world, while the crosscuts brusquely extend its logic into the ostensibly healthy realm of modern humans. Nosferatu himself, the embodiment of death, haunts the civilization of Western European culture, bringing mortality's radical otherness into Wisborg's sheltered community. Each of the three places that are crosscut in this short, two-minute sequence follows the same unseen consequence of life existing the world. Its materiality is that of the cosmos, for both cinema and the world belong together in their participation in animate, albeit precarious life. The Bulwer sequence teaches us that not only does the cinema allegorize this belongingness, this strange cosmopolitanism, but it also makes this thought possible in the first place.

In *Insect Media: An Archaeology of Animals and Technology*, the media scholar Jussi Parikka points to how Uexküll's description of animal perception opens the way toward other, non-Cartesian "wavelengths of sensation that would otherwise elude the human senses."[22] Parikka notes that the zoological study of non-human ways of perceiving inspires parallels with the camera's capacity for perception. In a footnote, he makes this parallel explicit: "such models of insects/technology proposed distributed subjectivities in which insects could function as new 'eyes' to the world, and camera eyes (Vertov) produced similar detachments from the phenomenological human being."[23] It is the musical approach that for Uexküll separates the creative, non-final becoming of life from the mechanistic, closed system of the machine. Parikka's analysis of "insects as media" cuts across radically non-human regimes of perception, showing how sensible worlds are constituted, not by a sovereign subject who receives stimuli from external reality, but through the mutual enfolding of the organism's interior with its exterior.

Moreover, Parikka makes clear that the bio-technical vocabulary of insects does not function simply as a metaphor of media technics, but that this vocabulary points to the production of potentialities, intensities, sensations, and passages that are instigated when life is lived within its *Umwelt*. He notes that perception does not take place when an image of a given, a priori world is projected into the organism, an image that is then processed as an object of cogitation. Perception is a capacity that is enabled by the contact of the human organism with her ecological surroundings, in the action between eye and image, the passage between mind and world. There is no ontological hierarchy between life and non-life. Bestial media archeology underscores the notion of an *Umwelt* as a surface of possibilities, upon which assemblages between the organic and inorganic may be improvised.

Blood is Life

The danger that draws nearer to Wisborg in this sequence from *Nosferatu* is the plague. Disease and pestilence accompany Nosferatu, his rats, and the experimental earth when they make their way into the port city. As the prison guard sweeps inside his cell, Knock quickly steals a piece of paper hanging out of the guard's back pocket. Explicitly entitled "Plague," the note reads:

> A plague epidemic has broken out in Transylvania and in the Black Sea ports of Narva and Galaz. Masses of young people are dying. All victims appear to have the same strange wounds on their necks, the origin of which is still a mystery to doctors.

The double-masted Empusa, carrying the coffins filled with dirt, is stricken with disease as sailors become delirious and die. When the ship lands in the post in Wisborg, the citizenry are quickly infected, then confined to their homes and commanded to bolt their windows and doors. A Christian cross, drawn in chalk on the door, indicates a home that has lost lives to the plague. Orlok enters Wisborg carrying his coffin of plague-infected dirt, the same that was used for Bulwer's experiments. We are informed, according to an intertitle, that vampires "draw their shadowy strength from the cursed earth in which they were buried." The encroaching contagion and representations of death throughout the second half of the film seem to reflect on the influenza epidemic, the "Spanish flu," that spread across the globe between 1918 and 1919. As a consequence of new means of transporting people and commodities across borders, as well as the close quarters of trench warfare in World War I, tens of millions were killed by this massive pandemic. A striking shot from *Nosferatu* shows a procession of pallbearers with coffins on their shoulders, marching through Wisborg to the cemetery.

Hutter's wife sees this procession from her window and realizes what she must do: give the gift of her own death, saving Wisborg from the plague, and grant the undead bringer of death permanent rest.

In many Cultural Studies approaches to Murnau's film, the representation of the vampire myth has been associated with anti-Semitic stereotypes of Jewishness, including notions of degeneracy and parasitism, as well as bodily features coded as Jewish.[24] Arguing along these lines, the historian Brenda

Figure 5.7 A frame from *Nosferatu*. (*Courtesy of Friedrich-Wilhelm-Murnau-Stiftung, Wiesbaden*)

Gardenour points to the stark contrast between the representations of Hutter and Orlok:

> Like the medieval Jew, Orlok is an inversion of the warm Christian male and as such is predominantly cold in humor. While young Hutter wears lightweight clothing appropriate to the season, Nosferatu bundles himself in layers of dark wool from head to toe in an attempt to maintain the little warmth necessary to his survival and to protect his frail flesh from any contact. Having scant bodily heat, no Christian ardor, and no vital pneumatic blood, the vampire's skin, like that of the imagined Jew, is pale and greyish white in pallor.[25]

In contrast to the healthy, Gentile Hutter, the vampire Nosferatu is associated with notions of contamination and criminality of Jews, thought to be sexually and economically parasitic on the communities they inhabit—the eternal, degenerate foreigner. As we know, the stigmatization of Jews intensified after the war as their increasing integration into German society seemed to compel ever more intricate, conspiratorial theories about the racial differences between Gentile and Jew.

In the same year as Uexküll published his *Theoretical Biology*, he also published a much more explicitly political text, called *Biology of the State*:

Anatomy, Physiology, Pathology of the State, where he outlines the state formation as a living organism. Here the zoologist provides a vocabulary for assessing the "health" of a state, while also identifying foreign elements that he calls "pathologies" to the living state-organism. Uexküll's characterizations of these pathologies seem to echo the degenerate representation of the Nosferatu in Murnau's film. Read in the light of other contemporaneous accounts of the state and biopower, including Karl Binding's *Zum Werden und Leben der Staaten* (1920) and Eberhard Dennert's *Der Staat als lebendiger Organismus* (1920), Uexküll's text articulates a seemingly shared reactionary, xenophobic attitude toward other life forms perceived to be hostile.

Biology of the State expresses a conjunction of life and politics that goes beyond the ancient metaphor of the body politic as well as the Hobbesian notion of the commonwealth headed by an absolute sovereign. Such metaphors describe abstract linkages between the sovereign and the organs of government and designate the institutions that assert power over the *de facto* state of nature (the war of all against all). In contrast, Uexküll illustrates how the biology of the state is continuous with nature, such that both are underpinned by nature's unifying principles. The proper role of the state is not only to express its possibility of being according to its specific organization, but also to bring about the ontological possibilities of each citizen according to his or her natural talent. As with the fly or the spider, the state must coordinate itself with its own internal, "morphological" capacities as well as the particular *Umwelt* already given to it, and this in order to secure its own survival.

To illustrate how a state organism lives, Uexküll describes a "chain of individuals" who contribute their specific abilities in conjunction with their *Umwelt* to produce bread. The farmer, miller, and the baker function as individual "organs," each carrying out their mutually exclusive roles to transform grain, flour, and yeast into nourishment for the inhabitants of the state. In doing so, each realizes their possibility of being by harmonizing with each other and contributing their specific talents to the state's continued existence. "The bread is distributed to the houses of the village to sustain its inhabitants. With this, the whole ["*das Ganze*"] is brought to a close."[26] Uexküll provides illustrations throughout his 55-page text that provide views of how individual citizens are related to the nation-state.

On the other hand, Uexküll seems keenly aware that these diagrams only provide an approximation of the goods that traffic between citizens, for they provide only the spatialized representation of this movement. What remains crucial is that this traffic occurs in time, and that it obeys a "temporal law" (*zeitliche Regel*) and not a spatial one. In this Uexküll emphasizes the activity of individuals in consort, not as archetypes with ossified characteristics, but as working together in a mutually determined process of transformation and creation. Fascinatingly, Uexküll refers once more to the cinematograph to illustrate the proper functioning of individual organs within the body of the state. In the following, he compares the two-dimensional space of a city map with that of the film screen:

> If we draw our attention on a certain area of the diagram and pursue the lines of exchange among the different organs of the state, we may obtain a perspective like that provided by a cinematograph, which projects various durational images on the same surface. In the cinema image, figures emerge and pass by according to a determined law [*nach einer bestimmten Regel*], on which the mechanics of the apparatus depends, and whose sprockets jerkily advance the film roll.[27]

Life obeys the law of nature and the cinema obeys a much more mechanical law. Yet, as Uexküll explains, both observe laws that dictate their unfolding in time. The unfolding of the moving image parallels the unfolding life of the state organism.

However, when Uexküll describes the "pathologies" and "parasites" that invade the state, other, more politically volatile resonances may be made to the allegorical vampire in Murnau's *Nosferatu*. In the latter sections of *Biology of the State*, the zoologist singles out enemies of the state such as the free press, Americanism, and the influx of foreign races, particularly those who originate from other nations and whose styles of being remain alien to Germany's. Such foreigners threaten the health of the state by interrupting the activity of the chain of individuals in the homeland, who already have a particular, organic relationship to their geographic *Umwelt*. Clearly informed by the discourses of modern, reactionary *Kulturkritik*, Uexküll opposes the *Volk* to the masses, and warns of the decadent effects of *Zivilisation* on organic *Kultur*.[28] Referring to the blindness to politics that is concomitant with the spread of commodity culture, Uexküll calls such elements "parasites" that "sap the national feeling"[29] that sustains the state:

> Genuine parasites that are dangerous to the state and are against its living participants may be called a foreign race. On the other hand, when they may be deemed useful to the state, one speaks not of parasitism, but of symbiosis.[30]

Repeating the reductive binary logic that often dictates Weimar *Kulturkritik*, Uexküll divides up foreign, "non-organic" inhabitants of a state into the irreducible binary between friend and enemy.[31] Indeed, he reserves some of his most caustic remarks for Germany's enemy in the Great War, England, whose citizens, according to Uexküll, would rather give bread to an English bulldog than a German child. "Of all the states of the earth, England should be considered the world-parasite and, with much cunning and ruthlessness, extracts resources from both friend and foe."[32] It seems that in 1920, perpetual peace among competing nations would be simply impossible. Just as it is innate that spiders entrap and consume flies,[33] which we saw in the montage sequence from Murnau's *Nosferatu*, so is it concomitant with nature's plan that one nation "consume" another. This was a bio-geopolitical situation that Uexküll clearly wanted to explain in his text. And despite his theorization of the biological state breaking from the Hobbesian model of the body politic, he nevertheless betrays his belief in a fundamentally insecure state of nature, a biopolitical perpetual struggle, and the war of all against all.

Thus if the state is a living organism, it must devise ways of immunizing itself from those internal and external elements that threaten to infect it. In the last section of *Biology of the State*, Uexküll calls for the founding of an institute that will train doctors of the state, who are charged with maintaining the hygiene of the state organism. This conclusion frighteningly foreshadows the fascist biocracy of the Nazi regime, the discourse of degeneracy, and its "anti-parasitic," recuperative final solution. While Uexküll does not explicate the meaning of "unworthy life" (described by Karl Binding in his *Die Freigabe der Vernichtung lebensunwerten Lebens*, also published in 1920), *Biology of the State* does deploy the vocabulary that would have been recognizable to early Weimar intellectuals. In this the underpinning idea is clear: the state should take it upon itself to monitor and regulate its citizenry, to ascribe quantifiable categories to individual bodies in order to make them available to state scrutiny, and to discipline the population with the aim of maximizing their productivity, deeming bodies either useful or useless to state biopower.

Conclusion

Murnau's *Nosferatu* and Uexküll's discussion of the organism presents us with the aporia of modern biopolitics.[34] On the one hand, the relationship of life to its *Umwelt* in *Theoretical Biology* provides a vocabulary to describe how life relates to its surrounding world. We have seen how this may be paralleled with the life of the cinema, specifically the crosscut and its capacity to present diverse locations simultaneity as a sequence of shots. Nature is unified through the movement and animation of the cinematic technology, unifying principles that also animate organisms living and dying in the world. On the other, this expanded definition of life raises questions regarding the power over life and the right to death. These questions center around the definition of the foreign body, its hygiene, and its subsequent affirmation or denigration. For *Nosferatu* raises a key ethical question for its spectator: how does one regard the uncanny, cinematic other, and it is possible to allow it hospitality, without condition, and to affirm its radical otherness as part and parcel of lived life? Uexküll's *Biology of the State* helps us see how Murnau's film raises

Figure 5.8 A frame from *Nosferatu*. (*Courtesy of Friedrich-Wilhelm-Murnau-Stiftung, Wiesbaden*)

these questions through the cinematic allegory, questions, moreover, that gain particular urgency in German culture following the experience of defeat.

Over 9.7 million soldiers died while engaged in military combat during World War I. In 1919, over 2 million German men did not return from the fighting on the war front. And many of those who did came back with physical wounds that left them permanently disabled. All were humiliated and traumatized by the effects of modern warfare. Machine gunnery, wireless communication, chemical warfare, armored tank artillery: these were technological developments that made possible the anonymous annihilation of the other. When Germany capitulated in 1918, the audacious heroicism of 1914 was forgotten and replaced by war weariness, desperation, and shame. In a historical account called *The Culture of Defeat*, the historian Wolfgang Schivelbusch writes, "People reacted not with manly composure, as the heroic vision would have it, but with everything from bewilderment to literal paralysis and nervous breakdown."[35] Defeat came as an unexpected shock to many Germans on the home front, who had been led to believe that they were winning the war. Schivelbusch reconstructs the crushing response to Ludendorff's call for a ceasefire, writing: "Eyewitnesses spoke of a 'devastating impression' and 'great despair,' and one described Social Democratic leader Friedrich Ebert as "seized with sobbing.'"[36] When *Nosferatu* played in cinemas in 1922, in the midst of extreme economic and political instability, its viewers were survivors who had also seen great loss: on the one hand military loss and defeat, but also the loss of national self-determination, the loss of the old Wilhelmine ways concomitant with the tipping of German culture toward modernity, and the great loss of millions of lives owing to war and postwar famine.

Is it possible to remain hospitable to Nosferatu's arrival and to the arrival of death? As long as the living spectator continues to disavow the possibility of his or her own finitude, the arrival of this stranger will continue to horrify. And as long as death is kept at bay, outside the biopower of the state, the vampire will continue to be seen to be trespassing. This is seemingly the invisible, uncanny fluctuation that Ellen repeatedly intuits throughout the film. It is the cinema that calls her to her destiny, to live out her potentiality as a living character in *Nosferatu*. Furthermore the cinematic technology presents the finite human spectator with this sobering *memento mori*: coming into being and dying away.[37] In giving the gift of her own death at the end of the film, Ellen in effect saves Wisborg from the plague. Her self-sacrifice also grants the undead Nosferatu his own path toward death. In one of the final scenes of the film, Orlok's body disappears with the streaming of sunlight through a window, fading like an overexposed photographic negative.

Notes

1. *Nosferatu: A Symphony of Horror (The Ultimate Two-Disc Edition)*, DVD, directed by F. W. Murnau, 1922, New York: Kino Video, 2007. All references to the film will be derived from this DVD release.
2. Stacey Abbott, *Celluloid Vampires: Life After Death in the Modern World* (Austin, TX: University of Texas Press, 2007), p. 57.
3. Indeed the cinema is apposite in this regard, for the crosscut dovetails nicely with the emergence of simultaneity and the reification of clock time within capitalist modernity. See Wolfgang Schivelbusch, *The Railway Journey: The Industrialization of Time and Space in the 19th Century* (Berkeley, Los Angeles, CA: University of California Press, 1986), particularly the chapter called "Railway Space and Railway Time."
4. Stacey Abbott, *Celluloid Vampires*, p. 43.
5. Gilles Deleuze, *Cinema 1: The Movement-Image* (trans. Hugh Tomlinson) (London, New York: Continuum, 1986), pp. 50–1.
6. Anton Kaes, *Kino-Debatte: Texte zum Verhältnis von Literatur u. Film 1909–1929* (Tübingen: Max Niemeyer, 1978).
7. Theophrastus Paracelsus, a Renaissance alchemist who studied the use of minerals in medicine, and who advocated the notion that not all toxins may be considered categorically poisonous to humans. In small doses, some of these ostensible toxins can even have medicinal effects. Around the time of Murnau's film, writer Erwin Guido Kolbenheyer wrote a trilogy of novels about Paracelsus, *Die Kindheit des Paracelsus* (1917), *Das Gestirn des Paracelsus* (1921), and *Das Dritte Reich des Paracelsus* (1926). As we know, during the years of the Third Reich, Kolbenheyer

would become a cultural spokesperson for the National Socialist regime.
8. See Tom Gunning, "To Scan a Ghost: The Ontology of Mediated Vision," *Grey Room*, Vol. 26, 2007, pp. 94–127. In this essay Gunning outlines a genealogy of ghosts and specters through the history of image production. His discussion begins with this intertitle from Murnau's film.
9. I have already referred to Stacey Abbott in this regard. For Lloyd Michaels, the uncanny vampire himself allegorizes "ontological status of the film image as a 'lost object' and a figure of the 'undead'" (Lloyd Michaels, *The Phantom of the Cinema: Character in Modern Film* (Albany, NY: SUNY Press, 1998), p. 241), linking the temporality inscribed on Orlok's body, its posthumous life after death, to the temporality of the filmic image, and the representation and revivification of the pro-filmic event already sunk into the past. "As Nosferatu drains his victims of blood," Michaels writes, "the film image deprives its referent of the materiality it once possessed when it appeared before the camera" (ibid. p. 248). Anton Kaes, in his magisterial interpretation of *Nosferatu*, corroborates this, writing: "In a horror film like *Nosferatu*, the symbolic function of film language expresses this rupture when hallucinations suddenly appear embodied. What is real? What is hallucinated? Film qua film—that is, it technological capacity for lifelike representation—is the ultimate double, an uncanny experience in itself to which we submit ourselves." Anton Kaes, *Shell Shock Cinema: Weimar Culture and the Wounds of War* (Princeton, NJ: Princeton University Press, 2009), p. 126.
10. Uexküll, *Theoretical Biology*, p. 315.
11. Ibid. p. 317.
12. For this reason, for Uexküll all life proceeds with purpose, in contrast to evolutionary theory, based as much on sheer serendipity as on the notion of the survival of the fittest. "In this respect," he writes, "there is no such thing as evolution: the lowest, just like the highest of living creatures are, as regards their micromechanics and microchemistry, equally perfect. In face of this fact, all attempt to explain living things as chance agglomerations of substances collapses utterly" (ibid. p. 114).
13. On page 223 he writes: "All subjects have a rule of function of their own, which expresses itself not only in the framework, given once and for all, and in the activity thereof but which also is able to repair all framework within certain limits; consequently, this rule represents a natural factor that is continually operative."
14. Ibid. p. 106.
15. Ibid. p. 107.
16. Judith Mayne, "Dracula in the Twilight: Murnau's *Nosferatu* (1922)," in Eric Rentschler (ed.), *German Film and Literature* (New York: Methuen, 1986), pp. 25–39, see p. 34.
17. Uexküll, *Theoretical Biology*, p. 283.
18. Ibid. p. 245.
19. Ibid. pp. 123–4.
20. Ibid. pp. 303–4.
21. Ibid. p. 29.
22. Jussi Parikka, *Insect Media: An Archaeology of Animals and Technology* (Minneapolis, MN: University of Minnesota Press, 2010), p. 68.
23. Ibid. pp. 235–6.
24. See, for example Judith Halberstam, "Technologies of Monstrosity: Bram Stoker's *Dracula*," in her *Skin Shows: Gothic Horror and the Technology of Monsters* (Durham, NC: Duke University Press, 1995), pp. 86–106.
25. Brenda Gardenour, "The Biology of Blood-Lust: Medieval Medicine, Theology, and the Vampire Jew," *Film & History*, Vol. 41, No. 2, 2011, pp. 51–63, see p. 56.

26. Jakob von Uexküll, *Staatsbiologie: Anatomie—Physologie—Pathologie des Staates* (Berlin: Paetel, 1920), p. 5.
27. Ibid. p. 16.
28. For an excellent cultural history of the *Kultur-Zivilisation* distinction in the German context, see Norbert Elias, *The Civilizing Process: Sociogenetic and Psychogenetic Investigations* (trans. Edmund Jephcott) (Oxford: Blackwell, 2000).
29. Jakob von Uexküll, *Staatsbiologie*, p. 50.
30. Ibid. p. 49.
31. A binary that is articulated most explicitly in Carl Schmitt's 1927 book, *Der Begriff des Politischen*.
32. Jakob von Uexküll, *Staatsbiologie*, p. 51.
33. Ibid. p. 52.
34. For a detailed discussion of this aporia, see Roberto Esposito, *Bios: Biopolitics and Philosophy* (trans. Timothy Campbell) (Minneapolis, MN: University of Minnesota Press, 2008).
35. Wolfgang Schivelbusch, *The Culture of Defeat: On National Trauma, Mourning, and Recovery* (trans. Jefferson Chase) (New York: Metropolitan Books, 2003), p. 197.
36. Ibid.
37. See Tom Gunning, "Re-Newing Old Technologies: Astonishment, Second Nature, and the Uncanny in Technology from the Previous Turn-of-the-Century," in David Thorburn and Henry Jenkins (eds.), *Rethinking Media Change: The Aesthetics of Transition* (Cambridge, MA: MIT Press, 2003), pp. 39–60.

6. *RASKOLNIKOW* (1923): RUSSIAN LITERATURE AS IMPETUS FOR GERMAN EXPRESSIONISM

John T. Soister

Fyodor Dostoevsky's *Crime and Punishment* is one of those classics that no one is ever reading *right now*; rather, it's one of those books that everyone claims to have read, eons ago, while they were still at school. While any educated person who can't come up with "Raskolnikov, in the pawnshop, with the hatchet" is not worth his salt—even the most casual of literati can reduce a novel such as this to pithy pronouncements straight out of *Clue*—few and far between are the *C&P* veterans who can recall many of the novel's sub-plots. A handful of those who slogged their way through one translation or another back when the world was a simpler place might recollect Rodion's being plagued by both a "Tell-Tale Heart"-type conscience and a nemesis right out of *Les Misérables*, but—if they do—it's likely that those are the only additional details that have, for them, survived the intervening decades. Still, one must be grateful nowadays for anyone who can remember even that much. (There are other folk for whom the passage of years has muddled the novelist's name and accomplishments with that of the author of *War and Peace*, and still others for whom Dostoevsky and Tolstoy are nothing more than two proper nouns that end in "y" and reek of Russianness.)

I raise these flags here, at the outset, because the "Raskolnikov, in the pawnshop, with the hatchet" business comes onscreen fairly early on in Robert Wiene's 1923 film (as it does in the literary unfolding), but soon gets lost in the flurry of relatives, relationships, recriminations, and redoubtable patronymics. (For reasons that are debatable—the addition of sound, perhaps, or the reimagining of screenwriter Joseph Anthony, or maybe the growing personality cult devoted to the über-quirky Peter Lorre—von Sternberg's talkie version focuses on Rodion's ... er ... *Roderick*'s classic lack of self-control to the near exclusion of the peripheral perambulations of the secondary cast. This simplification might explain the director's profound dissatisfaction with the 1935 Columbia release; indeed, von Sternberg is quoted hither, thither and yon as decrying his picture as "no more related to the true text of the novel than the corner of Sunset Boulevard and Gower is related to the Russian environment."[1])

In contrast to this later interpretation, the pivot of Wiene's version—the *Clue* formula, mentioned above—is greased with mothers and magnates, daughters and drunkards, painters and politicians, policeman and prostitutes, siblings, spies, blue bloods and οι πολλοί. As they do in the novel, these secondary-cast types offer much more in the way of off-kilter behavioral quirks than they do crucial bits of plot exposition, and their propensity to deliver lengthy disquisitions at the drop of a kopek does nothing to staunch the opinion held by many that the great Russian novelists were probably paid by the word. Inasmuch as Wiene's scenario rather doggedly followed the original novel, his Muscovites tend to bloviate frequently and at length, thus necessitating frequent (and fairly lengthy) intertitles, a surfeit of which might lead even the least perspicacious filmgoer to contend that *Crime and Punishment* might not be well suited to the silent screen.

In preparing this chapter, I viewed not only the Alpha DVD—drawn from faded and multifariously choppy preprint material, with sporadic, English-language intertitles that verge on Dickensian—but also (thanks to Henry Nicolella) a lengthier version, albeit with *Swedish* titles. The fact that neither I nor anyone of my acquaintance is even marginally conversant with Swedish momentarily vexed my attempts at comprehending the protracted expository pronouncements mouthed by Dostoevsky's/Wiene's Russians. Happily, however, I came upon a website that had archived the original titles, albeit in a Spanish translation. Assured that the Spanish texts were taken directly from the German, I proceeded by aligning these with the onscreen appearance of their Swedish counterparts, comparing them to the Victorian treatments on the Alpha disk (which more than once had seemingly been inserted into the action at random), and then cross-checked as best as I could with the text from my copy of the novel (a 1993 "Wordsworth Classic").[2]

For those for whom the secondary and tertiary and ... details of *Crime and Punishment* have faded into oblivion, the following synopsis may be helpful:

> Former student Rodion Romanovich Raskolnikov lives in penury in a tiny garret apartment in Saint Petersburg. [The unspooling shows that, from the get-go, he has been determined to test the limits of law and morality by committing a heinous crime. His proclivity here to stare

Figure 6.1 Publicity still for Robert Wiene's *Raskolnikow* (1923). (*Source: German Film Institute—DIF, Frankfurt*)

menacingly hither and yon and to strike the most uncomfortable of postures is quite unsettling and is early-on evidence of this criminality.] He walks to the flat of the old pawnbroker, Alona Ivanovna, not only to get what he regards as a pittance for his watch, but also to check out the surroundings in preparation for a possible future enterprise. Stopping at a bar for a drink on the way home, he is enthralled by the self-accusatory burblings of the whiskey-soaked Marmeladov, whose chronic drunkenness means that he has lost his job and that his wife (Katerina Ivanovna) and daughter (Sonya) have had to turn to prostitution to pay the bills. Rodion walks Marmeladov home and, in doing so, he meets Katerina Ivanovna, who exhibits signs of being quite ill.

After receiving a letter from his mother (Pulcheria Alexandrovna) telling him that his sister (Dunya) has become engaged to marry a government bureaucrat (Luzhin) and that the whole bunch of them will be moving shortly to Saint Petersburg, Rodion heads to *another* bar, where he hears *another* poverty-stricken former student opine that the world would be a better place without Alona Ivanovna. The next day finds

Rodion sewing a hatchet-holster into his jacket, snatching a hatchet from a conveniently unlocked garret, and making for the pawnbroker's apartment. Gaining entrance under the pretense that he's going to pawn something else, Rodion murders the old woman and her half-sister, Lizaveta, who has walked into the apartment in a most unfortunate act of serendipity. He steals a few items, escapes without being seen by anyone other than a couple of house painters, returns the hatchet, heads back to his garret, and collapses on his bed.

The following day is quite eventful. Having checked his clothes for bloodstains, Rodion must report to the police station, albeit not in connection with the murders; his landlady is pressing him for back rent. Nonetheless, when the subject of the murders arises, he faints; this causes the police to look at him askance. Back in his garret, he grabs the items he stole from the pawnshop and hides them under a rock some distance from his apartment house. Returning home, he collapses into a fever-ridden heap, and remains this way for four days. When he comes to, he discovers that his good friend, Razumikhin, and his housekeeper, Nastasya [*not* his landlady; even the desperately poor in Russia have "housekeepers"?], have been watching over him in the interim. What's more, a doctor (Zossimov) has been by to see him, and a police detective (Zamyotov) has been nosing around. Whenever the subject of the murders is broached, Rodion sort of freaks out, and this causes lots of people to look at him askance.

Into this brouhaha wanders Luzhin, Dunya's boyfriend, and the two men do *not* get along, almost immediately. Rodion heads out—to a café, this time—and bumps into Zamyotov (the detective), to whom he *almost* spills the beans. Heading home, Rodion decides to make a quick stop at the Scene of the Crime, and then comes upon the scene of an accident: Marmeladov, in the act of weaving across the street, has been hit by a carriage. Rodion helps get the drunkard back to his home, where he dies. Rodion meets Sonya (Marmeladov's daughter), gives her some money that his mother (Pulcheria Alexandrovna) had given him, and then makes for his garret, accompanied by his good friend, Razumikhin. When the men arrive at the garret, they find Dunya and Pulcheria Alexandrovna ensconced amid the clutter, and Rodion promptly faints (again). When he revives, he chases the women from the place, after having commanded Dunya to call off the wedding. This is fine with Razumikhin, as he has fallen for Dunya.

The next morning, Razumikhin, Dunya, and Pulcheria Alexandrovna return to Rodion's garret, following a meeting wherein Razumikhin tries to explain Rodion's personality quirks to the man's mother and sister. En route to the revelation that he is once again ruble-less, Rodion apologizes to the women for his behavior the previous evening; Dr Zossimov, who happens to be on hand, explains that the poverty-stricken former student has, indeed, "improved." Nonetheless, Rodion once again snarls that Dunya is to have nothing to do with Luzhin, whereupon Dunya invites Rodion to come to a meeting she's having with Luzhin that very evening, even though Luzhin has quite pointedly instructed Dunya not to invite her brother. Into this assemblage walks Sonya (Marmeladov's daughter), who invites Rodion to attend her father's funeral. After he agrees to attend, Sonya returns home, although without knowing that she is being followed by Svidrigailov, a former employer of Dunya (Rodion's sister), who has inappropriate yearnings for her.

Meanwhile, Rodion goes off to visit Porfiry Petrovich (a relation of Razumikhin, Rodion's best friend), who is the magistrate to whom the pawnshop murders have been assigned. Coincidentally, Zamyotov (the police detective) is there when Rodion arrives, pretending to be concerned about the status of the watch that he had pawned and that is now either lost or in the police evidence locker. After Rodion and Porfiry Petrovich speak fairly casually about the murders for a few moments, the conversation begins to take on the tone of a challenge, and Rodion suspects that Porfiry Petrovich suspects him; soon, Rodion and Razumikhin ponder whether Porfiry Petrovich does, indeed, harbor such a suspicion. Back home, Rodion learns that a man had been looking for him; since the man has just left, Rodion chases him down the street, where the man calls him a murderer. Sleeping uneasily that night, Rodion has nightmares about the killings; when he awakens suddenly, he finds there is a man standing right there, in his room.

It devolves that the man is Svidrigailov (the former employer of Dunya, etc.), who tells Rodion that he wants Dunya to break up with Luzhin, that he (Svidrigailov) will pay Dunya 10,000 rubles to marry him, and that his (Svidrigailov's) late wife, Marfa Petrovna, had left Dunya 3,000 rubles in her will. When Svidrigailov, who goes on at length about all this, begins to speak of his late wife's ghost, Rodion comes to the conclusion that the man is crazy, rejects any and all offers, and all but kicks him out of the garret.

Rodion and Razumikhin then make for the restaurant where Dunya is to meet Luzhin. Razumikhin tells his friend that he's all but sure that he (Rodion) is the police's prime suspect for the pawnshop murders. When the men arrive at the restaurant, they come upon Dunya, Luzhin, and Pulcheria Alexandrovna, and Luzhin is enormously upset that, despite his specific orders, Rodion is pulling up a chair at the table. After details of Svidrigailov's appearance and sundry monetary offers have been shared, Luzhin and Rodion commence arguing, whereupon Luzhin manages to alienate everyone already mentioned, and Dunya breaks off the engagement on the spot. Luzhin leaves in a huff, and everyone is tickled to death at his absence.

Sensing an opening with Dunya, Razumikhin begins speculating about some potential business prospects of his when Rodion announces that he doesn't ever want to see any of them, ever again, and he leaves in a huff. Everyone is shocked; Razumikhin chases after his friend, and catches up with him. At that moment, Razumikhin comes to understand that Rodion did, indeed, murder the old pawnbroker and her half-sister. Rodion stalks off, and Razumikhin returns to the table to attempt to explain once again Rodion's personality quirks to the man's mother and sister. Meanwhile, Rodion heads over to see Sonya Marmeladov, who—he soon finds out—had been friends with the pawnbroker's half-sister. In an uncharacteristic move, Rodion has Sonya read the New Testament story of Lazarus, so as to impress upon the young woman the fact that the dead do arise. In a coincidental moment that totally defies belief, this whole business is overheard by Svidrigailov, who (apparently) has taken up lodging in the apartment right next door[!].

The next morning (again) finds Rodion at the police department (again). The impoverished former student is ostensibly filing a formal request for the return of his watch; in reality, he's attempting to discover whether Porfiry Petrovich *does* suspect him. The two clever men go back and forth cat-and-mouse-like, and, just after Rodion pointblank accuses the police magistrate of playing mind-games with him, Nicolai—one of the apartment painters who had been on the scene the day of the killings—runs onto the scene to confess to the murders! Later, en route to the Marmeladov memorial funeral/dinner, Rodion confronts the mysterious man who had called him "a murderer," and finds that the man was just spouting off.

Meanwhile (again), Luzhin sits in his flat, snarling about Rodion and the broken engagement to his flat-mate, Lebezyatnikov. Deciding not to attend the Marmeladov memorial, Luzhin had instead invited Sonya (Marmeladov) to the flat, presumably for carnal reasons; he had given the young woman ten rubles. A bit later, over at the Marmeladov get-together, things are not going well, and—apart from Rodion—the few guests who have arrived are apparently every bit as inebriated as had been Marmeladov at any given point. Making things worse, in walks Luzhin, who accuses Sonya of having taken a *hundred*-ruble note from him, surreptitiously. Outrage ensues, only to have Luzhin—and not Sonya—bear the brunt of an honest explanation, when Lebezyatnikov also walks in and reveals he saw his flat-mate slip the hundred-ruble note into the young woman's pocket, surreptitiously. Rodion, who has been having feelings for the lovely Sonya, opines that Luzhin was probably trying to humiliate *him* (Rodion) by humiliating Sonya. Sonya's mother (Katerina Ivanovna) and landlady then begin quarreling over money.

In a quiet moment, Rodion confesses the murders to Sonya, who gets him to agree to confess to the police. However, Lebezyatnikov again walks in, this time with a less welcome announcement: Katerina Ivanovna—who has clearly gone off the deep end—is out in the street, singing and dancing and begging for money. Sonya runs out after her mother, Rodion heads back home to speak to Dunya, and Katerina Ivanovna has an altercation with a policeman. She collapses, is brought back into the Marmeladov flat, and dies. Rodion returns in time to witness this and to hear Svidrigailov [!] promise to pay for the funeral arrangements and the care of Sonya's young siblings. Rodion also hears Svidrigailov tell him that he (Svidrigailov) knows that he (Rodion) is a murderer. [The apartment next door, remember?]

In a daze, Rodion meanders through the streets, ending up back in the garret, where Razumikhin gives him hell for having caused so much misery for Dunya and the other one—you know, the mother. Then police magistrate Porfiry Petrovich shows up and (a) apologizes for being nasty to Rodion at the police station, (b) admits he doesn't believe for a second that Nicolai (the apartment painter) killed anybody, and (c) reveals that he (Porfiry Petrovich) *still* thinks that Rodion killed the women, but can't prove it (yet). If Rodion were to confess, though, it would go easier on him. Porfiry Petrovich leaves and so does Rodion, who has to find Svidrigailov, fast.

Find him he does, and the older man admits to being over Dunya to the point where he has taken up with a sixteen-year-old girl. Nonetheless, after leaving Rodion, Svidrigailov manages to get Dunya into his apartment where, after she turns down his proposal, he seems ready for rape. Producing a revolver, Dunya fires at him several times at pointblank range, and misses. He disarms her but lets her go free after finally realizing that the young woman despises him. It is now Svidrigailov's turn to wander hither, thither and yon through Saint Petersburg, doling out money hither, thither and yon (Dunya gets 3,000 rubles), and ending up in a hotel. The old man passes a tortured night in bed—as had Rodion, earlier—and then commits suicide come dawn.

After meeting his mother, Rodion meets up with Dunya and tells her that he's going to confess to his crimes. He then stops in to see Sonya who, returning the favor, New Testament-wise, gives him a cross. Despite all this, upon hearing of Svidrigailov's suicide, the young man considers reneging on his promise to Dunya and Sonya; he catches sight of the latter, though, and makes a clean breast of it to the police.

Owing to extenuating circumstances, questions as to his mental stability, and character witnesses, Rodion escapes the death penalty and is sentenced to eight years' hard labor at a camp in Siberia. Sonya has, in the interim, moved to a town near the camp and is visiting the prisoner on a regular basis. It devolves that, during that same interim, Pulcheria Alexandrovna passed away, and Razumikhin finally won over Dunya and has married her. Rodion comes to see the error of his ways and—it is hoped—all will eventually turn out well for the incarcerated former student some seven-plus years down the line.

The above synopsis of Dostoevsky's novel is as detail-oriented as it is because Robert Wiene moved virtually every bit of the plot—lock, stock, and ruble—to the expansiveness of the screen from the confines of the printed page. Not that the said confines have ever been too skimpy: any edition of the novel that runs to fewer than 450 pages is abridgement-suspect, and the Penguin paperback I read after watching the Swedish-titled silent feature is over 700 pages in length.

Such wondrous wealth of physical and philosophic detail did not, of course, necessarily translate well onto the silent screen. The 1917 Arrow five-reeler,

Figure 6.2 Publicity still for Robert Wiene's *Raskolnikow* (1923). (*Source: German Film Institute—DIF, Frankfurt*)

Crime and Punishment, was reduced to moving the whole kit 'n' caboodle—penniless student, pawnbroker and hatchet—to New York's Lower East Side, in the hope that their being unreeled against familiar climes might make the innumerable twists and turns more comprehensible to American viewers. Four years earlier, the Russians had taken the first whack (ouch!) at *Prestuplenie y nakazanie* and kept the goings-on local although many of Dostoevsky's minutiae were sacrificed to the exigencies of a two-reel length. And so it fell to Herr Wiene to bowdlerize (albeit, not by much) the novel while retaining (and not sacrificing much) most of the said minutiae for the entertainment and edification of the movie-going readership.

With the probable exception of its *original* readership—those legions of Tsar-following, Streltsy-fearing, literature-loving, middle-class Muscovites who probably saw in the author's brooding, convoluted style the paradigm for what would soon be lumped together as "Russian novels"—*Crime and Punishment* has most likely attracted worldwide attention more for its structure, canny psychoanalytical framework, and social commentary than for the innate qualities of its prose. The lengthy—in some places, overwrought—exposition that grinds Dostoevsky's action (and Wiene's *Raskolnikow*) to a fairly regular halt has won praise over the years as insightful, nuanced existentialism at its starkest, while the contemporary purchasers of first editions—perhaps poring over the book with a glass of vodka and both feet dangling in the Caspian Sea—may have viewed the occasionally turgid descriptive passages as accurate portrayals of the perennially inebriated and undeniably seamy lower classes. God only knows, the verbiage afforded Marmeladov's picturesque descent into debauchery could have withstood substantial winnowing from Day One. I for one have not—in over forty years—found a translation that contained Mama Raskolnikow's long-winded Chapter 3 plot wrinkles ("I must close. My two sheets are filled. I have no more room.") in fewer than seven pages.

When I took the requisite survey course on Russian literature during my undergraduate days, I dutifully worked my way through (among other titles) *C&P*, *The Idiot*, *The House of the Dead*, *The Brothers Karamazov*, and *The Gambler*, and emerged with both an undeniable appreciation for Dostoevsky's ability to probe psychological boundaries and an absolute dread of any of his interior monologues, dialogue exchanges, or public confessions that exceeded a paragraph in length. I don't know how much of his wit, charm, perspicacity, or stylistic genius is lost in translation, but I would venture to say that it is Dostoevsky's ingenious framing of the downside of the human condition that brought him his reputation, and not his characters' mind-numbing verbosity. (In fairness to Dostoevsky, I would also opine that one could count on the fingers of maybe two fingers those who have read *War and Peace* and have come away in awe of the realistic speech patterns of any of Leo Tolstoy's creations.)

Anyway, in the three years or so that separated *Raskolnikow* from *Das Cabinet des Dr. Caligari*, Robert Wiene was a busy man, with nearly a dozen films made for a handful of companies under his belt. Of these "interim" films, only 1920's *Genuine* could be tagged as an Expressionistic follow-up to the tale of somnambulism and murder. Released only seven months after *Caligari* (both Decla films premiered at the same theater: Berlin's Marmorhaus), *Genuine* shared a cinematographer (Willy Haymeister), a scenarist (Carl Mayer), and a studio lot (the Bioscop Atelier in Neubabelsberg) with its groundbreaking predecessor. Inasmuch as the film was the only one of Wiene's post-*Caligari* pictures to be produced in the Expressionist mode, it is obvious that neither the filmmaker nor the studio (nor the Stuart Webbs Film Company, Maxim Film, Ebner & Co., Ungofilm, or Leonardo Film—companies for which Wiene also worked during this brief period) regarded the style as being de rigueur for the nonce, or even markedly popular. Many contemporary reviewers felt that it was the novelty of presentation—seen not only as a clever cinematic offshoot of the then-appreciated art form, but also as the perfect visual reflection of the psychological imbalances of the main characters—that had won acclaim for *Caligari*. With *Genuine*, the bloom was off the rose:

> *Genuine* was an expressionistic film because expressionism was a success. But instead of being a method of composition, in a way it became the content of the film. Expressionistic film died from this paradoxical discrepancy. *Genuine* was official proof that these films were not working commercially. Their time was over.[3]

Despite this viewpoint, Robert Wiene may have seen Dostoevsky's novel as a perfect vehicle for Expressionistic interpretation, what with its dealing with madness and sundry other forms of askew behavior thematically; squalor (mostly) with respect to settings; and extreme personality types in terms of... well... personality types. His *Caligari* had drawn on all three elements and had made moviegoers sit up and take notice—in part, at least because of the natural affinity such fairly unnatural facets had with the unreal world of Expressionism. Missing from the dramatis personae of both *Caligari* and *Raskolnikow* is any sense of normalcy: all the characters are in various stages of suffering and misery, are deceitful or are being deceived, or pose a threat to or are threatened by others. When not unconscious owing to violence, seizures, or inebriation, the first (and second) cast members are either sleepwalkers or sleep-deprived when not actually in the arms of Morpheus; also, they are feared, hated, spurned, pitied, reviled, and/or menaced. Only the bit players and extras seem oblivious to—or are unaffected by—the operatic displays of emotion that whirl about them. If one could speak of the carbon-based life-forms shape-wise, only these latter persons appear to be rounded and three-dimensional; the principal characters in both films are as flat, vertical and angular as the designs painted on the canvas behind them—that is, they are *naturals* for Expressionism.

Grigori Chmara's title character, of course, is Expressionism personified. His (and Dostoevsky's) *Raskolnikow* is a cipher: at once totally black and white and yet—given instances of introspection that breathe life into the printed page yet add only title cards to silent celluloid—also a spectrum of endless shades of gray. We have to take Wiene's word that his protagonist is a penurious student; Raskolnikov regards himself as a superior being—a concept that disturbingly foreshadows the coming Age of the Übermensch— who would be justified even in committing crimes, so long as "mankind" would benefit. Thus the murder of Alona, the pawnbroker, whose stranglehold over society is depicted in a hallucinatory vignette. Her half-sister's death

Figure 6.3   Autographed postcard of Grigori Chmara in *Raskolnikow*. (*Courtesy of George Chastain*)

is unpremeditated, since the woman is slain solely because she is in the wrong place at the wrong time, a casually regrettable by-product of the Master Plan. Our eyes bear witness to Raskolnikov's poverty: his lifestyle—upon which the screenwriter and production designer feast—is a two-dimensional palette of filth highlighted by anger, paranoia and egocentricity. Again, Expressionism-wise, nothing wrong here.

The problem lay in the titular protagonist being really the only element in the story for which the bizarre art-form fits like a glove. Arguments can be made that his digs, the rooftop garret and its environs, the streets surrounding the murder scene, even the seemingly endless staircase to the pawnbroker's apartment that he navigates time and again—all of these locales might authentically be depicted in expressionist manner, as they are the sites that comprise the "floor-plan" (as it were) of the fatal machinations of a criminally diseased mind. (We might throw in the police station where Raskolnikov does some of his better fainting, but this is a bit of a stretch.) But the rest of the city? The dramatic pivot here does not turn on the menace of a traveling carnival, with the sort of bizarrely accoutered specters one might readily expect to be part of the show. Festooning sets meant to be barrooms in which wordy inebriates deliver autobiographical monologues so as to reflect the neurological slant of one of their clients is a bit much. As one of the contemporary reviews put it, "What was shown by the *style* [my emphasis] of the work in *Caligari* leads to a dichotomy between the character in the film and his environment."[4]

There has been argument as to whether Wiene's adding depth to his compositions—whether depth of focus or physical space—represents a forward movement in Expressionism. The film historian John Barlow[5] recounts how a restaurant set used in *Raskolnikow* adds not only a second and third vertical level to the setting, but also a three-dimensional effect via deep focus, a marked advance from *Caligari*. In their book-length study of the filmmaker, Uli Jung and Walter Schatzberg see an even greater significance in the scene:

> Barlow's evaluation of the deep focus is quite revealing. He fails to take note, however, of how Wiene's mise-en-scène makes use of it: After the conversation with Zamyotov, the police secretary, in which he taunts the officer, Raskolnikov leaves the restaurant, walks and then looks back at the officer, whom we see in the foreground sitting with a puzzled look. Wiene films the scene with a long shot that allows the audience an objective and comparative view of the subjective states of both men.[6]

Yet at what point does progressing *beyond* the two-dimensional palette, moving past the highly stylized visual plane, adding *depth* to Expressionism, cause the result to cease to be Expressionism? Adding the sort of blatant third dimension that Jung and Schatzberg praise in the above quotation is akin to adding spoken lines to opera: you now have something that is not quite opera.

Certainly, Chmara's Raskolnikov has shed the sort of face paint that Veidt's Cesare had worn not long before, when Expressionism and das Kino had made their acquaintance. Certainly, if there wasn't more camera movement in *Raskolnikow* than there had been in *Caligari*, the number of camera setups had increased. This in itself proves little except that the footage lengths submitted for censorship on the films had the 1923 picture not quite twice as long (3168 m vs 1703 m, per Jung and Schatzberg) as its predecessor; for all that, *Caligari* was listed at six reels, while *Raskolnikow* is on record at seven. The chiaroscuro lighting is very much in evidence in both pictures, albeit the surviving elements of the Dostoevsky adaptation are in every way fainter and more washed out than the constantly restored/upgraded *Caligari*. The sundry adjustments made between 1920 and 1923 (and we include here observations made upon screening the extant-albeit-abridged *Genuine*) seem to reflect Wiene's attempt at pushing the Expressionist envelope.

But why? To underscore the theme? These three films—that represent but a fraction of the filmmaker's output during that brief time span—deal in the macabre. It may well be that Wiene felt that the techniques that had seized the attention of so many of *Caligari*'s fans (and the film *did* have its detractors) would be best utilized again (and again) when the director would conspire to recreate the unreality that disrupts what we have taken to be "normal." But that was exactly the bizarre disruption that F. W. Murnau had exploited in his *Nosferatu* (1922), which was—for the most part—photographed in a fairly straightforward, realistic way. Undeniably, Murnau called for Expressionistic shots, and most of these involve shadow-play (on staircases, above beds) and tableaux arranged by the sudden appearance of the vampire, framed in a doorway or casket-lid. These touches work well, as they provide a departure from what were otherwise the "normal" facets of the story (and those bits of normalcy did include solitude, disease, and decay). Utilizing this sort of "selective Expressionism" might have benefited Wiene's *Raskolnikow*, if only to highlight visually the fact that the world in which Rodion saw himself was not that of the bourgeois Russian he so despised, or even that of the poorer citizens who were resigned to their fate.

All of this is, of course, speculation, and Herr Wiene may have opted to dive back into the Sea of Expressionism solely to catch those last waves. The studied mannerisms of the principal cast—some drawn from the Moscow Art Theater—together with the wealth of human strangeness on exhibit care of anyone with virtually any featured screen-time at all lend credence to the theory that the auteur felt that the sundry subplots were as worth of outré representation as was "Raskolnikov, in the pawnshop, with the hatchet."

In its review of the film, *Film-Kurier* appreciated the enormity of Wiene's task, yet felt that there might have been other possible avenues of approach:

The particular aim of a "Raskolnikow" film might consist in riding speedily along the waves of his psychic delirium, with the cinema projecting outwardly the mental intensity with which people like this live. In this way, what is the poet's would be rendered to the poet, and—at the same time—what is film's, to film. Or, one might have created the sort of weird and macabre ballad that is along the lines of a treatment that is characteristic of Wiene. In that case, more might stem from Edgar Allan Poe than from Dostoevsky, but it probably would result in a fascinating film, one which really comes to life. Here, though, we have a treatment that is faithful to Dostoevsky's text; a pictorial commentary, so to speak, to his words. In this case, it is a dangerous enterprise. As Dostoevsky the Grand Visionary is no master of composition, there is no reason why one might not change his approaches in the layout of this film. The anticipation of this objection appears to be the thought behind giving the film an Expressionist frame, a la Caligari, while putting on the story itself via simple realism.[7]

In the commentary that accompanies his "cigarette-card-photo" book on Silent Films,[8] the film historian Oskar Kalbus may have summed up what the public's take on Expressionism was by the time *Raskolnikow* hit the screens: "Expressionist films have given nothing uncomplicated to the movie-going public and everything for them to dislike." In light of the lack of appreciation for the "expansion" of Expressionism come the turn of the decade, we might argue that while it was certainly no *Caligari*, *Raskolnikow* was a fitting counterpart to *Genuine*, even if that is really not saying much.

Notes

1. <http://www.tcm.com/this-month/article/354843|0/Crime-and-Punishment.html>, <http://www.ovguide.com/crime-and-punishment-9202a8c04000641f800000000a890485>, and <http://www.imdb.com/title/tt0026246/trivia> (last accessed 20 August 2015), to name but hither, thither, and yon . . .
2. I would at this point like to thank my wife, Nancy, for not even once threatening to take a hatchet to me for spending this much time not papering the kitchen, plastering the ceiling in the bathroom, or cleaning out the attic.
3. Rudolf Kurtz, *Expressionismus und Film* (Berlin: Verlag der Lichtbild-Bühne, 1926), p. 73.
4. M—s [Heinz Michaelis], "Raskolnikow," *Film-Kurier*, No. 243, 29 October 1923.
5. John Barlow, *German Expressionist Film* (Boston, MA: Twayne, 1987), p. 56.
6. Uli Jung and Walter Schatzberg, *Beyond Caligari: The Films of Robert Wiene* (Oxford/New York: Berghahn, 1999), p. 99.
7. M—s, "Raskolnikow."
8. Oskar Kalbus, *Vom Werden deutscher Filmkunst. 1. Teil: Der stumme Film* (Altona-Bahrenfeld: Cigaretten-Bilderdienst, 1935), p. 107.

PART II

EXPRESSIONISM IN GLOBAL CINEMA

7. THE AUSTRIAN CONNECTION: THE FRAME STORY AND INSANITY IN PAUL CZINNER'S *INFERNO* (1919) AND FRITZ FREISLER'S *THE MANDARIN* (1918)

Olaf Brill

In 1920, *The Cabinet of Dr. Caligari* became a smash hit on the German screen. With its strange sets, the film, a story about murder and madness—and containing a diabolical twist—became known as "the first expressionist film." But as we know, and as Thomas Elsaesser wrote,

> there were few real "firsts" in the cinema: most so-called inventions of technique resulted from a series of diverse and more or less successful applications, often in films no longer remembered.[1]

The call for an "expressionist" film existed before *Caligari*, and if we look hard enough we can find forerunners which share some essential properties with the celebrated masterpiece. Some of the most interesting examples preceding *Caligari* were produced in Austria, especially one film which is considered to be lost, and another which was recently rediscovered. They not only address the topics of murder and insanity but also contain frame stories foreshadowing the much-discussed *Caligari* frame. Fritz Freisler's *The Mandarin*, especially, could very well have provided the inspiration for a revised version of the famous *Caligari* script which was adapted into the film we know in late 1919.[2]

GERMAN AND AUSTRIAN FILM INDUSTRIES AFTER WORLD WAR I

After World War I, German products were cut off from international markets, leading to, among other things, a growing domestic film industry. Concerns like PAGU (Projektions-AG "Union") and Ufa (Universum Film AG) expanded rapidly and gained control of the market. Small production companies merged into larger concerns. A good example is Decla (Decla Film-Gesellschaft), a relatively small company controlled by the producer Erich Pommer which, directly after the war, merged with Rudolf-Meinert-Film-Gesellschaft in 1919, then with Bioscop in 1920, and was later swallowed by Ufa. The ultimate aim in the late 1910s and early 1920s was to establish a powerful film industry which would not only be able to supply the complete domestic market with its products, but also could produce films which would succeed in foreign markets as soon as they were open to the sale of German products. The most famous German film of that period, Decla's *The Cabinet of Dr. Caligari*, was a product targeting exactly that aim. It was one of the first German films to be shown in France and the USA after the war, and was a vehicle for the international success of German film.

It seems obvious that the isolation of the German market after World War I was one of the main factors that spawned the industry's ultimate success. Without competition from foreign markets, products could be developed for a strong domestic market. The Germans, however, also scrutinized developments in foreign markets, because those were developments they would have to compete with once they started exporting their products again. Also, the strong German market became attractive for production companies and skilled personnel from smaller neighboring countries.

One such example was Austria, whose film industry was prospering after the war. From 1919 to 1922, Sascha-Film (Sascha-Filmindustrie AG) was the largest Austrian film production company and one of the biggest in Europe. Sascha-Film even flourished when most other Austrian film companies fell into a crisis in the mid-1920s because of growing competition, most especially from the American market. Nevertheless, even when the Austrian film industry was at its height at the end of the 1910s and the beginning of the 1920s, Germany was attractive in three ways: as a market for Austrian products, as a partner for co-productions, and as a place of employment for Austrian personnel, many of whom came to the capital Berlin to work in German film.

To recognize the Austrian influence on German film production in the years 1919 and following, one needs to look no further than the production team of *The Cabinet of Dr. Caligari*. The film's authors, Carl Mayer and Hans Janowitz, were both born in Austria-Hungary. While Janowitz grew up in Prague and fought in the war, Mayer was born in Graz and, disabled from a childhood injury, came to Berlin during the war to make a career in theater and, if possible, film business. Robert Wiene, the director, commuted between Germany and Austria and wrote and/or directed more than forty films prior to *Caligari*, mostly for Messter-Film GmbH, Berlin, but also a couple of films for Sascha-Film, Vienna. Rudolf Meinert, the film's long-forgotten executive

PAUL CZINNER'S *INFERNO* AND FRITZ FREISLER'S *THE MANDARIN*

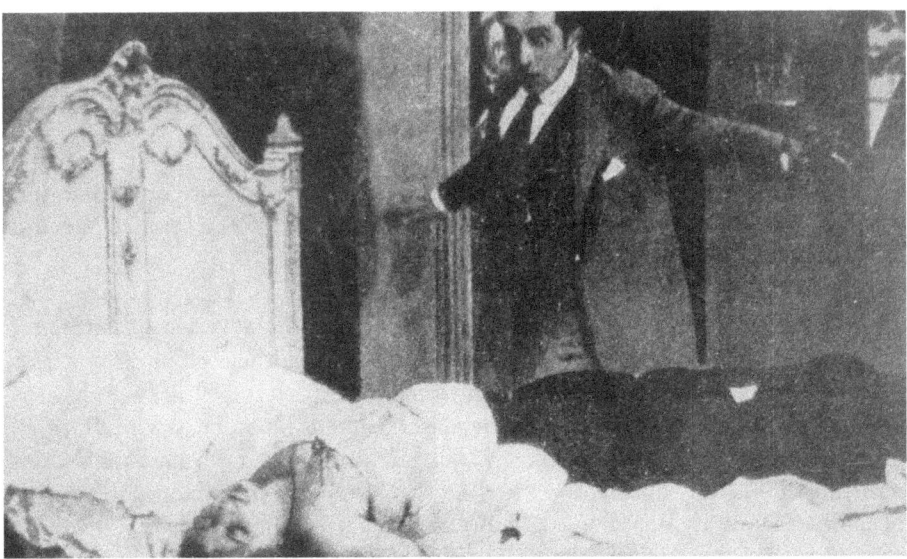

Figure 7.1   Franz Herterich and Grete Lundt in a publicity still for *Inferno* (1919).

producer, was also Austrian, born in Vienna, and came to Berlin after the war to found a film production company which merged with *Caligari*'s Decla in 1919. Leading actor Friedrich Fehér, who played Franzis, the person from whose point of view the whole story of the film is told, was also born in Vienna. He starred in German and Austrian films and was married to the famous Austrian film actress Magda Sonja.[3] Mayer, Janowitz, Wiene, Meinert, Fehér—many of *Caligari*'s pivotal personnel came from Austria to Berlin.

PAUL CZINNER'S *INFERNO* (1919)

Many more Austrians came to Germany who influenced German film production of that period, including the Viennese Fritz Lang, who started his career as a film director with Decla in exactly the same season as the very same company produced *The Cabinet of Dr. Caligari*, and fellow Viennese Paul Czinner (1890–1972), who prior to *Caligari* and before relocating to Berlin directed his first supposedly "expressionistic" film *Inferno* in Vienna, about which we know next to nothing and which is now considered lost. In 1970, Czinner remembered *Inferno* in an interview for Austrian TV:

> In Vienna, my most important film was a film called *Inferno*. That was an expressionistic film. The important thing for the Viennese at that time was that [Erik] Schmedes had played the lead, the greatest tenor in Vienna ... The film premiered in a concert hall, and I gave an introductory talk.[4]

According to Walter Fritz's history of Austrian film,[5] *Inferno* was indeed shown in a press screening at the Konzerthaus, Vienna, in December 1919. Czinner's talk was mentioned in the contemporary film trade press:

> He [Czinner] thinks that film as a pure art of expression is an especially appropriate medium to help manifesting a universal way of thinking, to give a bodily cover to the spiritual, not affected by the restrictive handcuffs of the word.[6]

Inferno then premiered on February 6, 1920 in Vienna, the very month *Caligari* hit the screens in Berlin. The film's plot is also given in the contemporary trade press as quoted by Fritz,[7] according to which the barkeeper Ulrik, who has just committed suicide and has newly arrived in Hell, tells his story to Satan himself. Ulrik was once an honorable citizen. But one day he found a half-starved girl named Eva on the roadside, took her into his home, fell in love, and for a while became a happy man. When malicious Eva married another man, Ulrik committed suicide. After having heard Ulrik's story, Satan decides to take revenge. He personally ascends to Earth, where he finds Eva and an astrologer, a happily married couple. Satan, in the shape of one Dr Natas, seduces Eva, but then drops her. Subsequently, Eva begins a double life whoring around at night. When her husband discovers her one night in a pub with lots of other men, he goes berserk and strangles her. According to additional information from a German censorship card,[8] the astrologer had previously foreseen this unfortunate outcome, and the last scene shows Eva arriving in Hell.

In that 1970 TV interview, Czinner also claimed that for *Inferno* he had devised a moving camera,[9] a technique later usually credited to *Caligari* scribe Carl Mayer and cameraman Karl Freund who invented the "unchained camera" for F. W. Murnau's *The Last Laugh* (1924). Unchained camera or not, and expressionistic style or not, *Inferno*'s plot as depicted in the trade press shows motifs which were also prominently used in German film of that period, and especially in expressionistic films to follow: murder, madness, a malicious woman who ruins a man's life, and a (here literally) satanic bad guy who pulls the strings. Even the frame story in which a man tells his story is a device, which is of course also found in *Caligari*.

Sadly, Czinner's film is believed to be lost. So this is really all we can say about it. But there is another Austrian film that even precedes both Czinner's film and *Caligari*. And that film bears a striking resemblance to the latter.

Fritz Freisler's *The Mandarin* (1918)

The Mandarin, produced by Sascha-Film, directed by Fritz Freisler (1881–1955), based on a stage-play by Paul Frank and starring Harry Walden and

Figure 7.2   German trade advertisement, published in *Der Film* (1919).

Carl Goetz, was released in theaters in Vienna on November 22, 1918 (with a press screening two days before), and is believed to have started its run in German cinemas in May 1919. Up until recently *The Mandarin* was considered lost, and we knew nearly as little about it as we know about Czinner's *Inferno*, until in the 2000s a nitro print resurfaced in the collection of the George Eastman House, Rochester. A screenable copy was made there in 2002 and was shown at the Pordenone Silent Film Festival in 2003. In 2004, the Austrian Film Museum in Vienna restored and showed it at an internal screening on February 29, 2004, then publicly on September 25, 2004. Subsequently, *The Mandarin* screened on a couple of occasions, among others at the Filmmuseum Biennal in Amsterdam on April 15, 2007, and at the Museum of Modern Art, New York, on March 6, 2014.

The print came from the estate of the Italian film collector Roberto Pallme (1893–1984). It is tinted in several colors; it contains Italian intertitles, and the title is *Il Mandarino (Storia di un pazzo)* (*The Mandarin—Story of a Madman*). Thus, it obviously originated from an Italian distributor, who probably

Figure 7.3 Vienna Insane Asylum in *The Mandarin* (1918). (*Courtesy of Austrian Film Museum, Vienna, frame enlargement: Georg Wasner*)

shortened the film to accommodate Italian audiences. The length of the surviving print is 1115 meters and it runs for approximately 61 minutes at 16 frames per second, which is less than two-thirds of its original length (1800 m).[10]

This is the story of *The Mandarin*, as depicted in the restored version:

> Like *Caligari*, the film begins with a frame story: Èrnesto Cristino, a writer researching his latest "psychological novel", is received by the director of a lunatic asylum (Carl Goetz). He asks to be shown around the institution, and the director introduces him to a number of insane patients, hinting the most interesting case would be that of Baron de Stroom (Harry Walden) who is sitting on a bench at a pond and is only uttering one word: "Man–da–rin!" So, the director tells the story of the baron.
>
> The baron is leading the life of a wealthy man in a huge house with a staff of servants. But for a year now he is madly in love with the famous singer Angela Gaalen, and is becoming franticly jealous when discovering she is meeting another man. When the baron is disturbing their latest rendezvous, she asks him: "Are you mad?"
>
> That night, the baron breaks into Angela's house and confronts her with his love. Coolly, she rejects him, again. And so his madness begins, an intertitle informs us. Appalled, he is sitting down on a park bench, when a street hawker is coming around offering his goods. At first, the baron is dismissive. But then he becomes enthusiastic about a little

Figure 7.4 Harry Walden and Carl Goetz in The *Mandarin* (1918). (*Courtesy of Austrian Film Museum, Vienna, frame enlargement: Georg Wasner*)

Chinese mandarin figurine. The hawker enthuses that if the baron would hold that figurine he'd become irresistible to every woman he desires.

The baron purchases the figurine, and back at his house, the little mandarin comes alive (also played by Carl Goetz). He offers his services to his master who then demands Angela's love. The mandarin disappears, leaving behind an astonished baron. But at the same night, Angela comes visiting the baron. She has indeed suddenly fallen in love with him.

On the next day, the mandarin reappears and assures that the baron now can have not only Angela but every woman. Next, with help of the mandarin the baron seduces the wife of an American businessman, then a young girl on a field. Even a woman from a painting on the wall is climbing out of her picture[11] and falling in love with the baron. The baron becomes overbearing now and tells the mandarin he would be able to seduce all women on his own, without the mandarin's help. But the mandarin warns him that now he cannot be successful without his help anymore, then disappears. Immediately, women are appalled by the formerly irresistible baron. Even café dancers and prostitutes reject him now. And when the mandarin reappears, then only to ridicule the baron. He is becoming increasingly mad and finally collapses on the street.

When several men take care of him, the baron claims one of them to be the malicious mandarin. Then he is taken to the asylum we know from the frame story. Again, he outrages and now claims the director is the mandarin. He is being sedated by the personnel.

End of frame story: having told the story of the baron to the writer, the director says that for a year now the protagonist of his story is a resident of his asylum. When they actually pass the baron who is still sitting at the pond, he suddenly attacks the director and accuses him to be the mandarin again. A member of staff captures him. Finally, the director explains that the baron is mentally ill, obsessed with the thought the director himself would be the mad mandarin responsible for his misfortune which was actually derived from an excessive life.

So far as we know, *The Mandarin* did not leave many traces in the contemporary German trade press, one of our main sources for information about German silent films of that period. There is, however, a small article in the weekly periodical *Lichtbild-Bühne*,[12] not even in the film reviews section but in the "business" section, which provided information for possible customers of the film distributor (in this case the company Hanewacker & Scheler, Berlin). The article provides a complete synopsis and so gives us some additional information about the plot. For instance, the girl seduced in a field by the baron is supposed to be a sixteen-year-old princess whom he had met at an exhibition (in a scene missing from the surviving print). The film works well without that scene, however. It seems quite possible that superfluous scenes have been deliberately cut to make the film "faster" for an Italian audience.

Figure 7.5 Harry Walden in *The Mandarin* (1918). (*Courtesy of Austrian Film Museum, Vienna, frame enlargement: Georg Wasner*)

The Mandarin and The Cabinet of Dr. Caligari

While *Caligari* became famous because of its stylized expressionistic sets, *The Mandarin*, being screened over a year before *Caligari*, contained no signs of such stylization. Also, unlike *Caligari*, *The Mandarin* was not shot entirely in a studio, but included many location shots in and around Vienna, most famously the Steinhof estate with its art nouveau church, which not only doubles for the film's "city of madmen" but was an actual mental asylum. A number of mental patients are shown in the film (certainly actors), arguably less multifaceted than their counterparts in the final scene of *Caligari*. But there are remarkable exceptions, such as a man in a cape holding a pumpkin, or a man who believes he is the Emperor of Greenland, sitting on a throne, dressed in a fancy fur coat, wearing a straw crown. Also it is interesting to note that in the asylum the baron is dressed all in white, while the director is dressed in black.

As to the techniques used in *The Mandarin*, the film contains various stop trick and double exposure effects reminiscent of Georges Méliès's magic cinematographic trickery—for example when the mandarin comes alive and starts growing, or the many occasions on which he suddenly appears or disappears into thin air. At one point, with a rotation of his body the mandarin transforms his Chinese look into that of a European man in contemporary dress. Also, a streetwalker and finally the director of the asylum transform into the mandarin. All these, of course, are tricks we know from Méliès's early films. So one could say that, instead of developing the future of cinema (Expressionism), *The Mandarin* is looking back at its past. Although *Caligari* very much does the same when telling a story of the fairground, a birthplace of cinema itself, arguably *Caligari*'s recourse to cinema's past is done self-consciously while *The Mandarin* is simply using well-known tricks from a decade before.

Another element which shows that Caligari is a more highly developed film than *The Mandarin* is the use of introductory pictures. At the beginning of *The Mandarin*, the main actors and their roles are introduced with title cards and a short film clip, which was common practice in the 1910s. *Caligari* abandons this traditional practice and more elegantly introduces its characters within the plot, while still using establishing shots.

So, *Caligari* is a more modern film, and of course it became the film which overshadowed all that came before it. But it is astonishing to see how *The Mandarin* anticipated some of *Caligari*'s most interesting features. When watching *The Mandarin* now, we find it incredible how close its story is to that of *The Cabinet of Dr. Caligari*, beginning with the insane asylum framework, then the motifs of murder and insanity; and of course both films toy with the question as to whether there is a hint of truth to the inner story. Is there a mystical mandarin who seduces the baron into leading an excessive life? Or is the mandarin only an invention of the baron's mind to excuse his socially unacceptable behavior? In short, is the mandarin real or only the imagining of a mad mind? If we substitute "the mandarin" for "Dr. Caligari," the same question is a central element of every interpretation of the *Caligari* film.

There even are hints that the integrity of the director in *The Mandarin* might be questioned. While the baron, as an inmate of the director's asylum, is dressed entirely in white, the director is clad in black. Could this be supposed to mean that the director is a bad character and his inmate an innocent? The supposedly insane baron identifies the director with the mandarin character of his back-story, and both are indeed played by the same actor (Curt Goetz). Is the director somehow the mandarin? So, could it be that the mandarin was indeed real and it was the director who framed the baron? But why? And how?

While much of *Caligari*'s charm stems from the film's ambiguity about the key question of whether the inmate is insane or the director, *The Mandarin*, despite some hints to the contrary as mentioned above, very much answers this question clearly. It is indeed the inmate who is insane. That is because *The Mandarin*, unlike *Caligari*, delivers no hints whatsoever as to why the director should be interested in framing the innocent. Also, there is no hint as to how the director should have managed to appear and disappear as the mandarin, making all the women fall in love with the baron, and so on. The plot of *The Mandarin* simply doesn't support the theory that the director might be insane. Instead, the film supports the rather conservative message that an excessive lifestyle might end in madness. It needed another film to go one step further.

Figure 7.6 Harry Walden in *The Mandarin* (1918). (*Courtesy of Austrian Film Museum, Vienna, frame enlargement: Georg Wasner*)

The Inspiration for *Caligari*?

The *Caligari* script is one of the most famous film scripts in the world. For more than fifty years, film historians could only speculate about its contents because it was believed to be lost forever. When an actual copy was found in the estate of actor Werner Krauß in the 1970s,[13] we saw that the script the two young authors delivered to Erich Pommer in April 1919 was still a far stretch from the finished film shot in September/October of the same year.[14] Especially the infamous frame story and all of the film's ambiguity about whether the patient is insane or the doctor must have been added between April and October. It was in that time, when it was decided to polish the script that *The Cabinet of Dr. Caligari* became the multi-layered piece of art we know.

Coincidentally, it was the same time when *The Mandarin* apparently was shown in Berlin cinemas. It didn't have much impact there. But it's certainly not too far-stretched to assume that some of the *Caligari* production team may have watched *The Mandarin* before the *Caligari* script was revised. It could very well be that it even was author Carl Mayer who within the next five years became the most important writer of Weimar cinema. Was it he who saw those few small hints in the insane asylum story of *The Mandarin* which would be used to full effect in the revised story of *The Cabinet of Dr. Caligari*? If we compare these two films today, *The Mandarin* certainly tells a more straightforward tale, where *Caligari* offers a complex narrative that leaves you thinking about it long after you've left the cinema. But it could very well be, that *The Mandarin* was not only a predecessor but also an inspiration for "the most famous German film," *The Cabinet of Dr. Caligari*.[15]

Notes

1. Thomas Elsaesser, "The New Film History," *Sight and Sound*, Autumn 1986, pp. 246–51, quoted p. 248.
2. *Caligari* was shot in September/October 1919, see my *Der Caligari-Komplex* (Munich: Belleville, 2012), p. 230.
3. Magda Sonja was probably also involved in Károly Lajthay's *Drakula halála* (1921); see Gary D. Rhodes' chapter in this volume.
4. *Filmgeschichten aus Österreich*, Ep. 3: *Hollywood am Laaerberg*, ORF (Austrian Broadcasting) 1970, quoted from: Michael Omasta and Brigitte Mayr (eds.), *Paul Czinner—Der Mann hinter Elisabeth Bergner* (Vienna: SYNEMA, 2013), p. 3.
5. Walter Fritz, *Kino in Österreich 1896–1930: Der Stummfilm* (Vienna: Österreichischer Bundesverlag, 1981), p. 113. See also Fritz's *Geschichte des österreichischen Films* (Vienna: Bergland, 1969), pp. 89–90, 230.
6. Fritz, *Kino in Österreich*, p. 113. Contrary to the reference given by Fritz, the correct original source is: *Neue Kino-Woche*, No. 12, December 1919, p. 6.
7. Ibid. p. 113.
8. Omasta and Mayr, *Paul Czinner*, p. 16.
9. Fritz, *Kino in Österreich*, p. 114.

10. According to censorship card.
11. An effect later repeated in *Caligari* successor *Genuine* (1920) when Fern Andra as Genuine is doing the same trick; see Mirjam Kappes's chapter in this volume.
12. *Lichtbild-Bühne*, No. 19, 10 May 1919, pp. 31–2.
13. Text published in: Helga Belach and Hans-Michael Bock (eds.), *Das Cabinet des Dr. Caligari—Drehbuch von Carl Mayer und Hans Janowitz zu Robert Wienes Film von 1919/20* (Munich: text + kritik, 1995).
14. For the production history of *The Cabinet of Dr. Caligari* see my *Der Caligari-Komplex*.
15. Many thanks to Oliver Hanley of the Austrian Film Museum, Vienna, for helpful information and the opportunity to watch *The Mandarin*. Also many thanks to George Riley, Hamburg, and to Brigitte Mayr and Michael Omasta, Vienna, for helpful remarks.

8. "THE REAWAKENING OF FRENCH CINEMA": EXPRESSION AND INNOVATION IN ABEL GANCE'S *J'ACCUSE* (1919)

Paul Cuff

Released in the immediate aftermath of the Great War, Abel Gance's epic drama *J'accuse* (1919) was a worldwide sensation. In France, the press reported the raw emotions the film provoked in audiences: men and women were seen alternately weeping in grief and cheering with enthusiasm.[1] The film skillfully combined an intimately "poignant" family melodrama with intense depictions of war's "rage and madness."[2] Gance's "sublime" and "terrifying visions"[3] emerged from, and fed back into, a public imagination haunted by personal and national grief. Not only did the film offer a potent evocation of the recent past, but its stylistic daring heralded cinema's future involvement with Modernist experimentation. For many critics, *J'accuse* was the "unquestionable" pinnacle of European film production: its impact was like a "strident trumpet-blast" that signaled "the reawakening of French cinema."[4]

Straddling avant-garde and mainstream film practice, *J'accuse* embodies its director's dream of expressing a radical artistic vision within popular cinema. Gance's rapidly developing talents can be seen in the film's shift from melodrama to the epic, the tension between realism and expressionism, and the challenge to existing formal techniques. Alongside *Broken Blossoms* (1919) and *Das Cabinet des Dr. Caligari* (1920), *J'accuse* was internationally recognized as one of the most ground-breaking productions of the immediate postwar period. It emulated the commercial scale of D. W. Griffith's film, as well as foreshadowing the break with aesthetic convention found in Robert Wiene's celebrated work. Its success across Europe and America propelled Gance to international fame and gave him the artistic and financial clout to make his two revolutionary masterpieces, *La Roue* (1922) and *Napoléon, vu par Abel Gance* (1927).

In this chapter, I want to examine how the form and content of *J'accuse* are shaped by its cultural and ideological contexts. The immediate aftermath of the Great War was one of the key periods in the birth of Modernism, witnessing an explosion of new ideas and divergent approaches to art. Few ages "have been more multiple, more promiscuous in artistic style,"[5] and *J'accuse* embodies exactly this sense of innovative energy. I will argue that Gance's film must be understood as the product of both commercial and artistic ambition, as well as the competing influences of Romanticism and Modernism, Expressionism and Impressionism. I aim to demonstrate the ways in which *J'accuse* sought to expand the boundaries of cinema's popular appeal and its expressive potential.

Figure 8.1   Romuald Joubé as Jean Diaz. (*Courtesy of Flicker Alley, LLC and Lobster Films*)

Art-film and Super-film

As with later Expressionist films, the Great War impacted upon *J'accuse* in multiple ways. The humanitarian crisis engendered by the conflict inspired Gance's narrative, while the conditions it created within the European film industry shaped the pattern of its distribution.

Gance began his filmmaking career in 1912; he achieved early commercial success with a number of impressive melodramas, but the scale of his work was held in check by restrictions of time and budget. His ambitions were galvanized when he saw the technical sophistication in Cecil B. DeMille's *The Cheat* (1915) and the sheer scale of Griffith's *Intolerance* (1916).[6] These new films suggested grander possibilities for the medium, but were also evidence of America's increasing commercial dominance. The economic impact of the war placed French filmmakers under severe financial strain, and would prove to be the deciding factor in the US dominance of cinema's world market. When Gance conceived a huge three-film series about the war in 1917, he intended not only to make a bold artistic statement, but also to demonstrate that French cinema could stand up to its US competitors in popular appeal.

It wasn't until 1918 that Gance convinced Charles Pathé to fund the first episode of this trilogy, but *J'accuse* proved to be a much larger undertaking than anticipated. His chief cameraman, Léonce-Henri Burel, later quipped that Gance used enough celluloid on *J'accuse* "to build an opera house."[7] The version of the film that premiered in March–April 1919 was some four hours in duration. This long-scale format was not simply a reflection of Gance's artistic grandiosity: it was designed to be in accord with commercial desire. The serial was a popular format with French audiences and exhibitors, and *J'accuse* was initially distributed in separate "parts," spread over multiple weeks.[8] (*La Roue* and *Napoléon* would also be released as multi-part films.)

Gance's blend of populist melodrama and high art is evident in the narrative content of *J'accuse*. The pacifist poet Jean Diaz (Romuald Joubé) is in love with Édith Laurin (Maryse Dauvray), a woman unhappily married to the brutish François (Séverin-Mars). When war is declared, the men's rivalry is transposed to the front line; Édith is captured and raped by German soldiers and later gives birth to an illegitimate child, Angèle (Angèle Guys). This tortuous love triangle may seem generic, but the film proceeds to confound our expectations. Firstly, Jean and François reconcile their differences on the battlefield. Later, Édith and Angèle arrive home, where they form an unconventional family unit with Jean as surrogate father/lover. (Though the "crisis of adoption"[9] is a common trope in French cinema of the postwar period, Gance's use of the device in *J'accuse* and *La Roue* contains a more personal dimension. He was himself an illegitimate child, and unconventional/incomplete families, oedipal relationships, and love triangles are recurrent themes in his work.) The end of *J'accuse* is even stranger: after François is killed, Jean is driven mad and leads an army of dead soldiers to accuse the villagers of being unworthy of the nation's sacrifice. Odder still, Gance initially planned to conclude the story with Jean still alive and living with Édith alongside the spirit of the dead François in a ghostly *ménage à trois*.[10]

Perhaps it is unsurprising that contemporary critics were appreciatively baffled by Gance's weird concoction. While some writers hailed *J'accuse* as "an astonishing revelation" that exceeded Griffith's achievements,[11] others felt that Gance had repeated the American director's "faults." Writing about *Broken Blossoms*, Léon Moussinac praises Griffith's attention to detail and "acute observation," as well as his grasp of subtle lighting effects and use of decor. However, he denounces Griffith's "bad taste" and "philosophical pretensions"; while his ideas are "debatable" his technique is "perfect."[12] Moussinac would have the same reservations about the director of *Napoléon*, and his words presage critics' longstanding ambivalence toward Gance.[13]

Nevertheless, *J'accuse* was successfully sold to exhibitors on the basis of its aesthetic quality as well as its commercial potential. Pathé's strategy for the foreign distribution of the film sought to emulate that of *Broken Blossoms* across America and Europe in 1919–20. Under Griffith's supervision, *Broken Blossoms* heralded itself as the first "super-film"; a mass of carefully orchestrated press reports preceded an exhibition run of unprecedented length and scale. Gance was as much influenced by Griffith's sales tactics as by his artistry. He wanted his distributors to "launch [*J'accuse*] like *Broken Blossoms* as a super-film."[14] In 1920, his film was exported to the UK, where a lavish press campaign was complemented by numerous publicity stunts from individual exhibitors.[15] As the first European production marketed as a super-film, Gance hoped *J'accuse* might be a "prototype" for future projects.[16]

Posters in the UK advertised *J'accuse* as "The Most Romantic Tragedy of Modern Times," an epithet whose contrasting tendencies toward the melodramatic and the epic were highlighted by the British press. Critics thought Gance's film contained "much confused thinking" and was "inclined to lack logical coherence," just as its love triangle "bears little relation to the real main theme of the story."[17] Though the plot of *J'accuse* "possesses nothing very remarkable," its "telling" was "unique in every way" and guaranteed that the film "will rank high among the very finest pictures ever made."[18] Some prudish writers worried that the "temperamental difference" of its continental origins would cause some Englishmen to flinch, but still felt *J'accuse* would be a "revelation" to the UK.[19]

It was Griffith himself who ensured the release of *J'accuse* in the USA, after being tremendously moved by the film's New York premiere in May 1921.[20] The film was eventually launched across the country by United Artists in 1922, accompanied by the slogan "A tremendous indictment of modern civilization!" Despite the confidence of such marketing, *J'accuse* suffered the same fate as *Caligari* in being textually censored upon its general release in the USA. Though Gance's film was the product of a wartime ally, the ambiguity of its accusations (examined later in this chapter) inspired numerous cuts and textual amendments. Similarly, the US trade press "aggressively" reshaped the reception of *Caligari* by rebranding it a "European" production (thus bypassing anti-German sentiment); exhibitors also tried to reframe its narrative through their mode of presentation.[21] However, even in its amended form, Gance's film was a great success—many theaters exceeded the contracted exhibition agreement to cater for demand.[22]

J'accuse was an important precedent for the export of European films. *Caligari* would follow close on its heels, becoming the first sensation of German Expressionist cinema and cementing the "novel" notion that "Art" could be a viable commercial product.[23] Despite the radical style of Wiene's film, it was nevertheless subject to the "rigid demands for the largest possible market."[24] As its producer Erich Pommer related, *Caligari* fitted in with what was "in vogue" with German public taste.[25] The film embodied both the "subjectivist traditions" of nineteenth-century Romanticism and the "radical disjunction and abstraction" of twentieth-century Modernism. Its innovative elements "emerge from and are dependent on the largely conventional form of the of the film's classic realist narrative."[26] *J'accuse* encouraged its maker to believe that high art and commercialism could be successfully welded together—as a result, it occupies the same "anomalous cultural space"[27] as *Caligari*, somewhere between the avant-garde and popular entertainment. While *Broken Blossoms* set new levels for the success of narrative realist cinema, and *Caligari* signaled the appearance of more radical formal experimentation, *J'accuse* sought to combine the qualities of both.

Toward a New Language

The ideological program that Gance wanted to introduce into his commercial super-film was nothing less than the reinvention of human communication. His previous two projects both dealt with the need for new forms of language.

The central sequence of *La Dixième Symphonie* (1918) is the realization of a new symphony by its composer, Enric Damor (Séverin-Mars). Gance cuts away from its performance to a series of images which embody the music itself. We see a masked shot of a dancer, diaphanously superimposed over a series of evocative landscapes. The masking is decorated with hand-tinted designs, and the combination of tints and tones creates an elaborate visual image—a clear predecessor to the visualization of Jean's poetry in *J'accuse*. *La Dixième Symphonie* demonstrated "a move toward non-narrative form, toward the expressive and the rhythmical"[28]—it was a mainstream film at whose heart was an avant-garde set-piece.

Soon after, Gance began a film that he would abandon after a few weeks of shooting. *Ecce Homo* (1918) was to be his first attempt at an epic theme: the transformation of mankind through a new world-philosophy. *Ecce Homo* featured a prophet named Novalic (Albert t'Serstevens), whose attempt to preach a message of universal fraternity was rejected by the cynical, materialist population. He is driven mad, but, thanks to the help of his son and a devoted female disciple, his sanity returns and he plans to use a new method to disseminate his religion of the future: cinema. From the surviving evidence, *Ecce Homo* was never going to be an Expressionist film, despite its familiar theme of madness and some superb visual effects.[29]

The extremely personal nature of its subject-matter marks a key connection between *Ecce Homo* and *J'accuse*, as does its portrayal of the central visionary. Just as Novalic would have been his screen persona in *Ecce Homo*, so Jean would be a kind of "double" for Gance in his subsequent project.[30] When he redrafted the script of *Ecce Homo* in the autumn of 1919, the finale contained a speech by Novalic addressing the film audience itself. Instead of relying on written works, he says, "I will employ a new language of the eyes, which, unlike other forms of communication, knows no boundaries."[31] Cinema would realize the dreams of the filmmaker and his fictional characters.

For Gance, human language was a bastardized, culturally divisive "translation" of the divine message, and the need to transcend it was one of his most urgent pleas: "The soul longs to speak without words."[32] Blending mysticism with scientific speculation, Gance believed that light was the ultimate expressive substance and that cinema's illuminative properties offered a unique opportunity to surpass the limitations of existing communication. As early as 1912, he envisioned spreading cinema's "faith" throughout the world—film was to be a new form of religion.[33] It was Novalic's vision of a prophetic discourse, a "language of the eyes," that Gance started to explore in *J'accuse*.

The film offers both graphic manipulations of the image and more complex visual representations of written or spoken text. While the Expressionistic font of *Caligari*'s titles announces a stylized mode of narration, the opening images of *J'accuse* display bold text-imagery. An extreme high-angle long-shot shows a mass of soldiers gathered on a plain. A masked shot of Jean blowing a whistle signals the soldiers to form the word "J'ACCUSE" in huge letters. Once in formation, they sit down in their ranks—as if refusing to move again and dispel their exclamation. This is a remarkably powerful opening. The soldiers used as extras were on leave from the Front and, as Gance later recalled, most would be killed when they returned[34]—their physical embodiment of accusation in the opening frames is viscerally felt. The transformation of text is also highly innovative. It breaks down the boundaries between subject and audience, the world of the film and the world beyond the film. Throughout, Jean's accusations are aimed as much at Gance's audience as his own. The manipulation of the *mise-en-scène* is Expressionist in its graphic alteration of the diegetic space, signaling the film's interest in transcending a realist narrative with a visionary sense of hallucination. Equally, only the cutting between Jean and the soldiers offers any connection between their otherwise incongruous *mise-en-scène*. Already, the film is transcending coherent continuity in favor of bold imagery.

The presentation of Jean's numerous exclamations of "J'accuse!" varies continually; the visualization of this titular word often involves superimpositions and the combination of graphic design and live-action. The least elaborate of such titles are painted images. One shows Paul Delaroche's *La jeune martyre* (1855), depicting a young Christian woman with tied hands in the River Tiber; in keeping with the Romanticism of the image, Gance superimposes the word "J'ACCUSE," formed by similarly bound female figures. This visual appropriation of nineteenth-century imagery makes the drowned girl both a tragic Ophelia-figure and a symbolic martyr: Édith and France. Similarly, the image of Death hovering above a huge crowd, scythe in hand ready to harvest the dead, is drawn from long-established representations of the "grim reaper." Such visualization is designed to embody the sentiments of characters and nation, appealing to a popular imagination with its easily identifiable images.

Gance repeatedly uses the more complex live-action *danse macabre*, with its ring of skeletons dancing around a central figure. They first appear during the declaration of war, providing an ironic undercurrent to the crowd's cheering enthusiasm. The shots of church bells sounding the arrival of war are greeted by most as a celebration, but the images of Death and gleefully circling skeletons are combined with painted images of other bells ringing a funereal toll. As the village begins to send its men to the Front, Jean imagines a skeletal hand clutching a scythe over his volume of "Pacifiques" and a vision of Death dissolves in over a view from his window. After Mme Diaz dies, her son's exclamation of "J'ACCUSE" (superimposed over the shot of him beside her deathbed) is followed by the image of dancing skeletons with the title: "War kills mothers as well as sons."

In other sequences, *J'accuse* offers uniquely cinematic alternatives to the purely textual form of language. The most obvious example of this occurs early in the film, when Jean reads his poetry (an "ode to the sun") to his mother. Instead of being shown the text of his speech, we are given a visual representation of his ideas. This series of lyrical images includes beautifully composed shots of sunlit exteriors, as well as painted images of idyllic scenes of nature and man in harmony. As in *La Dixième Symphonie*, this vision is summoned by the artist performing his work, a clear link to the filmmaker's ambition.

Yet there are also numerous instances of written text featuring prominently in the narrative of *J'accuse*—Gance's elaborate titles are very different from the "absolute brevity" found in *Caligari*.[35] Apart from the documents/letters that serve as narrative exposition, there are quotations from pre-existing literary sources. Earlier versions of *J'accuse* very likely contained more such material, as Gance's correspondence and 1917 screenplay refer to titles taken directly from Henri Barbusse's *Le Feu* (1916), a novel which was a key inspiration for the film. Unlike *La Roue*, which is filled with quotations from authors as diverse as D'Annunzio, Kipling, and Sophocles, the surviving version of *J'accuse* contains only two direct literary citations—from Alphonse de Lamartine and Pierre Corneille.[36]

Before the final battle sequence, we are shown extracts from soldiers' letters. Though the documents are genuine, they are actually taken from *Lettres d'un soldat* (1916), a published collection of letters from a fallen soldier. (Indeed, Gance narrowly avoided being sued for breach of copyright by the family's literary executive because the original prints gave no credit for their source.[37]) These letters are used as a form of realism, giving space for the soldiers' own words—a use of written text that remains deeply affecting. A related element of realism is the frequent use of soldiers' patois in intertitles. Earlier versions of the film may have contained more examples—the screenplay suggests Gance had wanted to deploy much more realistic dialogue (a noticeable feature of *Le Feu*).

As I have illustrated, it is difficult to categorize the film's multiple uses of

Figure 8.2   Séverin-Mars as François Laurin. (*Courtesy of Flicker Alley, LLC and Lobster Films*)

text. Text is used to convey narrative information, realism, poetry, and even the transcendence of written language. While some effects are strong examples of Expressionism, others are far more conservative. Gance would achieve a more cohesive integration of text and image in *La Roue*. Yet *J'accuse* already foreshadows another method that Gance's subsequent work would use to surpass language: rapid cutting.

From Expressionism to Impressionism

Fritz Lang and F. W. Murnau may be linked to the "unchained camera," but Expressionist cinema "effectively denied, or missed the opportunity of experimentation with the technology of the apparatus" until later in the 1920s.[38] The release of *Caligari* caused contemporary French critics to debate the move toward a potentially more "theatrical" mode of cinema. Writing in 1922, Lionel Landry felt the film marked a regression in the art's evolution. He branded *Caligari* anti-cinematic for relying on set-design instead of camerawork, and worried that other films might be "Caligarized" and follow suit.[39] Such views were also echoed by the poet Blaise Cendrars (who had been an extra in *J'accuse* and would be Gance's assistant on *La Roue*) in a brusque, bullet-point critique.[40] Yet for Émile Vuillermoz, *Caligari* offered "an interpreted world," one which was "sentient" and reflected the suffering of those who inhabited it.[41] These words seem to go some way toward reconciling Expressionistic subjectivity with the kind of animism Gance wished to proclaim.

Gance's earlier films had successively perfected a concise pattern of continuity editing. By the time he made *Mater Dolorosa* (1917), "the cutting within and between sequences is exceptionally clear and economical."[42] Yet with an expansion of dramatic/narrative breadth, Gance's style became more experimental. *J'accuse* was his most deliberate attempt to wrench cinema away from theatrical staging and imbue filmic language with a greater sense of movement, rhythm, and communicative range. It is this move from the graphic alteration of the *mise-en-scène* to the manipulation of the cinematic apparatus itself that (for some) marks a shift away from Expressionism toward Impressionism. However, such attempts to distinguish one artistic movement from another are not always helpful to review films which display characteristics of both. *J'accuse* is a case in point.

From its opening farandole sequence, the film is visibly striving to outstrip the existing grammar of cinema. The villagers are drinking and dancing around the fire-lit town. Close- and medium-shots are shown of various individuals and groups: musicians playing boisterously, an old couple nodding to the rhythm, young pairs laughing and drinking. There are a series of dissolves between close-ups of smiling female faces. The overlapping images create a sense of shared joy, "so [that] each person continues the laughter from the last."[43] From these techniques of montage, the audience shares in the visual rhythm of the music and the unitive quality of the occasion. After a complex series of close-ups and eye-line matches, we are introduced to Jean and his mother, as well as Édith, who watches from her window. At the climax of the sequence, these various spaces and images—close-ups of Jean, Mme Diaz, Édith, musicians, and dancers—are intercut with increasing speed, down to shots only a few frames in length. The cutting comes to an abrupt end as the dancing villagers encounter an owl, whose presence is taken as a bad omen.

The rhythm of the dance is both a celebration of community and an intimation of disaster. The rapid cutting gives the village festivities a suggestion of frenzy and fire that foreshadows the outbreak of war, just as the rhyme with the *danse macabre* casts the farandole in a dark light. That Édith and Jean are intercut with this dance shows that they too will be pulled into the imminent maelstrom. Though the rhythm of this sequence is very roughly developed, the intention of matching the emotional and musical sense of the scene through editing is clear. Even if the sequence seems crude by comparison with the masterful rapid montage sequences in *La Roue*, *J'accuse* is already moving away from the manipulation of *mise-en-scène* alone to express complex ideas.

The subsequent scenes in the village square, announcing the order for mobilization, possess an extremely effective visual rhythm. Gance's original screenplay states: "Tremendous emphasis on psychology. Intense expressions of stupor, joy, enthusiasm, fear."[44] The realized scene presents the thrilling spectacle of the village street crammed with people—the screen becomes a pulsing, seething crowd of faces. Gance's cutting punctuates these wider shots with telling details: a man singing the national anthem cannot see the look of concern on the face of the woman who clings to his side; an ancient woman wearing widower's black toothlessly repeats "Vive la France!" like a child; a young wife hides in the shadows away from the crowd and weeps with fear; Mme Diaz stands motionless amid the jostling sea of patriotism. The rhythmic precision of these shots demonstrates expert editorial organization, but the sequence still gives the overall impression of documentary verisimilitude. Gance exploits the fact that everyone onscreen had lived through the events of August 1914. His sequence becomes a disturbing re-enactment of the recent past: seen one hundred years after the event, the sea of faces is still palpably (almost uncomfortably) real. Made when the true cost of war was painfully evident, *J'accuse* possesses a rare and troubling self-consciousness.

In contrast to the boisterous display of public emotion at the declaration of war, Gance narrates the departure of men for the Front through moments of familial seclusion. In a beautiful sequence of close-ups, we see a series of tactile gestures set in relief against neutral backgrounds: a father's hands enclose those of his child, before slowly withdrawing from the frame; a mother and son raise their glasses in a final toast—his hand swiftly leaves the frame to drink, while hers unsteadily returns the wine to the table untouched; a pair of elderly hands clasp in prayer before a lighted candle. The method of visual isolation employed in this montage may draw attention to its representational artifice, but the emotional effect is all the stronger. Through the obscuring of the faces of those individuals involved, each gesture becomes loaded with the universal significance of separation; these hands could belong to people of any nation, at any time—Gance's evocation of personal loss remains extraordinarily poignant.

Elsewhere, the "half-fantastic, half-realistic spirit"[45] of *J'accuse* is felt in the transformation of documentary footage into stylized montage. Gance uses an intertitle to explain the veracity of material in the film's final battle scenes (the cameramen having accompanied the St Mihiel offensive in September 1918), yet incorporates it into an increasingly visionary narrative. The battle sequence uses whip-pans and an irregular pattern of quick cutting to induce in the audience a sense of disorientation felt by the soldiers onscreen, yet Gance also uses traditional imagery for added emotional resonance (the vision of the Marseillaise from the Arc de Triomphe as the men go over the top). There is also a fantastic visual expression of shellshock. Jean is seated in a trench when a shell explodes close by; suddenly, the tinting switches from black-and-white to red. A wider shot now focuses on Jean in the background as a blur of troops urgently pelt past in the foreground, punctuating the screen like the thud of gunfire and the repetitive tremors that seize his body as he shakes and laughs maniacally. Later, in Jean's hallucinatory view of the night-time fighting, imagery of the dancing skeletons is intercut with, and superimposed over, documentary footage of the battle. Gance had planned for the orchestra to play Saint-Saëns' orchestral tone poem *Danse Macabre* during this sequence—further evidence of his desire to transcend the real through rhythmic cutting, mobile camerawork, and evocative music.[46]

Just as striking as Gance's pursuit of rhythmic experimentation is his reliance on economic interior staging and a lyrical use of natural landscapes. While "Not a whiff of nature is allowed into the askew, spectral sets of *Caligari*,"[47] *J'accuse* and Gance's other silent films delight in the open-air. Even if careful lighting, composition, and color tinting/toning heighten the atmosphere beyond simple "naturalism," the basis of exteriors remains anchored in realism. In contrast to many of the studio-bound German Expressionist films, *J'accuse* contains a wealth of captivatingly beautiful exterior photography. The concentration on the lyrical joy of natural landscape serves to highlight the gulf between homestead and battlefield. If the village is far from idyllic (it is the backdrop to most of the film's romantic conflict), it remains physically unspoiled by the horrors of war. Just as Bonaparte (Albert Dieudonné) is connected to the natural landscape of Corsica in *Napoléon*, so Jean is linked with the rural setting of his village in *J'accuse*. Both visionaries come home to their mother from national conflict and there are sequences showing their relationship to their maternal landscape (Bonaparte rides across country, Jean lingers along the rural road back home). Similarly, Jean's visions of an ideal world in his poetry consist of images of the natural world.

Conversely, *J'accuse* frequently rejects the use of real locations in favor of pure stylization in an Expressionist mode. Several of Jean's visions are painted landscapes, consciously constructed images that stand in contrast to the location exteriors used elsewhere. Equally, many studio interiors look out onto what are very obviously painted backdrops (most noticeably in Jean's house, where characters are often framed by the large windows or the open door). Editing is used to unite (studio) interiors and (location) exteriors instead of sets built *en plein air*. In *La Roue*, however, Gance took particular (even extreme) care to unite interiors with exterior locations, enabling single shots to encompass both planes. Sets were built in the middle of railway yards so that every window looked out onto a tangibly real environment. Combined with a rhythmic visual orchestration, this sense of external reality could also evoke the internal worlds of characters' thoughts and feelings:

> *La Roue* marks a decisive evolution in Gance's style: *the transition from expressionism to impressionism*. By entirely forsaking the studio and becoming rooted in the very environment of its drama, Gance gave up the expressionist processes which had so far proved successful (and which *J'accuse* had realized in practice), seeking instead to *emotionally objectivize* states of soul, to force the spectator to become an actor in the drama and take part in the sufferings of its characters.[48]

There are already instances of this externalization in *J'accuse*. A good example of the simultaneous use of location photography, camera movement, and psychological expression occurs in the sequence where Édith has been tricked by François into thinking her young child Angèle has drowned. In a dramatic sequence of shots, we see Édith run to the river. During a tracking shot that precedes Édith along the village road, she calls out in terror: "Dead! She's dead!" There is a cut to a shot of the shimmering river—this subjective vision is emphasized by the iris mask that closes in on the rapidly flowing water. Gance then cuts back to another tracking shot in front of Édith, this time closer than before—linking Édith with the preceding image. After a static long-shot of Édith running past houses, there is another shot of the river, followed by Édith's appearance under a bridge. Édith's feverish state of mind is echoed in the wind-shaken trees, her billowing skirt, and the trembling surface of the water. Shots of the rushing current and the riverbank are intercut with midshots of her frantic gestures, heightening the suspense and creating a subjective sense of threat and panic. Finally, she sees Jean sitting alone on a fallen tree trunk by the river. After several moments of suspense (for Édith and for the audience), Angèle appears from behind Jean and giggles as he turns round to find her: a beautifully simple touch to end a remarkably effective sequence dominated by powerful editing and high drama. Its quick cutting to a series of subjective images foretells the evermore elaborate and sophisticated devices seen in *La Roue*, where the editing far surpasses that of *J'accuse* in Gance's pursuit of a cinema that would be "the music of light."[49]

Though *J'accuse* presaged some of Impressionism's techniques and *La Roue* was a profound influence on avant-garde cinema in France, Gance was never wholly associated with the artists he inspired. Advocates of "pure" cinema demanded he renounce melodrama in favor of formal experimentation, but Gance would always pursue wider audiences. Their divergent trends resulted in critics "pulling apart" his films in several different directions, unable to comprehend them as a whole.[50] That *J'accuse* contains "both a realistic element and a visionary rejection of realism"[51] can be most powerfully seen in its final scenes.

Figure 8.3   Jean Diaz stands guard over the dead, who await their resurrection. (*Courtesy of Flicker Alley, LLC and Lobster Films*)

Funereal Symphony

The "return of the dead" in *J'accuse* must rank as one of the most haunting and disturbing sequences in silent cinema. It also encapsulates much of what I have discussed so far: the blend of melodrama and the epic, the combination of image and written text, the use of bold editing, and the transformation of realism into Expressionism and supernaturalism. Above any other sequence, this finale removes *J'accuse* from commercial convention. These final scenes are crucial to understanding the paradoxical nature of the film's style and ideological content.

Jean has gathered the villagers at Édith's house, where he reveals that the dead have risen from the battlefield to see if the nation is worthy of their sacrifice. In these scenes, the intimate effect of low-key lighting visible in *Mater Dolorosa* and *La Dixième Symphonie* is pushed even further. Here, the figures are lit purely through firelight (original prints tinted these shots either red or orange[52]). The Expressionist chiaroscuro of vivid, low-key lighting produces a suitably febrile, nightmarish quality to Jean's speech. Gance cuts from this fire-lit interior to an extreme long-shot of a night-time exterior, illustrating Jean's tale through a complex flashback structure. The film proceeds to intercut past and present, battlefield and village, bringing these two time-spaces into eerie proximity. That Jean features in both halves of this parallel montage endows him with a cinematic omniscience that spans time and space: he is both protagonist and narrator of the film, summoning the images in which he himself appears. Gance thus blurs the distinction between on- and offscreen audiences; cinematizing the villagers' experience of Jean's account merges it with our own experience of the film.

We see Jean on the battlefield, surrounded by a huge plain of crosses. Imposed on the top half of the image is a matte-painting of a dark, brooding cloudscape. This artificial sky is the signal for our entry into a constructed passage of visionary narrative. Through a slow dissolve, the crosses appear to melt away and are replaced with bodies—conjured by Jean and replicated through the filmmaking process. A close-up of Jean, held in a tight iris-framed shot, shows the poet-soldier recoiling in horror at the vision of the rising dead; he stands against a bush whose sharp leaves quiver in the wind, a superbly evocative effect that vivifies the skin-tingling surreality of the scene.

The images of the marching dead are both realistic and supernatural. The soldiers are dirty and bloody, some are without limbs; they are dressed in battle-torn uniforms, swathed in bandages, and advance toward the retreating camera. Poetic intertitles are given pictorial designs to emphasize the visionary nature of their text, just as the masking around certain shots of the marching dead shape their progress into an elaborate visual manifestation. This is "visionary surrealism, a romantic language of nightmarish quality."[53] While the literary titles, lyrical superimpositions, and use of real locations speak of a kind of Romantic (even Gothic) sensibility, *J'accuse* also offers an Expressionist sense of shaped reality: "a radical transformation of the visible world, a projection of psychological states into highly constructed filmic spaces."[54]

Gance cuts between scenes of the dead following Jean along the road to the village and shots of the interior space where he is now warning of their approach. As Jean's exclamations grow in intensity, there are further cuts to scenes in which individual members of the dead confront their families. The structure of the narration makes the reality and continuity of these situations extremely ambiguous. Are we witnessing events from the past, present, or future? Are the images being actualized by Jean or are they taking place inside the minds of those he is accusing? Édith later wonders if Jean's audience was subject to a mass hallucination; Gance gives no answer as to the reality or unreality of this finale. The film's lack of definition here has a profoundly unsettling effect on its audience.

The actual confrontation between the living and the dead is equally ambiguous. The film holds back from a visual unification of its two separate strands: the parallel editing of the two spaces in this sequence delineate the villagers and the fallen. This is maintained even when the soldiers arrive at Édith's house and speak to their relatives: they are tinted a different color from that of the living, even though they inhabit the same exterior space. The dead are unable to embrace the living, recoiling when their loved ones approach. The film's apparent awkwardness in resolving such antithetical metaphysics is reminiscent of an earlier sequence. When Jean conjures visions of the ancient Gaul to inspire the French troops, a title states: "And the visionary told them many other things, profound and painful things, which mustn't emerge from the hellish mud through images, because the eyes are still too far from the heart to truly understand."[55] Such a description is both a reason and an excuse *not* to show something. In the finale, there is a similar moment of reticence. Jean speaks on behalf of the men, explaining that they are satisfied the nation is worthy of their death, just as Gance quotes Corneille rather than let the dead speak directly. A title then explains: "These great dead said many things more in the moonlight, mysterious words of the future that the living didn't understand, but which gave them joyful solace." This acts as an ellipsis for a situation that defies representation. The dead back away and, after the stunning image of them carrying their crosses into the horizon, we return to the interior of Édith's home. Jean has lost his mind, seemingly the victim of his own transcendent experience.

Just as the framing device of *Caligari* has been accused of rendering its revolutionary impulses "conformist,"[56] the ambiguities of authority and victimhood in *J'accuse* still provoke argument over Gance's political position regarding the Great War. If the film critiques the "moral blindness" of France's older generation, its "xenophobic elements" make it unclear whether "the filmmaker's pacifism overrides his patriotism."[57] The mix of nationalism and anti-war sentiment in *J'accuse* can be found in the sources from which Gance took inspiration. The film's inflammatory title originates with Émile Zola's open letter to the French President from 1898, as well as a book of the same name published anonymously in 1915 by the German pacifist Richard Grelling.[58] Gance was also influenced by the work of Henri Barbusse, a veteran of the war who later became a dedicated Communist. Grelling denounced the crimes of the Central Powers, Barbusse condemned European capitalism, and Zola attacked the military authorities over their handling of the infamous Dreyfus Affair. Though *J'accuse* clearly holds Germany to task for its imperial aggression, Gance's most forceful accusations are directed against French civilians. His condemnation of social complacency reflects the fact that many in the artistic community felt "revulsion" at France's exploitation of the fallen for nationalist propaganda after the Great War.[59] Barbusse was one of several socialist writers who portrayed the rising dead "taking revenge" against "the capitalist institutions whom they believed had promulgated the war."[60] In *J'accuse*, Jean's accusation against the homefront profiteers and industrialists expresses a common anger felt by soldiers. His fiery tirade is directed at those within France who have betrayed the soldiers and their fight for civilization: a terrifying accusation not only against the onscreen audience, but also against Gance's offscreen audience in 1919.

Just as the "return of the dead" unites the domestic and military aspects of *J'accuse*, so the "return of the undead" in German Expressionist films like *Der müde Tod* (1921) and *Nosferatu* (1922) signals a parallel concern with the trauma of war on a national and personal scale.[61] In *J'accuse*, the blend of the familial with the epic generates disturbing political ramifications. In the first instance, the film's obsession with incomplete/adoptive families defies the critical assertion that the work of Gance presents a patriotic representation of "the Nation as family."[62] Jean's adoption of the half-German Angèle is absorbed into (and complicated by) the narrative concern with revenge and forgiveness. After Édith shows him her child for the first time, there is an extraordinary moment when Jean half-protectively, half-threateningly holds Angèle's throat. Looking into her eyes, he tells her: "I'll teach you how to become French. Then you can find your own way to punish your father as he deserves."[63] *J'accuse* goes on to critique the effect of nationalist zeal on future generations in an alarming sequence where the village children bully Angèle. A local boy wearing a French soldier's kepi is blindfolded and lined up against a wall, whilst Angèle is forced to don a German pickelhaube and pretend to execute him. She refuses and bursts into terrified tears, whereupon her comrades viciously attack her; Angèle rushes home, bleeding and bruised, and burns the helmet on the fire. If this scene asserts that nationality is merely a difference of uniform, the suggestion elsewhere that the fatherless Jean may be Jewish offers a further comment on national/familial identity. A menorah is prominently featured in Mme Diaz's room in several scenes, raising intriguing questions about her son—a man who is introduced as embodying "all intelligence, all melancholy, all tenderness, all France." Rumors of Semitic ancestry caused many of his contemporaries to regard Gance as Jewish—an issue the right-wing press in France would maliciously exploit during the 1930s and subsequent Nazi occupation. Zola's "J'accuse!" attacked French anti-Semitism; as Gance's alter ego in *J'accuse*, is Jean a portrait of culturally repressed creativity and heroism?

The film's final accusation takes place when Jean returns home the day after the villagers have been confronted by the dead. Though present in an oblique, indirect fashion, this last sequence contains an accusation against the ultimate absent father in a film concerned with incomplete families: God. Jean enters his hallway and calls out "Jean! Jean!" by name—he has become divorced from his own identity. He stumbles across his book of pacifist poetry, laughing maniacally at his naïve former self; a title states: "The soldier in him had killed the poet." Jean destroys each page, yet when he reaches his "Ode to the Sun" he hesitates. Suddenly reacting with anger, he flings open the window and launches into a diatribe against the sun, during which he collapses and dies. These lines are not only the last words of the poet, but the last of Gance's film. Jean's ultimate utterance takes the form of a poem but, unlike his earlier "Ode to the Sun," these final (improvised) verses are not abstracted through visualization. Relying upon the stark scripture of white text and black background, Gance's character has abandoned the utopian project of pictorial language. In Jean's last stanza, his verbal articulacy defiantly confronts the sun's visual mutism:

> You lit up this appalling saga,
> Silent, placid, unhesitant,
> Your ghastly face and amputated tongue,
> A sadist on your azure balcony,
> Icily watching to the bitter end!

Jean's poem and final accusation are absent from the original screenplay and the published synopsis, which ends with Jean writing "J'accuse"—"the word of his life"—in chalk on the fireplace.[64] It seems that Gance was avoiding what would have been guaranteed censorship—firstly by excluding the film's climactic declamation from his script and publicity material, secondly by shifting blame onto "the sun" rather than "God." In the original script (and in Gance's correspondence), the poem is called "hymn to the sun," "hymn" being a more openly religious term than "ode," as it was later termed. Taking the logical step of replacing the word "sun" with "God," the accusation takes on a more focused emphasis. Indeed, one British critic suggested that the film's finale seemingly contained a "J'accuse thundered against the Almighty."[65] Given Gance's belief in the "theology of light,"[66] his accusation against the sun—

source of all light—is inescapably a declamation of divine culpability. Rather than posit a lack of God in the universe, it presents the even more terrifying possibility that God is present, but cruel, indifferent, or powerless.

Gance cuts from the interior of Jean's home to a long-shot of the setting sun. The beam of light that falls through the window slowly vanishes; the image fades to darkness, before we see the word "Fin" imposed over a painted title-design of the crucified Christ. This final image is a representation of human suffering: divine spirit made flesh, the son sacrificed by his father. The fatherless Jean dies screaming at the heavens for its malice and complicity in destroying a generation of youth. The poet, who has taken on the role of ombudsman between the living and the dead, curses God by another name—he then dies, rejecting a world where such barbarism is left unchecked.

The image of this ultimate sunset sinking into darkness is profoundly melancholic, if not outright pessimistic. This is in contrast to the final chapter of Barbusse's *Le Feu*, called "Dawn," the last line of which expresses hope that "the sun exists."[67] Though *J'accuse* depicts the transforming power of human kindness (François forgiving Édith and Jean, soldierly comradeship, adoption, etc.), it remains ambiguous concerning the social/political powers of authority. We see the old men naively pushing pins around a map of the Front, and we see the terrifying inheritance of violence in the children's attack on Angèle, but the most obvious absence is that of the generals and politicians behind the war. When an ultimate symbol of power is present, it is the sun itself—an image of natural authority takes the place of human agency. *J'accuse* offers an emotionally unsettling conclusion. Its final accusation is against the absence of power, the failure of an ultimate authority to prevent the slaughter of millions; if there is no explicit answer, there is an implicit question about where responsibility lies that is left for audiences to interpret. The outbursts of denunciation against multiple targets in *J'accuse* imbue it with a sense of maddened despair: anyone and everyone may be morally corrupt. Gance's film is aggressively pacifist, its anger transformed through imagery into an outraged, almost incoherent vision of loss. The impact of its scenes on contemporary audiences must have been overwhelmingly powerful.

Conclusion

Gance was a Romantic Modernist whose desire to synthesize high art with popular entertainment left a legacy of unique films. The conglomeration of styles and genres in *J'accuse* is typical of his belief in cinema's ability to embrace all artistic forms:

> it was the very heart of Gance's life project to overcome contradictions. A huge number of disparate elements are to be found in his films because

he put them there deliberately, so that his work could become the site of their reconciliation.[68]

For Gance and his colleagues—Ricciotto Canudo, Élie Faure, Marcel L'Herbier—cinema was the supreme *Gesamtkunstwerk*, a Wagnerian "synthesis of all the arts." As with numerous other elements of Romanticism, Gance embraced Richard Wagner's conception of art being able to "express the identity, the character, the cultural and mythic aspirations of an entire people, while uniting them in a common ritualistic and . . . religious experience."[69] Expressionism also fed on Wagner's theorization of art's ability to externalize repressed or secret thoughts in artistic form: his conception "foreshadowed, however unwittingly, a dichotomy central to expressionist thinking as to the nature and purpose of art."[70] As German Expressionist films were to do, *J'accuse* demonstrates the multifaceted lineage of experimental cinema.

Critics have often been unable or unwilling to negotiate between Gance's perceived contradictions. From the 1920s to the present day, the most common complaint is that the form and content of his films are irreconcilable. This has generated assumptions about the "reactionary ideology and formal brilliance"[71] of *Napoléon*, as well as more overarching claims that "Gance's technical developments, his stress on the novelty of the image, are seldom related to the meaning of his films."[72] The (Romantic) content of Gance's work is denigrated, yet its (Modernist) form is praised. The "interrelated" relationship between Romanticism and Expressionism is an accepted part of studies in silent German cinema,[73] yet this same connection is seen as problematic in Gance's work. Whilst it may be acknowledged that Gance and Murnau were "technological visionaries of romantic inclination,"[74] any criticism of Murnau's Romanticism has been far less vocal than that of Gance. The latter has become a kind of focus for criticism that established, canonical filmmakers of the silent period have escaped. Through this study of *J'accuse*, I hope to have demonstrated that Gance's filmmaking is considerably more complex and nuanced than has often been suggested.

The inability of some writers to reconcile the divergent aspects of Gance's work may be symptomatic of a wider critical trend. Commentators have sometimes been too eager to categorize artistic movements as belonging either to "a predominantly rational world-view" or to one of the "alternate spasms of irrational or subjective endeavour." The Modernist period has fallen victim to the temptation "to regard ages as being identifiably one or the other." Instead, as Malcolm Bradbury and James McFarlane argue:

> It may help us to understand Modernism if we recognize that these spirits can cross and interfuse . . . [This period shows] a compounding of all

these potentials: the interpenetration, the reconciliation, the coalescence, the fusion—perhaps an appallingly explosive fusion—of reason and un-reason, intellect and emotion, subjective and objective.[75]

The cultural value of *J'accuse* is not lessened because the film does not belong to any single category of cinematic art. Likewise, the "entirely" un-Expressionistic script of *Caligari* does not undermine the film's historical importance: its "most valuable contribution" was "the application of an avant-gardist art concept to the new medium of film."[76] In the 1920s, German cinema sought to create a culturally and economically viable model of film production in exactly the manner that Gance had attempted. The release of *J'accuse* immediately prefigures the growth of both the (German) Expressionist and (French) Impressionist branches of cinematic Modernism.

In 1922, Gance declared that cinema's "rapid technical evolution" had already rendered the protean experimentalism of *J'accuse* outdated. Though "no longer satisfied" with his work from 1919, at the start of the new decade he expresses his "absolute" conviction in "the miraculous powers of our art" and faith in the future of cinema to realize its potential.[77] By the time these comments were published, Gance was already working on the montage of *La Roue*, which would surpass *J'accuse* in scale and cinematic innovation. Jean Cocteau's comment that "[t]here is cinema before and after *La Roue* as there is painting before and after Picasso" confers on Gance a place alongside the great Modernists of fine art.[78] The release of *Napoléon* in 1927 marks the pinnacle of Gance's achievements: its form and content offer a resolution to the problems of national identity and stylistic uncertainties apparent in *J'accuse*. Both films demonstrate that Modernism was "disposed to apocalyptic, crisis-centred views of history,"[79] taking inspiration from epochal upheaval to express the possibility for social change. The French Revolution and the Great War were loci of supreme importance to Gance's conception of history. He transformed both events into mythic resurrections, his cinematic creations both Modernist and Romantic in their rush to proclaim a new vision of the past and the future. Gance's work exemplifies Modernism's "explosive fusion" of old and new ideas. The tensions within *J'accuse* may give it a sense of imbalance and imperfection, but they are fundamental to its impact. The sheer strangeness of its nature is what makes the film so compelling: it is a work of art that still possesses the power to fascinate and to shock.

Notes

1. *Hebdo-Film*, 5 April 1919.
2. *Le Courrier cinématographique*, 5 April 1919.
3. *Le Courrier cinématographique*, 3 May 1919.

4. *L'Ami*, 25 April 1919.
5. Malcolm Bradbury and James McFarlane, "The Name and Nature of Modernism," in Malcolm Bradbury and James McFarlane (eds.), *Modernism: A Guide to European literature, 1890–1930* (Hassocks: Harvester, 1978), p. 23.
6. *The Cheat* appeared in Paris in July–August 1916. There was a private screening of *Intolerance* in October 1917 (the film was not generally released in France until May 1919).
7. René Predal, "Souvenirs de L.-H. Burel," *Revue internationale d'histoire du cinema*, 3 (1975).
8. *J'accuse* premiered in a version that ran to 5250 meters, divided into four parts. For the film's general release in April–May, Gance cut the film down to 4350m in three parts. This was followed by substantial revision in 1921–2, after which the film was rereleased in a version running to 3200m. The latest restoration, begun in 2007 by the Nederlands Filmmuseum and released in September 2008 on a DVD produced by Flicker Alley, runs to 3525m. Despite the survival of Gance's original 1917 screenplay, we lack definitive information about the 1919 versions of the film and their differences to the restored edition.
9. Richard Abel, *French Cinema: The First Wave, 1915–1929* (Princeton, NJ: Princeton University Press, 1984), pp. 79–80. Abel believes the reason for French cinema's obsession with this theme may be "the terrible loss of men in the war as well as the decline in marriages and births during and after the war."
10. Abel Gance, "Pourquoi j'ai fait *J'accuse*," *Hebdo-Film*, 13 April 1922.
11. *The Bioscope*, 29 April 1920.
12. Léon Moussinac, "Cinématographie: *Le Lys brisé*," *Mercure de France*, 1 February 1921.
13. Moussinac calls *Napoléon* "indefensible on the level of content," but spends half of his review praising the film's "remarkable ... technical qualities" and formal innovation. Léon Moussinac, "Un film français: *Napoléon*," *L'humanité*, 23 and 30 April.
14. Abel Gance, Letter to Stouvenaut, 5 May 1920 [typescript], Fonds Abel Gance, GANCE559–B113, Bibliothèque du Film, Paris.
15. Just as some exhibitors had dressed up their theaters and employees in Chinese garb for *Broken Blossoms*, so staff wore French military uniforms and peasant outfits for screenings of *J'accuse*. (*Kine Weekly*, 3 March 1921.)
16. Abel Gance, Letter to Stouvenaut, 3 June 1920 [typescript], Fonds Abel Gance, GANCE559–B113, Bibliothèque du Film, Paris.
17. *The Bioscope*, 29 April 1920.
18. *Kinematograph Weekly*, 29 April 1920.
19. *Kinematograph Weekly*, 22 April 1920.
20. The story of Griffith's encounter with Gance and *J'accuse* can be found in Kevin Brownlow, *The Parade's Gone By* ... (New York: Knopf, 1968), pp. 338–9.
21. Michael Budd, "*The Cabinet of Doctor Caligari*: Production, Reception, History," in Peter Lehman (ed.), *Close viewings: An Anthology of New Film Criticism* (Tallahassee, FL: Florida State University Press, 1990), p. 346.
22. At least ten prints had to be recalled and destroyed in 1928 as they were being shown long after the agreed end-date of the release (Abel Gance and United Artists, Correspondence, 1920–8 [typescript/manuscript], Fonds Abel Gance, GANCE134–B46, Bibliothèque du Film, Paris).
23. David Robinson, *Das Cabinet des Dr. Caligari* (London: BFI, 1997), p. 43.
24. Budd, "*The Cabinet of Doctor Caligari*: Production, Reception, History," p. 335.
25. Robinson, *Das Cabinet des Dr. Caligari*, p. 11.
26. Budd, "*The Cabinet of Doctor Caligari*: Production, Reception, History," p. 335.

27. Ibid. p. 338.
28. Norman King, "The Sound of Silents," *Screen*, Vol. 25, No. 3 (1984), p. 5.
29. Remarkably, nearly three hours of footage survives from this project. (Abel Gance, *Ecce Homo*, 1918 [35 mm rushes], Cinémathèque Française, Fort de Saint-Cyr.)
30. Icart, *Abel Gance*, p. 107.
31. Abel Gance, Screenplay for *Ecce Homo*, 4 November 1919 [typescript], Fonds Abel Gance, 4–COL–36/550, Bibliothèque Nationale, Paris.
32. Abel Gance, *Prisme* (Paris: Gallimard, 1930), p. 69.
33. Abel Gance, "Qu'est-ce que le cinématographe? Un sixième art!," *Ciné-journal*, 9 March 1912.
34. Brownlow, *The Parade's Gone By . . .*, pp. 532–3.
35. Dietrich Scheunemann, "The Double, the Décor, and the Framing Device: Once More on Robert Weine's *The Cabinet of Dr Caligari*," in Dietrich Scheunemann (ed.), *Expressionist Film: New Perspectives* (Baltimore, MD: Camden House, 2007), p. 143.
36. Gance quotes the opening line of Lamartine's "Hymne à la douleur" (1830). He also cites the closing lines of Corneille's "Épitaphe sur la mort de damoiselle Elisabeth Ranquet" (1654).
37. Lemercier was a French soldier who had been killed in 1915. A collection of the letters he wrote to his mother and grandmother during the war was published the following year (Eugène-Emmanuel Lemercier, *Lettres d'un soldat, août 1914–avril 1915* (Paris: Chapelot, 1916)). Gance was contacted by the publishers to say that his use of six extracts from *Lettres d'un soldat* was illegal; but, owing to the "elevated nature of the film," Mme Lemercier (the author's mother) would allow their inclusion, as long as the intertitles were modified to include accreditation. (Librairie Chapelot-Paris, Letter to Abel Gance, 23 May 1919 [typescript], Fonds Abel Gance, 4–COL–36/551, Bibliothèque Nationale, Paris.)
38. Susan Hayward, *Cinema Studies: The Key Concepts*, 3rd edn (London: Routledge, 2006), p. 196.
39. Lionel Landry, "Caligarisme ou la revanche du théâtre," *Cinéa*, 28 April 1922.
40. Blaise Cendrars, "Sur *Le Cabinet du Docteur Caligari*," *Cinéa*, 2 June 1922.
41. Émile Vuillermoz, "*La Cabinet du Docteur Caligari*," *Cinémagazine*, 24 March 1922.
42. Richard Abel, *French Cinema: The First Wave*, p. 88.
43. Abel Gance, Screenplay for *J'accuse*, October 1917 [typescript/manuscript], Fonds Abel Gance. GANCE117–B45, Bibliothèque du Film, Paris.
44. Ibid.
45. *The Bioscope*, 29 April 1920.
46. Gance wanted to use sound recordings of machine-guns and artillery alongside moments of silence and specific pieces of music. His musical choices for *J'accuse* included: Bach, Beethoven, Berlioz, Bizet, Franck, Grieg, Rachmaninov, Saint-Saëns, Tchaikovsky, and Wagner. (Abel Gance, Notes for the use of music and sound in *J'accuse*, October 1920 [manuscript], Fonds Abel Gance, 4–COL–36/551, Bibliothèque Nationale, Paris.)
47. Gilberto Perez, *The Material Ghost: Films and their Medium* (Baltimore, MD: Johns Hopkins University Press, 2000), p. 123.
48. Icart, *Abel Gance*, p. 143.
49. Abel Gance, "La Cinématographie c'est la musique de la lumière," *Comœdia*, 16 March 1923.
50. Émile Vuillermoz, "*La Roue*," *Cinémagazine*, 23 February and 2 March 1923.
51. Jay Winter, *Sites of Memory, Sites of Mourning. The Great War in European Cultural History*, 2nd edn (Cambridge: Cambridge University Press, 2000), p. 133.

52. The last reasonably complete domestic print of *J'accuse*, tinted and toned, was preserved in the Cinémathèque française, but disappeared sometime in the 1980s. Alongside archival documentation, accounts of this lost print reveal discrepancies between its color scheme and that of the new restoration, which was based on a truncated tinted print. In the climactic sequence, the Cinémathèque print used purple tinting for the dead and red for the fire-lit interiors; the current restoration uses blue-tone-pink and orange.
53. Jay Winter, *Sites of Memory, Sites of Mourning*, p. 136.
54. Sabine Hake, *German National Cinema* (London: Routledge, 2001), p. 29.
55. This phrase is reminiscent of Gance's view that "In cinema, the heart is still too far from the eyes"—evidence of his continual search for better means of communicating the emotive, spiritual truth of reality through filmic means. (Abel Gance, "Autour du moi et du monde: le cinéma de demain," *Conférencia*, 5 September 1929.)
56. Siegfried Kracauer, *From Caligari to Hitler: A Psychological History of the German Film*, 2nd rev. edn (Princeton, NJ: Princeton University Press, 2004), p. 67.
57. Van Kelly, "The Ambiguity of Individual Gestures: Revisions of World War I in Abel Gance's *J'accuse*, Alain's *Mars ou La guerre jugé*, and Bertrand Tavernier's *La vie et rien d'autre*," *South Central Review*, Vol. 17, No. 3 (2000), pp. 11–12.
58. Émile Zola, "J'accuse ...!," *L'Aurore*, 13 January 1898; [Richard Grelling], *J'accuse, von einem Deutschen* (Lausanne: Payot, 1915).
59. Jay Winter, *Sites of Memory, Sites of Mourning*, p. 210. Winter's account analyses imagery of the living dead among nationalist writers like Maurice Barrès and Jacques Péricard, as well as in the work of left-wing writers like Roland Dorgelès and Barbusse.
60. Jean-Yves Le Naour, *Le Soldat Inconnu Vivant* (Paris: Hachette Littératures, 2008), pp. 88–91.
61. Anton Kaes, *Shell Shock Cinema: Weimar Culture and the Wounds of War* (Princeton, NJ: Princeton University Press, 2009), pp. 87–129.
62. Norman King, *Abel Gance: A Politics of spectacle* (London: BFI, 1984), p. 154.
63. This scene directly echoes one in *Mater Dolorosa*, where Gilles Berliac threateningly clasps the throat of his son after discovering that the child may not be his. The gesture is repeated by Sisif on his son in *La Roue* when his adopted daughter, with whom both men are in love, reappears and reignites the oedipal drama at the heart of the film.
64. *La Cinématographie Française*, 12 April 1919.
65. G. A. A., "Men with a message to the world," *Daily Express*, 1 June 1920.
66. Stephen Philip Kramer and James Michael Welsh, *Abel Gance* (Boston, MA: Twayne, 1978), p. 56.
67. Henri Barbusse, *Le Feu* (Paris: Flammarion, 1916), p. 378.
68. Alan Williams, *Republic of Images: A History of French Filmmaking* (Cambridge, MA: Harvard University Press, 1992), p. 90.
69. Peter Vergo, "The origins of Expressionism and the Notion of the *Gesamtkunstwerk*," in Shulamith Behr, David Fanning and Douglas Jarman (eds.), *Expressionism Reassessed* (Manchester: Manchester University Press, 1993), p. 13.
70. Ibid. p. 18.
71. Ginette Vincendeau, *The Companion to French Cinema* (London: BFI, 1996), p. 81.
72. David Thomson, *A Biographical Dictionary of Film*, 3rd edn (New York: Knopf, 1994), p. 273.
73. Lotte H. Eisner, *The Haunted Screen: Expressionism in the German Cinema and*

the Influence of Max Reinhardt (trans. Roger Greaves), 2nd edn (Berkeley, CA: University of California Press, 2008 [1952]), p. 15.
74. Malte Hagener, *Moving Forward, Looking Back. The European Avant-Garde and the Invention of Film Culture, 1919–1939* (Amsterdam: Amsterdam University Press, 2007), p. 80.
75. Malcolm Bradbury and James McFarlane, "The Name and Nature of Modernism," pp. 47–8.
76. Scheunemann, "The Double, the Décor, and the Framing Device," p. 139.
77. Gance, "Pourquoi j'ai fait *J'accuse*."
78. Sophia Daria, *Abel Gance: Hier et demain* (Paris: La Palatine, 1959), p. 82.
79. Bradbury and McFarlane, "The Name and Nature of Modernism," p. 20.

9. HERE AMONG THE DEAD: THE PHANTOM CARRIAGE (1921) AND THE CINEMA OF THE OCCULTED TABOO

Robert Guffey

"It's a spooky place to wait for midnight, here among the dead."
David Holm, *The Phantom Carriage*, 1921

THY SOUL SHALL BEAR WITNESS!

At its controversial best the cinema has always been about breaking taboos, and perhaps the biggest taboo of all is death. Victor Sjöström's 1921 touchstone film *The Phantom Carriage* combines both transgressive subjects into a single narrative that flips the binary opposites of the physical and the spiritual upside down. In Western civilization, explorations of metaphysical quandaries have always been somewhat frowned upon unless they are conducted in a socially acceptable context, that is, within the constraints of academia or a mainstream religion such as Christianity. As early as 1921, when cinema was just leaving its infancy stage, Sjöström dared to explore the nature of the spiritual and the physical in a context that appears, on the surface, to be socially acceptable, but in fact draws upon the esoteric philosophies of occult organizations that have never existed anywhere except on the fringe. *The Phantom Carriage* is an early example of filmmaking that cleverly camouflages its true intent, a tradition of the occulted taboo that continues to this day.

The main purpose of fiction, particularly the popular brand of fiction so prevalent in cinema, has always been about discussing the taboos of the day in a safe context—safe, that is, for both the audience and the author. The fictional veneer allows the audience to take in vital information without being offended while also allowing the author to hide his true purpose behind the excuse that the proceedings are all in jest. "We're just entertainers, Grand Inquisitor, that's all. Nothing to be too concerned about." A capital jest, indeed.

In the early 1600s a playwright named William Shakespeare knew this very well, and employed the technique to masterful effect in one crowd-pleasing production after another. Shakespeare's plays, of course, were never intended to be worshipped from afar by literary scholars as rarified pieces of High Art preserved under glass, but rather to be enjoyed as intense melodramas filled with blood and guts and bawdy humor. Shakespeare's plays were the seventeenth-century version of tent-pole summer blockbusters, complete with incessant, Quentin Tarantino-like violence, improbable plot twists and soap-opera-like revelations to keep the crowd's attention fixed to the stage. Shakespeare managed to intersperse within these crowd-pleasing spectacles covert messages of occult knowledge and political satire that would have resulted in imprisonment or even death for anyone attempting to utter such egregious pronouncements in an open and forthright manner. Shakespeare himself, rather puckishly, displays this method for all to see in the middle of *Hamlet* (1600) when the young and vengeful prince stages an ostensibly fictional melodrama, *The Murder of Gonzago*, for the benefit of the King in order to reveal the conspiratorial machinations with which he believes the King assassinated Hamlet's father for the purpose of attaining the throne.

At its core, Shakespeare's *Macbeth* (1606) is an occult allegory displaying the hermetic secrets of the third degree of Freemasonry in a fictional context, thus transmitting to a mass audience what would otherwise have been hidden information to which only Masonic initiates at the time would have been privy.[1] The purpose of popular fiction, the kind that lasts throughout the ages, has always been to transmit sensitive information to the masses in a form they can appreciate. The unconscious mind, that which hums secrets to us when we're asleep, often picks up far more information than the conscious mind, which so often struggles to understand concepts far beyond its grasp. Poetry, fiction, paintings, song—all of these art forms play on the subliminal brain without even trying. A strident reformer barking through a loud speaker on a street corner almost never succeeds in converting anyone to his cause. The conscious mind rejects him and his message merely owing to the fact that the average person resents being *talked* at. People want to be seduced. And what seduces better than the gentle caress and the whisper in the ear? Wrap your message in a catchy tune that rhymes and people will listen . . . and even pay to hear it again. People paid to hear and see Shakespeare's plays, and they still do when so many run-of-the-mill melodramas produced in the same year as *Macbeth* have long since faded into obscurity. There is a reason Bram Stoker's

1897 Gothic melodrama *Dracula* has survived into the twenty-first century while James Malcolm Rymer's vampire novel *Varney the Vampire* (1845–7) is rarely read today. Stoker did his research. *Dracula* manages to transmit genuine hermetic knowledge through a page-turning yarn filled with horrific sights and subliminal sexuality. The last two elements, however, are not the elements that have granted *Dracula* immortality. No, it's the genuine hermetic core of Stoker's novel that is the real achievement, that continues to speak to us through the grotesque and arabesque mask of entertainment.

Talents as diverse as Miguel de Cervantes, John Milton, Alexander Pope, Jonathan Swift, William Blake, Mary Shelley, Sir Walter Scott, Johann Wolfgang von Goethe, Edgar Allan Poe, Herman Melville, Lewis Carroll, Jules Verne, Oscar Wilde, L. Frank Baum, Edgar Rice Burroughs, Hermann Hesse, H. P. Lovecraft, William S. Burroughs, Richard Matheson, Ian Fleming, Philip K. Dick, Thomas Pynchon, Alan Moore, and J. K. Rowling have all understood this process and employ fiction for this exact purpose: to tell the hidden truth in an acceptable fashion, in a manner that will be embraced by the masses rather than rejected out of hand.

In the 1600s, Shakespeare used the most popular medium that existed in that day to "broadcast" his peculiar messages of transcendence.[2] Throughout the eighteenth and nineteenth centuries, however, the most popular medium became the novel, and thus Mary Shelley's bastard child of ancient black arts and cutting-edge scientific breakthroughs, *Frankenstein*, arose from the printed page rather than the stage of the Globe Theatre. Alice's tumble through the astral realms played out across the pages of a seemingly innocent children's book. Dorothy Gale's metaphysical journey similarly emerged from the nascent field of the American fairy tale.

When the Victorian era gave way to the twentieth century, the novel was eclipsed by a brand new art form as strange as the patchwork demon that emerged from Mary Shelley's imagination way back in 1818. Cinema evolved slowly over the first decades of the twentieth century, then began to mature to a drastic and impressive degree in the early 1920s. The more revolutionary-minded stage actors and playwrights saw the possibilities of this new form as a method of transmitting spiritual knowledge to the proletariat in a way no Catholic priest could ever attain behind a puny pulpit in even the largest urban cathedral. At the forefront of this burgeoning artistic revolution was Victor Sjöström, and his masterpiece in this taboo-breaking medium was his 1921 film *The Phantom Carriage*, an adaptation of Selma Lagerlöf's 1912 novel entitled *Thy Soul Shall Bear Witness!*[3]

What is most sly and impressive about Sjöström's considerable achievement is that he manages to retain Lagerlöf's occult message while disguising it in the form of a quasi-Christian morality play. When one scratches just the beneath the surface, however, one can see that *The Phantom Carriage* is in truth a transgressive allegory drawn from the teachings of Theosophy, of which Selma Lagerlöf was a committed student.

Theosophy is a philosophical-religious system adhered to by members of the Theosophical Society, an organization founded in New York in 1875 by Helena Blavatsky, Henry Steel Olcott and others. The purpose of the society, according to Lewis Spence's 1920 book *An Encyclopedia of Occultism*, is as follows:

> to promote the study of comparative religion and philosophy ... It is set forth in the Theosophical system that all the great religions of the world originated from one supreme source and that they are merely expressions of a central "Wisdom Religion" vouchsafed to various races of the earth in such a manner as was best suited to time and geographical circumstances. Underlying these was a secret doctrine or esoteric teaching which, it was stated, had been the possession for ages of certain *Mahatmas*, or adepts in mysticism and occultism. With these Madame Blavatsky claimed to be in direct communication ...[4]

During his audio commentary on the digitally restored Criterion DVD of *The Phantom Carriage*, released in the autumn of 2011, film historian Casper Tybjerg has this to say about Lagerlöf's interest in mysticism: "Lagerlöf was powerfully attracted by Theosophy and Spiritualism, and the influence of these esoteric doctrines is palpable ... Lagerlöf believed that Theosophy and Spiritualism held out the promise of bringing together religion and scientific theories, like the Theory of Evolution."[5] Here Tybjerg emphasizes Lagerlöf's intense desire to meld together concepts that many people assume to be polar opposites: religion and science. Significantly, reconciling extreme dualities is a prominent concern throughout Victor Sjöström's *The Phantom Carriage*.

The Phantom Carriage is filled with dualities, and thus reflective of Theosophy and Gnosticism in particular. From its beginning, Theosophy has been interwoven with Gnosticism, a suppressed form of Christianity with roots that extend at least as far back as the second century CE. To understand the dualities in *The Phantom Carriage*, it is important to understand the unique dualities inherent in Gnosticism. According to Dr Stephan Hoeller, Bishop of the Gnostic Church in Los Angeles:

> The Gnostic position ... might be called qualified dualism ... The Gnostics had their own myth about the origins of good and evil. It begins with a boundless, blissful Fullness—the Pleroma—that is beyond all manifest existence. The Pleroma is both the abode of and the essential nature of the True Ultimate God (*alethes theos*). Before time and before memory, this ineffable Fullness extended itself into the lower regions of being. In the course of this emanation, it manifested itself in a number of intermediate deities, *demiurgoi*, who were rather like great angels,

endowed with enormous talents of creativity and organization. Some of these beings, however, became alienated from their supernal source and so took on evil tendencies. They created a physical world long before the creation of humans, and they created it in the likeness of their own imperfect natures.

Thus the will that created the world was tainted with self-will, arrogance, and the hunger for power; through the works performed by these alienated beings, evil came to penetrate creation. Ever since then, as the Gnostic teacher Basilides reportedly said, "Evil adheres to created existence as rust adheres to iron." As part of the creation, human beings also reflect the flawed nature of the creators. The human body is subject to disease, death, and other evils; even the soul (psyche) is not free from imperfection. Only the spirit (pneuma), hidden deep within the human essence, remains free from the evil and tends toward the True God.[6]

The Phantom Carriage, rather like human beings in the Gnostic creation myth, is infused with paradoxes. The film is a strange and elegant mixture of realism and expressionism, Christianity and hermeticism, complexity and simplicity. Lagerlöf (as author) and Sjöström (as screenwriter/actor/director) weave together elements of both social realism and fairy-tale-like phantasmagoria into a seamless whole, a style of cinematic storytelling that has not been successfully realized on the screen in recent years, with the possible exception of Guillermo del Toro's 2006 film *Pan's Labyrinth*, which also juxtaposes scenes of brutal realism with images of the transcendent.

Despite a relatively complex story structure composed of flashbacks within flashbacks and stories within stories, the central conceit of *The Phantom Carriage* is not at all dissimilar to that of a traditional fairy tale. Once upon a time, on New Year's Eve, three men (old before their time) sit in a dilapidated cemetery passing a bottle of cheap liquor back and forth while talking about a local legend: that of Death's Driver. According to the prevailing myth, the last person killed on New Year's Eve must take over the reins of a horse-drawn carriage fashioned by Death himself. For the next year, that person must serve Death by collecting the souls of the recently deceased until the following New Year's Eve. Inevitably (at least according to the logic of fairy tales), our protagonist, an alcoholic ne'er-do-well named David Holm (played by Victor Sjöström), is murdered just before the stroke of midnight. Then comes Death's Driver, who just so happens to be a fellow derelict named Georges (Tore Svennberg), the man who first told Holm about the legend. Georges died exactly a year before in Holm's presence under very similar circumstances. As in all fairy tales, coincidence and fate play a crucial role in this film.

Georges removes Holm from his physical body, binds his astral body hand and foot with rope, and leads him on a soul-searing journey through the world of the living, forcing Holm to confront the consequences of his misspent life in a sermonizing manner that might remind one of Charles Dickens' *A Christmas Carol* (1843), but *The Phantom Carriage* lacks all of the sentimentalism so integral to Dickens' far more famous novel. This is what is most admirable about *The Phantom Carriage*. What at first seems to be a somewhat traditional moral fable inspired by typical Christian piety turns out, if one peers beneath the obvious, to be something far more subversive.

"Captive, Come Forth from thy Prison"

A clue to this esoteric subtext lies in the life of its author, the first female to win the Nobel Prize for Literature, Selma Lagerlöf. As mentioned before, Lagerlöf was a devoted student of Theosophy, in particular the writings of Helena Blavatsky, whose seminal work *Isis Unveiled* was first published in 1877 when Lagerlöf was only nineteen.[7] No doubt, *Isis Unveiled* had a major impact on the teenage Lagerlöf, as strong traces of it can be found both in Sjöström's *The Phantom Carriage* and in Lagerlöf's original source material. Sjöström was determined to bring to the screen a faithful adaptation of Lagerlöf's novel, and even performed the entire screenplay for her not long after its completion in order to win the author's approval. Except for a few minor criticisms, she did indeed grant him the approval he was seeking (Tybjerg).

Lagerlöf's novel is about spiritual evolution, an evolution that can only come about by freeing oneself from the confinements of the flesh. While traditional Christianity celebrates the human form (i.e. God is made manifest in the flesh, in the form of the Son, which is why the followers of Christ eat of His flesh symbolically every Sunday during the Eucharist), Gnosticism is quite different; it rejects the flesh and considers the material plane to be a realm of the unreal, not unlike Plato's view of the world as expressed in his "Allegory of the Caves" (380 BC) in which human beings and their material concerns are likened to shadows flitting about on a cave wall, the "real world" lying in the light beyond the entrance to the cave. In Gnosticism, the flesh, merely a cage that has temporarily trapped the divine spark buried deep in the core of every human being, must be overcome before true knowledge (*gnosis*) can be attained. In Christianity, anyone who accepts Christ into his or her heart has been saved. After that point, he or she knows everything that needs to be known; no further knowledge is required or even encouraged. In Gnosticism there are always much greater Mysteries waiting for those who are willing—or, in David Holm's case, forced—to walk the arduous path toward *gnosis* and the rejection of material concerns. This is the journey taken by David Holm in *The Phantom Carriage*.

A leading Theosophist, C. W. Leadbeater, wrote the following in his 1926 book *Glimpses of Masonic History* (later republished under the title *Ancient Mystic Rites*):

Even to-day it is quite commonly thought that Christianity had no mysteries, and some of its followers boast that in it nothing is hidden. That mistaken idea has been so sedulously impressed upon the world that it leads many people to feel a certain distaste for the wiser faiths which met all needs, and to think of them as unnecessarily hiding part of the truth or grudging it to the world. In the old days there was no such thought as this; it was recognized that only those who came up to a certain standard of life were fit to receive the higher instruction, and those who wished for it set to work to qualify themselves for it. Knowledge is power, and people must prove their fitness before they will be entrusted with power; for the object of the whole scheme is human evolution, and the interests of evolution would not be served by promiscuous publication of occult truth.

Those who maintain the above-mentioned opinion about Christianity are unacquainted with the history of the Church. Though many of the early Christian writers are bitterly hostile to the Mysteries, they indignantly deny the suggestion that in their Church they have nothing worthy of that name, and claim that their Mysteries are in every way as good and deep and far-reaching as those of their "pagan" opponents. S. Clement says: "He who has been purified in baptism and then initiated into the little Mysteries (has acquired, that is to say, the habits of self-control and reflection), becomes ripe for the greater Mysteries, for Epopteia or Gnosis, the scientific knowledge of God." The same writer also said: "It is not lawful to reveal to profane persons the Mysteries of the Logos."[8]

Unless, perhaps, such revelation arrives in the form of cinematic fiction?

When Georges, now Death's Driver, commands David Holm to abandon his body, he utters the sentence, "Captive, come forth from thy prison." This view of the flesh as a jail cell that is holding back the spiritual evolution of mankind is not an attitude one would find in traditional Christianity, whilst it is indeed an important aspect of Gnosticism. In *Thy Soul Shall Bear Witness!*, when Lagerlöf describes Holm's eventual return to his physical body, the material plane is referred to as "something suffocating and deadly" and Holm is worried that his "soul's fresh development [will] stop if he [becomes] a mortal once more." After his sojourn on the astral plane, Holm is now convinced that "All his happiness was awaiting him in another world."[9]

The evolution of the spirit is the core of Theosophy, which drew heavily from the ancient teachings of Gnosticism. (One need only consult Blavatsky's aforementioned *Isis Unveiled*, arguably the ultimate Theosophical text, to see the truth of that statement.) Perhaps this is why Charles Darwin's relatively new theory of evolution was supported by Blavatsky, no doubt one of the reasons so many intellectuals of the late nineteenth and early twentieth centuries, such as Selma Lagerlöf herself, saw Theosophy and Gnosticism as vital alternatives to what they perceived to be the backwards, anti-scientific views of the traditional Christian church.

In Chapter 2 of his concise but comprehensive 2002 book *Gnosticism: New Light on the Ancient Tradition of Inner Knowing*, Dr Hoeller writes:

> Gnosticism holds that human beings are essentially not the product of the material world. The important term in this statement is *essentially*, for Gnosticism focuses on the essence rather than the physical and mental containers that envelop this essence. Though the theory of biological evolution did not exist at the time of the ancient Gnostics, one might guess that unlike their mainstream Christian brethren, they would not have objected to it. For they believed that the human body originates on earth but the human spirit has come from afar, from the realm of the Fullness, where the true Godhead dwells . . .
>
> People are generally ignorant of the divine spark residing within them. This ignorance serves the interests of the archons,[10] who act as cosmic slave masters, keeping the light sparks in bondage. Anything that causes us to remain attached to earthly things, including the mental concepts we hold, keeps us in enslavement to these lesser cosmic rulers. The majority of men and women are like Adam, who was asleep in Paradise. Modern esoteric teachers (notably G. Gurdjieff) have capitalized on this Gnostic theme, representing humanity as a throng of sleepwalkers. Awakening from this sleep is the combined result of our desire for liberation and the supernal help extended to us.[11]

In Lagerlöf's narrative, Holm's "supernal help" takes the form of an etheric being who—thanks to his "cosmic master," Death—can pierce the veil between dimensional planes. Fortunately for Holm, Death's Driver is not enough of a slave that he is unable to exercise his own free will when he wants to, for ultimately it's the Driver's decision to allow Holm a final chance at life once the man's astral body—freed from its cage of flesh—has attained a sufficient amount of gnosis through the metaphysical journey imposed upon it by the phantom carriage and its "supernal" Driver. David Holm has, at last, evolved and Death's Driver is able to respond in kind.

From the perspective of Theosophists like Selma Lagerlöf and Helena Blavatsky, Charles Darwin's theory of the origin of the species—though hardly Theosophical in intent—offers sound advice to the unenlightened: evolve or die. This is the dilemma forced upon Holm just before the stroke of midnight when a glass bottle—significantly, a bottle filled with alcohol—wielded by an angered ruffian slams into the back of his skull, evicting his astral body from its physical shell, not unlike a fish pushed out of the ocean by volcanic activity and compelled to breath air for the first time, or a hominid forced to create fire from two sticks in order to survive a sudden blizzard.

In Chapter 5 of *Isis Unveiled Vol. I: Science*, entitled "The Ether, or 'Astral Light,'" Blavatsky has this to say about the metaphysical overtones of Darwinism:

> Modern science insists upon the doctrine of evolution; so do human reason and the "secret doctrine," and the idea is corroborated by the ancient legends and myths, and even by the Bible itself when it is read between the lines ... The word *evolution* speaks for itself. The germ of the present human race must have preexisted in the parent of this race, as the seed, in which lies hidden the flower of next summer, was developed in the capsule of its parent-flower; the parent may be but *slightly* different, but it still differs from its future progeny. The antediluvian ancestors of the present elephant and lizard were, perhaps, the mammoth and the plesiosaurus; why should not the progenitors of our human race have been the "giants" of the *Vedas*, the *Völuspa*, and the *Book of Genesis*? While it is positively absurd to believe the "transformation of species" to have taken place according to some of the more materialistic views of the evolutionists, it is but natural to think that each genus, beginning with the mollusks and ending with monkey-man, has modified from its own primordial and distinctive form.[12]

This was pretty strong stuff in 1877. Traditional Christianity is still unable to reconcile Darwin's century-old scientific theories with the core of their religion, but only eighteen years after the publication of *The Origin of Species* Blavatsky was already incorporating Darwin's work into her metaphysical framework. That Theosophy offered both a complex spiritual framework as well as an acceptance of the cutting-edge science of the day was attractive to writers, poets, painters, artists, and intellectuals of all sorts. Lagerlöf was by no means the only intellectual of the late nineteenth and early twentieth century drawn into Theosophy's fold. Jean Toomer, for example, author of the breakthrough 1923 novel *Cane*, was associated with Theosophy for most of his life.

Theosophy essentially updated the suppressed teachings of Gnosticism (i.e. the earliest form of Christianity before the tenets of the New Testament were reduced down to the present, legalistic, formalized structure we know today) and resurrected them for a modern intellectual audience that was losing its residual interest in organized religion and grasping for a deeper and more vital spiritual center to take its place. In the aforementioned *Glimpses of Masonic History*, C. W. Leadbeater sums up the entirety of traditional Christianity with this hypothetical commandment: "Thou shalt not think."[13] In contrast, Theosophy and Gnosticism celebrated the pursuit of knowledge, both intellectual and spiritual. But it is David Holm's *spiritual* evolution that most concerns

Lagerlöf and Sjöström. Spiritually, at the beginning of the film, Holm hasn't even reached the infant stage. He's still trapped in the womb, Plato's Cave of Shadows.

In *Isis Unveiled Vol. I*, Blavatsky paints a picture of a universe that has emerged from the process of evolution, replacing Darwin's scientific talk with the language of the poet and the mystic:

> at the creation of the *prima materia*, while the grossest portions of it were used for the physical embryo-world, the more divine essence of it pervaded the universe, invisibly permeating and enclosing within its ethereal waves the newly-born infant, developing and stimulating it to activity as it slowly evolved out of the eternal chaos.[14]

That chaos remains embedded in every molecule of our imperfect world, and in Lagerlöf's narrative David Holm becomes a symbol of that chaos. Holm has wasted his life on alcohol and the pleasures of the flesh, neglecting the spiritual bonds between his wife, Anna (Hilda Borgström), and their children. His younger brother, seduced into a life of alcohol by Holm's encouragement, ends up in prison on a murder charge owing to Holm's actions. This impediment, however, is not enough to sway Holm from his downward spiraling path and he is abandoned by his family. Holm is now consumed by anger and resentment, and his acts of self-destruction—his alcoholism, in particular—intensify, culminating in an incurable case of tuberculosis.

The prevalence of alcoholism in Lagerlöf's tale is not without Theosophical significance. Many Theosophists believe that alcohol is dangerous not just to the flesh, but to one's astral body as well. In his 1927 book *Chakras: A Monograph*, C. W. Leadbeater explains that human beings are surrounded by what he calls "the etheric web." The etheric web is "the protection provided by nature to prevent a premature opening up of communication between the planes—a development which could lead to nothing but injury."[15] Leadbeater goes on to say:

> The malpractices which may more gradually injure this protective web are of two classes—use of alcohol or narcotic drugs, and the deliberate endeavour to throw open the doors which nature has kept closed ... Certain drugs and drinks—notably alcohol and all the narcotics, including tobacco—contain matter which on breaking up volatizes, and some of it passes from the physical plane to the astral ...
>
> When this takes place in the body of man these constituents rush out through the chakras in the opposite direction to that for which they are intended, and in doing this repeatedly they seriously injure and finally destroy the delicate web. This deterioration or destruction may be

brought about in two different ways, according to the type of the person concerned and to the proportion of the constituents in his etheric and astral bodies. First, the rush of volatizing matter actually burns away the web, and therefore leaves the door open to all sorts of irregular forces and evil influences.[16]

When Leadbeater uses the phrase "evil influences," he is literally referring to non-physical entities from other dimensions that—according to Theosophists—can possess human beings who have laid themselves open to invasion through continual acts of debauchery and the harboring of various unhealthy obsessions. In both Lagerlöf's novel and Sjöström's film, these "evil influences" are symbolized by an incurable disease, the tuberculosis that ravages Holm's body. Just as possessing entities can pass on their evil influence to those who surround the possessed, Holm's tuberculosis threatens to reach out and destroy even the most pure of heart.

In one of the film's many flashbacks, a Salvation Army sister named Edit (Astrid Holm) chooses to risk her life for David Holm the night he appears on the Salvation Army's doorstep in an inebriated state. While Holm sleeps off his drink in a cot, Edit decides to sew up the numerous holes in his infected clothes, unknowingly picking up his disease. When Holm wakes up the next morning, we are shocked at his violent reaction to Edit's selflessness. He mocks her, laughs, and rips all the new patches off the coat while Edit can only stand and watch, horrified. Holm is so proud and arrogant that he would rather suffer extreme physical discomfort than be indebted to the sister's noble act of kindness. To Holm's disgust, however, this merely strengthens Edit's desire to save him. Her efforts do indeed pay off, but she doesn't live to see Holm's ultimate transformation (which occurs at the very end of the film). She dies just past the stroke of midnight, on January 1, from the tuberculosis to which David Holm had exposed her a year before.

This view of tuberculosis as a corrupting demon continues throughout *The Phantom Carriage*. In one particularly intense scene, David Holm threatens his wife (with whom he has been reunited thanks to Edit's efforts) by breathing into the faces of his sleeping children, attempting in his alcohol-induced madness to pass his infection onto his children. The chaos in the scene builds and builds, until at last Anne decides to take the children and flee once more. She locks Holm in the kitchen, then tries to wake the children and escape. Sjöström effectively uses crosscutting (still a new technique in 1921) to build the tension as Holm attempts to break through the locked door with an ax, a scene mirrored fifty-nine years later in Stanley Kubrick's 1980 film, *The Shining*, when Jack Torrance (Jack Nicholson) attempts to kill his family by cutting through a locked door with an ax. It's interesting to note that in *The Shining*, Nicholson's character (an alcoholic, like David Holm) is not just symbolically possessed by demons—he really *is* possessed. One cannot help but wonder what Theosophical significance C. W. Leadbeater, or even Selma Lagerlöf, would have seen in *The Shining*.

Just before Edit is about to die owing to the infection Holm has spread to her, Death's Driver arrives with Holm's astral body in tow. Before this point Holm has been unable to interact with the material world while in his nonphysical state . . . until the moment Holm expresses genuine sorrow at the pain he has wrought. Only in that second is his astral body capable of penetrating the planes and touching Edit's hand. His spiritual evolution has allowed him to transcend the barriers that separate most people from the higher realms of consciousness. Edit feels the touch and sees him. She is able to recognize the initial spark of transformation in his eyes before passing on.

In Lagerlöf's novel, the Theosophical subtext of this scene is even more obvious. Moments after Edit dies, Death's Driver addresses Holm:

> "Come with me hence at once," he went on; "we two have nothing further to do here. They who have to receive her are come."
>
> He dragged David Holm out with extreme violence. The latter thought that he saw the room suddenly filled with bright figures. He seemed to meet them on the stairs, and in the street—but he was whirled away at such a giddy pace that he could not distinguish them.[17]

Compare Lagerlöf's "bright figures" ascending the stairs with the following passage from Annie Besant's book, well-known to Theosophy's adherents, entitled *A Study in Consciousness*. In this excerpt Besant describes a group of supernatural beings whose task is to guide human beings away from spiritual devolution:

> They have received various names in the various religions, but all religions recognize the fact of their existence and of their work. The Sanskrit name Devas—the Shining Ones—is the most general, and aptly describes the most marked characteristics of their appearance, a brilliant luminous radiance. The Hebrew, Christian, and Muhammadan religions call them Archangels and Angels. The Theosophist—to avoid sectarian connotations—names them, after their habitat, Elementals; and this title has the further advantage that it reminds the student of their connection with the five "Elements" of the ancient world: Aether, Air, Fire, Water, and Earth . . . These beings have bodies formed out of the elemental essence of the kingdom to which they belong, flashing many-hued bodies, changing form at the will of the indwelling entity. They form a vast host, ever actively at work, labouring at the elemental essence to improve its quality, taking it to form their own bodies, throwing it off and taking

other portions of it, to render it more responsive; they are also constantly busied in the shaping of forms, in aiding human Egos on the way to reincarnation in building their new bodies, bringing materials of the needed kind and helping in its arrangements. The less advanced the Ego the greater the directive work of the Deva; with animals they do almost all the work, and practically all with vegetables and minerals. They are the active agents in the work of the Logos [the Word of God], carrying out all the details of His world-plan, and aiding the countless evolving lives to find the materials they need for their clothing. All antiquity recognized the indispensable work they do in the worlds, and China, Egypt, India, Persia, Greece, Rome, tell the same story. The belief in the higher of them is not only found in all religions, but memories of those of the desire and of the ethereal physical plane linger on in folk-lore, in stories of "Nature-spirits", "Fairies", "Gnomes", "Trolls", and under many other names, memories of days when men were less deeply enwrapped in material interests, and more sensitive to the influences that played upon them from the subtler worlds.[18]

A Study in Consciousness was published in 1904, only eight years before the publication of *Thy Soul Shall Bear Witness!* Lagerlöf undoubtedly read a great deal of Annie Besant's work, as Besant was elected President of the Theosophical Society in 1907.

Besant, as well as many other Theosophists, delved into the ancient rites of Freemasonry owing to its numerous Gnostic and Kabbalistic roots. In 1902, Besant was initiated into the International Order of Co-Freemasonry, eventually becoming its Grand Commander. Perhaps it is no surprise, therefore, that Lagerlöf's story—similar to Shakespeare's *Macbeth*—can be viewed as a quasi-Masonic allegory that subtly mirrors the rituals of the third degree of Freemasonry.

The third degree is a ritual in which the initiate is metaphorically killed with a violent blow to the back of the head delivered by fellow Masons acting as ruffians (not unlike the ne'er-do-wells we see lounging about in the cemetery at the beginning of *The Phantom Carriage*, one of whom kills Holm with a similar blow to the back of the head), resurrected by a command from the Master of the Lodge, then granted esoteric wisdom via a symbolism-laden, metaphysical journey enacted within the confines of the Lodge's ritual room. The initiate takes on the role of a poor, blind beggar clothed in rags whose sight is obstructed by a blindfold (representing spiritual desolation) and whose neck is bound with a "cable tow" (or a noose), just as Holm's wrists are bound by Death's Driver at the beginning of his odyssey. Only after he has been "killed" and then resurrected is the initiate's blindfold and cable tow removed, just as Holm must burst free from the ropes binding his wrists before he can slip back through to the physical plane and make contact with Sister Edit in the seconds before she passes on. In *The Phantom Carriage*, Death's Driver acts as a stand-in for the Master of the Lodge. After all, though Death's Driver is the servant of a higher "master," he is at the same time Holm's Master. Such pyramidal relationships mirror the evolutionary scales of the human soul in Theosophical thought.

At the conclusion of *The Phantom Carriage*, the last words spoken by David Holm are: "Lord, please let my soul come to maturity before it is reaped." The casual observer might interpret these words as Christian at base, but when one understands the hermetic overtones that Lagerlöf and Sjöström have layered onto their narrative one begins to realize that this film is structured like an Egyptian pyramid: esoteric secrets are layered, one on top of the other, with even deeper secrets buried within the architecture itself, there to be uncovered for those viewers intuitive enough—or determined enough—to pick up on the hidden meanings. But one can appreciate the architectural wonders of the Great Pyramid without understanding what it means. Lagerlöf and Sjöström knew this, creating a structure that could stand the test of time because its most valuable secrets are those that are revealed to the unconscious. Like ethereal images flickering on a movie screen, the secrets of the mind are often best seen in the dark.

Figure 9.1 Victor Sjöström's innovative use of double exposure dramatically brings to life the legend that lies at the heart of *The Phantom Carriage*: the phantasmagoric notion that the last person killed on New Year's Eve must take over the reins of a horse-drawn carriage fashioned by Death itself. (*Source: German Film Institute—DIF, Frankfurt*)

Double Exposure (and Other Dualities)

Though darkness permeates *The Phantom Carriage*, this does not occlude the light of *gnosis* that emerges from David Holm's soul in the final reel. These binary opposites, darkness and light, are realized in the film thanks to the breakthrough special effects that Sjöström integrates seamlessly into Lagerlöf's plot.

The technical aspects of the film were a major reason for *The Phantom Carriage*'s initial international success and remain one of its most impressive qualities. Needless to say, the wizardry of 1921 cinema pales in comparison to the latest advances in make-up and special effects on display in such recent Swedish dark fantasies as Tomas Alfredson's 2008 film, *Let the Right One In* (which owes a considerable debt to the ground first broken in fantastic cinema by *The Phantom Carriage*). Nonetheless, there is something quite endearing about the crude and yet effective in-camera effects used by Sjöström to bring Lagerlöf's parable to life. No matter how sophisticated the graphics, there is something rather cold and unappealing about the computer-generated effects so prevalent in recent films of the *fantastique*; however, there is an ineffable quality about the most basic effects (i.e. those performed in-camera) that lend phantasmagoric films a veneer of authenticity, that tricks the human brain into thinking that the chimerical events unfolding before our eyes are indeed possible. Perhaps our brain knows, subliminally, that a *human hand* was involved in the creation of these effects, thus emphasizing the realistic over the fantastic.

It is appropriate and poetic, thematically, that Sjöström used *double* exposure to bring this dream/nightmare (nightmare/dream) to fruition. The process of double exposure involves filming the background image first, then rewinding the film and shooting the spectral beings and objects (i.e. Death's Driver, his skeletal horse, David Holm's astral body, and the carriage itself) against a black background. This process mirrors the theme of duality found throughout the film. The purgatorial world inhabited by Holm's astral double is similar to the twilight realm in which the film itself dwells. *The Phantom Carriage* hovers gracefully between two worlds, between the extremes of phantasmagoric expressionism and stark realism.

It must be remembered that *The Phantom Carriage* emerged during a period in which the seductive shadow of expressionism hung over the cinema. Two of the most important expressionist films ever made, Robert Wiene's *The Cabinet of Dr. Caligari* and Paul Wegener and Carl Boese's *The Golem*, had been released only a year earlier. F. W. Murnau's equally iconic film, *Nosferatu*, went into production the same year *The Phantom Carriage* was released. It's unlikely, therefore, that Sjöström did not have to contend with this shadow while conceiving how best to bring *The Phantom Carriage* to life. Lagerlöf's novel could very well have lent itself to a purely expressionist interpretation, similar to *The Cabinet of Dr. Caligari*. Though it's intriguing to imagine what such a film would have been like, Sjöström must have known that this approach would have emphasized the phantasmagoria of Lagerlöf's story over the tangible strains of social realism. In order to represent the theme of Gnostic duality so prevalent in *Thy Soul Shall Bear Witness!*, Sjöström had to balance the darkness with the light, the expressionistic with the realistic.

Having no doubt seen contemporary Expressionist films, such as those mentioned above, Sjöström would have recognized expressionism's potential to manifest images of what Sigmund Freud called "the uncanny." In his 1919 essay "The Uncanny," Freud applied his psychoanalytic theories to such fantasy tales as E.T.A. Hoffmann's "The Sand-Man," contending that stories like these are built around emotions and images that are (paradoxically) both strange and familiar at once, unearthing repressed and primal impulses buried deep within us:

> this uncanny is in reality nothing new or alien, but something which is familiar and old-established in the mind and which has become alienated from it only through the process of repression. This reference to the factor of repression enables us, furthermore, to understand [the] definition of the uncanny as something which ought to have remained hidden but has come to light.[19]

The most famous works of Expressionism of the early 1920s all invoked this transgressive world of the uncanny and the supernatural at a time when, in Hollywood, the prevailing wisdom was that the virgin pure medium of film—a *populist* medium at heart—was not the proper home for such taboo stories. The masses simply would not accept tales of the uncanny in the form of film, insisted the Powers That Be, which explains why so many American movies of the 1920s featured ostensibly supernatural events that always turned out to be prosaic in the end. The examples are numerous, but the most prominent of these films would include Rupert Julian's *The Phantom of the Opera* (1925), Roland West's *The Bat* (1926), Paul Leni's *The Cat and the Canary* (1927), and Tod Browning's *London After Midnight* (1927). Some critics even insist to this day that *The Phantom Carriage* falls into this category, that the phantasmagoria in the film is a result of David Holm's disordered brain after he has been knocked unconscious by the ruffian's bottle in the graveyard; however, I think I have already demonstrated, via Lagerlöf's personal beliefs, that the uncanny elements of the tale are intended to be literal representations of reality—a form of "magic realism," as it were, long before that term was coined in the 1950s. And perhaps "magic realism" is the best term that could be applied to Sjöström's film, for it's clear that Lagerlöf believed a little magic was sometimes the only means by which one could access the inner realms of the soul and thus light oneself up with the quotidian wonders of reality.

Sjöström somehow evokes this world of "magic realism" by emphasizing the real over the magical, choosing to shoot many of the scenes in natural surroundings rather than on a soundstage. As Casper Tybjerg says during his Criterion commentary, "To fully grasp how atmospheric *The Phantom Carriage* would have seemed to contemporaries, we need to understand that few (if any) previous films had been enveloped in the darkness of night the way this one is." Indeed, almost every scene takes place in the dark, with night-for-night shooting that is exquisitely vivid, a feat that required superior technical skills for the time period. The near-permanent darkness not only adds to the spookiness of the naturalistic graveyard scenes at the beginning of the film, but also acts as a contrast to the light (i.e. the Gnostic illumination) that will swell up within Holm at the end of his spiritual journey. This final illumination would be difficult for the viewer to accept if so much darkness had not preceded it.

This duality, this melding of light and dark, is encapsulated in a single shot that occurs nineteen minutes into the film: a silhouette of Death's Driver creeping over the horizon of a shadowy, desolate hill. Almost the entire screen is filled with the ragged landscape, symbolic of the darkness the carriage has left in its wake. Though our eyes are overwhelmed by this blackness, one cannot help but be drawn toward the band of waning light at the top of the screen, representative of the faint—but very real—light that awaits us all if we heed Lagerlöf's warning and mature our souls before they are reaped.

The overall realism of the film renders the magical moments even more startling when they appear. The most expressionistic sequence in *The Phantom Carriage* is the one that lingers in the mind long after the memory of the final scene has faded away. Almost exactly eighteen minutes into the film, we are introduced to a story within a story within a story—a series of visual vignettes that could stand on their own as an experimental short film about the travails endured by the single human unfortunate enough to be initiated by Death into the dual role of Driver and Soul Collector. The carriage and its ghostly servant are brought to life through meticulous double exposures that must have been grueling for Sjöström and his crew to pull off in the early 1920s. We see Death's Driver forced to collect the soul of a rich but desperate man who has just blown his brains out with a pistol. We next see the Driver and his skeletal horse trundling across the surface of the ocean. The Driver leaves the carriage in order to descend beneath the waves and collect the fresh soul of a drowned sailor lying peacefully on the ocean floor. The sailor almost appears to be sleeping, his battered skull using a large white rock as a final pillow. These are the most famous scenes in the film, and serve to establish not only the depressing horror of the Driver's task, but the fact that no man on Earth (rich or poor), no place on Earth (on land or at sea), is inviolate to Death's touch.

The double exposure technique had been employed before to bring incredible sights to the silver screen (Georges Méliès had used the technique as early as 1898 in his short film *The Four Troublesome Heads*), but never in such an appropriately foreboding context. It was the perfect technique to realize Lagerlöf's uncanny fantasy. Perhaps for the first time in cinema, special effects and emotional content came together to create a unique and harrowing frisson.

Cinema of the Occulted Taboo

The effects (and affects) of *The Phantom Carriage* can be seen in the cinema to this day, even among filmmakers who may never have encountered Victor Sjöström's masterpiece, a film that in 1924 Charlie Chaplin hailed as "the best film ever made." Chaplin also referred to Sjöström as "the greatest director in the world" (Tybjerg). Ingmar Bergman often insisted that his first viewing of *The Phantom Carriage* at the age of fourteen sparked his initial desire to become

Figure 9.2   At midnight on New Year's Eve, David Holm (Victor Sjöström) comes face to face with Death's Driver (Tore Svennberg), who commands Holm to abandon his body, then guides him on a metaphysical journey laden with Theosophical overtones. (*Source: German Film Institute—DIF, Frankfurt*)

a filmmaker, no doubt the reason he cast Sjöström in two of his films, including the 1957 classic *Wild Strawberries*. The influence of *The Phantom Carriage* on Bergman's *The Seventh Seal*—a 1957 film about a medieval knight who challenges Death to a chess game during the Black Plague—is unmistakable.

The Phantom Carriage is part of a long storytelling tradition that appears to be unstoppable. Many esotericists have recognized the immense potential cinema possesses with regard to unobtrusively disseminating occult information to the average man and woman. Consider the example of Manly P. Hall, founder of the Philosophical Research Society in Los Angeles and author of dozens of encyclopedic volumes about the history of the occult. At first, Hall attempted to use periodical fiction for this purpose. In the first two decades of the twentieth century one couldn't find a better medium for mass communication than the numerous magazines that filled up newsstands all across the country and featured brand new short stories every week. Many of these publications were open to the subject of the supernatural, just as long as it was broached in the context of fiction. Hall presented to the public little gems of esoteric wisdom in the form of elegantly crafted pulp short stories. Some of these pieces Hall later collected in a 1925 book entitled *Shadow Forms*, in the introduction to which he writes, "In an erratic moment we conceived the notion of attempting to portray certain great occult truths through the medium of fiction. We believe many people will read stories who would never consider a philosophical dissertation on the subject."[20] One such occult-related project Hall succeeded in bringing to the screen was a mystery entitled *When Were You Born?* (1938), directed by William C. McGann and starring Anna May Wong as a Chinese woman in San Francisco who solves a murder using the techniques of astrology. The film begins with a five-minute-long prologue by Hall in which he briefly explains the history of astrology.

But Hall was not the only esotericist who brought to the cinema his unique insight into the world of the occult. Jean Cocteau, among the most acclaimed directors of the twentieth century, reshaped ancient myth and folklore into powerful visual tone poems such as *Beauty and the Beast* (1946) and *Orpheus* (1950). According to the 1982 bestselling nonfiction book *Holy Blood, Holy Grail* by Michael Baigent, Richard Leigh and Henry Lincoln, Cocteau was the Grand Master of a centuries-old occult secret society known as the Prieuré de Sion.[21] Whether this tantalizing claim is accurate or not, it is evident from his work that Cocteau did indeed possess a deep and intimate understanding of hermeticism. Kenneth Anger, an acknowledged follower of Aleister Crowley's religion, Thelema, poured his occult knowledge into such avant-garde films as *The Inauguration of the Pleasure Dome* (1954), *Invocation of My Demon Brother* (1969) and *Lucifer Rising* (1972). Anger's contemporary, Alejandro Jodorowsky, is not only a knowledgeable practitioner of alchemy and the tarot (in fact, he has created his own spiritual system called "psychoshamanism," which he writes about extensively in his 2010 book *Psychomagic: The*

Transformative Power of Shamanic Psychotherapy), but he also happens to be one of the most visionary film directors alive today. Since 1970 he has written and directed the most illuminating metaphysical allegories ever committed to celluloid, foremost among them *El Topo* (1970), *The Holy Mountain* (1973), *Santa Sangre* (1989), and *The Dance of Reality* (2013), all of which seethe and overbrim with unbridled *gnosis*.

Hall, Cocteau, Anger, Jodorwosky, Lagerlöf and Sjöström were neither the first nor the last artists to exploit the power of the cinema for the purpose of disseminating occult knowledge. The examples read like a list of some of the most cutting-edge films to emerge from the cinema during the past ten decades. Some of these films you may have watched but never really *seen*, and some you may never even have heard of, but all are blessed with at least a touch of genuine magic: Giuseppe de Liguoro's *L'Inferno* (1911), Benjamin Christensen's *Häxan* (1922), Rex Ingram's *The Magician* (1926), James Whale's *Frankenstein* (1931) and *Bride of Frankenstein* (1935), Carl Dreyer's *Vampyr* (1932), Karl Freund's *The Mummy* (1932), Walt Disney's *Snow White and the Seven Dwarfs* (1937), *Pinocchio* (1940), *Fantasia* (1940), *Peter Pan* (1953), *Sleeping Beauty* (1959) and *Alice in Wonderland* (1951), Victor Fleming's *The Wizard of Oz* (1939), Jacques Tourneur's *I Walked with a Zombie* (1943) and *Night of the Demon* (1957), Luis Buñuel's *The Exterminating Angel* (1962), Orson Welles' *The Trial* (1962), Federico Fellini's *8 ½* (1963), Robert Stevenson's *Mary Poppins* (1964), Michelangelo Antonioni's *Blow-up* (1966), Stanley Kubrick's *2001: A Space Odyssey* (1968) and *Eyes Wide Shut* (1999), Terence Fisher's *The Devil Rides Out* (1968), George Lucas' *THX 1138* (1971) and *Star Wars* (1977), Robin Hardy's *The Wicker Man* (1973), John Huston's *The Man Who Would Be King* (1975), Jeannot Szwarc's *Somewhere in Time* (1980), Ken Russell's *Altered States* (1980), Ridley Scott's *Blade Runner* (1982), David Lynch's *Blue Velvet* (1986), *Twin Peaks: Fire Walk with Me* (1992) and *Mulholland Drive* (2001), Jan Svankmajer's *Alice* (1988) and *Faust* (1994), Peter Greenaway's *Prospero's Books* (1991), David Cronenberg's *Naked Lunch* (1991) and *eXistenZ* (1999), Hayao Miyazaki's *Porco Rosso* (1992), *Spirited Away* (2001) and *Ponyo* (2008), Jim Jarmusch's *Dead Man* (1995), Darren Aronofsky's *Pi* (1998) and *The Fountain* (2006), Alex Proyas' *Dark City* (1998), the Wachowskis' *The Matrix Trilogy* (1999–2003), Richard Kelly's *Donnie Darko* (2001), the Hughes Brothers' *From Hell* (2001), Matthew Barney's *The Cremaster Cycle* (2003), Francisco Athie's *Vera* (2003), Christiane Cegavske's *Blood Tea and Red String* (2006), Christopher Nolan's *Inception* (2010), and the various *Harry Potter* films (2001–11). These examples could all be placed under a single category that one might call the "Cinema of the Occulted Taboo."

This type of film, which disguises its true purpose behind the seductive veneer of entertainment, pervades the cinema even today: subtle movies that continue to creep across the landscape of the twentieth century and beyond, like an army of phantom carriages steered by implacable drivers intent on fulfilling their sacred tasks, quietly disseminating seeds of ancient wisdom through shadow shows projected on blank screens all across the globe, hopefully paving the way for new paradigms and new dreams and new nightmares . . . new worlds of gods and monsters.

Notes

1. For an in-depth analysis of *Macbeth's* Masonic overtones, see Chapter 9 of my book *Cryptoscatology: Conspiracy Theory as Art Form* (Walterville, OR: TrineDay, 2012).
2. For further examples, see *A Midsummer Night's Dream* (1590) and *The Tempest* (1610), two hermetic allegories that would have been banned by the Catholic Church if Shakespeare had chosen instead to write non-fiction essays about the Gnostic themes embedded at the core of both fictions.
3. Selma Lagerlöf, *Thy Soul Shall Bear Witness!* (trans. William Frederick Harvey) (London: Odham's, 1921[1912]).
4. Lewis Spence, *An Encyclopedia of Occultism* (New York: Citadel, 1993 [1920]), p. 411.
5. Casper Tybjerg, "Audio Commentary" (prod. Karen Stetler), *The Phantom Carriage* (DVD, The Criterion Collection, 2011).
6. Stephen A. Hoeller, *Gnosticism: New Light on the Ancient Tradition of Inner Knowing* (Wheaton, IL: Quest Books, 2002), pp. 76–7.
7. Helen P. Blavatsky, *Isis Unveiled Vol. I: Science* (Pasadena, CA: Theosophical University Press, 1988 [1877]).
8. C. W. Leadbeater, *Ancient Mystic Rites* (Wheaton, IL: The Theosophical Publishing House, 1986 [originally published under the title *Glimpses of Masonic History*, 1926], pp. 114.
9. Lagerlöf, *Thy Soul Shall Bear Witness!*, p. 180.
10. According to Dr Hoeller, an archon is an "inferior cosmic being ruling over and imposing limitations on creation" (*Gnosticism*, p. 257).
11. Ibid. p. 17–18.
12. Blavatsky, *Isis Unveiled*, pp. 152–3.
13. C. W. Leadbeater, *Ancient Mystic Rites*, p. 115.
14. Blavatsky, *Isis Unveiled*, p. 157.
15. C. W. Leadbeater, *Chakras: A Monograph* (Wheaton, IL: The Theosophical Publishing House, 1969 [1927]), p. 62.
16. Ibid. p. 63.
17. Lagerlöf, *Thy Soul Shall Bear Witness!*, pp. 128–9.
18. Annie Besant, *A Study in Consciousness* (Wheaton, IL: The Theosophical Publishing House, 1967 [1904]), pp. 62–4.
19. Sigmund Freud, *The Complete Psychological Works of Sigmund Freud Vol. XVII* (London: Hogarth, 1955), p. 241.
20. Manly P. Hall, *Shadow Forms: A Collection of Occult Stories* (Los Angeles, CA: The Philosophical Research Society, 1979 [1925]), p. 5.
21. Michael Baigent, Richard Leigh and Henry Lincoln, *Holy Blood, Holy Grail* (New York: Dell, 1983), p. 131.

10. *DRAKULA HALÁLA* (1921): THE CINEMA'S FIRST DRACULA

Gary D. Rhodes

In recent years, a number of film historians have discovered that F. W. Murnau's *Nosferatu* (1922) did not, as was long believed, represent the first occasion on which Bram Stoker's *Dracula* was adapted for the screen.[1] Instead, Hungarian director Károly Lajthay's *Drakula halála*, even though it was hardly faithful to the novel, marked the character's earliest film appearance, incorporating Stoker's vampire character into a tale that also drew heavily on Robert Wiene's *Das Cabinet des Dr. Caligari* (1920). Despite the growing awareness of *Drakula halála*, however, little is known of the film's production or its storyline, particularly in English-language texts.

Announcing that the film was being produced, the Hungarian trade publication *Képes Mozivilág* wrote in 1921:

> About twenty years ago, H. G. Wells' novel *Drakula*, one of his most interesting and exciting stories, was published as a serial in the *Budapesti hírlap*, and then later published here as a book. The novel was highly acclaimed at the time, because the reader was fully absorbed into its exciting plot that featured so many unexpected turns.[2]

Though the publication mistakenly named Wells as the author rather than Stoker, it did indicate that Lajthay intended to translate the "basic ideas" of Stoker's *Dracula* onto the screen. Even if it would not become a direct adaptation of the novel, *Drakula halála* would rely heavily upon it for story ideas. Its Drakula was not based on Vlad the Impaler or some new character: Bram Stoker's Dracula would become Károly Lajthay's Drakula.

Born in Marosvásárhely, Károly Lajthay (1885–1945) became an important figure in the Hungarian film industry during the 1910s. At times he was a writer (as for *Átok vára* in 1918 and *Júlisa kisasszony* in 1919), and on at least one occasion before *Drakula halála* he was a producer (for *Tláni, az elvarázsolt hercegasszony* in 1920). But the bulk of his credits were as director and as an actor; Lajthay used the screen name Charles Lederle in some thirteen Hungarian feature films (including *Nászdal* in 1917, which co-starred Bela Lugosi).

According to censorship records, the Lapa Film Studio produced Lajthay's *Drakula halála*.[3] In late 1920, Lajthay visited Budapest in order to rent space at the Corvin Film Studio for a film that bore the working title *Drakula*. By that time, the theater magazine *Színházi Élet* noted that Lajthay was one of several leading Hungarians who had left the Budapest film industry for Vienna. In an interview with the same publication, Lajthay said:

> Film production in Vienna is virtually under Hungarian control, because Hungarian directors dominate the industry there. [Sándor] Korda and [Mihály] Kertész are extremely successful there ... Now I am directing my film entitled *Drakula* [for a Vienna-based company].[4]

Lajthay had co-written the *Drakula* script with Mihály Kertész, who had already been a prominent film director in Budapest, having worked at Phönix with Bela Lugosi on such films as *99* (1918). By the time of *Drakula halála* (as the film became known at some point during its production), Kertész was making films in Austria; years later, using the name Michael Curtiz, he would direct such Hollywood movies as *Dr. X* (1932), *Mystery of the Wax Museum* (1933), and *Casablanca* (1943).

As for his crew, Lajthay employed Eduard Hoesch, whom he called the "best cameraman in Vienna."[5] Hoesch would shoot *Drakula*'s interiors, though later credits suggest he was only one of two cinematographers who worked on the film. The other was Lajos Gasser, who had previously shot *Júlisa kisasszony*.[6] Unfortunately, no known records indicate the names of other crewmembers.

For the role of Drakula, Lajthay cast Paul Askonas (1872–1935), a member of the Deutsches Volkstheater in Vienna. Among other films, Askonas had previously appeared as Svengali in Jacob and Luise Fleck's *Trilby* (1912). In the years following his work as Drakula, Askonas would portray Dr Mirakel in Max Neufeld's *Hoffmanns Erzählungen* (1923) and a servant in Robert Wiene's *Orlac's Hände* (1924). As for the other two key roles in *Drakula halála*, Lajthay cast Deszö Kertész (Mihály's brother) as the young male lead George, and Margit Lux as the heroine Mary Land. Lux had previously appeared in such films as Pál Fejös' *Lidércnyomás* (1920) and Mihály Kertész's *Alraune* (1918, co-directed with Edmund Fritz).

Margit Lux's appearance in *Drakula halála* has been the matter of a minor controversy, as the January 1921 issue of *Képes Mozivilág* claimed that Lene Myl (who was in fact a Serbian named Miléne Pavlovic) would play "the role of the heroine"; they remarked on her "impressive appearance," and went so far as to say that she would "ensure the success" of *Drakula halála*.[7] Though she was essentially unknown, Myl had appeared in small film roles at studios in Rome and Berlin. Lajthay presumably spotted her in the Austrian film *Königin Draga* (1920), in which she had a supporting role alongside Askonas. However, every other publication during 1921-3 claimed that Lux was Mary Land, not Myl.[8] Moreover, it is definitely Lux who appears with Askonas in a *Drakula halála* publicity still published in *Szinház és Mozi* in 1921; its caption specifically credits Lux as portraying Mary.

Perhaps some cast changes occurred during pre-production, but it is equally, if not more, possible that *Képes Mozivilág*—the same publication that had incorrectly claimed that H. G. Wells wrote the novel *Dracula*—simply made an error. It seems highly probable that Lux portrayed Mary Land, and that Myl portrayed some other, lesser role. For example, 1921, Lajthay actually said, "The major parts are played by Margit Lux, Lene Myl, and Askonas"; a cast list published circa 1924 by Lajos Pánczél also listed Lux as Mary Land, with Lene Myl in a small role.[9] Given *Drakula halála*'s storyline, Myl likely appeared either as a nurse or—more likely, if an extant publicity photograph of her for the film accurately reflects her onscreen costume—as one of Drakula's brides.[10]

With Askonas, Kertész, and (apparently) Lux in the lead roles, Lajthay cast such actors as Lajos Réthey—who had costarred with Bela Lugosi in *99* (1918)—as the "Fake surgeon," and Karl Götz—aka Carl Goetz, who starred in Fritz Freisler's *The Mandarin* (1918) and would later appear as Schigolch in *Pandora's Box* (1929)—as the "Funny Man." Others included Elemér Thury, who had acted in Hungarian films since at least 1912, and Aladár Ihász, who appeared in a small number of films between 1913 and 1944.

Script in hand and cast and crew in place, Lajthay shot some of the film's exteriors in and around Vienna, including in the village of Melk, in December 1920.[11] The following month, beginning on January 2, 1921, he shot the interior scenes at the Corvin Film Studio in Budapest, which he believed was "better equipped than any studio in Vienna."[12] Afterwards, he returned to Vienna to shoot additional exteriors in the nearby Wachau Valley.[13]

During the Corvin shoot, a journalist from the publication *Színház és Mozi* visited the set and wrote a story about the film's production, the most in-depth that was published:

> It was not one of our famous prima donnas' weddings, nor one of our celebrated actors, or for that matter one of successful writers, poets,

Figure 10.1   Paul Askonas and Margit Lux in *Drakula halála*.

sculptors, or painters; however, I nonetheless must insist that I attended a wedding. Firstly, because I de facto did; secondly, because it was the most unusual and extraordinary wedding ever witnessed by anyone.

I attended a wedding—at the Corvin Film Studio. The bridegroom—an actor—was none other than Asconas [sic], the most celebrated actor in Vienna, and the bride—an actress, of course—is Margit Lux, the nice, talented film actress who has been so highly acclaimed for crying so realistically on the screen.

Asconas [sic], Drakula *in persona*—a phantastic creature, some kind of modern bluebeard—brings a new woman into his amazing castle, this new woman being played by Margit Lux. He stops at nothing in order to possess the woman: he summons demons and spirits and strange creatures to gain control over her, but then a cross around her neck comes into view ... and Drakula, this wonderful, and at the same time mysterious creature, is dispelled by it.

That's how Drakula's wedding took place—in the Corvin studio, namely. Since I might not be able to give away anything by admitting now that *Drakula* is a film, I will say that it is a film destined to become sensational, the plot of which must not be told due to the extraordinary excitement it conveys and the fact it will depend upon suspense when it appears on the screen.

Drakula's wedding gives a taste of the film's energies. There is an immense hall, dressed in marble, with a very, very long and dark corridor in the middle. That is where Drakula lives his mysterious life. It is night. The flutter and shrieks of a multitude of beasts can be heard, and the door in the middle of the hall opens. Beautiful women parade through it, all dressed in dreamlike costumes, all of them being Drakula's wives. But now Drakula awaits his new woman, the most beautiful and desirable of all. She will be welcomed with a rain of flowers.

How beautiful it will appear on the screen, I thought to myself while watching *Drakula* being shot at Corvin. Károly Lajthay, the great film director, worked all day without interruption to have Drakula welcome his new bride; when the film is finished, this scene will constitute just a small section of a four-act film. On the screen, this scene will not last more than five minutes, whereas it takes a full day's work to produce. The viewer, sitting in the theatre, will have no idea what extraordinary talent was required from the director to rehearse, shoot, and edit the sequences one by one.[14]

Színház és Mozi then quoted Lajthay as claiming the film would be a "super production," which were coincidentally the same words that Universal Studios used a decade later to describe their *Dracula* (1931).

But then the press information seems to stop. *Drakula halála* allegedly premiered in Vienna in February 1921, though no data has yet surfaced in Austrian trade publications or Vienna newspapers. If such a premiere occurred, the film likely would have born a German title, and even then it might not have been a direct translation; the name "Drakula" could have been removed and an altogether new title used. More primary research in Austria will be critical to understanding *Drakula halála*'s distribution.

Why the film did not premiere in Budapest in 1921 is unknown. Perhaps there were legal problems or troubles with censors, but no record exists of either. At any rate—according to a "Calendar of Events" listing in the April 1923 issue of *Mozi és Film*—distributor Jenö Tuchten presented *Drakula halála* to Hungarian audiences for the first time on April 14, 1923.[15] At that time, the film ran to 1448 meters in length. In the same issue of *Mozi és Film*, an advertisement promoted yet another screening in Budapest:

> Drakula is coming
> THE REAL DRAKULA IS NOT DEAD!
> but he continues his triumph in full health, and appears again on May 12 or 19

AT THE ROYAL-APOLLO!
Due to what promises to be an enormous demand, film exhibitors are advised to immediately book available dates![16]

But the enormous demand seems not to have occurred. For reasons unknown, the film quickly disappeared from theater screens in Hungary and Austria. No evidence has yet surfaced that *Drakula halála* was ever rereleased in either country, or that it was screened in any other country. The film seems to have vanished after the spring of 1923.

That disappearance includes film prints of *Drakula halála*, none of which survive. However, four publicity photographs have surfaced in Hungary in recent years. Two of them are portraits: one of Lene Myl, and the other of Askonas as Drakula, clad in black, his eyes glaring, his eyebrows accentuated by makeup, and his dark hair forming a widow's peak on his forehead. What is fascinating is that Lajthay apparently deviated from Stoker's description of Dracula, which included a "long white moustache." The clean-shaven Askonas thus appears none too different from how Raymond Huntley would in the London stage version of *Dracula* in 1927, or Bela Lugosi in the Broadway version that same year, as well as in the 1931 Universal Studios film.

Though it is difficult to discern much information from the two surviving scene stills—and it is certainly dangerous to generalize too much on the basis of them—they tantalizingly suggest that the film bore the influence of Expressionism, which may not be entirely surprising given the apparent influence that *Caligari* had on the film's script. One of them shows Drakula and Mary Land with his brides; the other shows Drakula peering through a window (or open door, perhaps) at Mary. Both include some evocative shadows, and the latter depicts an artistically painted flat, showing a building and dreary sky in the distance. Though certainly not as stylized or exaggerated as *Caligari*, the image evokes an eerie and unreal landscape.

Only one other artifact survives that can help us understand the screen's first Dracula: a short novella that acted as a kind of "book-of-the-film." Apparently written by Lajos Pánczél (who had in fact been a friend of Bela Lugosi's before Lugosi left Budapest in 1918), the novella *Drakula halála* was copyrighted and published in Temesvár in 1924, though there is the possibility an earlier edition appeared in either 1921 or 1923. How closely Pánczél's novella adapted the film's storyline is unknown, but it was evidently intended to be quite faithful, as it was promoted as "Number 6 in a Series of Film Books." Moreover, Pánczel begins the book by discussing the film and offering a list of its cast members.

The full text of Pánczél's novella is printed below in an English translation.[17]

Figure 10.2 Paul Askonas (left) in *Drakula halála*. This scene likely depicts the wedding ceremony between Drakula and Mary Land.

The Death of Drakula:
A Novella of the Phantasy Film
by Lajos Pánczél
[Translated by Péter Litván and Gary D. Rhodes[18]]

Preface

This mystical story ushers us into the bizarre realm of unrestrained human fantasy. Entering into this stormy night of dreams and magic, we are faced with an ominous tale of frightening black shadows, of the dying, and of the living dead . . .

In the midst of this piteous ensemble, there grows a budding, young girl; she is like an oasis in a barren desert wasteland, but unbridled madness savagely threatens her fragile existence. The weak little soul is a helpless captive of fate, which unmercifully forces her into life's raging waters, down its cascades toward impending doom, until—after much suffering—the golden gate opens, and the heroine reaches the shores of a bright and happy future.

This is a brief summary of *Drakula*'s enthralling plot, the film version of which is a product of the great Hungarian cinema industry. Written and directed by Károly Lajthay, the film is enacted by the following cast:

Drakula	Paul Askonas
Mary	Margit Lux
George	Deszö Kertész
The Chief Surgeon	Elemér Thury
The Fake Surgeon	Lajos Réthey
His Assistant	Aladár Ihász
Funny Man	Karl Götz

Also featuring Lajos Szalkay, Károly Hatvani, Oszkár Perczel, Béla Timár, Paula Kende and Lene Myl.

I The Tragedy of Old Mr. Land

In the midst of some giant mountains covered with everlasting snow could be found a little Alpine village. Here, in majestic silence, far from the bustle of the world, lived little Mary Land, a poor seamstress. Each day in the life of this little lady passed sadly. Mary tried to overcome her loneliness and her heart's endless sorrow by devoting herself to work. She toiled unceasingly, night and day, in order to earn a meagre salary, which she used to support her sick father who was kept in the mental asylum in nearby capitol city.

In the poor little house where Mary lived, the sewing machine was forever buzzing; her soft, fragile little fingers were always moving.

Outside of Mary's home, the wintry landscape seemed to gleam with power. Surrounded by snowy mountains, the little village lived its own dreamlike life like a tiny island surrounded by the sea's endless waters. A deep calm enshrouded the village, its peaceful citizens taking a rest from the year's hardships.

Mary's tiny house, where she had been born 16 years earlier, had once been a home to great happiness. Her parents were wealthy; their home was free of sorrow, filled instead with laughter and joy. However, during a recent spring, Mary's mother fell ill, and not too long afterwards, Death delivered the poor woman from her misery.

Mary's heart bled for her deceased mother, and old Mr. Land's grief was indescribable. The tragedy had such a terrible impact on him that he eventually lost his mind, causing Mary to follow the doctors' advice and have him committed to a mental asylum.

From that time onward, Mary lived a lonely existence in her home at the end of the village. She worked without rest in order to earn a living and pay for her father's care. After two sad years, though she was worn down by hard work, Mary's will power did not weaken. She would have sacrificed her own life to help her father. But regrettably, two years of care in the asylum did not improve old Mr. Land's condition. He lingered inside the asylum like a living corpse. The doctors eventually came to the conclusion that his mental state was beyond repair, that he had mere days to live, and that a quick death would be an act of mercy for such a broken, suffering old man.

Mary visited her father every week, causing Mr. Land's confused eyes to light up, beaming with renewed energy. When he would see his daughter, the old man nearly broke into euphoria: he hugged, kissed, and caressed his only child, because in secret he knew that the end was near and that he would soon have to bid his treasured daughter farewell. For her part, Mary tried to comfort her father, and, even when she was reduced to tears, she tried to remain silent. She bravely endured the painful goodbyes, and neither of them openly admitted that their world would never be the same . . . They beguiled one another . . . Their tearful glances were lies, promising a happy future and the hope of a new life, but deep inside they both heard the sorrowful sound of "Fare-thee-well."

Both of them spent their time yearning for their next encounter, but when they parted, they did so with the terrible feeling in their hearts of those who know, who *feel*, that death is at hand, and that they might see each other never more . . .

II Mary and George

During those sad, wearisome days, Mary's only comfort was George Marlup, who eventually became her fiancée. He loved her, and his heart brimmed with affection for the blossoming young girl. Though George worked as a woodcutter in the neighbouring village, he still called to see Mary every day. Those became her few happy hours . . . It was only then that Mary's heart was freed from sorrow. It was only then that she could forget about her pain and imagine a happy future, one that would make up for all the agony she had suffered.

George devoted himself to Mary with tender love and attention. He also tried to spare his little bride-to-be from exhaustion, warning her that she was too obsessed with work and that it was too much a burden for her sensitive nature. But Mary would not yield; she would not stop working. When George visited her on the holy day of Christmas, he could not believe that she was still working, working as hard as ever.

"Again you have been awake, working all night, my little Mary! Why don't you take better care of yourself? After all, today is a holiday, the holy day of Christmas, and I brought you this little tree. When I come back this evening, we will decorate it together."

"My destiny is labor and self-denial," Mary answered in a solemn voice. "But I am not complaining . . . I have had to deal with my situation in my own way . . . I must keep carrying life's heavy burden."

Then a tear welled in Mary's sad eyes . . . The young man put the little fir-tree on the table, bestowed a kiss on her lips, and departed.

"God be with you, my sweetheart!" George said, turning back to look at her before leaving. "Goodbye!"

* * * * *

That same night, George returned to his bride-to-be, and together they decorated the fir-tree, a beautiful symbol of peace and love . . . Then they prayed to the Lord in Heaven with their hearts full of gratitude, and as they prayed, they heard the chapel bells in the little village begin to chime, summoning the pious to midnight Mass.

They had already decorated the little fir-tree with many glittering ornaments and candles, which cast a silvery light onto the two lovers. It seemed to create a halo around Mary's golden hair . . .

At that minute, they heard someone mysteriously knocking on the door. George answered it to greet the unexpected visitor, who turned out to be the town's postman, delivering a registered letter for Mary.

The maiden hastily opened the envelope:

To Miss Mary Land.

We regret to inform you that your father's condition has worsened. You should attempt to visit him as soon as possible.

Yours sincerely,
Municipal Mental Asylum
Dr. Faigner, Head Surgeon,
and Director.

Mary's eyes, which had been gleaming with joy, ran wet with tears . . . Although she was well aware and prepared for the fact that her father had limited time, she was still taken aback by the news and tearfully placed her head on George's shoulder.

Then she quickly raised her head and said: "We must not miss the midnight Mass. Let's hurry, George!"

Without saying a word, the young man took his fiancée by the arm. The little chapel's bell was still ringing throughout the village, and its devout citizens were busily making their way to the worship service . . .

Neither Mary nor George would have missed the midnight Mass. The maiden and her fiancé looked to Almighty God, praying from the depth of their hearts that He might prolong old Mr. Land's days . . .

When the service was over, Mary nervously said to her fiancé: "My dear, wonderful father! Who knows whether he will still be alive when I reach the asylum? The next train leaves in the morning . . . I'm scared that I might be too late."

George understood Mary's fears and tried to comfort her: "Not a minute must be lost, Mary! Let me harness the horses, and then we will set out! Dawn will see us arrive at the asylum!"

Quick as it was thought, it was done. George readied the horses and a sleigh, and within a few minutes he was outside Mary's house, ready for departure. With great care, the young man seated the sad maiden in the sled, her own thoughts consumed by worry and fear.

The horses raced along with the lovers in full gallop. The little sleigh boldly glided down the frozen, snowy path, and the fairylike chime of its silver bells echoed throughout the darkness of the night . . .

For hours, heavy, thick snowflakes floated down from the skies . . . It was long after midnight. Worn out by grief, Mary lay down in the sleigh in order to sleep.

* * * * *

The rising sun was already casting its golden rays when the lovers approached the city. With a few minutes, they reached the gates of the mental asylum. It was morning . . . a crisp, fresh, winter morning. But soon the light of the sun struggled to beam through an increasingly dismal, cloudy sky . . .

Frowning gloomily down at the young couple was an immense, sad, desolate building: the madhouse.

Mary shuddered, "Oh!"

George embraced her tightly and sheltered the fainting maiden in his arms: "What happened, my dear? What is wrong?"

"Every time I arrive at this place, I am nearly overcome. I am reminded that my poor father must live here, his life empty and his mind hardly conscious. Oh, George, what a terrible fate! This house is the realm of the living dead; the most unhappy of men dwell here, and among them is my father! I could never forget the way he was. His wonderful face, his tender look, and the great devotion he had towards me. He raised me with so much love, and yet he's ended up here! Is this the end of his journey?"

George tried to comfort his fiancée, softly explaining: "Be calm, dear. We cannot know the ways of providence, and we must live with God's will, however painful it is. Now be brave. I am confident that your father is still alive."

George's words calmed Mary, and soon the couple reached the door of the madhouse.

Before entering, Mary said: "Thank you, George, for bringing me here. I will return home on the evening train. Goodbye, my sweetheart!"

The lovers parted with a gentle kiss.

"Please do not be late, Mary," George said at last. "God be with you. Goodbye!"

Then the girl entered the house of sorrow. As she nervously walked through its archway, her heart filled with grief and her spirits sank. She was shaking with fear over her father's fate.

Mary anxiously asked the first man that crossed her path: "Could I speak to Doctor Tillner, please?"

As soon as she asked for him, Doctor Tillner appeared. One of the most important doctors at the asylum, Tillner was wearing a white coat, preparing for his morning rounds. By that time, Mary knew Tillner quite well, because her father was a member of his ward.

With her eyes wide open, Mary questioned the doctor: "How is my father? Is he alive? Please doctor, tell me everything!"

Tillner remained silent for a moment, and then he tried to calm down his desperate visitor by saying: "Take comfort, Miss! Death will

Figure 10.3. Paul Askonas in *Drakula halála*.

be salvation for your poor father. Come along and have a look at my patients. What a pitiful life these poor wretches must live!"

III Humans Reduced to Shadows

With an air of curiosity, Mary followed him. Doctor Tillner ushered her into the garden of the hospital, where so many of the inmates were gathered. They instinctively wanted to be outside on such a bright winter morning, which had a calming effect on their dead nerves and paralyzed spirits.

With scared and troubled eyes, a host of inmates stared at Mary, the unknown and unexpected interloper, as if they were all part of some picturesque panopticon. She kept close to the doctor, because—even though she did recognize a few of the patients from her previous visits—she was scared by the bizarre appearance of them gathered together. Her fear heightened when some of them moved towards her. Their eyes radiated with madness, and their slow steps dragged frail, wrecked bodies towards her as if she was their enemy.

Growing aware of the danger, Doctor Tillner motioned for the patients to withdraw. They moved away, but their gaze revealed a hateful, murderous light.

"Do not be afraid, my dear child," Tillner said, trying to reassure Mary. "They are all innocent people who wouldn't hurt a fly. It is only their appearance that is threatening. They are cowards, who would shrink back at the mere rustle of a leaf."

Mary remained fearful of the poor, death-bound pariahs, and so the doctor continued to speak to her as he approached one of the inmates: "This man here," he said, "was a famous scientist, who now has the belief that his foot is made of glass and prone to break if he steps on it."

Doctor Tillner then pointed out the fact that his feet were wrapped in thick scarves: "Now he believes that he is the Minister of Finance. He constantly doles out checks worth billions to his friends."

Mary observed the thin, haggard man dressed in bizarre clothes; he manically wrote in his notebook and then tore out pages from it, giving them to other inmates who passed his way. Each time he did, his pale face lit up with joy and happiness.

Then she became aware of a tall, gaunt man with bushy hair and a face that resembled Beelzebub. Turning to the doctor, she asked, "Who is this formidable man? He is staring at me as if I am his prey. He virtually swallows me with his eyes, which are ablaze with all the terrible colours of Hell."

"He used to be an excellent composer," Tillner replied. "Now he believes himself to be a ruler. He wouldn't part from his royal cloak even to go to sleep."

"He resembles the organ player who some years ago taught me how to sing," Mary said.

"If you are not afraid, you are certainly welcome to speak to him," the doctor said. "I ask him questions in vain. He will not reply."

IV Drakula

Encouraged by the doctor, Mary slowly approached the man dressed in the cloak, who gazed upon her with a terrifying smile. Growing more confident among the patients, she asked him: "How are you, master? ... Don't you remember me? My name is Mary Land ... Five years ago in the school ..."

"I don't remember," the horrible man replied. "I do not remember anything. I am Drakula ... the immortal!"

A wild fire then flared inside the man's heart. In a commanding voice, he exclaimed once again: "Yes! I am Drakula ... the immortal!"

Mary Land shuddered at the sight of the awful man. She quickly regretted having spoken to him, but continued the conversation: "Try to remember, master ... I was in the second row ... I sang soprano, and you often stroked my hair as a token of affection ... a long time has passed, but I can still remember everything."

The madman shuddered: "I have been alive for a thousand years and I will live forever ... Mine is immortality ... Immortality! I possess eternal life ... People will die, the world will be destroyed, but I will keep living!

Deeply shaken, Mary shrunk away from Drakula, who continued speaking: "My life is a life eternal! Death will never come for me! Oh, do not believe that I, too, am mad! I stay here only because I love the living dead. I deeply pity them, and I want to give all of them life!"

Mary listened nervously to Drakula, the human monster, whose voice sounded like a roar from Hell, and whose deep fiery black eyes glowed with dark flames. Then he towered over fragile little Mary as if he was going to squeeze her to death with one single movement.

Doctor Tillner, who had been watching the scene from a distance, rescued Mary and escorted her back into the hospital. The doctor ushered the girl into an operation room and said to her: "Please, take a seat here while I have a word with the director about giving your father a room of his own."

Mary replied in a trembling voice, "I am so very disturbed by that terrible man dressed in black ... Drakula."

"Please relax," the doctor told her. "Drakula only looks terrifying. You mustn't be scared of him. Calm down."

Mary nervously sat down in the sterile, white operation room. She was still shuddering. Faced with an irrepressible and unceasing image, her thoughts struggled with Drakula. And while she was waiting, consumed by her thoughts, one of the doors opened and a man who appeared to be a doctor entered quietly.

Mary grabbed at her chair. She was terrified by the stranger's weird looks. Though he wore a doctor's white coat, the man was one of the inmates. He was tall and had a bony face. The madman believed he was a doctor, always wore a doctor's coat, and always arrogantly tried to examine and operate on the other patients.

"I am Professor Wells," he told Mary. "A doctor of universal medicine. If you don't mind, Miss, I will examine you." He then sat down next to her, staring at her with his eyes wide open.

V The Two Doctors

Mary had no idea that "Professor Wells" was a madman disguised as a doctor, but she instinctively felt that danger was near. She feared, abhorred, and then shrank from this man who gazed her with great intensity.

"Tell me, please, do your eyes not hurt?" the madman said, breaking the silence, and all of a sudden he started to examine her. "My diagnosis is very clear! You are suffering from severe eye disease, Miss," the fake doctor pronounced. "If we do not operate at once, you will go blind!"

Mary was taken aback. Her doubts about the man vanished. She believed him and was convinced that he was indeed a doctor.

At that very moment, the door opened and another man wearing a doctor's coat entered. Professor Wells' face lit up and he said to Mary: "If you don't believe me, ask my colleague," and he pointed to the man who had just entered.

The other pseudo-doctor scrutinized Mary's eyes and produced his diagnosis: "Vulpis doloris! To be operated on without delay!"

Utterly terrified, Mary changed her opinion once more and tried to get away from the two men. But they grabbed the young maiden and threw her onto the operating table. They strapped down her hands and feet. Professor Wells then appeared over her brandishing a surgical knife that he had removed from one of the cupboards. All of this occurred within a few moments.

A terrible shriek then escaped from Mary's throat: "For God's sake... Let me go! Help!"

"Be quiet!" one of the fake doctors shouted at her.

"You should be glad that we have chosen to operate on you!" the other madman exclaimed. "You will owe us your life, your eyesight . . . It will take only a minute or two, and then it will be over!"

Mary cried: "No! I won't let you do it! Let me go! Please, let me go!"

But the two madmen, their eyes wildly ablaze, swooped down on the maiden, who was now fighting with all her might. She desperately wanted to escape from the operating table, and while she was struggling, she kept crying: "Help! Help!"

Her words echoed throughout the white operating room, but fate seemed determined to keep her where she was. Like a bird caught in a net, she was helplessly trapped in the claws of the two madmen. As an ominous, cruel silence fell across the room, Mary suddenly quit crying. The two madmen were just about to pierce open her eyes, when Doctor Tillner and his assistants rushed into the operation room, grabbed hold of the madmen, and freed the maiden from her straps.

Mary was lying there, swooning. She didn't recover consciousness for more than an hour. Doctor Tillner watched over her, checking her heavy breath and the convulsions of her body, which was still heavily affected by the terrifying adventure she had experienced. Eventually, she opened her eyes.

"What happened to me?" she asked with a frightened voice, her eyes full of terror. "Have I dreamt an evil dream, or did those awful things actually happen to me?"

The doctor tried to comfort her as best he could. "There is nothing that can hurt you now, little Mary!" he said. "Forget what happened; consider it nothing more than an ugly dream."

"It's so awful to think about!"

"You shouldn't have been in here alone, Mary, but nobody could have guessed that you might attract such strange visitors."

Hoping to banish the terrible memories from her mind, Mary wiped her forehead, and then she left the operation room with Doctor Tillner's help.

Finally Mary went to see her father, who was near death. Though weak, he embraced his daughter. Mary's tears washed down her face . . . then she heard a loud groan . . . the father's outstretched arms lost their strength . . . his bony fingers stiffened . . . his head dropped to one side . . . his confused eyes were forever shut . . .

In tears, Mary held onto her father's corpse. Doctor Tillner raised her and took the sad, shaken young maiden out of the ward. Had his death, and her strange adventure with the two doctors, really happened, or were they simply a dream?

The doctor helped the poor, fainting creature into a little room adjacent to the director's office and laid her on a couch so she could a rest. But Mary longed to get away. To run from this house of Hell, where she had suffered so utterly, where the most horrendous memories of her life had been born.

"Away ... I want to go away ... to escape ... My life is threatened here! Let me go!" the frightened little maiden kept crying.

Doctor Tillner was hardly able to keep Mary from fleeing: "In such a terrible state of mind, you cannot leave," the doctor said. "stay here for the night and have a rest. In the morning you will be fine, and then you can leave for home."

The maiden felt inclined to follow the doctor's kind advice. She lay down on the couch, but said in a frightened voice, "I beg you ... don't hurt me ... I haven't done anything." Her eyelids then closed, and she fell asleep.

VI Drakula's Assault

Mary had been asleep for several hours ... When the tower clock struck midnight, Drakula appeared in the room like a ghost from Hell. He

Figure 10.4. Károly Lajthay in *Vorrei morir* (1918)

quietly approached the sleeping girl and then touched her shoulder with his long, bony fingers, which caused Mary to awaken. Taken aback, she looked up at Drakula, whose eyes burned with all the horrendous colours of Hell. A satanic smile formed on his lips before he grabbed the girl and began to drag her across the room.

"Follow me!" he commanded. "We are going to my castle, the home of lust and delight! I want to save you! All of these men here are evil. They want to destroy you just like they destroyed your father!

Mary listened in terror while Drakula continued: "Flee this Hell! Follow me and trust me. I am immortal, and I possess supernatural powers! Come!"

"No! ... For God's sake, leave me alone," Mary protested. Then she nervously asked him a flurry of questions: "Who are you? What do you want of me? By what right do you command me to follow you? Where do you want to take me?"

Without responding, Drakula grabbed her and set off for his castle like a whirlwind so that they would reach it before dawn.

Outside, the mysterious veil of night enshrouded the town. Large, soft snowflakes fell to the earth, and this black-and-white panorama created a weird, haunting effect.

The human monster dragged Mary into the night as if she was a helpless puppet ... Their desperate journey lasted for hours, until they finally reached a strange, enormous building: Drakula's Castle.

Mary shuddered. Shaking in the icy wind, she was completely bewildered by her weird companion. She wanted to escape from Drakula's arms, but the monster was holding her firmly.

"Hah, my dear," he laughed in his satanic voice. "Joy and ecstasy are awaiting you! Why would you try to flee?"

"Let me go! Let me go!"

"You, too, will enter the realm of immortality, the palace of wonders: Drakula's Castle! Do not be afraid; do not shudder! Be happy instead, for bliss is awaiting you! Come!"

And so the young maiden's protests were all in vain. Drakula's power overcame her.

Then an immense stone gate creaked open before them. Drakula had reached home with his prey.

Though scared, Mary was curious, and so she looked around in the interior of the palace. Its weird architecture, its phantastic illumination reminded her of the strange realms that appear in fairy tales.

And then she smelled a weird and rank odor in Drakula's castle, the smell of death and decay. And this heavy, suffocating smell nearly intoxicated the mentally broken young maiden.

"But why have you brought me here?" Mary finally asked. "What do you want from me?"

Drakula replied triumphantly: "You will never be able to flee! Tomorrow we will celebrate our engagement! You will be my bride! I will marry you with an immortal kiss, and you will stay here with my other wives, all of whom possess eternal life!"

Then, with a wave of Drakula's hand, the marble floor in the middle of the palace opened. A blue-violet light appeared from below . . . the lush sounds of supernatural music could be heard . . . and twelve beautiful women could be seen, who, with their attractive bodies covered in veils, danced to the rhythm of the soft music . . .

Drakula told Mary: "Before the sun rises twice, you will be among my subterranean residents!"

"No . . . I don't want to be here, not for all the treasures in the world," Mary screamed. Filled with despair, she grabbed the cross hanging around her neck and beseeched God to save her from such horrors.

"Damnation! . . . Hell! . . . The only means by which my power is paralyzed! . . . Away with it!" Drakula shouted after seeing the crucifix.

VII The Wedding

Soon the palace was lit up by the first light of dawn. As he began to flee, Drakula scowled, "I hate the sunlight! It forces me away. But I shall see you again, tonight!"

Drakula disappeared, and all the gates of the palace closed behind him. Mary was left alone in the mysterious castle, and yet in every corner she could still see Drakula's satanic image grinning at her . . . She wanted to flee from the terrible phantom, but her actions were all in vain . . . Drakula's power prevented her from escaping.

Hours of agony passed . . . Mary helplessly moved around in her prison . . . She dragged her trembling limbs from one room to the next, in search of some relief, but to no avail . . . The horrendous image of Drakula's cruel, grinning face seemed to be everywhere.

Evening was soon at hand . . . Mary ran down into the park of the palace . . . Just as she did, the great gate opened with majesty and Drakula entered . . .

"How kind of you to receive me!" he said to the terrified maiden.

Drakula took Mary by her arm and led her through the palace. He told her: "Go now, and dress for our marriage ceremony."

Drakula then waved to his slave women, who surrounded Mary and led her into a beautiful, flowery room. Inside it was a wedding dress adorned with gold, silver and priceless jewels. The slave women dressed

Mary, and when they had finished, Drakula's newest bride was led into the great hall of the palace, where the devil's son was eagerly expecting her.

Drakula approached her, offering her a lustful smile. Deprived of her own will, as if trapped in a dream, Mary yielded to the power of the satanic man.

"You are welcome, my beautiful bride," Drakula flattered Mary. "We are now celebrating a feast of joy, the eve of our nuptials!"

Shrill music was then heard... It was the loud, weird music of some devilish wedding march, to which some strangely costumed ballerinas offered a wanton dance. The whole palace was covered in a mystical light... Shocking colors interchanged. A flash of colorful light appeared and then faded, only to be followed by the next one. Drakula's engagement feast was luxurious, but strange.

"After the rain of flowers, my kiss will unite us for ever!" the bridegroom said to the bride.

In the wake of these words, thousands and thousands of flowers fell from the ceiling of the palace, like summer rain, covering the floor. Horrible, death-like odors filled the enormous hall. Then, Drakula bent his head towards Mary in order to bestow a kiss onto her lips. His mouth trembled from wild desire, and he opened his arms to embrace her.

But at that very moment Mary pushed Drakula away, reached for the cross hanging around her neck, and bravely revealed it to him, her eyes flashing as she did.

"The cross!... The cross!" Drakula roared, shrinking back from the girl in terror.

At the sight of the crucifix, the entire hall was seized with panic... Drakula and all of the other evil spirits fled. Mary seized her opportunity. She rushed through the castle gate and into the snowy night.

VIII Down the Path of Death

Mary fled from Drakula and the palace of Hell, but her tired legs could not take her very far. Fainting, she fell on some snowy ground beside a tree trunk; the rays of dawn were just starting to shine upon her. Later that same morning, a nice family discovered her and took her back to their house so she could rest. But they were unable to revive her.

Mary Land was unconscious, though a fever had taken control of her mind. She was tormented by cruel, gruesome images. Drakula's hellish face never ceased grinning at her. His eerie eyes, his satanic features, and his terrible hands seemed always ready to possess her. Those images danced in front of her unconscious eyes.

Figure 10.5 Actor Carl Goetz, aka Karl Götz. (*Courtesy of George Chastain*)

"No ... no ... Don't hurt me!" Sometimes a word or two escaped from between her parched lips, causing Mary's rescuers to watch her with great sympathy.

"We must call a doctor," the head of the household decided. "We won't learn anything from her until she regains consciousness. There might be information we need to know before then." His younger brother then journeyed into the town to call a doctor.

All the while, Mary's agony persisted. She was tormented by nightmares that seemed as if they might destroy her. The family covered her burning forehead and face with snow in an effort to help ease her fever.

Hours later, the room was almost silent. Only poor Mary's panting could be heard. But the quiet was broken when the door opened unexpectedly. Mary's rescuers saw a visitor clad in black standing at the threshold. It was Drakula. The devilish creature made the family shudder in fear.

Outside the wind was howling and thrashing snow into the room. Without saying a word, Drakula closed the door behind him and quietly approached Mary. He paid no attention to the family members staring with wonder at his appearance.

"I am here because she requires medical help. Nothing else is more important," Drakula informed the onlookers.

"But who sent you?" the head of the household asked. "How did you know to come here? My brother has left to get a doctor from the town."

Drakula chose not to answer. Instead, he approached the still-unconscious Mary, looked at her briefly, and then said: "This young maiden is insane and must have escaped from a mental asylum. She must be removed from here as soon as possible, since she is a threat to herself and those around her."

Those standing nearby fell under the spell of Drakula's powerful words. An awkward silence followed. Drakula's blazing eyes hypnotized the family, who helplessly suffered as a result. Then it seemed as if he would never remove his violet, flashing eyes from Mary's poor body, which had become more and more disturbed since Drakula's arrival.

"Don't surrender me! Rescue me! Help ...! He is killing me!" she screamed, trapped in a state of extreme terror. Then Drakula displayed once again his cruel, hellish smile.

With his arms crossed, he stood beside Mary, while the horrified family watched.

Meanwhile the head of the household's brother arrived with a real doctor from the town.

"This doctor considers the young woman to be a dangerous maniac," the head of the household said to the new doctor.

After examining Mary, the real doctor turned to Drakula and said: "You seem to be wrong, dear colleague. All I can perceive are wounds ... and a fever." Then he proceeded to say: "This seems to be quite an extraordinary case! Whatever it is, I will remain here, in order to watch over her."

Disgusted by the real doctor's words, Drakula immediately disappeared from the house.

*****

Days passed ... Mary struggled to regain her health, and after a week had gone by, she was in much better form. She was cheerful again, as if nothing had happened. In fact, she could hardly recall the horrible events that had transpired. She just felt as if she had awoken from a terrible nightmare, but one that she could hardly really remember. The family continued to watch over Mary as if she was one of their own relatives.

One day, after examining the little patient, the doctor happily announced: "Mary is definitely getting better. Soon she will be fully recovered!"

IX A Cruel Night

One night, when everyone in the household was sitting together, a man arrived at their door. "You have been requested," he said to the surgeon. "somebody has had an accident at the sports field! They are waiting for you!"

"Who are you?" the doctor inquired.

"I am a coachman," man replied. "It is me who takes the hotel guests to the train and back."

"But it is pitch dark outside," the doctor said with a concerned voice.

"You needn't be afraid, doctor! I know the road by heart, and my horse is very reliable," the coachman said reassuringly.

The doctor understood his duty and left with the coachman. He promised Mary and the others that he would return as soon as he had finished his work.

Outside the sky was pitch black and a heavy fog blanketed the landscape. The snow crunched under the two men's steps. The doctor took a seat inside the little carriage, the coachman sat on the box, lashed the horses, and the wooden frame was set into motion.

The doctor turned back to look behind them. The bright window of the nice little house became an increasingly distant image as the carriage moved forward through the white snow.

The coachman drove faster and faster; the carriage seemed to fly on wings, as the road it traveled over could not be seen. The blackness of night and the thick fog seemed to hide everything. As he smoked his cigar during the long journey, the doctor thought about Mary, and he rejoiced in the fact that he helped the blossoming young woman regain her life.

The carriage continued its journey, faster and faster, and the sound of the horses suggested a hint of life in the otherwise desolate and mysterious night. After a quarter of an hour had passed, the doctor asked the coachman, "Where are you actually headed?"

Perhaps the question escaped the coachman's attention, or perhaps he chose not to hear it, as he kept silent and continued to drive the horses. The doctor was puzzled and so he asked even more loudly: "Where are you heading for? Where are you taking me? Stop!" But this call, too, was lost in the night. The doctor then felt his pockets; he had no weapon. He was aware now that his guide was part of some cruel plan.

However, the doctor did not lose faith. Encouraged by a sense of urgency and danger, the doctor once again raised his voice: "Tell me, will you, where you are taking me? What is our destination?"

At that very moment, the little carriage reached a hazardous stretch of road that ran alongside an deep abyss ... Even a slight landslide would cause the carriage to fall to its doom.

Realizing the risk they faced, the coachman admitted: "A strange man clad in black gave me a gold coin and ordered me to bring you here, doctor."

"You miserable man! Turn back at once!" the doctor said. "Our lives are in danger!"

The graveness of the situation and the doctor's warning did not fail to have an effect on the coachman who had been bribed by Drakula. He cautiously turned the carriage around and took his passenger back to the home where Mary now resided.

On the return journey, the doctor questioned the coachman further, but he was unable to give anything more than a vague description of his employer. Nonetheless, his information was enough for the doctor to realize that the man who bribed the coachman was the same "doctor" that he had met at Mary's sick bed. That man had suggested that Mary should go to a mental institute as a ruse to kidnap her. But all of this information was of limited help, since the doctor did not know where the mysterious stranger lived.

Meanwhile, the family's house was enshrouded by the deep silence of the night. The whole family was asleep; only little Mary was restless ... At about midnight, Mary awoke to an odd, frightening sound ... It was as if she heard the ghostlike wail of an owl ... Her entire body shuddered ... She looked around in the half-lit gloom of the house ... Her eyes turned towards a dim lamp ... She looked for the source of the mysterious sounds, but she saw nothing. Mary then sank back to her bed and tried to sleep.

The wind outside howled viciously, and so Mary was unable to close her eyes. The dim light of the lamp cast strange images around the room, and Mary believed she could see shadows flickering on a white wall.

Drakula invaded her thoughts ...

The kind family and the good doctor had helped her forget about the horrors of the past: its terrible memory had grown distant, but this horrible night brought it back to the forefront of her mind.

"To-whoo ... To-whoo ... To-whoo ..." Mary heard the hoots of an owl, but she did not know whether she really heard it or if it was just another delusion ... And the dark shadows kept creeping around the room. Sweat beaded from her forehead; her body was burning with fever. Overcome with distress and terror, she tossed around in her bed.

Mary desperately tried to forget everything, keeping her eyes closed in stubborn determination and pushing her head into the pillows. She wanted sleep, nothing but sleep. Her lips murmured prayers, beseeching God to grant her a deep and restful sleep.

But try as she might, her eyes did not close. On the contrary, no matter how hard she tried, her eyelids remained open. "My God . . . don't leave me!" she whispered, feeling that her fate was about to reach a terrible turning point.

Outside the wind howled more horribly than ever. It caused the windows to shake with a vengeance. Mary felt she could hear countless cries echoed in the roaring wind.

The minutes passed slowly, which weighed on the poor maiden as if they were hours.

When Mary looked once again into the vanishing lamplight, it crashed down onto the floor, flames erupting in its wake, setting the carpet on fire and spreading across the little room. Jumping out of her bed, Mary fled from the sea of fire into the cold winter night . . .

Figure 10.6   Actress Magda Sonja, who likely played one of Drakula's brides. (*Courtesy of George Chastain*)

As if pursued by something, she ran and ran through night ... She didn't feel the cold of the snow or the lashes of the icy wind. She just ran and ran and ran ...

X The Devil Has Flown Away

At last the terrible nightmare ended.

Mary woke up and, with her frightened eyes, she looked around the operation room, where the snow-white furnishings and the operating table were reminiscent of death. They had a ghastly effect on the poor creature, who had just been freed from her terrible dream ...

The red rays of the rising sun appeared. Nature was waking up, and the hospital, too, with its wretched patients, was also coming to life. Looking worried, Mary ran across the room. She raised her frail hand to stroke her forehead.

Shuddering, she remembered her awful experiences, but her soul cheered up at the thought that they had only been a dream.

But then a terrible fear gripped her, and Mary began to worry once more. Since she had entered the madhouse, so many bizarre things had happened: the incident in the operation room and the cruel nightmare that seemed so real. Her nerves began jumping, and her heart was beating heavily. Then she heard a horrible sound that seemed to come from the asylum's garden.

Remembering her poor father, who had lost his mind, Mary grew worried. The icy hand of suspicion crept across her body. "What if ... what if ... if I too ...?" she shuddered.

At that moment, the door of the operation room began to creak open, but Mary wasn't strong enough to look at who entered.

* * * * *

Doctor Tillner's morning rounds brought him to the operation room. Mary was still lying on the couch. Her eyes were open, but she was too weak to get up. The nurse standing beside her approached the doctor.

'she must have had very horrible dreams. She was crying out all night," the nurse explained.

Doctor Tillner tenderly held the maiden, who was still shaking with fear and distress and looking about in the room, still in tremor from the satanic Drakula ...

"What is it ... what happened to me?" Mary nervously asked the doctor. "Am I awake ... or I am still trapped in that awful nightmare?"

"Calm down, my dear," Tillner said to her. "It was just a dream; please try to forget about it."

XI Drakula's Death

The mental patients had already gathered in the garden of the asylum. They continued with their strange habits. The scientist feared for his "glass leg," the "Minister of Finance" doled out checks, and Drakula, the one-time composer, gave a speech about his immortality to a group of patients who quickly grew bored with him.

Among these living dead stood a heavyset little man who wore a tall, pointed top hat. A pair of enormous spectacles weighed down on his thick nose. His old, parchment-colored face displayed a permanent smile, as if he was forever caught in a distorted laugh. He never ceased making strange jokes and was always kidding his companions. He liked to fool the others, though they were long used to his ways.

This morning, the "Funny Man," as he was nicknamed, had somehow discovered a loaded revolver, which he began pointing at his panicked companions. The armed madman then appeared before Drakula, pointed his gun at him, and laughed with that distorted grin.

Drakula nearly erupted with joy, telling the Funny Man: "At last I can prove that I am immortal! Shoot!"

Drakula's voice boomed throughout the garden, causing the other patients to gather around them.

Drakula then thundered: "What are you waiting for, you cowardly mongrel! All of you have always stared at me like fools, not believing in my immortality. Now, come here all of you, gather around and witness the truth! Drakula is safe from your bullets; they will not penetrate my body. Drakula is immortal! Hahaha! Come . . . here . . . all of you! And you . . . raise your revolver!"

The Funny Man nervously began to back away from Drakula.

"No . . . I dare not do it . . . I dare not do it!"—he said, slowly lowering the revolver.

'so you are afraid? You coward! Shoot, as I command you to do! Here—aim at my chest!" Drakula shouted.

The terrified group that surrounded the two madmen surveyed the scene with heightened interest. Then, obeying his stern command, the Funny Man cocked the trigger of his pistol and fired . . .

The bullet hit Drakula in the heart and killed him at once. His blood poured forth, staining the fresh snow with the color red.

After the gun was fired, the terror-stricken patients scattered throughout the garden. Within moments, Doctor Tillner and his assistants stood beside Drakula's body.

"Drakula is dead," one of the assistants told the doctor after examining him. "The Funny Man has killed him with a stolen gun."

At the sight of his gruesome deed, the mad murderer was at first seized with panic, but soon he began giggling once again. While the assistants tied him up and took him back to his cell, the Funny Man's face grew even more disfigured by his insane laughter.

XII Down the Road of Love

A sleigh stopped in front of the madhouse. It was George, Mary's fiancé, who climbed out of it. After having waited in vain for his bride-to-be the previous night, he had rushed to the city, in order to find her and take her back home.

Overjoyed at the sight of George, Mary ran up to him, fell into his arms, and then the two lovers shared a long kiss . . .

"Thanks God," the young man said with the sound of relief and happiness in his voice. "At last we are reunited . . . I was so worried . . . so anxious that something might have happened to you! . . . But please tell me, why didn't you come back last night? What kept you?"

A flood of questions poured out of George's lips, but Mary did not have the time or desire to answer them: Doctor Tillner was approaching. He bade the young couple farewell, and they set out across the garden to leave the hospital. As they were walking arm in arm, they came across two assistants who were carrying Drakula's corpse on a stretcher. When the procession passed in front of her, Mary caught sight of Drakula's formidable face, which caused her even more fright than when he was alive. Nearly fainting, she drew close to George. Not knowing about her horrible dream, George was puzzled by her reaction.

The assistants carried Drakula away. As they did, a notebook dropped out of his pocket. George picked it up and examined the cover:

> A DIARY OF MY IMMORTAL LIFE
> AND OF MY ADVENTURES
> —DRAKULA

Glimpsing the title and growing even more frightened, Mary she demanded: "Throw it away at once! I don't want to look at it! This man was the cause of my terrible dream!"

George followed her wishes. He threw the diary away, took Mary by the arm, and then helped her into his sleigh. Its little wooden frame then carried the lovers back home, back to happiness and to bliss.

During the journey, George repeatedly tried to get Mary to talk, but her lips remained sealed. She did not tell him a single word about the agony she had suffered because of the terrible dream. George would not

Figure 10.7   The cover of Lajos Pánczél's novella adaption of *Drakula halála*.

learn what had happened. Realizing she wished to remain quiet, he never spoke about it again.
The End

Notes

1. See, for example, Jenö Farkas' "Nosferatu Elött: A Magyar Drakula," *Filmvilág*, December 1997. Available at <http://www.filmvilag.hu/xista_frame.php?cikk_id=1714> (last accessed 20 January 2015). I would note that all modern researches seem to have been greatly assisted by the hard work and research of Gyöngyi Balogh at the Hungarian Film Insitute in Budapest.

2. "*Drakula*—Károly Lajthay's Latest Film," *Képes Mozivilág*, 16 January 1921, p. 21.
3. I am very grateful to Gyöngyi Balogh for this information.
4. "Hungarian Film Directors in Vienna," *Színházi Élet*, No. 52, 1920.
5. Ibid.
6. Ibid.
7. "*Drakula*—Károly Lajthay's Latest Film," p. 21.
8. It should also be noted that *Képes Mozivilág* never actually says that Myl would portray Mary Land. Rather, the publication claims she would play the "heroine."
9. "I Attended a Wedding," *Színház és Mozi*, January 1921, pp. 26–7.
10. Anna Marie Hegener and Magda Sonja might well have portrayed Drakula's other brides; both are named in "Hungarian Film Directors in Vienna."
11. Ibid. pp. 26–7. In this publication, Lajthay notes that he "completed external shots last month," meaning December 1920, "near Vienna." The article "Hungarian Film Directors in Vienna" was more specific, quoting Lajthay as mentioning he had shot in Melk. However, in "*Drakula*—Károly Lajthay's Latest Film," *Képes Mozivilág* reported that—following the interiors at the Corvin Film Studio—Lajthay would "resume the external shots in the Wachau near Vienna" (p. 21).
12. "I Attended a Wedding," p. 27.
13. "Hungarian Film Directors in Vienna."
14. "I Attended a Wedding," pp. 26–7.
15. "Calendar of Events," *Mozie és Film*, April 1923, p. 23.
16. Advertisement, *Mozi és Film*, April 1923, p. 4.
17. With regard to my research on both the film and the novella of *Drakula halála*, I offer great thanks to my dear friend Gyöngyi Balogh of the Hungarian Film Institute in Budapest, who is certainly the leading expert on Hungarian silent cinema. I also wish to thank my colleague János Szántai in Timisoara, Olaf Brill at Cinegraph in Bremen, and Brigitte Mayr at Synema, the Society for Film and Media in Vienna. With regard to the translation of the text from Hungarian to English, I offer my deepest appreciation to Péter Litván, whose kindness, patience, and assistance were invaluable.
18. Translation copyright Gary D. Rhodes, 2009.

11. *LE BRASIER ARDENT* (1923): IVAN MOSJOUKINE'S *CLIN D'ŒIL* TO GERMAN EXPRESSIONISM

Bernard McCarron

Figure 11.1 Ivan Mosjoukine.

Ivan Mosjoukine's regrettably little-known film *Le Brasier ardent* (1923) represents an important amalgam of formalist and stylistic patterns from a number of national cinemas.[1] These include France, Germany, and (though it will not be interrogated in this chapter, given its focus) Russia.[2] In tandem with visual motifs and aesthetic strategies that drew upon filmmaking schools prevalent during the 1920s (including of such French Impressionist directors as Abel Gance, Louis Delluc, Marcel L'Herbier, Jean Epstein and Germaine Dulac), *Le Brasier ardent* features a small number of scenes that reveal the influence of German Expressionism.

While the overall film appropriates and responds to Impressionism, it does so through a form of pastiche that offers "flourishes" of Expressionism (to borrow a term from Lotte Eisner) in order to make its point—a kind of postmodern *clin d'œil* before the fact.[3] The key objective of this chapter is to probe the Expressionist aspects of *Le Brasier ardent* by engaging in a neo-formalist analysis of the film's *mise-en-scène*.

The chapter explores synergies between *Le Brasier ardent* and notable Expressionist films that predate its production, specifically Robert Wiene's *Das Cabinet des Caligari/The Cabinet of Dr. Caligari* (1920) and *Genuine, die Tragödie eines seltsamen Hauses/Genuine, the Tragedy of a Strange House* (1920), Karlheinz Martin's *Von morgens bis Mitternacht/From Morning to Midnight* (1920, released 1922), and other significant films of the Weimar period which are not strictly Expressionist, but employ Expressionist motifs, particularly Fritz Lang's *Dr. Mabuse, der Spieler/Dr. Mabuse the Gambler* (1922). In adopting this strategy, the chapter mounts a case for *Le Brasier ardent* as being an early example of the influence of Expressionist cinema outside of Germany.

In order to undertake this analysis, this chapter will present some background information on *Le Brasier ardent* and its somewhat cryptic narrative. It will also interrogate the film's debt to French Impressionism. The purpose here is to distinguish the given artistic influences on specific scenes, the juxtaposition of which makes the (admittedly limited) use of Expressionism more pronounced, as well as to note the unexpected convergence of the two traditions at given intervals in the film.

PRODUCTION BACKGROUND

Produced in Paris in 1923, *Le Brasier ardent* ranks among the important French Impressionist films of that year, along with *L'auberge rouge* (*The Red Inn* [Jean Epstein, 1923]), *Don Juan et Faust* (*Don Juan and Faust* [Marcel L'Herbier, 1923]), *La Souriante Madame Beudet* (*The Smiling Madame Beudet* [Germaine Dulac, 1923]), *Coeur fidèle* (*Faithful Heart* [Jean Epstein, 1923]), *Crainquebille* (*Coster Bill of Paris* [Jacques Feyder, 1923]), *Le Marchand de*

Plaisir (*The Seller of Pleasure* [Jaque Catelain, 1923]), and *Gossette* (*The Little Kid* [Germaine Dulac, 1923]).

Though it was certainly a French film, *Le Brasier ardent* was the product of Russian émigrés who had fled the Soviet Union. In many respects, its origins lie in the arrival of Joseph N. Ermolieff and a number of his colleagues at Marseilles during the summer of 1920. They housed their productions in an old Pathé studio in the Parisian suburb of Montreuil-sous-Bois. Yakov Protazanov's *L'Angoissante aventure* (*The Distressing Adventure*) (1920, later titled *The Narrow Escape*) became the studio's first production.[4]

Although it received only a lukewarm reception from critics and audiences, *L'Angoissante aventure* led the way to a number of subsequent Franco-Russian productions, films that were arguably different and more dynamic than the standard French fare that had become increasingly insipid in the immediate aftermath of World War I. Paul Theimann, another Russian émigré, enlisted Protazanov to make three films, including *Le sens de la mort* (*The Sense of Death*) (1922). Ladislas Starevich made a number of puppet animation films, including *Le roman de renard* (*The Tale of the Fox*). In addition, Viatcheslav Tourjansky directed eight films and Alexandre Volkoff directed four.[5]

Lenny Borger rightly argues that there is a tendency among film historians to reduce the varied outputs of Russian émigrés in Paris at this time to the Ermolieff–Albatros company, whereas the Russian cinematic contribution in France was far more complex.[6] For example, the first subdivision of the company occurred in 1922 when Joseph Ermolieff moved to Germany and sold his studio holdings to Alexandre Kamenka and Noë Bloch; they, in turn, formed a new company called Les Films Albatros that integrated with the distributor Les Films Armor.[7] Between 1923 and 1924, the company produced twelve films. Ivan Mosjoukine—best-known at the time as an actor, who was then living in France—was very much the face of that studio, starring in a number of successful productions, including three directed by Volkoff: *La maison du mystère* (1923), *Kean* (1924), and *Les ombres qui passent* (1924).

But *Le Brasier ardent* proved unique among the Le Film Albatros' output. Mosjoukine not only starred in the film but directed it as well. It marked his debut in that capacity and would in fact be the only film he would ever direct, perhaps not surprising given the negative reaction accorded *Le Brasier ardent* by most viewers in 1923. Its breathtaking range of styles and its plot structure dumbfounded many audiences and critics alike on its release.

Released on June 8, 1923, *Le Brasier ardent* led Jean Renoir to exclaim: "One day . . . I saw *le brasier ardent* [sic], directed and acted by Mosjoukine and produced by the courageous Alexandre Kamenka. The audience howled and whistled, shocked by a film so different from their usual fare. I was ecstatic . . . I decided to abandon my trade, ceramics, to try to make films."[8]

But perhaps *Le Brasier ardent*'s crowning achievement is how it discovers and organizes synergies between the French avant-garde and German Expressionism. These stylistic aspects make the film a hub for the various artistic ideas prevalent within European filmmaking traditions at the time. Mosjoukine's film consolidates the disparate features of these national avant-gardes into an entity that mutates from one scene to the next. As Richard Abel has noted:

> *Le Brasier ardent* certainly has the most extravagant mixture of style or mode . . . That is due in part to Mosjoukine's performance as nearly a dozen different characters. In the opening nightmare alone, he plays a heretic burning at the stake, an elegant gentleman, a bishop and a beggar. In the rest of the film, he shifts among a series of contradictory personae—a brilliant detective, a silly buffoon, a cruel dancing master, a shy lover, and a mamma's boy. The decors . . . also change radically to complement these and other character shifts.[9]

As Abel suggests, *Le Brasier ardent* features a playful quality from the presence of Mosjoukine being behind the camera, as well as in front of it. As Mosjoukine shifts from character to character during the course of the film, as well as from one premise to another, no stable reference point emerges for the bizarre narrative. As a result, Mosjoukine's roles abound in the plurality of meaning created by the absence of a fixed identity.

To this end, *Le Brasier ardent* brims with Mosjoukine's sense of dynamism, one in which identity remains in flux. The film's narrative follows the exploits of a number of characters, including a lady named Elle (played by Nathalie Lissenko, a Russian actress), "the husband" (Nicolas Koline, a Russian actor) and Detective Z (Mosjoukine). The film centers on themes of dissatisfaction and jealously, particularly in the relationship between Elle and her husband.

Figure 11.2 and 11.3. The Expressionist Gaze: Elle and Z's intimacy, as depicted in the nightmare sequence at the beginning of the film.

Initially this dissatisfaction occurs during a dream sequence in which Elle struggles to escape from an unknown man who follows her. She awakens and realizes that a book that she has been reading—the memoirs of a famous detective known simply as Z—inspired her nightmare. The images in the book appear in the form of a rebus, clearing up the various sources of her anxiety within the nightmare sequence. After she realizes the triviality of the dream's source material, she turns her attentions to her marital problems.

Elle's husband has grown jealous of her flirtations with a group of male revelers and as a result becomes desperate to relocate her to an isolated estate in the *banlieue*, a move that she resists at all costs. She loves Paris too much to leave it. To retaliate against her husband's plans, Elle steals their marriage contract. The husband thus engages a detective so as to recover the document and to regain at least a modicum of control over his wife. The man he employs turns out to be Detective Z. Well aware of Z's identity, Elle tries to seduce the detective during the course of his investigation.

Z resists her attempts, and after completing his work he returns home to spend time with his grandmother, a decision that undercuts his credibility as a fearless investigator to humorous effect. At the conclusion of *Le Brasier ardent*, the husband realizes that he cannot force Elle to love him and concedes that she should be with Z in order to attain true happiness.

The film takes place across a number of locales, including the underground, the Parisian social scene, and various domestic and private spaces of Paris during the 1920s. In the process, *Le Brasier ardent* traverses a number of formal qualities and aesthetic traditions of France and Germany. It is this (quite playful) fusion that allows the film to take on multiple modes of cinematic expression and make use of German Expressionism and French Impressionism.

Impressionism

Prior to investigating the usage of Expressionism in *Le Brasier ardent*, it is necessary to examine its engagement with Impressionism. Like the term "Expressionism," the term "Impressionist" itself is contentious when applied to the cinema. It is critiqued on the basis that many so-called Impressionist films vary wildly in terms of their aesthetic and narrative form. Nevertheless, one of the key aspects of Impressionist cinema is how character subjectivity is made possible through techniques of *photogénie*. Thompson and Bordwell chronicle a number of techniques that allow for the conveyance of a character's thoughts or memories, including superimpositions, filtering and defocusing the camera lens.[10] Whilst it is difficult to agree upon an exact definition of *photogénie*, what is apparent is that techniques that create subjectivity enhance its properties.

Within this context, then, the bulk of *Le Brasier ardent* can be regarded as Impressionistic. This is apparent not only in its avant-garde storyline, but also by observing the key aesthetic criteria of Impressionist cinema formulated by Thompson and Bordwell, that is to say, the subjective mode of narration that germinates from the perspective of Elle, the film's lead female character. *Le Brasier ardent* attempts to capture the inherent beauty of Paris, employing various visual effects that make Elle's subjective view discernible.

Such effects include flashbacks, particularly in the final third of the film. For example, following a disagreement between Elle and Z and an impromptu dance competition that results in an apparent fatality (owing to the extreme tempo of the music), Z takes Elle back to her home. Z's face dissolves into a flashback of him dressed as a bishop from the nightmare seen at the beginning of the film, at which point he tells Elle to go home. Returning to his own house, Z suffers a toothache and falls asleep on his grandmother's shoulder. Then another flashback from the nightmare appears, an image of Z as a destitute man. Here the flashbacks serve as a means to demystify the enigmatic phantasms in Elle's dream. *Photogénie* in this sequence represents an avant-garde mode of storytelling that aligns *Le Brasier ardent* with other Impressionist films of the era.

Augmenting these visual effects, Mosjoukine uses location shooting and nonfiction footage to his advantage. In a number of Paris exteriors, shot on location, *Le Brasier ardent* conveys the emotional impressions and sensations associated with *photogénie*. Again these are expressed through Elle's perspective and through the depiction of her experiences of Paris. One of the sequences presents Elle and her husband on the streets of Paris. She exclaims: "Paris! What more beautiful city could there be?" In the shot that follows this intertitle, Elle and her husband are framed in front of the Place de la Concorde. Here, and in a number of other places during the film, Mosjoukine incorporates actuality footage taken in and around Paris, at times featuring actors in the film and at other times featuring actual Parisians, including when Mosjoukine illustrates the husband's daydreams about Elle's infidelity.

Paris in this sense is presented as being overwhelming, something more than the sum of its parts. Through Mosjoukine's cinematic representation of the city, the spectator is encouraged to see what Elle sees and feels. Viewing the world through Elle's perspective, the spectator shares in her *jouissance* for Paris, which attains a mystical, almost Stendhalian status. Certain framings are key here. For example, point-of-view shots allow Mosjoukine to show how Elle's mood changes from the anger she displays at her husband when he explains that he is selling their estate to the feeling of inspiration she experiences when looking out of her room onto the fountain in the Place de la Concorde.

During one sequence, Elle conveys her deep love of Parisian life to Z, which Mosjoukine illustrates by use of an interplay between images and intertitles.

This sequence begins with Z and Elle discussing their mutual adoration of the city's features, including:

> The Bois du Boulogne and its flow of automobiles. The Grands Boulevards at night in the rain. Notre-dame Cathedral. The Eiffel Tower! The music hall revues ... Symphonies of color ... Boldness of lines ... The rhythm of the trapeze ... The harmony of muscles ...

Following these verbal exchanges a number of other conceptions about Parisian life are conveyed with corresponding onscreen images, such as "The Park Monceau on a Spring Morning and the Tuileries in the autumn sunset!" The varying graphic relations within these sequences are indicative of what are generally understood to be the basic poetics of the Impressionist film.

More than any of the other films made or influenced by the personnel of Ermolieff's company, Mosjoukine's film resembles Dulac's avant-garde character study *La Souriante Madame Beudet*. In much the same way as Dulac's film features a female character (Madame Beudet, played by Germaine Dermoz) doomed to fulfill a loveless marriage to a maniacal husband, Mosjoukine's film, too, remarkably features a very similar character in Elle. Both characters experience a series of subjective visions. Aside from the sequences in which Elle daydreams (apart from her opening nightmare), a number of images exist externally to her imagination, images that are similar to Beudet's fantasies. These are, according to Judith Mayne, "indications of some kind of alterna-

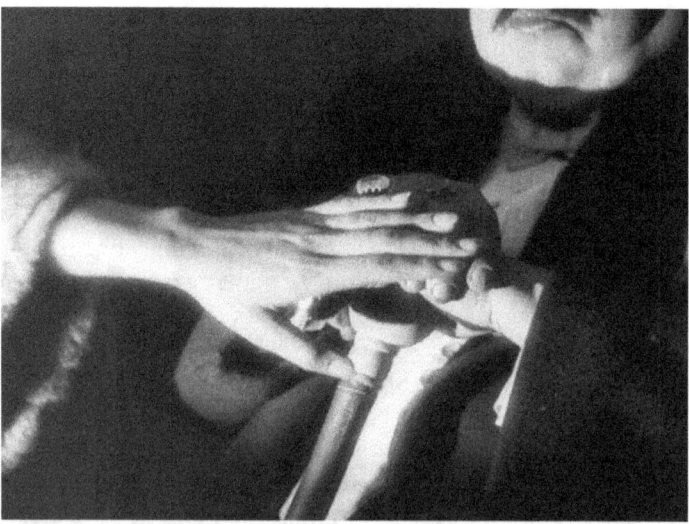

Figure 11.4 Dark desires exposed: in Elle's nightmare, a wealthy man is solicited on the seedy backstreets of Paris.

tive to the claustrophobic world of the Beudet apartment. If private and public spheres are relatively autonomous of each other ... this world outside constantly beckons."[11] Mosjoukine's film adopts a similar formal approach.

Whereas filmmakers like Dulac and L'Herbier aspired to "pure cinema" (*cinéma pur*), one featuring formal, temporal, graphic and non-narrative forms, Thompson and Bordwell claim that "[m]ost impressionists took a less radical course, making films that explored the medium of cinema."[12] *Le Brasier ardent* concurs with this engagement with Impressionism, not only in how it mimics the narrative structure of *La Souriante Madame Beudet*, but also in how it explores other cinematic movements.

Expressionism

While the bulk of *Le Brasier ardent*'s running time exemplifies cinematic Impressionism, two particular sequences use Expressionistic motifs, specifically Elle's nightmare and, much more so, "The Seekers Club," which Elle's husband visits in a bid to regain his runaway wife. Important similarities exist between Mosjoukine's film and at least a few German films that predate it, including Lang's *Dr. Mabuse, der Spieler* (which was released approximately one year prior to *Le Brasier ardent*).

To begin, *Le Brasier ardent* adopts the same mode of Expressionism that Dietrich Scheunemann finds to be at work in *Dr. Mabuse the Gambler*. For him, the key evidence of *Dr. Mabuse*'s engagement with Expressionism unfolds in a conversation between Mabuse (Rudolf Klein-Rogge) and Count Told (Alfred Abel) when the two meet at a gambling party known as "The Great Game":

> Count Told: "What is your attitude toward Expressionism, Doctor?"
>
> Dr. Mabuse: "Expressionism is a mere pastime—but why not?—*Everything* today is pastime—!"
>
> Count Told: "Since everything is a pastime, Doctor, I hope you will not hold it against me if we now go over to play poker ..."

In a sardonic manner, Lang seems to reveal his stance on Expressionism and its associated uses and abuses. Scheunemann makes an important observation about Lang's appropriation of the playful character of Expressionism. On these grounds, *Le Brasier ardent* is making the same overtures pertaining to play, desire and irrationalism.

Nowhere in *Le Brasier ardent* are the film's allusions to *Dr. Mabuse* more apparent than when the husband pursues Elle. The Seekers Club warehouse is fitted with conveyor belts and various other items of automated technology. Its

Figure 11.5 "The husband" gains admission to "The Seekers Club."

Figure 11.6 "The husband" faces a panel of psychologists in the committee room.

individual rooms feature disembodied sensory organs. One room is filled with ears to suggest covert listening, or bugging; another room is filled with a slew of eyes, which also give the impression of surveillance, not unlike that which is sometimes associated with Mabuse. The Seekers Club's objective is to grant wish fulfillment to its clients. The building itself displays a series of absurd signs featuring lettering that reads: "Heaven of the Fleeced. Find All Agency. Thieves Hell. Return of Missing Wives."

The club's committee room illustrates a set design evocative of a number of Expressionist films, including the scantly austere *mise-en-scène* of *Von morgens bis Mitternacht*. The similarities between the two films are particularly apparent in Mosjoukine's use of high contrast, as in the door through which the husband enters and the interior of the committee room itself, in particular a carpet composed of black and white shapes that include diamonds, rectangles and curved lines. The husband enters through a door emblazoned with a number of symbols and text reading "Return of Missing Wives." This includes a miniature set of piano keys that the doorman plays in order to admit the husband. The door also includes a number of white arrows against a dark background. Later in this sequence, when the husband stares at each committee member, he is framed against a blank background. These reverse shots in particular recall the barren set design of *Von morgens bis mitternachts*, where the bank clerk is regularly framed against a plain blank background.

Likewise, the committee members—who are psychologists—appear mechanized and inhuman. Deformed and sneering in appearance, their faces exemplify the distorted and angular aspects of German Expressionist films of the period. The Seekers Club thus reveals the existence of an experimental film inside the narrative film. The polyvalent nature of the club (and the fluidity of identity at play in the film as a whole) is made abundantly clear with the inclusion of a series of comedic effects in the form of the committee members' strange facial gestures and synchronized movements that function to parody, disarm, and even gentrify the threat and horror of Expressionism. Put another way, here is a kind of apocalyptic adolescence.[13]

Character similarities are also present between the two films, particularly between Mabuse and Detective Z. One of the key ways Detective Z resembles Mabuse is in the multiple dimensions of his character. Z's ambiguous nature is communicated through Expressionistic settings inside Elle's nightmare, including the seedy backstreets of Paris, which are a far cry from Elle's quotidian city experience. Within the initial nightmare sequence, Detective Z exerts control over Elle in a manner similar to that of the master criminals of German Expressionism, specifically Mabuse and Caligari. Outside of this nightmare and for the remainder of the film, Detective Z is revealed as less mysterious and less of a threat. Elle does not come under his control so much as he comes under hers. *Le Brasier ardent* is at times accommodating to the demands of Expressionism; its characters are totally irrational and crude, to a perverse degree.

While there is a temptation to view Elle's autonomy within the film as an early example of feminism on the French screen, she can also be read as emblematic of the licentious female that marked many important films in Weimar cinema.[14] Elle's personality is split along the dual desires of lust and long-term happiness. This explains her attraction to Detective Z, who is himself a changeling of sorts. Here the normative, quiet and lavish life of the bourgeoisie is threatened by the intrusion of other values, standing in stark opposition to that of the Parisian upper crust. In this sense, the film reveals its darker theme, which is not at all dissimilar to what Siegfried Kracauer identified in German Expressionism.

Indeed, it could well be argued that the character of Elle exerts a strange power over Detective Z, her husband, and all of her various male companions in a manner that resembles the eponymous female lead in Wiene's *Genuine* (portrayed by Fern Andra), who is both a vampire and a malevolent force. Parallels are discernible between Elle's social entrapment by her husband, who seems to want to keep her hidden away from the rest of society, and Genuine's situation. *Genuine* is captured as a savage, bought by an older man, and held in captivity. This arouses the suspicions of the community before she begins to exert her mystical control over the young men in the film. Much the same is true of Elle, who is rescued from savages by her husband.

While most of *Le Brasier ardent* is characterized by high-key lighting (including at The Seekers Club), Mosjoukine does make use of low-key lighting, albeit sparingly. In particular, low-key lighting is employed during the initial nightmare sequence, for example when the light source is trained on the faces of Elle and Z when they are depicted as heretics. There is also a discernible use of low-key lighting in the streets into which Elle runs after she escapes the scenario at the burning stake. When she enters the Parisian back streets, low-key lighting is used to underscore the austerity and corruption associated with these non-places.

But perhaps Mosjoukine's most innovative use of Expressionism occurs during the editing of one particular sequence, that in which Z plays piano in a bar and Elle's emotional turbulence surfaces. Mosjoukine builds suspense in the scene as it moves through a number of styles, from a very slow shot/reverse shot in which Z and Elle look into each other's eyes to a rapid sequence at the end of the scene, when an extremely high volume of shots unfold, the average shot length of which is between only one and two seconds. The editing is used to create an explosion of neurotic jealousy experienced by the would-be lovers. This sequence conveys not just these feelings of emotional disturbance experienced by the lead characters, but also the wild sexual excitement of the audience, comprising licentious females and aroused males who dance to the increasing tempo of Z's piano playing.

Editing is less often examined as a feature of German Expressionist cinema, but that is indeed its purpose at this point in *Le Brasier ardent*. The fast and pronounced editing style—as well as the particular images being cut—generates a form of expressionist editing that communicates individual and mass neuroses

Figure 11.7 The dance contest begins: Elle looks on as Z begins playing the piano. (*Courtesy of Flicker Alley, LLC and Film Preservation Associates*)

and sexual desire. The result, to borrow a phrase from Béla Balázs, conveys the crowd's most "expressive expression."[15] Put another way, here is editing that—as Kasimir Edschmid might say—"grasps what is behind" the characters—their increasing sexual desires—and rips them frenetically to the surface.[16]

Convergence

Mosjoukine's variegated approach to the cinema yields specific moments in which a convergence of Impressionist and Expressionist styles can be said to occur. For example, Mosjoukine alludes to Elle's backstory through the use of photonegative imagery. The use of this technique encapsulates the subjective nature of both the French Impressionist films of the period (in terms of how it attempts to represent an act of recollection as an experience of mind using experimental techniques) and German Expressionist cinema (in terms of its status as "a double" image; a negative that illustrates the suggestion of deviancy within a character who, on the surface, appears to belong to a sophisticated bourgeois set). Just as the photonegative calls to mind some French films of the period, so too is it evocative of certain German films, such as *Nosferatu* (1922).

Le Brasier ardent also illustrates a shared connection between Impressionist and Expressionist film structures in its use of framing devices. *Le Brasier ardent* includes a number of psychological framings akin to the most famous of framing stories in German Expressionist cinema, *Das Cabinet des Dr. Caligari*. Mosjoukine presents his narrative as a type of triptych that includes the perspective of Elle, her husband and Z throughout. In fact, the film's overall lyrical quality emerges from the kinetic play that occurs in and between these various psychological perspectives held together in Mosjoukine's unique sequencing of the film's montages.

One of the most notable examples of the film's use of framing devices occurs when Elle suspects Z of having another female admirer. Mosjoukine sets this up in order to further characterize Elle and her attraction to Z. When Z makes a phone call to an unknown woman, shortly after telling the husband his prognosis (that Elle's problem is her obsession with Paris), Elle's jealousy of the other woman to whom Z declares his love is revealed to be unnecessary. Z in fact is merely arranging a rendezvous with his grandmother. This rather comedic framing device, however (like the nightmare sequence at the beginning of the film), functions within the narrative as a means of figuring Elle's irrationality and therefore drawing the viewer's attention to the play of surfaces at work within the overall film. In the main, this is achieved through Elle's subjective point of view. This device undercuts the spectator's position by delaying the outcomes of an otherwise linear narrative. Montage sequences serve to frame and reframe the narrative and create a lateral experience of the

Figure 11.8　Licentious female dancers affected by the dance contest.

film's events through Elle's irrational anxiety that feeds her inexorable desire for Z. The entire plot of *Le Brasier ardent* is entirely dependent upon this mechanism, one that seems to draw upon both Impressionist and Expressionist traditions.

Conclusion

For Volkoff's *Kean*, produced one year after *Le Brasier ardent*, Mosjoukine collaborated in order to create a lead role for himself that shares many similarities with Detective Z. Mosjoukine's unique persona is characterized by his involvement with a variety of popular European literary and filmic styles of the time. His status as a trans-European personality is epitomized by roles like Edmund Kean, where he, a Russian actor, holds the lead role in a French film about an English stage performer. In it, he essays the famous Shakespearean actor, one who (in the film's plot) suffers an identity crisis in the wake of a romantic affair.

Mosjoukine's career remains in urgent need of intervention, particularly in the English language. Here is an important actor who traversed various national cinemas during his life and career. Films like *Kean* remain worthy of investigation, as does Mosjoukine's biography. However, no Mosjoukine film was more dynamic, electric, or innovative than the single film he directed himself.

While much of the *Le Brasier ardent*'s *mise-en-scène* is ornate, similar to other Impressionist films in other places, the film delivers a number of Expressionistic flourishes in a manner similar to those observable in Lang's *Dr. Mabuse the Gambler*. In *Le Brasier ardent* this is largely communicated through *mise-en-scène* that is composed of angular designs and characters who are distorted both physically and mentally. This is particularly apparent in the nightmare sequence at the beginning of the film and in the Seekers Club sequence, but also within particular aspects of the film's editing styles.

The mutative tendencies of *Le Brasier ardent* create a protean dimension that renders the film's appearances entirely uncertain, thereby lending the overall film a phantasmagorical quality. Mosjoukine experiments with and alternates between aspects of French Impressionism, German Expressionism, and his own idea of how *Le Brasier ardent* can exceed his audience's expectations. It is this ironic play that dictates the direction, tempo and the overall design of the film as it efficiently and effectively shuttles between impressionist and expressionist modes of address.

Notes

1. This chapter chooses to use the spelling "Ivan Mosjoukine," given that it is the spelling used on the credits of *Le Brasier ardent*. It is true that other spellings and variations of Mosjoukine's name were used during his career, including "Mozzhukhin" and (in the USA) "Moskine."
2. In some respects, *Le Brasier ardent* presents a distinctly Russian identity. The sequences where Detective Z and Elle gaze at each other demonstrate an editing pace and pattern more akin to those of the early Russian cinema, as seen in a Boris Barnet film. Indeed, Mosjoukine's film exhibits certain shots and sequences that concur with Yuri Tsivian's observations on the early Russian cinema regarding the speed of the action. In parts, it reflects the uniquely Russian ideal to "film story, not drama," the motto, we are told, of Russian film style during World War I. This view was so entrenched it became a type of genre that broke with the conventions of cinematographic pictures in the sense that it repudiated movement. See Yuri Tsivian, "Early Russian Cinema: Some Observations" in Richard Taylor and Ian Christie, *Inside the Film Factory: New Approaches to Russian and Soviet Cinema* (New York, London: Routledge, 1994), pp. 7–31, quoted p. 14.
3. Lotte H. Eisner, *The Haunted Screen: Expressionism in the German Cinema and the Influence of Max Reinhardt* (trans. Roger Graeves) (Berkeley, CA: University of California Press, 1969 [1952]).
4. Lenny Borger, "From Moscow to Montreuil," pp. 3–4 [DVD booklet] in *French Masterworks: Russian Émigrés in Paris, 1923–1928* (DVD, Flicker Alley, 2013).
5. Ibid. p. 3.
6. Lenny Borger and Catherine Morel, "L'angoissante aventure. L'apport russe de l'entre-deux-guerres," *Positif—Revue mensuelle de cinema* (January 1988; International Index to Performing Arts), p. 38.
7. Borger, p. 8.
8. Jean Renoir, "Memories," *Le Point*, Vol. 18, December 1938, reprinted in André Bazin, *Jean Renoir* (New York: Simon & Schuster, 1973), pp. 151–2.
9. Richard Abel, *French Cinema: the First Wave, 1915–1929* (Princeton, NJ: Princeton University Press, 1984), pp. 367–73.
10. Kristin Thompson and David Bordwell, *Film History: An Introduction* (New York: McGraw-Hill, 1994), pp. 78–80.
11. Judith Mayne, "The Woman at the Keyhole: Women's Cinema and Feminist Criticism," *New German Critique* 23, Spring–Summer 1981, pp. 27–43.
12. Thompson and Bordwell, *Film History*, p. 90.
13. In this instance, I am borrowing terminology from Eisner, who was herself quoting Expressionist artists, Eisner, *The Haunted Screen*, p. 15.
14. Siegfried Kracauer, "The Shock of Freedom" in his *From Caligari to Hitler: A Psychological History of German Film* (Princeton, NJ: Princeton University Press, 1947), pp. 43–61.
15. Quoted in Eisner, *The Haunted Screen*, p. 11.
16. Ibid.

12. NIETZSCHE'S FINGERPRINTS ON *THE HANDS OF ORLAC* (1924)

Phillip Sipiora

For it is only as *an aesthetic phenomenon* that existence and the world are eternally *justified*.

Friedrich Nietzsche

Dionysian art, too, wishes to convince us of the eternal joy of existence: only we are not to seek this joy in phenomena, but behind them. We are to recognize that all that comes into being must be ready for a sorrowful end; we are forced to look into the terrors of the individual existence—yet we are not to become rigid with fear.

Friedrich Nietzsche

What might Friedrich Nietzsche have to do with a 1924 silent film, even one that might be considered an exemplary representation of German Expressionism? Nietzsche wrote extensively about art and drama, of course, but his life was cut short at the beginning of the new century when moving pictures were only in gestation. I would like to suggest that there are currents in Nietzsche's thought that may be connected to Expressionism in general, and in particular to Robert Wiene's grotesque film, *The Hands of Orlac* (*Orlac's Hände*). It is not my intention to suggest direct linkage connecting *Orlac*, Nietzsche, and classical art. What I attempt to explore is Nietzsche's reading of classical tragedy as it relates to the spirit and tensions growing out of the binary distinction between the Apollonian and the Dionysian (intimately intertwined), and the ways in which Nietzsche's theoretical impulses may relate to

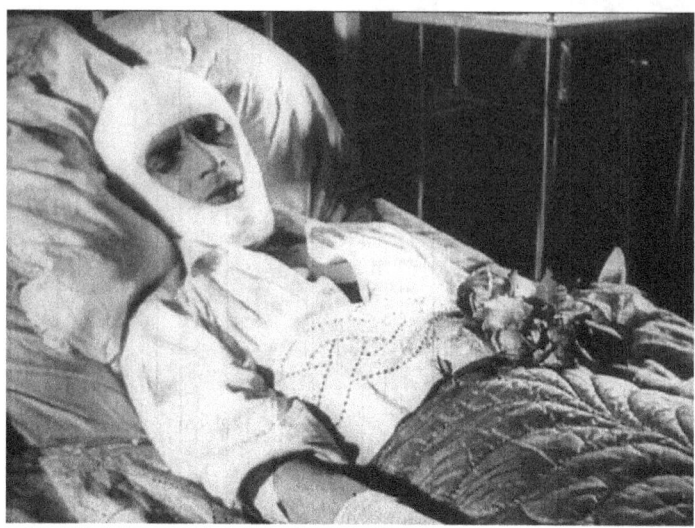

Figure 12.1   Orlac's furrowed brow reveals his new identity. (*Courtesy of Friedrich-Wilhelm-Murnau-Stiftung, Wiesbaden*)

German Expressionism. This chapter is not intended as a source study; rather, it seeks to serve as a speculative inquiry into fragments of Nietzschean gesture, sensibility, and sensitivity as they relate to a powerful and seductive film that I consider a fertile synecdoche of global Expressionism. Paul Orlac is an existential figure expressing Apollonian and Dionysian antipodes within himself, but he also lives the life of his times, as he must, in which these dialectical tensions born in antiquity find release in mid-1920s German culture, thus nurturing the festering impulses deep inside, and not only within the individual but also very much within the fabric of emerging Modernist culture.

Nietzsche's analyses of the numerous metaphysical issues he interrogated so intensely resist reductive summary. Any summative exposition of most of Nietzsche's work is surely a redoubtable task. Yet many readers of Nietzsche recognize that his early work *The Birth of Tragedy* (1872, reissued 1886) examines Greek tragedy and the interactive relationship between the influence of two gods: Apollo and Dionysius. Scholars have long debated positions attributed to Nietzsche, but there are some general concepts that are relevant in the Apollonian/Dionysian binary. One of these general concepts is the role of illusion, yet the relevance of illusion to Expressionism is not a simple case of reconciling opposing movements or clearing up false illusions. Appearance, or illusion, is a critical component in Nietzsche's always-evolving worldview, and the maze of appearances that cloak "reality" is problematic at multiple levels in his analysis, including the role of language in reading the world around us. Nietzsche was very familiar with classical rhetoric and he believed in the rhetorical (figural) undergirding of all language in its representation of concepts. From this arises his well-known stance on the eternal presence of metaphor in the machinery of human understanding, including metaphysics:

> What then is truth? A mobile army of metaphors, metonyms, and anthropomorphisms—in short, a sum of human relations, which have been enhanced, transposed, and embellished poetically and rhetorically, and which after long use seem firm, canonical, and obligatory to a people: truths are illusions about which one has forgotten that is what they are; metaphors which are worn out and without sensuous power; coins which have lost their pictures and now matter only as metal, no longer as coins. We still do not know where the urge for truth comes from; for as yet we have heard only of the obligation imposed by society that it should exist: to be truthful means using the customary metaphors—in moral terms, the obligation to lie according to fixed convention, to lie herd-like in a style obligatory for all.[1]

Intellectual Revolution

Nietzsche's iconoclastic analysis of the self and its relationship to the intellectual and cultural architecture of nineteenth-century society clearly anticipates

Figure 12.2   Pure evil. (*Courtesy of Friedrich-Wilhelm-Murnau-Stiftung, Wiesbaden*)

(and influences) the explosive birth of Modernism at the dawn of the twentieth century. Nietzsche dies, ironically, in 1900, the same year as the publication of Freud's *The Interpretation of Dreams*, one of the seminal works of the new century that dramatically changed intellectual history. The cumulative residue of the revolutionary work of Darwin, Marx, Freud, Einstein, and Heisenberg catalyzed the dethroning of the intellectual architecture of Western history. The subconscious mind was awakening to consciousness in the art and intellectual/cultural mores of Modernism. Nietzsche's *cri de coeur* "God is dead" sets the stage for Pound's rallying call, "Make it New," not only in literature but, more expansively, in modern art. This full-throated emphasis on innovation clearly worked its way into the marrow of much intellectual thought one century ago—and into the very fabric of evolving intellectual history.

The presence of aesthetic illusion, a critical dimension of Apollonian/Dionysian conflict, is generally seen by Nietzsche as a positive force because it is protection against the inevitable harsh realities of life, although those darker sides of life contain their own strings of illusions, necessary to their very make-up. *Orlac* would seem an exemplary example of art infused with the darkness of life, a struggle between appearance and reality, an aleatory intoxication that is part rational, part irrational. Paul Orlac carries both Apollonian and Dionysian traits in his expressionist genetic code, and his narrative is a battleground that exists in the margins and borders between unmediated predispositions. At times he is understandably irrational, fully believing himself to have assumed the identity of his murderous hands. At other times, he expresses a leaning to reason and logic. Paul exists within a dichotomy of forces, and he represents intertwined tensions between the Apollonian and Dionysian. Thus the dramatic interplay between the Apollonian and Dionysian nurtures and molds Paul Orlac's character into a frenzied expressionistic caricature.

The film's linear chronology is relatively simple. Paul Orlac, a concert pianist, is in a train wreck and loses his hands. Vasseur, a convicted murderer of a moneylender, is executed in the same area at approximately the same time. Dr Serral successfully transplants the killer's hands to Paul Orlac. Paul fears that his new hands will take control of his heart, mind, and body and these fears come alive in his dreams (nightmares). He fears that he will kill someone. As the storyline progresses, Paul's father, Vater Orlac, is killed with the same knife that killed the moneylender. Vasseur's fingerprints (now attributed to Paul) are found at the murder scene and Paul is wrongfully arrested for the murder of his father. As the narrative reaches its climax, it is revealed that Nera, Dr Serral's former assistant, murdered Vater Orlac and is attempting to blackmail Paul and his wife Yvonne. The truth, however, comes out at the end, when Nera is confronted by the police, who learn that Nera had murdered the moneylender, framed Vasseur, and then murdered Vater Orlac. Nera thus functions as a *deus ex machina* and his admissions set Paul free. The

Figure 12.3 Orlac grasps his fate but struggles to understand why. (*Courtesy of Friedrich-Wilhelm-Murnau-Stiftung, Wiesbaden*)

chronology spans several years, although that length of time is not implicit in the cinematic plot segmentation. Transplanted murdering hands makes for a terrifying trope of a topic and the story has not failed to captivate viewers,[2] as attested to by the several remakes of this powerful narrative. Paul begins as a type—a professional pianist—and is transformed into a surreal human entity, one who suffers what Nietzsche calls "the agonies of individuation ... This dismemberment, the properly Dionysian suffering ... [means] that we are therefore to regard the state of individuation as the origin and primal cause of all suffering, as something objectionable in itself."[3] As Nietzsche expands his examination of the Dionysian he seems to come to the conclusion that, at the very least, it is an embrace of life and its most terrifying, inexplicable moments.

The heart of the story, at least in my reading, is Paul's tortured mental state, which is both initiated by and resultative of his illusions. From the time he is in hospital recovering from his injuries, he is a deeply troubled man. Perhaps his intense obsession with music adds to his psychological instability (echoing Platonic notions of music and poetry as destabilizing to effective living, except for religious forms). Paul's intensified and conflicted mental state is illustrated by his dreams, which contain fear and terror. Life is not worth living for Paul and Yvonne Orlac, as they live in constant dread that Paul's murderer's hands will control his heart and mind and murder again in the body of his Vasseur surrogate. Paul experiences a veil of illusion, a destructive, malevolent veil rather than one of protection.

Nietzsche explores unveiled, unprotected horror, deriving his thought from Schopenhauer and others (Goethe, Schiller, Heine):

> Schopenhauer has depicted for us the tremendous terror that seizes man when he is suddenly dumbfounded by the cognitive form of phenomena because the principle of sufficient reason, in some one of its manifestations, seems to suffer an exception. If we add to this terror the blissful ecstasy that wells from the innermost depths of man, indeed of nature, at this collapse of the *principium individuationis*, we steal a glimpse into the nature of the Dionysian, which is brought home to us most intimately by the analogy of intoxication.[4]

Nietzsche deftly intertwines the antipodal representations of Apollo and Dionysus into a metaphysical conjunction that leads to artistic expression. As Dietrich Fischer-Dieskau argues, "For Nietzsche, the antithesis of the two notions (Apollonian and Dionysian) became a synthesis in Greek Drama. The hostile Greek gods Apollo and Dionysus joined into a necessary independence."[5] Synthesis does not connote reconciliation but suggests something closer to intertwined tension—a confrontation that may lead to productive conflict.

There is at least a double play movement in *Orlac*. The primary characters, Paul and Yvonne, are frightened and influenced by what appears to be a horrifying reality—Paul's hands are killers and Paul *is* his hands. Nietzsche

Figure 12.4   Orlac holds his identity in his hands. (*Courtesy of Friedrich-Wilhelm-Murnau-Stiftung, Wiesbaden*)

equates the classical chorus to the "*dramatic* proto-phenomenon: to see oneself transformed before one's eyes and to begin to act as if one had actually entered into another body, another character."[6] This transmogrification eerily suggests Paul's character. Yet the viewer cannot be ignored in the matrix of illusion. The film is horror cinema precisely because there is a willing suspension of disbelief—Paul's murderous hands may have taken control of Paul's heart and mind. Yet there exists a counter-illusion, an Apollonian/Socratic dimension implying that Paul's situation is anti-rational and therefore non-threatening. Illusions in conflict would seem to play a strategic role in all art. Which motif is more common that the specter of appearance and reality? And the aesthetic construct is never merely the sum of its parts. It must be more, because of the catalyzing release of always-evolving contexts. By the film's end the viewer is given a comforting adjudication: when the truth comes out, everyone now understands that Paul was never a threat to anyone, so that illusion has been destroyed. And neither was Vasseur ever a threat, since he was framed by Nera, obviously the major (and only) malevolent character in the drama. Vater Orlac is a selfish misanthrope, of course, but that does not make him evil in any significant way. The summative conclusion of *Orlac* results in an affirmation of life on the part of Paul, Yvonne, and Dr Serral. Metaphysical justice has been served. Subsequently, there are at least two layers/levels of drama being acted out. The torment and suffering of Paul *and* the restoration of order have been resolved by the film's end, as in a fine Shakespearian tragedy. Evil has been expunged and good has been restored. Paul's reputation is fully restored as he returns to Yvonne's loving embrace, free to use his hands to caress Yvonne, no longer fearful that he might strangle her. Adjudication is complete and social harmony is the residue. Illusions have been neutralized, at least temporarily.

The film begins, however, with a scene of ironic sentimentality. Yvonne lies in her bed reading a love note from Paul in which he promises to return home soon. His letter states, "I will embrace you . . . my hands will glide over your hair . . . and I will feel your body beneath my hands."[7] Gentle caressing and lovemaking, however, are not destined to happen upon Paul's return. The next scene reveals Paul as a concert pianist, replete with a newspaper headline proclaiming his talent. Yvonne eagerly dresses for Paul's return on the evening train. The musical background is light and comforting. However, Yvonne learns of the wreck and frantically travels to the scene, her eyes bulging in horror at what she might find.

The derailed train carrying Paul sets in motion the terrifying plot, and the results are absolutely chaotic, scenes from hell. People are running from and around the scene of devastation, which looks like the carnage seen in war. Characters are depersonalized. There is cringing fear and horror everywhere. Survivors' eyes are bulging with intensity and there is a glare of flaming lights offset by overarching shadows. It is a wasteland scene, one of massive

Figure 12.5 The eyes are a window to the soul. (*Courtesy of Friedrich-Wilhelm-Murnau-Stiftung, Wiesbaden*)

desolation and fear. Fleeing survivors look more like terrified animals than railroad passengers. Piano chords become louder and more cacophonous, macabre. Crying violins pervade the scenes. Torches and intermittent fires illuminate the dark night of the horrifying landscape, partially hidden in clouds of smoke. The flares and cressets are almost like weapons aligning with the horror because they publicize the horror. Stretchers are everywhere, laden with bodies dead and alive. Yvonne miraculously discovers Paul, an early hint of the fantastic, as she silently screams, "He's alive." However, Yvonne herself appears hysterical, physically displaced and a little deranged, someone otherworldly. Cries of terror filling the air are piercing in spite of intermittent silence. The catastrophic scenes are clearly classical Expressionist exaggeration, hyperbole, hypersensitivity, and grotesque exposure of terror and fright. The train wreck is a metaphor for the man wreck to come that will be the birthing of a monster. When the wreckage fades, as it must, the disaster scenes, *ad seriatim*, seamlessly flow into a brief shot of a man in disarray sitting on a makeshift bench, holding his head in one hand, abandoned in a Dionysian world. His world is not only lost to chaos but is unintelligible. Carnage melts into solitude.

Yet the horror of the wreck is only the beginning for Paul. When Paul is brought to Dr Serral, the surgeon tells Yvonne that there is hope—but Paul may lose his hands. Yvonne is devastated, distraught, weeping, clothes falling low as she falls into the doctor's arms. Her undergarment straps are off her

Figure 12.6 Orlac has insight into his transformed nature. (*Courtesy of Friedrich-Wilhelm-Murnau-Stiftung, Wiesbaden*)

shoulders. She is unkempt and freakily overdramatic, wild hysterical orbs above her nose—all essential qualities of Expressionistic distortion. Yvonne pleads with the doctor, "save his hands . . . his hands are his life . . . His hands are more than his life." Yvonne's fear is prophetic and she intuits Nietzsche's prophecy: "Contradiction, the bliss born of pain, spoke out from the very heart of nature. And so, wherever the Dionysian prevailed, the Apollonian was checked and destroyed."[8] This movement works both ways, of course, and when Dionysus is countered, Apollo emerges as frightening and powerful. Dr Serral and Yvonne are Apollonian forces pitted against Nera, who is quintessentially evil. The battleground is in Paul's head and heart, of course, as these forces oppose one another. Dr Serral's eyes show utter despair in looking—not at her, but into a cold, barren world, bereft of meaningful life. There is considerable "eye acting" in *Orlac*, which is piercing, ominous. Yvonne becomes hysterical when told that Paul's hands are lost. The doctor's eyes "see" into the abyss, the dark void, the underworld, as he says to her, "I'll try." Her eyes piercingly and adoringly look up and into him as if he were a deity. Yvonne falls into physical rapture, a form of intoxication. In the Dionysian world, music evoked fear and terror, and these effects are the residue of funereal atmospherics in *Orlac*.

Dr Serral visits Orlac and eagerly examines Paul's new hands. The doctor asks, "Tell me, what's under these bandages? What kind of secret are they hiding?" The Secret is Dionysian—magical and mystical. The doctor unwraps them and reveals the secret. Paul asks, "Will these hands ever be able to play again?" An obvious pun on "play": one meaning for a concert pianist and quite another for a strangler. Dr Serral replies, "The spirit rules the hand . . . nature and a strong will can overcome anything." The wise doctor clearly knows and understands the realities of a rational world—he is a man of science, after all. Paul then stares at his hands as if they are foreign, yet they are part of him but not of him. Yvonne restlessly waits for Paul at home, anticipating the "first stroking of his beloved hands." Paul's dreams present visions of Vasseur's grisly face (actually Nera's face, but Paul does not know that) displaying a macabre look, a twisted grimace, a ghostly apparition—the face of fear. A giant fist then appears and is held over Paul and plunges into his body before fading out. Shortly thereafter, the January 15 newspaper that Paul located contained the story of Vasseur's appearance in court. Paul reads of Vasseur's conviction based upon the discovery of his fingerprints on the knife that he used to murder a storekeeper. Paul realizes, shockingly, that the murderer's fingerprints are now his fingerprints. He falls into a reverie prior to finding a mysterious note on his lap (presumably placed by the thrusting fist): "Your hands couldn't be saved. Dr. Serral gave you different hands . . . the hands of the executed robber and murderer Vasseur!" Mesmerized, Paul's new hands have taken control as he gyrates into a grotesque figure before collapsing to the floor. The realization of what has happened—the parts have indeed become the whole—terrifies him into unconsciousness. Later, Paul appears in Dr Serral's office, looking like the monstrous fiend that he has become. Paul asks, "Is it true? Do I have the hands of the robber and murderer, Vasseur?" His eyes and face are grotesquely distorted.

Orlac is fundamentally a Modernist horror film, staged in Gothic sets with traditional expressionistic techniques of lighting: shadows and stark illumination, particularly in the café scene with direct lighting over Paul's face, surrounded by shadows and a shadowy waiter. There is much face acting, including hyperbolic grimaces, bulging eyes, and grotesque visages with exaggerated body movements. It is a stark film that derives its essential energy from a narrative that focuses on the darker sides of life—the hideous macabre in continuous distortion. Such is the life force that sustains *Orlac*.[9] Yet one horrifying dimension of the film involves Paul Orlac's terrifying dreams, which tend toward irony within the layers of Nietzsche's Apollonian/Dionysian distinction. Nietzsche sees Apollo as the god of life-sustaining dreams: "the deity of light is also ruler over the beautiful illusion of the inner world of fantasy."[10] Paul Orlac's horrifying, ruling nightmares are in sharp contrast to beautiful illusions and do not serve to ameliorate his wrecked existence. As Nietzsche questions, "Can frenzy be viewed as something that is *not* a symptom of decay, disorder, and over ripeness?"[11] These characteristics would seem to profile a number of Expressionistic films beyond *Orlac*.

NIETZSCHE'S FINGERPRINTS ON *THE HANDS OF ORLAC*

Paul Orlac is indeed caught between rational and irrational impulses, yet intoxicated by unrelenting fear, which does not end until there is a rational adjudication of his crime and he is proven to be an innocent man. Paul is free at last as the film ends with a tender embrace between man and wife. Reconciliation is the residue of forces in conflict. As Nietzsche writes, "Under the spell of the Dionysian, not only is the alliance between man and man restored: but Nature, estranged, hostile, or subjugated, celebrates anew her feast of reconciliation with her prodigal son."[12] Paul is an actor in a mysterious drama that he does not comprehend because his mind and spirit are functioning at an irrational, primal stage. His role is reminiscent of Nietzsche's comment about Shakespeare's understanding of self-perception: "The Dionysian man resembles Hamlet: both have once looked truly into the essence of things, they have *gained knowledge*, and nausea inhibits action; for their action could not change anything in the eternal nature of things."[13] Paul has gained knowledge about his horrifying nature—he believes that he is a killer—but only because his hands have determined the moral essence of the man. Synecdoche is not only an allusion; it is also reality and it is not temporary. This flower of language has become a figure of nature that defines Paul's inexorable fate. In his analysis of tragedy, Nietzsche could have been describing Paul's existence: "Now no comfort avails any more; longing transcends a world after death . . . existence is negated . . . Conscious of the truth he has once seen, man now sees everywhere only the horror or absurdity of existence."[14] Paul is a distant cousin of the classical satyr. Although he is educated, in a way he is still a "man of the

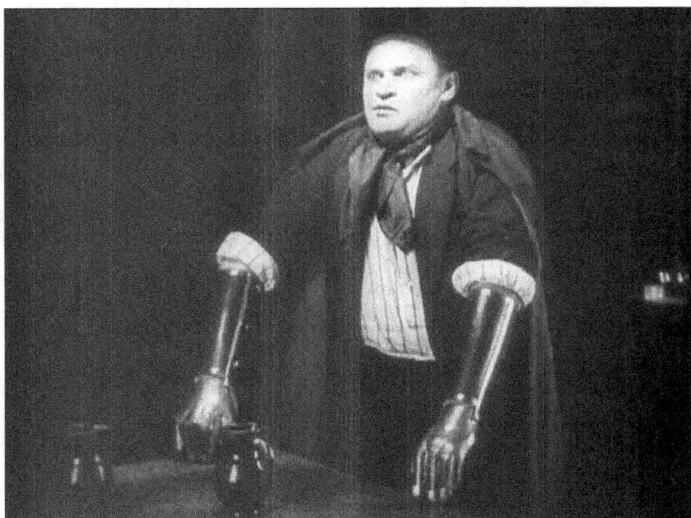

Figure 12.7 Grotesquerie in the service of evil. (*Courtesy of Friedrich-Wilhelm-Murnau-Stiftung, Wiesbaden*)

woods," somewhat infantile, impulsive, and a creature of his perceived urges. Nietzsche describes the satyr as "the archetype of man, the embodiment of his highest and most intense emotions."[15] For Nietzsche, metaphor creates its own kind of reality that reflects a phenomenological perspective: "For a genuine poet, metaphor is not a rhetorical figure but a vicarious image that he actually beholds in place of a concept. A character is for him not a whole he has composed out of particular traits, picked up here and there, but an obtrusively alive person before his very eyes."[16] *Orlac*, a towering master trope in full blossom, reveals a state of intoxicated reality as savage instincts are unleashed in Paul in the metaphysical nether regions of his mind and spirit, especially cruelty in its highest form—murder. As Allan Megill points out, "The Apollonian and Dionysian are symbols rather than concepts, multivalent centers of meaning rather than denotatively exact tokens designating a determinate 'X' and a determinate 'Y.'"[17] Rather than generating answers, they serve to sharpen questions.

My synoptic analysis carries within it an implicit chain of questions: is *Orlac* a form of tragedy, and is Paul a tragic figure? I do not see *Orlac* as representative of tragedy in the usual sense of the genre, but I do think that there is a tragic spirit embedded within it. The forces of tragedy that constitute the conflict between the Apollonian and the Dionysian are clearly insufficient to place *Orlac* within the tragic tradition—but Paul is a fascinating figure. He is a good man who has fallen, yet not because of pride or any other any constitutional flaw (with the exception of his predilection toward the irrational, which might be seen as an intellectual and emotional deficiency). What has prompted Paul to embrace the irrational and demonic with unmistakable, surrendering enthusiasm? Part of the answer may lurk within Nietzsche's exploration of the subterranean world of frenzy, irrationality, and, of course, horror.

Notes

1. Friedrich Nietzsche, "On Truth and Lie in an Extra-Moral sense," in Walter Kaufman (trans. and ed.), *The Portable Nietzsche* (New York: Penguin, 1959), pp. 46–7, quoted p. 47.
2. The other characters function as a kind of "Greek chorus" as they provide continuous meta-commentary on Paul's condition. Limits of space constrain an inquiry here, but it would seem to be worth pursuing considering Nietzsche's interest in the concept of chorus as "ideal spectator." Viewers, of course, would seem to be another loop in the chorus line.
3. Friedrich Nietzsche, *The Birth of Tragedy*, quoted from *Basic Writings of Nietzsche* (trans. and ed.Walter Kaufmann) (New York: Modern Library, 1992), p. 73.
4. Ibid. p. 36.
5. Dietrich Fischer-Dieskau, *Wagner and Nietzsche* (trans. Joachim Neugroschel) (New York: Seabury, 1974), p. 63.
6. Nietzsche, *The Birth of Tragedy*, p. 64.
7. My references are to the Kino International restored version of 113 minutes.

8. Ibid. 46–7.
9. One of the ironies in applying Nietzsche's Apollonian/Dionysian distinction to *Orlac* is that Nietzsche sees Apollo as the god of life-sustaining dreams: "[T]he deity of light is also ruler over the beautiful illusion of the inner world of fantasy" (*Birth of Tragedy*, p. 35). He also notes the salubrious quality of the Apollonian view: "The higher truth (the beautiful illusion of the inner world of fantasy), the perfection of these states in contrast to the completely intelligible everyday world, this deep consciousness of nature, healing and helping in sleep and dreams, is at the same time the symbolic analogue of the soothsaying faculty and of the arts generally, which make life possible and worth living" (ibid.).
10. Ibid.
11. Ibid. p. 8.
12. Quoted in Fischer-Dieskau, *Wagner and Nietzsche*, p. 63.
13. Nietzsche, *The Birth of Tragedy*, p. 60.
14. Ibid.
15. Ibid. p. 61.
16. Ibid. p. 63.
17. Allan Megill, *Prophets of Extremity: Nietzsche, Heidegger, Foucault, Derrida* (Berkeley, CA: University of California Press, 1987), p. 38. Megill goes on to say that these categories contain within them internal oppositions. These internal tensions would seem to destabilize their identities as stable critical genres but not their function as interpretive catalysts.

13. "TRUE, NERVOUS": AMERICAN EXPRESSIONIST CINEMA AND THE DESTABILIZED MALE

Robert Singer

The madman is not the man who has lost his reason. The madman is the man who has lost everything except his reason.

Chesterton, *The Maniac*

Expressionism revels in troubled, paroxystic souls. Some of the most compelling representations of the tense, affected male, a being and body in physical and metaphysical space, have occurred in both classic German and American expressionist and neo-expressionist cinema where a subverting male nervousness is a recurring trope. Many of these films are psychologically unsettling, constructed narratives of nervous men afflicted by fixed ideas and internal terrors: the substance of waking, protracted bad dreams. This study will initially focus on two select avant-garde expressionist American film narratives, produced during the Weimar era in Germany (1918–33), and then will comparatively analyze the trope of the nervous male in three modern American film narratives in which a neo-expressionist visual and thematic design is appropriated via industrial, generic structures. American cinema has (principally but not exclusively) produced phases of interrelated expressionist cinematic culture: the first phase an avant-garde expressionist film narrative produced during the silent era, and the second phase (produced principally post-World War II) neo-expressionism, which characteristically referenced and appropriated expressionist themes and forms in select shot sequences recalling and revising the silent era aesthetic, involving such styles and genres as film noir, adaptation, horror, and the melodrama.[1]

The American expressionist film is a hypertextual narrative, part of an international movement. When, in "Modernism and the Cinema: *Metropolis* and the Expressionist Aesthetic," Richard Murphy comprehensively surveys the compositional strategy of Fritz Lang's pivotal German expressionist narrative *Metropolis* (1927), he especially notes principal characteristics of the expressionist film narrative that are equally applicable to two contemporary American expressionist narratives, Melville Webber and James Watson's *The Fall of the House of Usher* (1928) and Charles Klein's *The Telltale Heart* (1928),[2] namely, the distortion of temporal and spatial relationships and a destabilization of the viewer's position and knowledge as a product of guilt-driven nervousness. Murphy concludes, "within the broader context of modernism ... destabilization of the coordinates of time, space and causality affects the recipient's sense of interpretive mastery."[3] The audience perceives the expressionist narrative, its story and performance, but the viewer consistently acts in a re-perceptive mode, revising and renewing narrative data, essentially "re-seeing," and interpreting in order to detect and compose meaning, from both internal (the character's point of view) and external (spatial and set designs, camera angles and movement) fields of perception.

In *Metropolis*, when Freder, son of the industrialist master of the city, journeys into the bowels of the city to see how the other half lives—the workers and workings of the city—he experiences a type of nervous, feverish breakdown before the chthonic machinery that produces progress for the elect, but ceaseless labor for the workers, and consequently, Freder has a vision of sacrificial offerings to the devouring symbol of Moloch, a consuming deity. While the audience sees the nightmarish, occult vision as Freder, the wandering nervous male, experiences it, neither is real. The industrial accident precipitated by an exhausted worker leads to a chaotic and deadly series of events, but Freder's moment of destabilized perception of Moloch and the machinery of the city is a vision of the loss of life. He "re-sees" workers and machines, and via a nervous deformation of perception, Freder (and the audience) experiences a more complex, visually charged, heightened view of the exploitive, political real.[4]

Hausenstein asks, "What is expressionism? Who is an expressionist?" and then succinctly states: "what constitutes expressionism has not been established. There is something like a signature of expressionism, perhaps a scheme underlying it. One could define it roughly like this: form from deformation."[5] Like Freder, Webber and Watson's Roderick Usher and Klein's insane man in *The Telltale Heart*, among other expressionist figures, are the ideal conveyors of this process, as each is an agitated, impulsive, and extremely nervous character whose debilitating vision leads to what Herbert Ihering has described as the "sensational experiment" of the expressionist film narrative.[6]

Klein's compositional strategy of frenzied, nervous destabilization in *The Telltale Heart* invites comparison with Lang's *Metropolis*. In his essay "The

First American Film Avant-Garde, 1919–1945," Jan-Christopher Horak analyzes the expressionist compositional strategies located in the Klein adaptation:

> The film relates an insane young man's killing of an old man, and his eventual mental breakdown and confession to a pair of detectives questioning him. Two particularly interesting devices are the use of words burned into the image (similar to *Caligari*), and the intercutting of single-frame images flashing back to the murder to illustrate the subjective state of the protagonist. Another expressionist device is the extremely distorted close up of the killer, as seen through a magnifying glass by the detectives ... the close up of the old man's eyes and the superimposition of an image of a beating hammer that become visual tropes for Poe's literary device of the victim's beating heart.[7]

Although Horak identifies Charles Klein's *The Telltale Heart* as "another very low budget off-Hollywood production reprising German Expressionist cinema," he is careful to point out that Klein's film and others "are not simply copies of European art films. Their thematic concerns are for the most part American, their stylistic sensibilities a mixture of sophistication and naïveté, their aesthetics against the grain of Hollywood narrative."[8] This suggests an initial avant-garde classificatory status.

According to the nineteenth-century psychologist George Beard, "American nervousness is the product of American civilization."[9] Perhaps no author or figure in nineteenth-century American culture has exerted as great an influence on American expressionist cinema as Edgar Allan Poe. American expressionist silent cinema is intertextually linked to Poe's Gothic prose. An informal listing of Poe's "gothic inheritance" indicates an evolution and presence of recurring visual and psychological tropes: a ruined, sinister physical space (home, castle), shadows and restless spirits, stylized Gothic-style printed text, dreadful, magical events in the past, coming again in the future, and compromised, distressed souls, nervous figures, averse to people, sounds, memories, and the proprieties of normalcy. Whether the film narrative is an avant-garde adaptation-appropriation of a select Poe short story, such as Webber and Watson's or Klein's silent films, or indicated as intertextual citations as in Alfred Hitchcock's noir melodrama *The Wrong Man* (1956), Woody Allen's stylized comedy *Shadows and Fog* (1992), and Stanley Kubrick's adaptation, *Eyes Wide Shut* (1999), Poe's fiction, primary among other national and international referents, establishes a core narrative presence, a series of signifying tropes related to the nervous, post-Gothic disjointed expressionist male.

According to Horak, Webber and Watson's *The Fall of the House of Usher* and Klein's *The Telltale Heart* confirm Poe's position in the historical processing of the Gothic into an American expressionist aesthetic. In her study of the films of Watson and Webber, Lisa Cartwright underscores this process in her discussion of the compositional design of their *The Fall of the House of Usher*:

> Framed by brief shots of the visitor entering and leaving, the fifteen-minute film takes place almost exclusively within the interior space of the house of Usher, a space constructed by Webber out of cardboard and paint ... The set [design] was ... a strategy also suggestive of an Expressionist use of light to fragment and destabilize conventional perspective and form. However, the disjunctive and optically fragmented space of the house also suggests a scene described quite explicitly in the Poe story itself.[10]

The unsettling presence in Poe's narratives of the fixed idea, an implacable notion that unsettles normalcy and collapses the spaces between the external world and internal processes, becomes a catalyst, an informing energy. In Webber and Watson's *The Fall of the House of Usher*, near-spectral visions—in the form of the cursed, decaying mansion with its jarring noises and images—disturb Roderick Usher; he is convinced that his wife (in Poe's story, his sister) is doomed, and he prematurely, nervously acts upon this notion. Roderick intuits death in life. As the fixed idea—however irrational or disturbing—expresses itself, the ensuing expressionist moment begins to fully manifest. As early as 1892, the psychologist Pierre Janet wrote extensively about the fixed idea and the expression of nervousness and general conditions of mental illness:

> Fixed ideas are ... psychological phenomena which are developed in the mind in an automatic manner, outside the will and the personal perceptions of the patient ... ideas of this kind have been described at length in the case of patients described as lunatics. They went under the name of obsessions, impulsions, phobias ... A lunatic tormented with fixed ideas, whether he accords them full credence or struggles against the encroaching delirium, has always an exact knowledge of the thoughts, which torment him.[11]

When the individual's fixed idea has erupted or deflated, both spatial and psychological reality unsettles. It is the moment of the expressionist shudder, how the psychological terror—real or imaginary—is rendered palpable:

> The imaginary floats, moreover, about humanity, like the atoms in the air it breathes. The fantastic, the macabre, the mystery, the shudder, surround us, constrain, master us ... Every man who, returning from a ball or from the play, has found himself alone on coming home, and has

by chance, in his empty room, seen his own image reflected in the glass after lamp or candle is lighted, has inevitably experienced a strange sensation of disquiet if not of terror.[12]

The hypersensitive Roderick Usher breathes erratically and exhibits physical expressions of nervous cognition. The stimmung, a palpable but immaterial projection-manifestation generated by expressionist film narrative, significantly affects viewer perception, and expresses the moment of the collapsing fixed idea, leading to this shudder, the exhalation of terror. Nervousness is the sign. The subject/object male in these films is linked to the pervasive expressionist stimmung via his afflicted, visual/physical presence. The nervous, tormented male functions in a real space—a body—as a destabilized, problematic entity. The destabilized individual functions like an object, a failing fixed idea in motion, framed in an incorporeal quandary. As Lang concludes in "The Future of the Feature Film in Germany," acting in the expressionist film signifies a movement "from carriers of the plot to *carriers of an idea.*"[13] These ideas often function as waking nightmares.

Charles Klein's *The Telltale Heart* is another case study of expressionist destabilization, as the nervous, "insane man"—without name, identity, or inferential causalities—fixates on the blank, dead eye of the old man lying in bed in a dark room. The insane man's shadow and the old man's eye are both arguable presences in the film, along with the two stolid officers of the law. These officers, reminiscent of Kafka's intrusive authority figures at the beginning of his expressionist novel *The Trial*, knock on the door like an insistent heartbeat and enter the room as a response to a cry heard in the night, thus initiating a new phase of the nightmare, the revelation process:

> As the bell sounded the hour, there came a knocking at the street door. I went down to open it with a light heart,—for what had I now to fear? There entered three men, who introduced themselves, with perfect suavity, as officers of the police. A shriek had been heard by a neighbor during the night; suspicion of foul play had been aroused; information had been lodged at the police office, and they (the officers) had been deputed to search the premises.[14]

Klein's insane man establishes a story to falsely confirm that he is innocent, and convinces the investigators that he is not guilty of anything since the old man's gold remains in a chest, safe and accounted for. As he relates his false story to the authorities, after his symbolic stepping over the grave of his victim, the disassembling of self occurs as he inevitably re-experiences (thus destabilizing his and the audience's perceptions) the crime and its ugliness—in the form of the heartbeat only he hears—and he too collapses, a victim of guilt

Figure 13.1 *The Telltale Heart*; the insane man.

and exposed nerves. This is an especially significant moment. Poe and Klein's narrators destabilize as one voice:

> No doubt I now grew very pale;—but I talked more fluently, and with a heightened voice. Yet the sound increased—and what could I do? It was a low, dull, quick sound—much such a sound as a watch makes when enveloped in cotton. I gasped for breath—and yet the officers heard it not. I talked more quickly—more vehemently; but the noise steadily increased. I arose and argued about trifles, in a high key and with violent gesticulations; but the noise steadily increased. Why would they not be gone? I paced the floor to and fro with heavy strides, as if excited to fury by the observations of the men—but the noise steadily increased. Oh God! what could I do? I foamed—I raved—I swore! I swung the chair upon which I had been sitting, and grated it upon the boards, but the noise arose over all and continually increased. It grew louder—louder—louder! And still the men chatted pleasantly, and smiled. Was it possible they heard not? Almighty God!—no, no! They heard!—they suspected!—they knew!—they were making a mockery of my horror!—this I thought, and this I think. But anything was better than this agony![15]

These are the sounds and activities of the near-hallucinatory, enacted before an audience. As Poe and Klein's nervous, afflicted narrators begin to lose control and enact their delusional and violent behavior, the crime is revealed in a frenzied psychological space and time, via associative words and symbols,

253

in both the literary and film narratives. The series of nervous reactions Klein's narrator experiences—his facial contortions, gesturing, and movement across the room—suggest the inner workings of the rage and anxiety he feels. In the montage-revelation sequence, Klein's expressionist adaptation creates an atmospheric, enclosed space for the insane man's exposure, destabilizing his and the audience's perspective; there is no place to escape. Poe's nervous narrator involuntarily reveals the inner workings of the mind in an expressionist montage of guilt-infused images and projections—the "ghostly" presence of things past—as his collapse from exhaustion is a frenzied confession. The dead heart beat one last time.[16]

Murphy notes in his essay that, in expressionist cinema, "harshly contrasting lighting, the extreme stylization of the production, or the excessive gestures, costume and make-up of the actors" (basically, the formal, compositional design, the expressionist *mise-en-scène*) are thus linked with the internal conflicts and psychologically destabilized personality of the expressionist performer. Murphy adds that expressionist cinema incorporates "emotional and psychological values" which signify "the inner life of the central figure."[17] Poe's insane man, as renewed in Klein's expressionist adaptation, reveals his inner life in this stylized context: the nervous man in an irrational space. The idea of not being detected comes crashing into the real world of punitive exposure.

However perturbed the insane man feels as he re-experiences the stultifying series of events for which he is responsible, the audience feels him feeling it, jarring our individual and collective sensibilities. The vision is participatory. This reception process denotes the avant-garde status of expressionist cinema. The real has been defamiliarized and more than a surface of things is connoted in both the physical and psychological landscape and portraiture. The world—the real—is subjectively perceived and processed via narrative, often by the troubled, the deformed, or the lost individual. Perhaps the single most critical component of the expressionist film aesthetic is the presence of stimmung, that unsettling, metaphysical mood generated in the film narrative; it is the presence of a disquieting feeling, experienced by both audience and protagonist.

The classic phase of expressionist narrative, in production in both Germany and America until the demise of Weimar, and the subsequent rise of the independent cineaste and studio film system in America, are directly linked to the postwar, modern neo-expressionist film narrative which recalls and revises core classical expressionist formalist and psychological precepts as defamiliarized citations via genre. Neo-expressionist American films differ from their predecessors as each utilizes compositional strategies, shot sequences, and dynamic characterizations, while being more appropriately classified among related film genres, such as melodrama, horror, adaptation, the "bio-pic," and even comedy.[18]

The neo-expressionist film narrative, such as Hitchcock's *The Wrong Man*, Allen's *Shadows and Fog*, and Kubrick's *Eyes Wide Shut*, situates an expressionist moment or series of moments—shots and shot sequences—most often as studies in destabilized space and identity; the emotionally and physically afflicted, the lost, the "broken," and the sexually depressed or enraged have a film presence, however distorted. In these films, nervousness also indicates a moment of social exposure, of guilt, of humiliation, and of failure. Each film narrative produces the surface expression of nervous effects in a neo-expressionist compositional context. Whether in film, literary or the visual arts, an expressionist machine is not always just a machine, and a face is not only a face. The neo-expressionist film may contain a critical shot sequence, a series of stylized moments, that are often the product of generic fusion; for example, a literary adaptation-crime ("bad cop") narrative such as Welles' *Touch of Evil* (1958), or an original composition, like Welles' *Citizen Kane* (1941) are plausibly read in this context.[19]

A prominent sign of narrative destabilization involves the expression of nervousness, as it affects the susceptible male character, signifying the expressionist moment. In Hitchcock's crime-noir melodrama *The Wrong Man*, as Manny, an innocent man (however guilty of escapist gambling fantasies), is questioned and detained by the police, he realizes that he is not going home and that he is in significant trouble. A process of stripping away at his identity begins. Manny may literally be the wrong man, but it is his face that betrays him. As with the unjustly accused and imprisoned Captain Dreyfus in turn-of-the-century France, Manny's handwriting compromises him before the authorities, as the police use these signs as indicators of guilt. The audience witnesses the victimized musician Manny as he slowly deteriorates (he is initially passive, stripped of belongings and held in a cell) as he—concurrently, slowly—begins to destabilize internally. Manny's wife, a sickly, troubled figure, and his mother, an ethnic stereotype of religious fervor, contribute to Manny's already claustrophobic existence as a working-class father; his family's nervousness precedes and informs his decline, like catalytic agencies, because he must also worry about them. As Manny's social status deteriorates and evidence of his guilt builds, his ensuing nervousness is portrayed by Hitchcock in tightly composed close-up shots in starkly lit, shadowy sets, exposing Manny's vulnerability as a neo-expressionist male whose identity is no longer fixed and safe. His response to this downward spiraling ranges from concern, to enervation, and finally to an overwhelming nervousness.

Once apprehended by the police, Manny must obey the authority figures. He is not allowed to communicate with his family; he has his fingerprints taken, stands in a suspects' lineup, removes his personal items, and is eventually led to a stifling holding cell. The camera placement and movement indicate a confining, vertiginous series of shots that express his interior conflict and anxiety.

Figure 13.2 *The Wrong Man*; Manny is questioned by the police.

As Manny appears to become unnerved and look perturbed, the police, who assume that his encroaching nervousness is related to his guilt, pursue him more aggressively. They press forward, questioning him and then accusing him to ensure their mistaken victory. Every nervous exhale is a sign of fear, and Manny's imminent enclosure in the space of the cell is an expressionist graphic in which form and content seemingly merge. While *The Wrong Man* possesses a near-documentary quality depicting the streets, subways, and stores of the 1950s, Hitchcock's film clearly displays neo-expressionist formalist designs: stark black and white photography, montage, camera placement-movement and angle positioning, eccentric lighting, and the functional close-up shot as expressive, suggestive indicators of signs which suggest a contrasting presence, an underside to this urban environment. Manny's social standing, his identity, has been constrained by the nearly supernatural powers of the authorities in dreadful places: the precinct and the courtroom. In "Hitchcock and Kafka: Expressionist Themes in *Strangers on a Train*," Peter J. Dellolio notes Hitchcock's expressionist strategies in that film which are equally applicable to *The Wrong Man*:

> The narrative and stylistic organization of the film (based on the notion of inner-directed elements controlling the objective world) is deeply

influenced by some of the precepts of Expressionism. Hitchcock's style harnesses many of the rules of visual communication derived from expressionist concepts. His films are not traditional or textbook examples of expressionist cinema, yet they systematically utilize much of the aesthetic phrasing of expressionist thinking.[20]

Like Kafka's Josef K. and Manny, Kleinman, the "little man" of Allen's neo-expressionist comedy *Shadows and Fog*, learns that being guiltless is not the same thing as being innocent, as that notion crumbles before an imposed, deleterious reality. Kleinman, a diffident clerk, lives in a protracted nightmare of perennial night, and he is awakened, like the authorities awaken a slumbering Josef K., by a hostile group of urban vigilantes. In what world, what city, what place or time does *Shadows and Fog* take place? Allen's film links itself to the silent era's avant-garde narratives—the nightmarish landscape—both thematically and visually, making *Shadows and Fog* a unique comedic neo-expressionist narrative, that recalls the unfamiliar, disturbing city and streets of Robert Wiene's *The Cabinet of Dr. Caligari* (1920). Vincent Canby has noted the presence of such an expressionist design in Allen's film:

> Kleinman (Mr. Allen) is a timid clerk in the kind of unidentified Middle European city once so beloved by Kafka, Kafka's imitators, the masters of the German Expressionist cinema of the 1920's and their imitators. It is always night in this closed world of miasmic fog, cobbled alleys and street lamps that shed too little light but cast photogenically deep shadows ... Authority here is absolute and inscrutable. It may be represented by the police, by angry mobs or by Kleinman's petit bourgeois employer, whom Kleinman addresses with deference. He calls him "your grace."[21]

While Kleinman humorously—therefore, subversively—cringes before the mob, there is a murderer still on the loose in a neo-expressionist setting that reactivates the *mise-en-scène* of its American and Germanic predecessors; in Kleinman's waking nightmare, the real criminal exists in a world of unsettling, shadowy moments, while imposing authority figures, equally intimidating, add to the pervasive display of Kleinman's nervousness. *Shadows and Fog* utilizes the night-town searching of a little man in a drolly terrifying, otherworldly milieu.[22]

As Kleinman walks the streets looking for signs of the plan to catch the criminal, he encounters the assorted historical, expressionist staples: prostitutes, lonely women, alcoholics, the foolish, and the enraged. It is an unreal city, a place of expressionist improprieties. George Beard noted, "we are under constant strain, mostly unconscious, oftentimes in sleeping as well as in

Figure 13.3 *Shadows and Fog*; Kleinman is questioned.

waking hours, to get somewhere or do something at some definite moment," but for Kleinman, the goal of re-establishing his innocence and place in this society is as illusory as the set design.[23] He is not alone in this compulsion.

In *Traumnovelle (The Dream Novel)* (1926), expressionist novelist Arthur Schnitzler's young doctor, Fridolin, experiences sexual alienation and night-town escapades in an expressionist stimmung that is an erotic, nightmarish landscape. As transposed onto the screen by Stanley Kubrick in a series of unsettling, urban atmospherics, *Eyes Wide Shut* is a modern, neo-expressionist adaptation in which color assumes a nearly abstracted, painterly presence, a quality of the unreal, especially in two critical shot sequences: the bedroom confrontation, and the masked ball in the mansion. According to Charles H. Helmetag, in *Eyes Wide Shut*, "Kubrick's striking blues, reds, and yellows seem the perfect vehicle for Schnitzler's prose and for [the couple's] state of mind."[24] Kubrick's neo-expressionism stands at the edge of the psychologically discomforting for both characters and audience, like witnessing a parade of well-dressed, colorful grotesqueries.

Precipitating Dr Harford's (Fridolin's) misadventures at the masked ball in the mansion, at a critical and humiliating moment in Kubrick's exceptionally underrated adaptation, the doctor experiences the spoken adulterous yearnings of his wife as she relates her drug-laced sexual fantasies to him after an evening at a Christmas party. This discussion upsets his already repressed sense of self; he too feels sexually drawn to others but fights these impulses and resists, yet he was unprepared for his wife's innermost fancies to be expressed; these are expressions of dangerous erotica that unsettle his belief system in fidelity and jar his privileged sense of place and secured identity.

The bedroom shot sequence exposes the raw nerves of sexual repression and fantasy and occurs when Dr Harford's wife, feeling the effects of a late-night marijuana cigarette prior to lovemaking, directly inquires "Did you fuck them?," referring to the two young women she saw her husband speaking to at the Christmas party. Except for an occasional two-shot of husband and wife, Kubrick utilizes a series of confrontational-passive reverse shots in this extended, confessional sequence; husband and wife are not in the same frame, although they are in the same room. Space and time have begun to shift to a more psychological, dizzying perspective; they are separated. As she initially questions his fidelity and later reveals her own fantasy of infidelity while he sits alone, she winds up sitting on the floor, surrounded by red curtains, as in a theatrical performance. This sequence recalls Edvard Munch's *Ashes* (1894), an expressionist portrait of despair in the boudoir in which a woman in white, unbuttoned and upset, stands apart from a male figure, sitting with his head in his hand, in the painting's foreground.[25]

In Kubrick's adaptation, as Dr Harford remains passively posed on the bed, unaware of his wife's deep resentment and desires, the doctor listens to her pose the rhetorical statement "if you only knew," which refers to female longing. The set design in this confessional sequence is full of red, blue and brown colors, which highlight the whiteness of their bodies. Color complements their contrasting moods: a slow burning fire, and a deep, bluish, yet decomposing cool surface. As she nearly finishes speaking about her sexual desire, his deep exhalation indicates a potential shudder of recognition; he really may not know her. Once the phone rings to interrupt this scenario, summoning him to a dying patient, he rides away in a cab and fantasizes about his wife making love to another man. This inserted, graphic shot is a black and white vision of unrestrained betrayal that unsettles him. Thus begins the night-town experience on the streets of Kubrick's neo-expressionist New York of the Gothic imagination, full of mobs, prostitutes, ominous buildings, and perfectly (un)respectable people. This is not even Manny's noirish city; this is an eroticized landscape.

After a series of implausible events, Dr Harford winds up in a contemporary Gothic mansion, full of beautiful perversities and masked men. This is not a *carnivalesque* moment in the film narrative. In this extended sequence, Kubrick's set design and neo-expressionism have more in common with the masked ball in Poe's *Masque of the Red Death* (1842), in which the damned converge for an evening's pleasure in rooms decorated with different colors. Kubrick's mansion is a stylized quasi-brothel/masked ball for escapees from that society. The neo-Gothic mansion, like the doctor's bedroom, is a neo-expressionist site of fantasy and anxiety, because the doctor is estranged from both and flees from each one, into the city at night. Kubrick's *Eyes Wide Shut* is a unique neo-expressionist

Figure 13.4   Edvard Munch, *Ashes* (1894).

narrative, as it delineates the nervous, colorful nightmares of a man apparently lost in space and time, acting without reason. I believe this indicates a movement recalling the expressionism of the painterly canvas.

The art historian Bram Dijkstra has noted the relationship between the Gothic and the American expressionist canvas:

> The "Gothic" qualities in the writing ... of Poe ... and the highly unstable physical environments to be found in the works of [American expressionist] painters ... are, in essence, a result of their belief in the potential materialization of the moral conditions of the human soul. As proto-psychoanalytical delineations of the human psyche manifested in the material world, these sources were instrumental in the development of American expressionism.[26]

Dr Harford is a soul in distress, and he wanders about a city that appears to be alien and disturbing. There is no peace or place for him on the uninviting

Figure 13.5 Ernst Ludwig Kirchner, *Nollendorfplatz* (1912).

street, which recalls the dark urban landscape envisioned by Ernst Ludwig Kirchner in his expressionist painting *Nollendorfplatz* (1912), comprising unspecified bodies and misshapen buildings. Dr Harford has no place to go, yet remains a part of the picture.[27]

In the essay "Collaborative Dreaming: Schnitzler's *Traumnovelle*, Kubrick's *Eyes Wide Shut*, and the 'Paradox of the Ordinary,'" Judy Pocock has likewise denoted the adaptation's expressionist legacy:

> In Kubrick's hands, film, at one and the same time the most realistic and dreamlike of art forms proves to be the perfect medium to capture and develop Schnitzler's vision . . . Kubrick appropriates Schnitzler's turn-of-the-century flâneur-like protagonists and transports him and his urban quest . . . exploring terrain that is so familiar and at the same time, so foreign and strange.[28]

For neo-expressionist male figures, the streets possess an alchemical, unsettling danger. Dr Harford, Kleinman, and Manny collectively undergo the nocturnal, ambulatory and secretive activities, the dark, experiential romanticism of the perturbed soul, as expressed by the voice of Whitman's *flâneur* in the poem "The Sleepers" (1855). Whitman's speaker experiences the restless, dreamlike, night-time activities and fantasies of the streets:

> I wander all night in my vision,
> Stepping with light feet, swiftly and noiselessly stepping and stopping,
> ... Wandering and confused, lost to myself, ill-assorted, contradictory,
> Pausing, gazing, bending and stopping.²⁹

These drifting souls find the streets of the city to be dangerously engaging at night, often, with a promise of peril, but also, with repressed pleasures surfacing. According to R. W. French:

> It ["The Sleepers"] has a clear plot much in the manner of dream visions... It begins with the poet in a state of confusion and distress... What the poet sees in his wanderings reinforces the reader's sense of a soul in distress; for the people he visits in the night are so overwhelmingly among humanity's unfortunates that suffering and isolation would appear to be the norm.³⁰

As with Whitman's wandering voice and vision, in these American neo-expressionist film narratives the streets and city are near-sentient, sinister, dark sites, which reflect and reveal internal and external states of despair for men like Dr Harford, Kleinman, and Manny. In both Schnitzler's novel and Kubrick's adaptation, the distressed, nervous doctor encounters the unfamiliar city at night, with its streets, people, and liabilities that unsettle internalized notions of place and propriety, especially the sexual. "Both novel and film have a dream-like quality and we are never sure where reality ends and fantasy begins."³¹ At least the distressed Dr Harford will find his way home to his expressively eroticized wife. They even make plans for intercourse.

In the essay "Art as Technique," the Russian formalist critic Victor Shklovsky noted how, "after we see an object several times, we begin to recognize it... Art removes objects from the automatism of perception." The perception is not a singular sensory experience yielding a totality; the audience re-addresses the subject/object and intuits the immaterial:

> An image is not a permanent referent for those mutable complexities of life which are revealed through it; its purpose is not to make us perceive meaning, but to create a special perception of the object—*it creates a "vision" of the object instead of serving as a means for knowing it.*³²

In expressionist cinema, a modernist movement linked to the experimentalism of the twentieth century, film consciously exploits its visual capacity to generate representations, perceptions of reality and suggestive poses, and destabilizing these cinematic moments is a critical precept. Meaning is symbolic and fluid, and this remains an aesthetic criterion from the turn of century in expressionist literature, painting, and especially, film narratives. Shklovsky concludes:

Art exists ... to make one feel things, to make the stone *stony*. The purpose of art is to impart the sensation of things as they are perceived and not as they are known. The technique of art is to make objects "unfamiliar," to make forms difficult, to increase the difficulty and length of perception because the process of perception is an aesthetic end in itself and must be prolonged. Art is a way of experiencing the artfulness of an object; the object is not important.[33]

Expressionist and neo-expressionist cinema make the viewer see the new, the different, and the covert potential of the previously seen. The films discussed feature the psychologically-politically destabilized male character in the midst of an alienating formalist design based in the real world of objects, people, and places. Poe's narratives of nervous men hold a special place in the adaptation practices of the avant-garde in American silent expressionist film, as each film is the geometrically conceived study of Gothic contrivances, completed by a nervous, disassembling voice, in space and time. The later, neo-expressionist films cohere as composed studies, working in and across various film genres, and reflect parts of an aesthetic whole appropriated from historical narratives in expressionist cinema, painting, and literature. Whether facing controlling authority figures, the machinery of the state, or the waking nightmare of the street and unfamiliar faces of people, in American expressionist/neo-expressionist cinema, nervous men are case studies in decline, as identity is a commodity to be "un-fixed" by experience.

Notes

1. This is a study of the trope of the nervous male, focusing on aesthetic compositional strategies and the dissemination of expressionism in American film culture. It is not a survey of hysteria in film or literary narrative. Hysteria is a linguistically charged, quasi-medical term replete with historically and politically divisive strategies and consequences. Hysteria is a collection of various forms of illnesses, real or not, represented in an exceptionally gendered terminology. In select American expressionist and neo-expressionist films, the nervous is a visible, primary manifestation of irregular, effectively heightened behavior, whereas hysteria may be a more complex, interior catalyst for such erratic, often explosive behavior. The conceptual application of a reactive, politicized, psychoanalytical hysteria is discussed by Mark S. Micale in *Hysterical Men: The Hidden History of Male Nervous Illness* (Cambridge, MA: Harvard University Press, 2008), and by Elaine Showalter in her essay "On Hysterical Narrative," *Narrative*, Vol. 1, January 1993, pp. 24–35, in which she concludes, "hysterical narrative has become the waste-basket term of literary criticism, applied to a wide and diffuse range of textual techniques and, most alarmingly, taken as a synonym for women's writing." In his major study of hysteria and German expressionist war films, *Shell Shock Cinema: Weimar Culture and the Wounds of War* (Princeton, NJ: Princeton University Press, 2009), Anton Kaes links hysteria to wartime battlefield experiences. Some other highly recommended works examining the hysteria dialectic include Francis M. Sharp,

"Expressionism and Psychoanalysis," *Pacific Coast Philology*, Vol. 13, October 1978, pp. 94–100; Ursula Link-Herr and Jamie Owen Daniel, "'Male Hysteria': A Discourse Analysis," *Cultural Critique*, No. 15, Spring 1990, pp. 191–220; and Jan Goldstein, "The Uses of Male Hysteria: Medical and Literary Discourse in Nineteenth-Century France," *Representations*, No. 34, Spring 1991, pp. 134–65.
2. While Webber and Watson's *The Fall of the House of Usher* has been the subject of significant critical exegesis, Klein's film narrative has been inadequately represented as a prominent expressionist film text.
3. Richard Murphy, "Modernism and the Cinema: *Metropolis* and the Expressionist Aesthetic," *Comparative Critical Studies*, Vol. 4, No. 1, 2007, pp. 105–20, see p. 110.
4. American expressionist playwrights Sophie Treadwell's *Machinal* (1928) and Elmer Rice's *The Adding Machine* (1923) also feature toxic machines in the form of an electric chair and an adding machine, respectively, leading to disastrous, fatal results for the afflicted nervous. Like Kafka's penetrating needles in the expressionist, nightmarish machinery of execution from *In the Penal Colony* (1919), machines represent judgmental authority. These aesthetic precepts recur in later neo-expressionist narratives as well.
5. Wilhelm Hausenstein, "Art at This Moment" (1919–20), reprinted in Anton Kaes, Martin Jay, and Edward Dimendberg (eds.), *The Weimar Republic Sourcebook* (Berkeley, CA: University of California Press, 1995), p. 479.
6. Herbert Jhering, "An Expressionist Film" (1920), reprinted in Kaes, Jay, Dimendberg (eds.), *The Weimar Republic Sourcebook*, p. 620.
7. Jan-Christopher Horak, "The First American Film Avant-Garde, 1919–1945," in his (ed.) *Lovers of Cinema: The First American Film Avant-Garde, 1919–1945* (Madison, WI: University of Wisconsin Press, 1996), pp. 14–66, see p. 48.
8. Ibid. p. 50.
9. George Beard, *American Nervousness* (New York: Putnam, 1881), p. 176.
10. Lisa Cartwright, "U.S. Modernism and the Emergence of 'The Right Wing of Film Art': The Films of James Sibley Watson, Jr., and Melville Webber," in Jan-Christopher Horak, *Lovers of Cinema: The First American Film Avant-Garde*, p. 161.
11. Pierre Janet, *The Mental State of Hystericals* (1892), ed. Daniel N. Robinson (Washington, DC: University Publications of America, 1977), pp. 278–9. This edition is a reprint of a translation by Caroline Corson; Putnam, 1901.
12. Jules Claretie, "The Shudder in Literature," *The North American Review*, Vol. 155, No. 429, August 1892, p. 140.
13. Fritz Lang, "The Future of the Feature Film in Germany," reprinted in Kaes, Jay and Dimendberg (eds.), *The Weimar Republic Sourcebook*, p. 620.
14. Edgar Allan Poe, "The Tell-Tale Heart" (1843). Available at <http://xroads.virginia.edu/~hyper/poe/telltale.html> (last accessed 22 January 2015).
15. Ibid.
16. In D. W. Griffith's adaptation of "The Tell-Tale Heart," renamed as *The Avenging Conscience* (1914), this breakdown-into-confessional shot sequence is a highlight of the film, with a marvelously suggestive series of ghosts, close-ups, nightmarish images, and the general destabilization performance of Henry Walthall as the (dreaming only) murderer in Griffith's revised melodrama.
17. Richard Murphy, "Modernism and the Cinema," p. 114.
18. This study will exclude those film narratives categorized as film noir, which may be viewed as a *stylized* and industrial movement lasting primarily from 1941–58.
19. Welles' *Citizen Kane* (1941), as well as his adaptation *The Trial* (1962), have both been the subject of so much historical and contemporary critical analyses

that focus on expressionist design and themes that I would avoid, for the sheer physical space it merits, including either in this study. For a contemporary reading of *Citizen Kane* and American expressionism, see Alicia Kozma's unpublished thesis, "Deconstructing American Mythic Identity: Citizen Kane and American Expressionism" (2009), at the CUNY Graduate Center.
20. Peter J. Dellolio, "Hitchcock and Kafka: Expressionist Themes in *Strangers on a Train*," *Midwest Quarterly: A Journal of Contemporary Thought*, Vol. 45, No. 3, Spring 2004, p. 240.
21. Vincent Canby, "Shadows and Fog" (film review), *The New York Times*, 20 March 1992. Available at <http://movies.nytimes.com/movie/review?res=9E0CE5DC123 FF933A15750C0A964958260> (last accessed 22 January 2015).
22. Kleinman is reminiscent of another nervous male dominated by the presence of power, Kafka's servile but all-too-human Block, the perennially waiting figure in need of his lawyer's counsel in *The Trial*. People speak about Kleinman in his presence as if he were invisible, perhaps guilty of something; Block also becomes the subject of attention between Josef and Leni, the woman at the lawyer's office, and his future lover: "[K.] asked, 'Who is this man?' Leni put one hand around K. as she stirred the soup with the other, she drew him forward toward herself and said, 'He's a pitiful character, a poor businessman by the name of Block. Just look at him . . . He's as talkative as he is sweet. Maybe that's why the lawyer can't stand him.'" A copy of Kafka's novel is available at <http://www.gutenberg.org/cache/epub/7849/pg7849.html> (last accessed 22 January 2015).
23. George Beard, *American Nervousness*, p. 104.
24. Charles H. Helmetag, "Dream Odysseys: Schnitzler's *Traumnovelle* and Kubrick's *Eyes Wide Shut*," *Literature and Film Quarterly*, Vol. 31, No. 4, January 2003, pp. 276–86, see p. 279.
25. A good reproduction of the original painting is available at <http://www.edvardmunch.org/ashes.jsp> (last accessed 22 January 2015).
26. Bram Dijkstra, *American Expressionism: Art and Social Change 1920–1950* (New York: Harry N. Abrams, 2003), p. 72.
27. For a more complete view of the Kirchner painting, see http://bit.ly/1Png9f3 (last accessed 20 August 2015).
28. Judy Pocock, "Collaborative Dreaming: Schnitzler's *Traumnnovelle*, Kubrick's *Eyes Wide Shut*, and the 'Paradox of the Ordinary,'" *Arachnē: An Interdisciplinary Journal of the Humanities*, Vol. 7, Nos. 1–2, 2000, pp. 76–93, see p. 77.
29. I cite Whitman's "deathbed" edition (1881), available at <http://bailiwick.lib.uiowa.edu/whitman/sleepers/poem1881.html> (last accessed 22 January 2015).
30. R. W. French, "Whitman's Dream Vision: A Reading of *The Sleepers*," *Walt Whitman Quarterly Review*, Vol. 8, Summer 1990, pp. 1–2.
31. Judy Pocock, "Collaborative Dreaming," p. 81.
32. Victor Shklovsky, "Art as Technique," in Lee T. Lemon and Marion J. Reis (eds.), *Russian Formalist Criticism: Four Essays* (Lincoln, NE: University of Nebraska Press, 1965), pp. 3–24, see pp. 13, 18. These are the original italics.
33. Shklovsky, "Art as Technique," p. 12.

14. *DOS MONJES* (1934) AND THE TORTURED SEARCH FOR TRUTH[1]

David J. Hogan

The hothouse of unhappy emotion that is Mexican writer-director Juan Bustillo Oro's *Dos monjes* (*Two Monks*, 1934)[2] ruminates on the differences between art and reality, and the misleading and potentially disastrous collisions of reality and perception. The film is also a reflection of many cultural markers, some unique to Mexico, others not: echoes of the 1910 Mexican revolution; a brewing Mexican nationalism; *moderne* Mexican stage aesthetics; the Social Realism art movement; split personality; and the cross-continental influence of Weimar Germany, specifically, Expressionist filmmaking.

Expressionist art, whether on canvas, on stage, or on film, is pointedly self-referential. It is conscious of its own form, and invites exaggerated viewer attention to the medium. For filmmakers, Expressionist thought and concomitant techniques bring a new—and wholly intentional—artifice.

Film provides a false image of the world. We do not witness screen characters empirically. We are not there with them. Motion pictures—like all photography—put us at a remove from reality. The American documentarian Errol Morris wrote, "We *imagine* that photographs provide a magic path to the truth ... With the advent of photography, images ... became more like dreams."[3]

Expressionist films do not merely tell stories; they manipulate camera movement, point of view, and narrative structure, so that dreamlike and other psychological (frequently, psycho*sexual*) effects are called to the fore, and heightened. And Expressionist film frequently imagines—that is, creates—images suggestive of disturbed or aberrant mental and emotional conditions.

Frequently, as in Robert Wiene's great German psychodrama *Das Cabinet des Dr. Caligari* (*The Cabinet of Dr. Caligari*; 1920), Expressionist technique is so potent, so stylized, that the viewer is pushed away from the experience, even as he or she is engaged, realizing, *I'm watching a movie. This isn't real, but it's compelling because I've been invited to experience that character's thoughts.*

A great deal of Expressionist art invokes struggles for identity, and one's place in the world. In this, the movement parallels some of the political and artistic activity going on in Mexico in the twenty years prior to *Dos monjes*.

DIAZ, THE MOVIES, AND REVOLUTIONARY THOUGHT IN MEXICO

The distinguished Mexican soldier Porfirio Diaz was Mexico's self-appointed president from 1876 to 1910 (excluding the years 1880–4, when a Diaz puppet was installed in the office). The length of Diaz's tenure is, by itself, sufficient to mark him as the most influential figure in Mexican life and politics during those years.

Diaz was born in 1830, and during his adult lifetime he experienced the Mexican–American War of 1848, and the subsequent grab by the USA of an enormous portion of Mexican territory. That act inflamed Diaz's nationalistic fervor, which was exceeded only by his personal ambition. During the 1860s, he led Mexican forces in successful campaigns against the French (including the victory now celebrated as Cinco de Mayo), and built up considerable political and military capital. In 1876, federal forces that answered to a one-time Diaz ally, President Benito Juarez, were defeated by Diaz's opposition troops.

A significant portion of Mexico's history pivots on the nation's relationship with the USA. Diaz resented imperialism, but wasn't blind to the advantages of a prosperous and educated middle-class citizenry. Because he knew that Mexico was woefully behind its northern neighbor, and Europe, he instituted a modernization program in 1885, remaking Mexico City, forcing industrialization, and encouraging education among the nascent middle class. However, Diaz had little regard for indigenous Mexican culture, and worked hard to erase it. He was embarrassed by Mexico's *peones*, and controlled that population with restrictive legislation and an active police and military presence in rural areas.

So preoccupied was Diaz with American and European material culture that he remade himself, as well, becoming less and less Mexican in his outlook, and even his appearance. Diaz elevated his own power by keeping local governments in check, and allowed American and European interests to purchase enormous stakes in Mexican oil, copper, and railroads.

All of this brought undeniable material benefit to many in Mexico, including Diaz, his inner circle and other cronies, and the growing middle class. Film and other media also benefited. If Diaz was to strengthen his grip on the nation, he had to modernize and direct Mexican popular communication. The technological push that allowed the Mexican film industry to begin to flourish in the first two decades of the twentieth century, then, is attributable in large part to Diaz's self-serving initiatives.

But while President Diaz clouded Mexican identity and oppressed the nation's have-nots, opposition politicians found a wedge issue that played very strongly on these questions: What is a Mexican? What is the true Mexican culture? Who are we?

Revolt

The Mexican Revolution of 1910 was a response to Diaz's essentially anti-Mexican, authoritarian rule. A key opponent, Francisco I. Madero, championed democracy and led revolutionary troops into battle against federal forces throughout the early part of 1911. In May of that year, Madero drove Diaz from office (and all the way to exile in Spain). Madero became Mexico's president the following month. Although he instituted land reform and other progressive programs, he was ultimately hobbled by the government's insider tangle of conflicting agendas and loyalties, and by the growing dissatisfaction of his former revolutionary allies, Emilio Zapata and Pancho Villa. Madera was finally betrayed by one of his generals, and executed by forces sympathetic to the Diaz family in February 1913.

Art for All

Despite Madera's overthrow, Mexico continued on its course of expanding the middle class. The nation also undertook a formal effort to recognize the importance of its own history. The Mexican presidential election of 1920 was won by Alvara Obregón, a general whose troops, including Yaqui Indians, had performed well during the Revolution. Working closely with his secretary of public education, José Vasconcelos, Obregón placed new emphasis on pre-Hispanic Mexican culture. Vanconcelos utilized the mandate to conceive a mural project that would install nationalistic public art across Mexico. By 1921, Mexico's mural movement was thriving.

Vasconcelos fancied "pure art," and was disappointed when many of the commissioned murals, particularly those by José Clemente Orozco, David Alfaro Siqueiros, and the famed Marxist fresco artist Diego Rivera, displayed obvious political underpinnings. But what else could Vasconcelos have expected from art born of revolution?

Unhappiness with the aesthetics of certain murals was not limited to politicians. During 1923–4, numerous murals across Mexico were physically attacked by prep school students, who called the works "monstrosities." Regardless, the Obregón government was convinced that art and education, combined, would elevate Mexico in the Americas, and on the world stage. But in 1924, shortly before he resigned under public pressure, Vasconcelos ended the mural program. However, Rivera and the other Social Realists had made their mark, sharply influencing the tone of Mexican painting.

Virtually simultaneous with the late stage of the mural movement was the first issue of a Socialist-Communist arts magazine, *El Machete*. It was edited by Siqueiros, with contributions by Orozco and Rivera. Siqueiros insisted that Mexican art fulfill a social function. He had been on board with the murals program, but now he agitated for something grander, a communal "monumental art" movement. This had particular appeal for Rivera, whose work (and the work of his wife, Frida Kahlo) was rooted in indigenous art traditions of Mexican Indians.

This scrum of political, economic, cultural, and nationalistic impulses bubbled in a stew that, during 1910–20, made Mexico a lively (if unpredictable) environment. Young people interested in motion pictures had myriad cultural influences from which to draw: local, national, and international. Equally significant is the Mexican government's continuing interest in the various uses of film. During the 1934–40 government of the liberal nationalist president Lázaro Cárdenas, new protectionist laws encouraged loans for film production. Further, domestic film productions could now enjoy tax exemptions. Private financing became possible with the establishment of the Financiadora de Películas.

Mexican cinema's technical growth continued. Sound arrived in 1929; ten sound features were released during 1929–30. These initiatives and developments, and a general air of excitement about moviemaking, gave budding screenwriters and directors hope that a Mexican film industry would exist when they were ready to take their turn.

Oro's Formative Years

Juan Bustillo Oro, the writer-director of *Dos monjes*, was born in Mexico City in 1904. He was an active, commercially successful filmmaker from 1927 to 1966. He directed sixty films, and remained busy as a screenwriter until 1969. He wrote many of the pictures he directed, scripting sixty-six in all.

Because Oro's father, Don Juan Bustillo Bridat, managed Mexico City's Teatro Colón, it's not surprising that Oro's early narrative interest was theater-based. Oro eventually became a playwright, writing *Una lección para los esposos* (*A Lesson for Husbands*) and *Tiburón* (*Shark*, from Ben Jonson's satirical *Volpone*). But Oro was also captivated by the movies. As a youngster, he had been impressed by French filmmaker Georges Méliès, German Expressionism, and films from the USA and the Continent.

Oro attended the Universidad Nacional Autonoma de Mexico in the 1920s and earned a law degree. Before completing his studies, he took a correspondence course on story and film adaptation. Tenuous as this was, it accounts for the totality of Oro's formal training as a filmmaker.

In 1925, Oro took a psychology course taught by the philosopher Samuel Ramos. The course apparently freed up Oro's thoughts about events from earlier in his life. Oro said:

> I was very interested when I heard that the course would deal with Freud's ideas, which ended up not surprising me, but disturbing me. They brought back to me with a renewed intensity the horror I felt at the end of my childhood, when I saw *The Strange Case of Dr. Jekyll and Mr. Hyde* [*Den Skæbnesvangre Opfindelse*], the [1910] Danish film based on Stevenson's novel.[4]

It is not known whether Ramos delved into Jekyll and Hyde personalities in the course attended by Oro, but that may well have been the case. Ramos was intrigued by split personality, particularly as it related to the fragmentary nature of Mexican national identity. He lamented the nation's shift from a rural to an urban emphasis, suggesting that city life created an unnaturally self-conscious, even destructive, national character. Ramos lamented that many rural Mexicans could not negotiate city life successfully, which exacerbated preexisting feelings of inferiority.

Oro wrote his first script, *Yo soy tu padre* (*I Am Your Father*), in 1927. This adaptation of French author Maurice Leblanc's 1925 novel *La Vie extravagante de Balthazar* (*The Extravagant Life of Balthazar*) is a romantic comedy predicated on class and misapprehensions about wealth. After financing was secured, Oro directed the film, a silent. The same year, Oro hoped to film musical numbers from Lyric Theatre revues starring Roberto Solo. These were to be the backbone of what would have been Mexico's first talkie, but the project was stillborn.

In 1932, Oro and a prominent playwright and journalist, Mauricio Magdeleno, founded Mexico City's Teatro de Ahora (Theatre Now), which mounted many plays with revolutionary political overtones. That was a reflection of Oro's growing list of professional and personal preoccupations, which included the Indians, Mexican sovereignty, US economic abuse of his country, migration, and judicial and governmental corruption. Oro's theater work focused frequently on the Mexican Revolution's achievements and shortcomings. In all of this, Oro's art was inextricably entwined with his politics.

Building on a European Aesthetic

Not all of Oro's political influences were Mexican. He was taken with the Socialist-uplift theories of theater propounded by German actor-director Erwin Piscator, a creative force in Weimar Munich and Berlin. Simultaneous with Bertolt Brecht, Piscator (who collaborated with Brecht in 1927) developed the notion of epic theater, by which onstage narratives were keenly instructional, even didactic, rather than purely dramatic. In some iterations, plays would be "interrupted" so that actors could directly address the audience, breaking the fourth wall, and emphasizing theater's inherent artificiality (and, of course, the inherent artificiality of all art—and even, perhaps, the artificiality of human perception). Via this technique, Piscator, Brecht, and other practitioners of epic theater elevated ideas at the expense of audience involvement with characters or "plot." Piscator's Expressionistic staging, and occasional use of film clips, light effects, and loudspeakers, heightened the essential artificiality of the experience, and further emphasized ideas.

In 1931, Oro said that Teatro de Ahora's "full dramatic technique in subjective and objective alternatives [functions] in a constant mixture of reality and fantasy."[5] Teatro de Ahora enjoyed public approval from Narciso Bassols, a sociologist who founded a Mexican Socialist political party, Partido Popular. Bassols was also Mexico's secretary of public education, and Mexican ambassador to the UK.

Oro was making his mark in serious Mexican theater, but his interests were wide-ranging; during 1932, for instance, he staged music hall revues. In 1932–3, while living in Spain, Oro wrote two plays, *Tropico de Magdaleno* (*Tropic of Magdaleno*) and *San Miguel de las espinas* (*St Miguel of Thorns*). The latter looks at Mexican peasants who try desperately to manage a drought by building a dam. They fail and continue to suffer; Oro's point was that, despite the Revolution, little helpful change had come to Mexico's vast rural areas.

In 1934, beginning with the regime of Lázaro Cárdenas, Mexico entered a period of progressive reform that lasted until Cardenas left office in 1940. Mexican film prior to about 1930 had been encouraged to be strongly nationalistic, but a general broadening of governmental outlook during the Cárdenas years, and the already-mentioned growth of the Mexican middle class that had begun around 1885, helped make *Dos monjes* possible. The film launched Oro's long career as a writer-director of movies, brought Expressionism to Mexican cinema, and helped usher in the fifteen-year golden age of Mexican moviemaking.

Figure 14.1 The disturbed composer Javier (Carlos Villatoro) longs so fiercely for love that his reality shifts, and assumes a sinister aspect. (*Courtesy of the Agrasánchez Film Archive*)

Dos monjes and Disastrous Romance

In late nineteenth-century Mexico, a tubercular composer named Javier (Carlos Villatoro) lives in a comfortable but modest flat with his solicitous mother (Emma Roldán). Javier has written a sweeping *romanza* inspired by Ana (Magda Haller), a beautiful young woman who lives across the courtyard. Javier does not know her; indeed, the inference during the early portion of *Dos monjes* is that he may never even have spoken to her. Instead, he secretly gazes at her through the latticework of the window that illuminates his elevated piano platform. Doubly framed by Javier's window and her own, Ana seems very much a perfect work of art. But art has subtexts, and so does Ana's existence, namely, her overbearing parents, who have apparently arranged a romantic relationship for their daughter. Disturbed by this, but essentially passive, Javier observes Ana and the young man as they embrace in silhouette. When Ana resists the embrace, Javier is at once heartened and upset.

Shortly, in an abrupt and frankly dreamlike turn of events, Javier and Ana are a couple, and Javier is introducing the girl to his mother. Thereafter, Ana is frequently in the house (having been practically thrown there by her furious father), and Javier continues to write music for her. Javier's cough is less frequent, and he and Ana speak freely about marriage.

But Ana is preoccupied with thoughts of another man, and when Javier dreams of his long-absent friend, Juan (Victor Urruchúa), it becomes clear to us that the two men are going to be rivals.

The friends are joyously reunited. Juan has become wealthy during his time away, and promises to support Javier in his music.

Javier's affect changes after he introduces Juan to Ana. Javier inexplicably begins to talk of winter and his own death. His health grows worse, and by spring he's disturbed because Juan no longer visits. "I ask him [why he doesn't come]," Javier tells his mother, "and he avoids the issue. He has something to hide from me."

The film's narrative and visual tensions increase. A complicated interlude during which Juan says he is about to leave on a long journey culminates when Javier witnesses Juan and Ana in embrace. Javier shouts that Juan is a swine, and slashes his face with a cane. Juan, as if prepared for trouble, pulls a revolver. He fires carelessly and hits Ana, who falls dead in Javier's arms. When Javier's mother enters, she, too, is shot by Juan.

Three Tales to Tell

Thus far, the events of *Dos monjes* are blunt and starkly melodramatic. The love triangle that culminates in violence is as old as drama itself. But nothing here is as simple as it seems. The film has a framing device, set in a monastery. As *Dos monjes* begins, Javier is a monk whose tormented blaspheming has upset his brother monks. They are convinced that Javier has been possessed by Satan. Another young monk, Brother Servando, is sent to calm Javier, but his presence only aggravates Javier's agitated condition—and little wonder, because Servando is Juan, installed in the monastery following Ana's death and the (unexplained) destruction of his fortune.

Javier, wracked by despair and illness, is convinced that Servando/Juan is the devil. Javier tells the Prior (M. Beltran Heder) how he "discovered [Juan's] treacherous soul," and then relates his story, which has been designed by Oro as a flashback (described above). "I decided to try and forget my sorrows, shutting myself away in this monastery," Javier concludes.

The Prior grasps Javier's misery, but informs Javier that absolution cannot be granted until the Prior hears Juan's version of the events.

In his own cell, Juan/Servando admits, "My sins are great," but adds that "Friar Javier's truth is just a partial truth." With that, *Dos monjes* suggests that there are limits to human perception, and that the events of human lives are not necessarily as they appear. Juan goes on: "It's a truth seen through

[Javier's] eyes only. The sinner Juan [here Servando/Juan refers to himself] has *his* truth, also, the one he lived."

Juan's recollection establishes that he knew Ana intimately before he was introduced to her by Javier. Juan had purposely removed himself from Ana's life, and now here he is—in her presence again.

When Javier is occupied elsewhere, Ana clutches Juan, telling him that she's loved him all along. She's never loved Javier romantically. "For him I feel a sister's love," she tells Juan, "gratitude, anything but the love I feel for you."

Javier's mother overhears, and confronts Juan and Ana. Javier remains ignorant of the affair, but is consumed by an unnamable dread. His health fails, and (as in Javier's own account) he frets about the onset of winter.

In a key moment, the doctor tells Juan and Ana that Javier is very ill, and will not live for many more months. With this bit of recollection—whether honest or not—Juan fashions his story so that his affair with Ana is explained and perhaps even justified: Any romance Ana might have with Javier would be truncated and pointless. But Ana is struck with guilt, and convinces Juan that they must part from each other. If they do not, Javier will suffer, and possibly die even sooner than expected.

All of that is noble enough, but during a final goodbye, Juan weakens, and reiterates his love. Ana mounts a feeble, momentary resistance, and then gives in as well. They embrace.

When Javier enters with a gun, Juan makes the mistake of daring him to shoot. Javier fires the gun and Ana is killed. Was Javier's shot intended for her, or for Javier? This question will remain unanswered.

Juan gets to the final part of his recollection. Javier retreats to the monastery's organ, and when the other monks gather to confront him there, Javier hallucinates, imagining them as grotesque, judgmental fiends. He collapses and dies, but not before Juan begs him for forgiveness.

All of what is recounted above accounts for two tales. The third is the tale told by *Dos monjes*, the tale we will create from our own perceptions and judgments.

Art and the Unreal

Because of the preoccupation with Ana that is shared by Javier and Juan, and the fact that the actors who play the parts (Carlos Villatoro and Victor Urruchúa, respectively) strongly resemble one another, it's easy and reasonable to assume that Oro intended the characters to be regarded as different aspects of a single personality. (Remember that Oro had been struck by a film adaptation of *The Strange Case of Dr. Jekyll and Mr. Hyde*.) The "Javier" component is introspective and naively romantic; the "Juan" element is assertive and driven more by the flesh than the soul. Given Mexico's efforts to disentangle

Figure 14.2 Javier secretly watches his beloved Ana (Magda Haller), who appears to give her heart to Javier's rival, Juan (Victor Urruchúa). (*Courtesy of the Agrasánchez Film Archive*)

itself from foreign oppressors, and establish a unique identity, this reading of *Dos monjes* has timeliness on its side.

Further, Javier and Juan both forsake former lives to become monks. Juan even assumes a new name. Each man has voluntarily divided his persona, which adds a sub-level of split personality to *Dos monjes*.

On the other hand, the film's narrative presents the physical reality of two discrete men. Although we may be tempted to accept Juan's recollection as the credible one (mainly because Juan seems less "mad" than his friend), Javier—dissipated cough and all—is the central, and most sympathetically intriguing, figure of *Dos monjes*. He is a creature of artifice (he creates music) whose life is dominated by physical illness and his own imagination (his music, and his paranoia). Music, as a creative response to life, is inherently artificial and subjective. It is also easily codified, via notation drawn or printed on score sheets. Of course, what can be seen and held isn't the totality of music, but it does give music a physical presence.

Javier's music, then, is his reality. Even as contemporaneous, real-life Mexicans grappled with national identity and the purposes of art, Javier fashions a reality that, although artificial, nevertheless suits him. When he (in his own recollection) tells Ana, "You're like the daybreak which looms in my soul," he doesn't speak to her. Instead, he *sings* to the melody of the distinctly European *romanza*. Normal communication seems beyond his capabilities. He goes on, singing: "Flower from a sublime dream, with a subtle scent which adorns my window."

With the lyric "sublime dream," Javier hits on the ferociously (if essentially innocent) selfishness that will be his undoing. The Ana he sees isn't the Ana that walks and eats and sleeps. Javier's Ana is a wishful confabulation.

In a symbolic conceit that director Oro executes with far more subtlety than one might expect, Javier wears white throughout his recollection, while Juan wears black. The black presages Juan's eventual crimes, of course, but the white of Javier's attire is more important because it encourages us to think well of Javier, and to assume that his personal and narrative points of view are noble as well as credible. Near the climax of Javier's recollection, when he comes upon Juan's black coat and ebony hat in Ana's foyer, the clothing suggests the black stain of deceit.

In a neat reversal, Juan's recollection places him in white outfits, and Javier in black. Near the climax of Juan's account, the white of Javier's coat and hat suggests—what? A visualization of all victims of betrayal? Perhaps the white suggests that Javier's innocence was destined to be shattered. But there are two versions of the climactic event. Is *anyone* innocent?

At the beginning and the end of Juan's recollection, he speaks to the Prior in the third person. "Javier never knew the drama existing between his friend Juan and Ana," Juan begins. He has been a monk for an unspecified time, and while one may assume that he now sees himself primarily as Brother Servando, his third-person reference to himself is jarring. In keeping with the Expressionistic visuals of *Dos monjes*, this disassociation is an indicator of Juan's psychological and emotional confusion. His mind cannot adequately catalogue the events in his tale, so he briefly "exits" the persona called Juan and becomes somebody else. That other person happens to be Servando; it hardly matters. The point is that although Javier has been tormented by visual hallucinations, Juan's mind is no less fractured. Juan/Servando closes his story with, "He [Juan] traveled. He tried to forget. It was useless. Only the hardships of the monastery and the discipline of the penance brought consolation to his heart."

Truth and reflection—even when they are bitter—are necessary for the attainment of self-knowledge. It's no accident that *Dos monjes* isn't called *Javier y Juan*. The film opens and closes at the monastery. Thinking and praying go on there. Self-denial is practiced there. Little that happens in the monastery is traditionally comfortable or pleasing. The film's opening sequence highlights the claustrophobic dimness of the place, and presages the darkness of the heart and soul that will follow. The end sequence, no less literally and figuratively dark than the earlier one, reiterates the trap Juan and Javier create for themselves in the main narrative.

In each man's version of events, Juan asks Javier to look after some papers that he will shortly bring. (Javier lives by the reality of his score sheets. Now, additional paper may enter his life.) We never learn precisely what these papers are, but they could represent Juan's struggle with his own exculpation. Perhaps the papers are Juan's confession of his affair with Ana. Perhaps they award Javier the money Juan earned during his long, hazily explained absence. Or maybe there are no papers at all, and Juan is simply trying to verbalize something he'd *like* to do.

Mind and Movie: Off-kilter

The Expressionist flourishes of *Dos monjes* build slowly but steadily. During the first scenes in the monastery (that is, during the initial part of the film's framing device), the screen is dominated by group shots of chanting monks. The chant, "May the Devil get out from the House of God" (repeated three times), shortly adopts another rhythm when the screen is interspersed with quick close-ups on the hooded faces of individuals, with the words divided among individuals: "May the Devil/get out/from the House/of God/from the house of God/from the house of God . . ." During the chant, the camera cuts to a setup dominated by a single, robed monk, seen from the back with outstretched arms. In this pose, he resembles the Christian crucifix. Admittedly dramatic, the image also has an unavoidable, and purposeful, impertinence, even in the context of the monastery.

When we first see the distraught Javier, the frame is initially dominated by the bright flare of an overhead light. We're unable to see anything else in the room; if we were actually present, we'd be blinded. Is this the omniscient eye of God? Javier's (presumed) psychosis? More likely, the light is the pitiless burn of Javier's paranoia, for he raves in his cell about "that man" (Juan) whom he's spied in the corridors.

The monastery's main gathering area is shadowed and foreboding, and when the scene shifts to the office of the Prior, the desk behind which he sits is tilted in the frame, the higher end at frame left. This imagery signals the psychological disarray that will dominate Javier and Juan's recollections, and their present situations.

Javier finally catches up with Juan, and cries "sacrilege!" His outburst is underscored by two things: a cut to a reaction shot of the shocked Prior, with camera tilted (this time, in a reversal, with the higher point at frame right); and Javier's subsequent striking of Juan with a crucifix. (The mark left by the blow anticipates a similar mark that Javier will make on Juan's face later in the film, with a cane.) With the crucifix, Oro's religious impertinence continues, and is made uncomfortably personal with quick cuts between the faces of Juan and Javier. The early sound technology—indeed, numerous moments of *Dos monjes* were apparently shot silent—cause the emotionalism of the sequence to become all the more potent. Visual frisson is found in close-ups on the men's faces, which are dominated by staring eyes and mouths that look like holes. (In this, the faces recall the hyper-dramatic close-ups created in Russia, a decade earlier, by Eisenstein.)

Two other significant visual elements occur during the opening monastery sequence. The monks seem lumpish and off-balance in their heavy robes, allowing Oro to force a visual contrast with the precisely upright stone pillars that support the place's ceilings. The geometry of the stone, that is, the faith that put the building together, is rigid and exact. But the men who interpret that faith are random and formless. They are just men.

When Javier begins to relate his tale to the Prior, the camera executes a dramatic, elevated pullback that leaves Javier alone in a spot of light amid blackness. The man is clearly isolated, and we get the impression that isolation is common to all people. This interpretation is another hint at determinism, which would render Javier and Juan's discrete accounts pointless rather than meaningless. Can a man resist a preordained fate? Well, he can try. Javier tells the Prior, "I ardently dedicated myself to music." His music protected him, and gave him the illusive strength needed to avoid interacting with the world. And then he saw Ana.

We've already noted the heavy, cross-hatched latticework of Javier's window. Ana's window is similarly adorned, and in a bravura dolly shot, the camera moves completely through Javier's window frame and across the narrow courtyard to a close-up of Ana. Javier is enraptured, but the sudden appearance in the frame (the frame of the screen and the dual frames of the windows) of Ana's perturbed parents introduces a jolt of unease.

Javier's music keeps his sensibilities in check. His piano is on an elevated platform in the flat's main room, and is accessible by three or four horizontally wide steps. It's a dominant physical position utilized ironically by Oro, to emphasize Javier's gradual disintegration. He cannot control his imagination. His elevated perch gives him neither stature nor comfort.

Oro's narrative progression is purposely artificial, pulling us forward through time via fades, and horizontal and diagonal wipes. This is mechanical technique that announces itself as such. Oro wants us to remember that we are watching a *recollection*, and that, knowingly or unknowingly, Javier will omit events and compress time. The nature and special capabilities of film itself are used to illustrate the strengths and limits of the human memory, and personal narrative.

Figure 14.3 Driven to despair and, possibly, madness, Javier retreats to the monastery's organ. His music may redeem him, but first he must suffer the torments of hallucinations. (*Courtesy of the Agrasánchez Film Archive*)

A Protective Canopy of Art

In one of the bright moments of his recollection, Javier unintentionally gives Ana a backhanded compliment: "Now I can really trust you!" And he may, but primarily because they have become linked by art. Whatever Javier composes, he composes for Ana. Like the stone pillars that support the monastery, Javier's neatly ordered score sheets and melodies buttress his love for Ana, his muse. She has become an integral part of his art, and thus, his faith.

According to Javier's version of events, Ana may possess vaguely supernatural powers. After Javier suffers a fit of coughing, Ana declares (in another of the film's religious impertinences), "You'll see how I'll end up healing you completely!" Although Ana may intend her "healing" declamation to be received in a relatively mundane way—as a promise of simple, general rejuvenation—Javier's response suggests a faith in Ana's ability to effect a near-mystical resurrection of his body and soul:

> Javier: Yes, Anita! Your love is my health and my happiness! Everything. When we're married, I'll live again.
>
> Ana: Javier!

With that exchange (and Javier's possible fundamental misunderstanding) the lovers embrace, becoming the only visible elements in a black void. For a long moment, the image is beatific—and then another man appears in the background. It is Juan, dressed in black. The "love-as-healer" notion suddenly seems childish.

Javier tells his mother than Juan has "appeared in strange form" in his dreams. Javier misses his friend, and wants him to return, but whatever it is about the dream-Juan that seems strange is yet another portent of the disaster to come. Juan finally shows up, after Javier has brooded at his desk, the curved pendulum of the clock dominating the frame. Why is the pendulum curved? And why is the fireplace surround free-form-organic rather than traditionally square? Perhaps Javier is still sleeping, and his dream is still unfolding. One visual clue suggesting that this may be the case is Oro's return to the tilted camera, which forces us to bend our heads rightward in order to take in Javier and Juan's reunion.

Later, when springtime encourages Javier to brood some more, his mother innocently suggests that Juan and Ana may have grown too close. It's a not unreasonable comment, but because Oro frames part of the scene through the familiarly tilted latticework, the remark's effect on Javier is heightened. In this camera setup, though, the room's floor is level; *only the latticework is tilted.* Oro lets us see that Javier's reality has tipped. The young composer is slipping away from the rational world.

Javier's health subsequently—and very quickly—declines, leaving him in a precarious emotional and physical state that culminates with his cane attack on Juan and his accidental shooting of Ana. Shocked by what he has done, Javier flees to the streets, which are dark and empty at night, and bracketed by stone walls and curved doors that evoke the contours and emotional tone of the monastery.

And the monastery is where we return after Javier's account. When Juan begins his own tale in the third person ("Javier never knew the drama existing between his friend Juan and Ana.") the camera pans to the window of Juan's cell. Significantly, it is barred. Bars, latticework, windows that torment as well as illuminate—all of it suggests imprisonment, whether the characters are at home or sequestered elsewhere.

Juan's recollection, although a confession of sorts, is self-serving. Despite his eagerness to reveal the truth, he casts himself as Servando in order to lessen the emotional friction. He also casts himself as the injured party, and Javier as the villain. As Juan recalls things, he's been helpless, not least because Ana flirts with him, even when she's in the arms of Javier.

When the doctor speaks of Javier's health, the camera is very close on his lips, which look like writhing worms. Javier's discovery of the embracing Ana and Juan is announced with progressive jump cuts to Javier's face, closer each time, as Javier moves forward. These cuts are another pointed utilization of the peculiarly artificial elements of cinema.

Faces of Terror

Appropriately enough, Oro saved his most obviously Expressionist stylistics for the film's climax, by which time both versions of the story have been told, and Javier has retreated deep into the monastery and climbed the steps to the organ. There, locked behind a wrought iron gate and with his back to the assembled monks, he furiously plays his *romanza*. The physical elevation of the organ naturally recalls the elevated positioning of Javier's piano. Paradoxically, the organ provides a release that the piano never fully did. Javier has been driven to the edge, and he has retreated to the one thing that matters most, and that he had hoped to create from and for Ana: art.

We have already seen the literal tilt of Javier's home, so now Oro pulls a reversal: As Javier forces the *romanza* from the organ's pipes, he is partially framed against the gray wall by a perfectly straight, vertical bar of light. When Javier turns from the organ to peer at the other monks, his face is haunted, but the geometric precision of the rectangle of light makes the possibility of madness questionable, and even suggests a queer sort of coherence.

But then Javier's emotional disintegration asserts itself, and most of what remains of *Dos monjes* is delivered to us subjectively, from Javier's point of view. The camera (Javier's gaze) roams along the walls to rest on roughly carved statuary. The monks come closer, their faces set in frowns. A cut to an objective shot of Javier tilts the organ's pipes leftward in the frame, recalling the unnerving latticework of earlier sequences, and exploding whatever comfort we've taken from that neatly vertical shaft of light.

With a return to the subjective camera, Javier is assaulted by a progression of darkly robed monks whose faces are distorted, chalky-white masks with wizened eyes, deep frown lines, and grotesquely mashed noses. Javier manages a sickly laugh, and then the immobile faces come at him faster, faster, as if revolving on a drum, the eyes of one mask open, the eyes of the next one closed, and so on, maddeningly. Javier slowly closes his eyes (like Cesare in *Das Cabinet des Dr. Caligari*). He wants to escape this; he wants to be a dreamer again.

In a briefly visualized flurry of memory, Javier reviews his attack on Juan. The key dramatic moments are there, but the great speed at which they are presented, and Javier's apparent somnambulant state, relieve the events of much of their emotional impact. Now, in Javier's memory, the events are merely impediments to be reviewed and overcome.

The subjective camera shows Javier's fresh view of the monks, who slowly come into focus before him (via the inherent artificiality of focus-pulling). The monk's faces are normal, and worried.

The film's few remaining moments are depicted via the objective camera. Juan enters and kneels before Javier, asking forgiveness. Will he receive it? We don't know, for Javier collapses and dies. Juan steps down from the altar (as he had many times stepped down from Javier's piano). Oro's camera tilts up to a cross on the monastery wall, and then dollys in, accenting the shadows cast by this emotionally charged totem. A fade to a crucifix is followed by a medium-shot of Juan, viewed from behind, as he kneels at the altar, praying, his body framed by a pair of inwardly tilted pillars. This is a sort of nave, and Juan is a supplicant who wants to acknowledge his sins.

Behind him, the monks chorus, "Amen."

Oro's Collaborators

Oro's producers, brothers José and Manuel San Vicente, were responsible for only one other film, *El tesoro de Pancho Villa* (*The Treasure of Pancho Villa*, 1935), directed by Arcady Boytler. The *Dos monjes* cinematographer, Augustin Jiménez, had more staying power. Between 1934 and 1973, he shot 170 films. Although *Dos monjes* was his first feature, his initial work as a cinematographer had come much earlier, with a pair of shorts released in 1904. During his nearly forty years of activity, Jiménez shot romances, biopics, science fiction, rural dramas, and sexploitation. Cultists are familiar with his *La mujer murciélago* (*The Batwoman*, 1968), a campy superhero thriller directed by René Cardona, and starring Maura Monti.

The *Dos monjes* score is the work of Max Urban, who was born in Germany, lived in Mexico, and later in Reno, Nevada. Active in the movies during 1932–54, Urban worked as a composer, arranger, and conductor. He scored dramas, thrillers, and comedies. Later, he was a key recording engineer with Inglewood, California's Tape-Athon, a provider of canned music in the style of Muzak. Urban's *Dos monjes* score is dominated by the *romanza* theme, which derives from the romantic impulses of some late nineteenth-century European music. The soaring, faintly melancholy melodic line swells at appropriate places, but the score becomes darkly portentous when that sort of suggestion is needed, as when Ana (in Juan's recollection) tries to extricate her heart from Juan's.

The Masks

The striking masks that enliven the climax of *Dos monjes* were created by Mexican artist Germán Cueto. Largely self-taught, Cueto was preoccupied with caricature masks executed in bold colors on heavy card stock. (His *Dos monjes* creations were designed, of course, for black-and-white film stock.) When he worked with Oro, Cueto had already been a highly visible artist for nearly a decade. His involvement in Estridentismo (Stridentism), an avant-garde literary and art movement that renounced symbolism and promoted public art, informed much of his work. Of course, the rejection of symbolism would seem to be at odds with the thematic and aesthetic purposes of the *Dos monjes* masks that torment Javier. Estridentismo favored a severe kind of literalism. Why, then, would Cueto involve himself in Expressionist maskmaking? The likely answer is that Estridentismo wanted artists and writers to move away from religiosity. The poet Manuel Maples Arce, a leader in Estridentismo circles, was particularly emphatic about this in a manifesto published in 1921, in the first issue of the avant-garde magazine *Actual*. Although the framing of *Dos monjes* is set inside a monastery, the film is certainly no advertisement for the efficacy of religion. The masks are at odds with the supposed contemplative and sympathetic nature of faith and a life of meditation. Cueto would almost certainly have found that appealing.

Oro after *Dos monjes*

Contrary to what would characterize the rest of Oro's career, *Dos monjes* was a box-office failure. Audiences who expected to be thrilled by sound may have been disappointed by the film's sparse dialogue—an amusing development in retrospect because, throughout most of his movie career, Oro was taken to task for heavy dialogue. But Oro's second film, *Monja casada, virgen y mártir* (*Nun, Married, Virgin and Martyr*, 1935), was well received by the public, and was profitable.

Oro wrote, but did not direct, *El fantasma del convento* (*The Phantom of the Convent*, 1934). Like *Dos monjes*, the film concerns a love triangle—in this instance, one that begins inside a strange, crumbling monastery that is visited by a married couple and their male friend. The three visitors learn that, at the monastery many years before, a monk sold his soul to Satan in order to seduce and keep the wife of his closest friend. Sin caused the monk's body to waste away, and although he was buried, his body continually reappeared in his cell. In an eerie replication of the monk's sin, the unmarried visitor tries to seduce his friend's wife. At the climax (with the adulterous relationship unconsummated), the friend discovers the monk's rotted body inside the monastery, still unable to find peace.

Oro returned to Expressionism with *El misterio del rostro pálido* (*The Mystery of the Ghastly Face*, 1935). In 1937, Oro and his business partner, Grovas Jesus, founded the Gold Grovas production company, which enjoyed commercial success with *Amapola del camino* (*Poppy Road*, 1937), *Huapango* (1938), *Don Porfirio times* (*In the Times of Don Porfirio*, 1939), *Al son de la marimba* (*To the Sound of the Marimba*, 1940), and *El ángel negro* (*The Black Angel*, 1943).

A 1938 release, *Cada loco con su tema* (*Every Madman to His Specialty*), is in Hollywood's familiar "old dark house" vein, with an assembled group of unhappy suspects and innocents, and moody cinematography that's often suggestive of a single light source.

The director's *Ahí está el detalle* (*That's the Point*, 1940) introduced the comic actor Cantinflas, who eventually achieved international stardom. Oro's *Mexico de mis recuerdes* (*Mexico of My Memories*, 1943) is a well-mounted period picture (set during the Porfirio period) that combines romance, politics, and music hall entertainment. Oro also directed musicals, *ranchera* (rural romances), and domestic dramas. A 1955 release, *El asesino X* (*The Murderer X*), is a film noir thriller set in the USA, with a plot propelled by amnesia.

Oro's work grew increasingly more commercial as the years passed, and he enjoyed critical and box-office success with such films as *El hombre sin rostro* (*The Man Without a Face*, 1950), *La huella de unos labios* (*The Footprint Lips*, 1952), *El medallión del crimen* (*The Medallion Crime*, 1956), and a screwball romantic comedy with overtones of *Romeo and Juliet*, *Asi amaron nuestros padres* (*So Loved Our Fathers*, 1964).

Oro retired in 1969, and published a memoir, *Vientos de los veintes* (*The Winds of the Twenties*), in 1973. Juan Bustillo Oro passed away, in Mexico City, in 1989.

The Current State of *Dos monjes*

Dos monjes was released in Mexico on November 26, 1934. An American release, under the title *Two Monks*, followed on January 20, 1935. The English-language title aside, whether the film was dubbed or subtitled for the American market remains unclear. If dubbed or subtitled prints exist today, they are elusive. All available prints are scratched and grainy, and carry the original *Dos monjes* title. Obvious bootlegs lack the logo of Proa Producciones SA, but the trademark is present on the print viewed by this writer.

Perhaps the movie would today be better known, and exist in better condition, if it were an easily categorized genre piece. Some sources erroneously classify *Dos monjes* as a horror movie. That isn't just off the mark, but regrettably misleading. Oro had deeper ambitions. The French poet and Surrealist André Breton looked at *Dos monjes* and called it "a bold and unusual experiment."[6]

Oro himself said, "I wanted to give the film a surreal atmosphere, entering an Expressionistic place. I felt I could ... achieve uncommon cinematic effects, and reflect the profound influence that the German masters sealed in my imagination."[7]

MEXICO LOOKS BACK AT ORO, AND AT EXPRESSIONISM

In 1980, the Mexican Academy of Film gave Oro the prestigious Ariel Award for his decades of work as a producer, director, and writer. Five years later, Oro received the Salvador Toscano Medal for lifetime achievement; the award was named for a pioneer of Mexican cinema. Nineteen eighty-five also brought a short novel by Oro, *Lucinda del polvo lunar* (*Lucinda Moondust*).

New York's Museum of Modern Art screened *Dos monjes* in July 1993, as part of a "Views from Latin American Archives" series.

A major exhibition of German Expressionist art was mounted in 2012 at Mexico City's Museo del Palacio de Bellas Artes. Among the artists represented were Max Beckmann, Otto Dix, Egon Schiele, Ernst Ludwig Kirchner, Vasily Kandinsky, and Oskar Kokoschka. One gallery was dominated by a dozen like-sized black-and-white pieces by Max Pechstein, which were exhibited in two horizontal rows of six. The effect was very much like a comic strip or, more usefully for our purposes, the storyboards for a film.

Black-and-white imagery, executed in pastel, pencil, charcoal, and black paint, dominated this exhibition, and dominates much of Expressionism in general. Oro utilized the aesthetic well in *Dos monjes*, and with laudable restraint, hoarding his best effects and delivering an emotionally and visually agitated meditation on perception, guilt, and identity that is simultaneously local (an emerging, frequently violent Mexico) and universal.

The film's final image of the stricken Juan divorces *Dos monjes* from the postmodernist notion that truth is relative. Juan's cry for absolution is a confirmation of a specific, actual course of events. Javier's decline into temporary madness does nothing to change that.

Perspective is relative. Truth exists.

NOTES

1. The author thanks Henry Nicolella and Gary D. Rhodes for supplying a copy of *Dos monjes*, and Bernard McCarron for providing a printout of the film's dialogue in English.
2. *Dos monjes* (*Two Monks*, Mexico 1934), Director: Juan Bustillo Oro. Cast: Carlos Villatoro (Javier), Victor Urruchúa (Juan), Magda Haller (Ana), M. Beltran Heder (Prior), Emma Roldán (Gertrudis, Mother). Writer: Jose Manuel Cordero. Adaptation: Juan Bustillo Oro. Editor: Juan Bustillo Oro. Titles: C. Vejar, Jr. Cinematographer: Augustin Jiménez. Music: Max Urban, Song ("Anita") by

Manuel M. Ponce and Raul Lavista. Sound: B. J. Kroger. Set designers: Mariano Rodriguez and Granada Carlos Toussaint. Maskmaker: Germán Cueto. Producers: José San Vicente and Manual San Vicente. Black and white, 35 mm, 1.37:1, 85 minutes, Proa Producciones SA.

3. Errol Morris, *Believing is Seeing (Observations on the Mysteries of Photography)* (New York: Penguin, 2011), p. 92 [emphasis in original].
4. Fernando Fabio Sanchez, *Artful Assassins: Murder as Art in Modern Mexico* (Nashville, TN: Vanderbilt University Press, 2010), p. 66.
5. Available at <http://www.escritores.cinemexicano.unam.mx> "Juan Bustillo Oro" (last accessed 22 January 2015).
6. Available at <http://www.listal.com/movie/two-monks> (last accessed 22 January 2015).
7. Available at <http://www.cinemexicano.mty.itesm.mx/peliculas/monjes> (last accessed 22 January 2015).

15. MAYA DEREN IN PERSON IN EXPRESSIONISM

Graeme Harper

Critical explorations of expressionist cinema sometimes produce profound ambiguities. Given the individual contexts of Expressionism, perhaps that is natural. Most of these ambiguities occur as critics negotiate defining expressionist film in general terms. On the evidence, it appears that some traps also lie in remembering at least to acknowledge the likelihood of creative authorial intention in any individual filmmaker's output. For example, Marc Silberman, writing in his essay "What Is German in German Cinema?" says this, expertly and yet somewhat paradoxically:

> Expressionism in all the arts was committed to abstraction, to highlighting the artificial, precarious identity of image and referent. The cinema offered a new scale for the abstraction of referential meaning through the presence of the image. Stark lines and lack of depth are traits that characterize the two-dimensional sense of surface and space in these films.[1]

Silberman's analysis of German cinema is articulate and strong. But where here in his summary is the relationship between the authorial individuals and the aesthetic? Other notes in his essay suggest that Silberman is aware that personal relationships are significant in expressionist cinema, and that every expressionist film has at its core an exploration of a personal world as much as it has at its heart a response to the stark, mechanized intrusions of modernism into the external environment. Yet, when he explores the starkness of line in expressionist film he appears momentarily to forget that expressionism is, most certainly, profoundly about persons as much as it is about the place and the conditions it considers.

This is not really a strong criticism of Silberman. Beyond the fact that his essay is excellent in spite of this anomaly, he is also in good company in such a momentary absence of mind. He shares this absence with one of America's most renowned, and sadly recently deceased, film critics, Andrew Sarris. Death is often said to be a great leveler and one aspect it most certainly levels is that of nationality and culture. Regardless of the rituals around them, the dead persistently remain deceased. Thus, that Sarris writes mostly about American cinema and Silberman writes mostly about German cinema is of no consequence in the story of Sarris's death, or necessarily either in the connection between Sarris's critical apparatus and Silberman's. In both cases, what is missing in their analyses is a continuance of clear observation regarding the role of individuals in effecting a film's aesthetic meld, its bringing together of persons and the mass, as cinema references persons involved in its production and the individual person in an audience while also referencing an audience as a collective or mass.

Ultimately, what can be told in an exploration of expressionism and the films of Maya Deren—most particularly here *Meshes of the Afternoon*—is a story of four deaths and one life. A story that thus fits very well with (dare I say?) expressionism's profound and personal "play of light and shadow."[2] Telling this story as one involving a particular filmic grasping of an association between life and death is not at all a random choice. Rachel Palfreyman, writing on the work of the German animator Lotte Reiniger (1899–1981)

Figure 15.1 The play of light and shadow.

explains that "her understanding of the silhouette as uncannily positioned between life and death offers a way of reading her work as occupying a unique position between the shadows of Weimar Expressionism and the conceptual enquiry of experimental animation."[3] So it is that expressionism often situates itself in those uncannily positioned silhouettes. The first death here, in this particular uncanny story, is that of Andrew Sarris.

Sarris died in June 2012 at the age of 83. Richard Brody, writing in *The New Yorker* on June 20, said this on the occasion of his death:

> In the classic split between hedgehogs and foxes, [Sarris] was the great hedgehog of American criticism. He knew one big thing: the colossal gravitational pull of the director, the true star that held all in its orbit and gave its light to reflect.[4]

Sarris's death marks the end of an era, in terms of what film was before the enormous technological changes of the last twenty years and, in a key way, in terms of how American film criticism examined the role or roles of individuals in filmmaking. This was an era that owed much to a trans-Atlantic exchange; specifically, the influence of François Truffaut on Sarris. Truffaut's death in 1984—Truffaut dying as the result of a brain tumor at the age of 52—is indeed the second death in this story. Many reading here will know the story: that is, that Sarris's essay "Notes on the Auteur Theory in 1962" picked up the flowing European current of François Truffaut's "A Certain Tendency in French Cinema," from 1954, and directed that current into American film criticism.

But Brody, writing in *The New Yorker*, also says this about Sarris, which extends this story, and perhaps fortuitously relates well to questions about the appearance and persistence of expressionism in Maya Deren's filmmaking:

> Sarris may have suffered for staring too long and too fixedly into the directorial sun, but before he showed everyone which way to look, *hardly anybody knew that it was there at all* [my italics]. Which is why, on this sad occasion, it seems fitting to talk about the idea and the word with which his name will always be linked.[5]

That phrase "hardly anybody knew that it was there at all" is intriguing. Authorship, the author: that of course is what Brody is talking about. But much as we see in Silberman a momentary absence of mind with regard to expressionism, so we did in Sarris, as he pursued a sense of directorial identity with a tendency toward absolutism that missed film's less absolute human engagements—paradoxically in a valiant attempt to highlight an authorial human presence in filmmaking.

In essence (though somewhat boldly stated given the combined punching weight of the critical targets), while Sarris and Truffaut knew what film authorship might be, because both were ardent and intelligent cinephiles, neither man was able to fully articulate what he was feeling, though each had an influence on what I would call "critical film enthusiasm" that has been immeasurable. In contrast, a woman writing about filmmaking a dozen years earlier than Truffaut and nearly twenty years earlier than Sarris, a woman whose films were ultimately known to very few compared to Truffaut's, and whose critical writings were known to very few compared to the critical writings of Andrew Sarris, wrote about film authorship with a clarity that is further reflected in her own, often expressionist, interests. Hers was a clarity that related not to a pathological or monstrous sense, as many have intimated in relation to both her and her work, but to her ability to avoid authorial absolutism while highlighting the ideals and understandings of individuals.

Maya Deren was born Eleanora Derenkowsky in Kiev in 1917. Though she and her parents had moved to the USA by the early 1920s, Deren herself returned to Europe eight years later, where she attended the League of Nations School in Geneva. Her mother moved to Paris to be with her daughter, and the two women lived there from 1930 to 1933. When Deren returned to the USA again, this time she studied at the New School for Social Research. She later graduated from Smith College with a Masters degree entitled "The Influence of the French Symbolist School on Anglo-American Poetry." Active in Socialist causes in New York, she identified herself as European in her circle of émigré friends, as well as in her outward appearance, and by the early 1940s she was connected also with other art forms, such as dance and still photography.

Such are the most commonly related facts of Maya Deren's short life. But while she and her work have been discussed in relation to surrealism and the aesthetics of surrealist art, while her life and works have been examined in relation to women filmmakers in the American avant-garde, she is much more rarely included in an exploration of expressionist film. So little has this happened that what remains today the most wide-ranging collection of essays on her work, Bill Nichols's *Maya Deren and the American Avant-Garde* (2001), does not even include the term "expressionism" in its index.

That duly noted, Theresa L. Geller, a PhD candidate at Rutgers University at the time of her writing, observes in 2006 that "Deren's films have a great deal in common with the expressionist attempts at film autobiography."[6] This is an observation that reaches some way toward the recognition of expressionism in such films as *Meshes of the Afternoon*, though I would resist blocking the personal here into the corral of "autobiography," as this to me limits exchange, the "auto-" becoming resistant to more open conversation.

Geller's note points likewise toward the recognition of expressionist

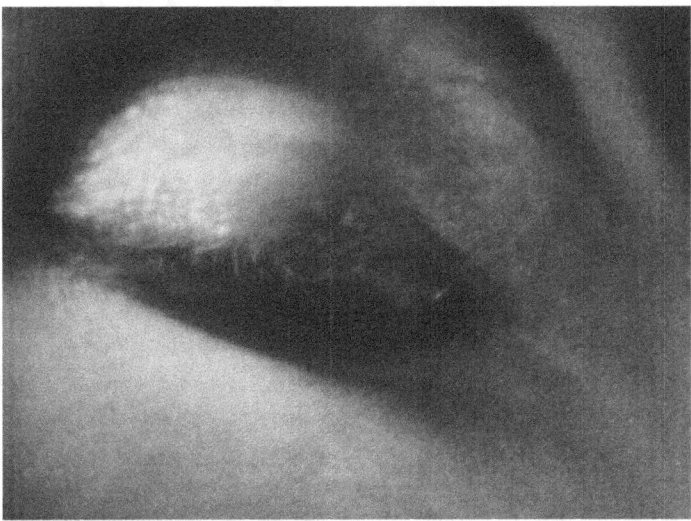

Figure 15.2 Dreams in a dreamscape.

aesthetics in *Meshes* as part of a broader persistence of what Silberman explains is expressionism's "ability to articulate the anxieties of modern subjectivity through a profound rethinking of the nature of representation in image and gesture."[7] Drawing on the work of Elizabeth Bruss, Geller further suggests that *Meshes* "employs abstract expressionism, fantasy, or surrealism." She argues that these "convey the Imaginary, to map the very psychic structures that predate and predetermine both the 'eye' and the 'I'",[8] and she relates this directly to modes of feminine autobiography.

Silberman is correct in noting that "expressionist plots, directing style or editing are hard to enumerate with precision and do not suffice as traits for defining an entire film period."[9] So it is that Deren's *Meshes of the Afternoon*, appearing in 1943, employs expressionist abstraction, lighting, artificiality and stylization—qualities, Silberman observes, which some have considered ended in the mid-1920s:

> the "end" of expressionist cinema has been dated anywhere from the production of *Das Wachsfigurenkabinett* (1923, release 1924) or *Die Nibelungen* (1923–24) or *Varieté* (1925) or *Faust and Metropolis*.[10]

Meshes, with its "interiority" and focus on the "psychologized," thus assists us in coming to understand the continuance of expressionism, to avoid what Silberman observes are the "problems" of "drawing chronological boundaries,"[11] and to wonder on what expressionist qualities represent for filmmakers and audiences alike, who appear to have enthusiastically embraced those qualities. Could it be that Theresa Geller's inclusion of the word "personal" in the title of her article provides an excellent clue, and that by extending a discussion of the personal observations of those who have used expressionism we can get closer to the core of that enthusiasm or even suggest a reason for expressionism's ongoing appearance in film? Indeed, I believe that to be the case.

The Museum of Modern Art in New York summarizes *Meshes of the Afternoon*, which was in fact made by Deren in collaboration with her then husband, the cinematographer Alexander Hammid, in this way:

> A non-narrative work, it [*Meshes*] has been identified as a key example of the "trance film," in which a protagonist appears in a dreamlike state, and where the camera conveys his or her subjective focus. The central figure in *Meshes of the Afternoon*, played by Deren, is attuned to her unconscious mind and caught in a web of dream events that spill over into reality. Symbolic objects, such as a key and a knife, recur throughout the film; events are open-ended and interrupted. Deren explained that she wanted "to put on film the feeling which a human being experiences about an incident, rather than to record the incident accurately".[12]

This is as useful a summary of the film as any, with the majority of critics echoing this summary, focusing on such elements of the film as its "dreamscape," the role of the woman who pursues a hooded figure, the hooded figure with its mirror for a face, the falling key, the knife, the flower, the woman becoming multiple instances of herself, the role of the man who wakes the woman, who at that point has been trying to kill her sleeping self. They comment too, as part of the narrative and in relation to their sense of the film, on her ultimate death. This is the third death in our story.

Marc Silberman, in his essay "What Is German in German Cinema?," plainly asks a question, and through this clearly stated question explores the nature and history of Germanness. We might ask in turn "what is Expressionist in *Meshes of the Afternoon?*," and in doing so also ask "what is Expressionist in Expressionist cinema?" Robin Wood gives us further food for thought regarding that question, commenting:

> Expressionism evades simple definition, but a central impulse was clearly an attempt to "express" emotional states, through a distortion of deformation of objective reality, "expression" taking precedence over representation.[13]

The accuracy of Wood's assessment is demonstrable in *Meshes*, and the film's attention to emotional states reiterates well something of the precedence to which Wood refers. But it is the role of individuals that also emerges in Wood's comment, the considerable importance of beginning our understanding of expressionist film from the point of view of shared human perceptions, or, as we might say in relation to *Meshes*, of a "pairing of sharing" brought about by the contributions of Deren and of Hammid.

How far we wish to treat *Meshes* as foundationally influenced by Deren and how far we must treat it as influenced equally by Deren and Hammid is open to consideration, but we might return in this to Deren's practical and critical roles in writing, editing and producing the film, as well as her shared roles in directing and starring in it. Mark Durant adds further to this consideration when he says:

> In a biographical statement from 1953, she [Deren] wrote: "It was like finally finding a glove that fits. When I was writing poetry, I had, constantly, to transcribe my essentially visual images . . . into verbal form. In motion pictures, I no longer had to translate . . . and I could move directly from my imagination onto film".[14]

So it was that Deren found an individual medium for personal expression that felt both natural and significant, and so it was too that she went on to make more films, with each aiming for this "direct" movement from her imagination to the film itself. This seems to take on Wood's observation about expressionism's "central impulse," if that central impulse might also be seen as something that could be shared or exchanged between people. Additionally, as

Figure 15.3 The hooded figure.

John Titford has pointed out, expressionist cinema has a specific quality also because of "its concern, directly and indirectly, with the filmic process itself."[15]

I would offer Deren's filmmaking as seen in *Meshes* and its expressionist ideals as an exemplar in that regard. On the other hand, reacting to Wood's point about expressionism's "central impulse" appears to occasionally result in critical assumptions that are not so easily supportable. For example, Peter Dellolio, who draws on Wood, though not uncritically, suggests:

> Another important ingredient of Expressionism is its attack upon the primordial issue of identity, often resulting in the alienation of the individual from what was formerly incontrovertible and familiar.[16]

If we are not entirely sure to whom Dellolio refers, a closer reading allows a sense of it to begin to emerge. The process of determining his meaning is also instructive. If it is the audience he is suggesting is being "alienated," then much is being assumed in terms of how a film audience is constructed, what role individualism plays in film reception, and what is ultimately familiar to any given audience at any given time. With the range of these questions persisting, it seems more likely that Dellolio is referring to the filmmaker, or more accurately to the methods by which any filmmaker presents their filmic aesthetic, their formal and structural choices, even what we might call their "appeal to the audience."

On that basis, Deren's expressionism, or the expressionism employed in films in which Deren is a key creative and critical force, is not the expressionism to which Dellolio refers. It is impossible for that expressionism to be Dellolio's expressionism, because Deren is not so much alienated by her filmmaking techniques, or by her maker–audience communications, as she is empowered by them. What *Meshes* reveals is expressionism's contribution not to *separating* the individual from the familiar but to further engaging the individual with the familiar and projecting that engagement into a realm of wider human exchange. In this sense, *Meshes* reveals just how much expressionism is a form committed to the sharing of personal perceptions, emotions and dispositions. This might be a key reason (indeed, perhaps *the* key reason) for expressionism's persistence. Put simply, expressionism is able to convey and share the individual in a medium known more often and more generally for its appeals to a (seemingly) individualized mass.

I would return us to Geller's well-observed points on feminine autobiography, which, while perhaps too defined by the relativity of the "auto" in autobiography, offers a keenly observed analysis of what "infuses"[17] the film. Additionally, even if I do not employ a psychoanalytic frame here, I'd point also to the ways in which *Meshes* emphasizes again and again that individuality is not absence but shared physic presence, that the psychologized

Figure 15.4 Maya Deren.

aspects of expressionism are also the psychodynamic, and that this dynamism comes about through exchange, not through internalized self-reference. It does this, while not being entirely based in the singular unconscious as some have suggested (for example, Palfreyman suggests in that vein that there is an "Expressionist binary of self and other."[18]

Meshes is thus not a film that seeks to alienate, nor is Deren a filmmaker who is alienated—though many of the commonly reported facts of her life seem to be reported to portray her as an alien creature. Rather, *Meshes* is a film full of what I would call expressionism's *anxiety about the importance and possibilities of self-hood*, a film therefore that is clearly about self-determination. Unfortunately, that is not how critical reception of the film has most often portrayed it—and that has happened largely because of critics missing or misinterpreting its expressionism.

Maya Deren has frequently been described, even by those who are clearly seeking to recognize her filmic importance, as having "fierce convictions."[19] This observation is presented as if this constitutes a description of a flaw, a point of personal weakness, perhaps one even bound up in her European origins and her émigré status. Such a description seems in itself a kind of death, in that its inference is one tainted with at least some irrationality, and if surrealism has been the chosen description of her aesthetic, as most often it has been, then the inference is that such a critical choice over any other was a result of her subversive, peripheral or irrational frame of mind.

We have seen this kind of depiction with other influential women, and influential women in the arts most notably. With expressionism highlighting the personal and with Wood's observation about its referencing of "the primordial issue of identity,"[20] we're faced with the difficult premise that while expressionism indeed offered (and offers) filmmakers a personal mode of expression in a mass medium, in the case of women filmmakers such as Deren it has sometimes meant not celebration of this but a critical pathologizing of it. Rather than an understanding of the expressionist aesthetic, this has meant, in Deren's case, either a critical denial of it (e.g. defining her as almost purely "surrealist" instead) or a linking of the form in her hands to a kind of personally uncontrollable irrationality. Other than the damage this does to our understanding of expressionist cinema more generally, I am specifically reminded in this of one of our most famous alleged artistic madwomen, Virginia Woolf, and how such critical denial is reminiscent of some critical reception of her work.

Strong in intellect, but allegedly dubious as to disposition, Adeline Virginia Stephen (as once Virginia Woolf was known) was much more than a mad woman, or much less of a stereotype of women and ferocity than some critics would have us believe. As with Deren, we see in the story of Woolf's critical reception something of patriarchy's problem with gender. It might be that this reception and pathologizing has links to what Barbara Creed so wonderfully explored in her work of film criticism *The Monstrous-Feminine* (1993), where the urtexts of the monstrous are discussed, though the arguments being explored here are directly associated with expressionism itself, and the notions around pathology are perhaps less interesting in their directness. To set the expressionist scene: beyond those gender debates, we find the literary critic Robert Scholes writing:

> I want to suggest that what these art historians were calling "expressionism," a movement that was explicitly linked to a revival of interest in baroque art and to the discovery and revaluation of primitive art, entered modern prose narrative most powerfully in the form of the monstrous personal chronicle."[21]

So expressionism—albeit in "art," not specifically in film—becomes not just a personal chronicle but a monstrous one. It is not that some of the filmic images or attitudes of expressionism could not be defined as monstrous—in size and shape and even in what some might consider their appearance of *in*humanity. It is not, either, that Scholes locates this monstrousness in the feminine or, indeed, in specific writing by specific women writers—he doesn't. Rather, he speaks of a number of writers, a number of works, and he constructs an argument concerning these and the nature and contexts of the time in which these writers were writing, all the while exploring the relationship between this and Modernism. However, Scholes does indeed leave us with a critical point not unlike Creed's but perhaps less veracious, when he concludes his essay with an observation about Anaïs Nin that she was "the monstrous mother of all the others."[22] Motherhood and monstrousness thus find themselves occupying the same textual space.

The University of Cambridge, King's College archivist Patricia McGuire, commenting in *The Guardian* in 2010, after the discovery of new letters about Woolf's suicide, says this of Rosamond Lehmann, additionally pointing toward Woolf and the other women in the Bloomsbury Group:

> They had well-developed points of view, were articulate about their emotions and at the same time struggled with their bohemian lifestyles and the more conservative, older generation.[23]

Candidly, this doesn't sound like madness at all to me, nor at all monstrous—at least not in any accurate clinical or definitional sense of either of these things. The same sense of the irrational or, more accurately, pathological is applied by critics to Maya Deren and her works, and while that analysis might indeed be attempting to map the anxieties of the period, the macro concerns that accompanied the political, economic, and technological elements of the early part of the twentieth century, the issues being raised by many critics appear more directly related to their reactions to this individual and her gender than they do to the period or indeed to the approaches of Expressionism.

In the widely distributed assessment of Maya Deren's death, as well as in the assessment of her life and her works, we hear exactly the same inferences of

Figure 15.5 Attention to emotional states.

the pathological and the monstrous that we hear in reports on Woolf's death, inferences that are at least partly evident in what Robert Scholes observes in his essay "The Monstrous Personal Chronicle of the Thirties":

> during the period that extends from just before the first World War to just after the second, much of the best writing that appeared in English prose took the form of extended chronicles in which the personal was neither suppressed nor transcended in the approved modernist manner, but was kept in the foreground, sometimes flaunted, but always acknowledged, and ... this attention to the personal compensates for the modernist attention to form and structure that is so obviously lacking. This was also a genre in which women worked very well.[24]

Compare Scholes' piece—with its focus on "women" rather than a woman—with the report on Deren's death and how it continues to be recalled, in widely distributed popular sources and in critical assessments, as some kind of definition no less than as a piece of unbiased reportage:

> Deren died in 1961, at the age of 44, from a brain hemorrhage brought on by extreme malnutrition. Her condition was also weakened by the amphetamines she had been taking ... Deren was taking amphetamines and sleeping pills on a daily basis when she died. Her father suffered from high blood pressure, which she may have had as well.[25]

So we have the drug-addled, malnourished but ferocious woman who, if we read her life primarily in a macro-historical context and believe she employed expressionist techniques, tropes and aesthetics, primarily did so because of her monstrous nature buoyed by its existence in a monstrous time. The feisty, surrealist émigré Ukrainian, for whom film, it is so often said, was an experimental form—not a personal form with echoic importance for her exchange with others, not a form in which she finally found the medium and the mode that suited her creative and critical senses, but an "experimental" medium—is marginalized not once but twice from anything we might see as significant for a wider audience.

How might we thus reconsider *Meshes of the Afternoon*? We might differentiate Deren's enthusiasm for film and her critical and creative understanding of it from the critical enthusiasms of Andrew Sarris and François Truffaut, if only to give voice to the human context of expressionism rather than to the supposed inhumanity of it. We might venture it forward in our analysis of the continuation of expressionist ideas, ideals and aesthetics by highlighting points of exchange and styles of communication rather than assuming that by "psychologized" we mean internalized, inaccessible and even absence. We might recognize, and indeed recognize not before time, that film authorship remains a significant area of critical investigation and consideration, and that much that has been said about it—perhaps said, indeed, by Andrew Sarris and François Truffaut—has not entirely reached the truth of this authorship, which has been so influential now for well over a century. But this, of course, is a story about four deaths and one life. And there is one death more, a famous (or more accurately an infamous) death. It is concluded like this:

> The [film audience] has never been the concern of classical criticism; for it, there is no other [wo]man in film but the one who makes it. We are now beginning to be the dupes no longer of such antiphrases, by which our society proudly champions precisely what it dismisses, ignores, smothers or destroys; we know that to restore to [film] its future, we must reverse its myth: the birth of the [film audience] must be ransomed by the death of the [filmmaker].[26]

This is my adaptation of the conclusion of Barthes's most famous essay on authorial death. That authorial death, which influenced so many in literary studies and, because of our own histories as film scholars, which were often drawn from that literary realm in the earliest days of film scholarship, much scholarship in film as well, came at the price of understanding the relationships between the internal lives of the authors and the internal lives of the audience. It came at the price of understanding the fluidity of culture and its participants, and the shared sense of human existence that has been fundamental to making and reception of cinema. It came at the price of recognizing the collaborative nature of human existence.

Though Barthes was an evolutionary writer, a critic who moved about the realms of thinking, the constant presence of an inferred (if not always determined) structuralism was the same in him as it was in Andrew Sarris. I would turn, then, in this story, a story I am telling here almost as a mirror image of the popular film *Four Weddings and a Funeral*—here "Four Funerals and a Wedding"—I'd turn then to life, the life that is the life of Maya Deren, and ask her to respond for herself.

"The function of film [is] to create experience"[27] she once wrote, while in her 1947 notebooks she writes:

> here, suddenly, is the strange fever and excitement. Is it because in holding film in one's hand one holds life in one's hand?[28]

In her 1946 theoretical essay *An Anagram of Ideas on Art, Form and Film*, she says:

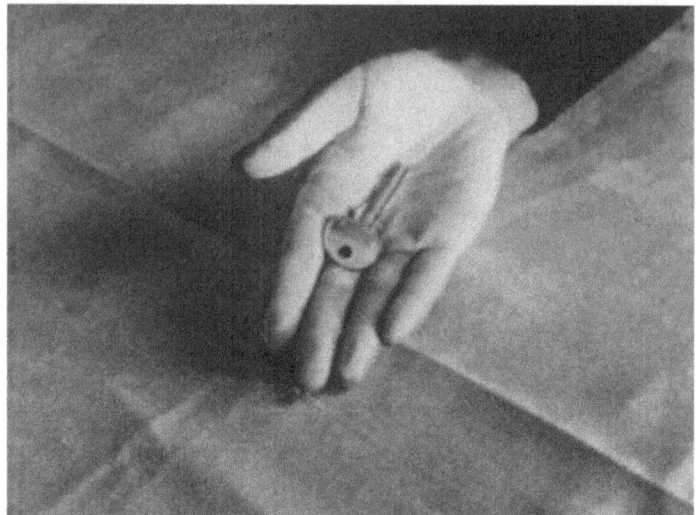

Figure 15.6 Symbolic objects.

> As a matter of fact, the very methods which result in the failure of the other art forms in film may be the basis of creative action in film itself, once the effort to carry over the values of one to the other is abandoned. Such inversion is possible largely because film is a time–space complex of a unique kind.[29]

A time–space complex of a unique kind? Is this not a very fine insight into film, and one that continues to be true? So too is this, if we remember that she is saying this in 1946, not in the twenty-first century:

> It is not only the film artist who must struggle to discover the esthetic principles of the first new art form in centuries; it is the audience, too, which must develop a receptive attitude designed specifically for film and free of the critical criteria which have been evolved for all the older art forms.[30]

So, finally, is this:

> Art is the result of the relationship of three elements: the reality to which (someone) has access—directly and through the researches of all (others); the crucible of (their) own imagination and intellect; and the art instrument by which (they) realize, through skillful exercise and control, (their) imaginative manipulations. To limit, deliberately or through

neglect, any of these functions is to limit the potential of the work of art itself.³¹

We certainly need to look more closely at Maya Deren's creative and critical engagements with film authorship. We need to look more closely at the ways in which, around the mid-twentieth century, what was once called "the old world" of Europe and the "new world" of North America came jointly to define the debate in film authorship as a sort of victory over the relationship between the self and others—to see how this influenced the ways in which filmic expressionism was perceived, and perhaps even prevented an understanding and observation of its continuing influence. We need to see that Maya Deren enthusiastically employed expressionism, not least in *Meshes of the Afternoon*. Maya Deren knew film authorship from the point of view of personal intention and will and from the point of view of individuals exchanging with individuals. This made her filmmaking not the irrational monstrous communications inferred by some, but an important exemplar of film's ability to express our human dispositions, emotions and ideals. In a period today in which Maya Deren seems to know more about the association between the self and culture, filmmaking and film audiences, technological art and technological audience, expression and form, we need to look again, so that from four deaths come not just one life, but many.

NOTES

1. Marc Silberman, "What Is German in German Cinema?," *Film History*, Vol. 8, 1996, pp. 297–315, quoted pp. 308–9.
2. Cynthia Walk, "German Expression Cinema: The World of Light and Shadow" (review), *Monatshefte*, Vol. 102, No. 3, Fall 2010, pp. 420–1.
3. Rachel Palfreyman, "Life and Death in the Shadows: Lotte Reiniger's *Die Abenteuer des Prinzen Achmed*," *German Life and Letters*, Vol. 64, No. 1, January 2011, pp. 6–18, quoted p. 6.
4. Richard Brody, "Andrew Sarris and the 'A' Word," *The New Yorker*, 20 June 2012.
5. Ibid.
6. Theresa L. Geller, "The Personal Cinema of Maya Deren: Meshes of the Afternoon and Its Critical Reception in the History of the Avant-Garde," *Biography*, Vol. 29, No. 1, Winter 2006, pp. 140–58, see p. 147.
7. Marc Silberman, "What Is German in German Cinema?," p. 311.
8. Theresa L. Geller, "The Personal Cinema," p. 143.
9. Marc Silberman, "What Is German in German Cinema?," p. 307.
10. Ibid. p. 207.
11. Ibid.
12. Available at < http://www.moma.org/collection/object.php?object_id=89283> (last accessed 23 January 2015).
13. Robin Wood, *Hitchcock's Films* (New York: Paperback Library, 1970), p. 27.
14. Mark Alice Durant, "Maya Deren: A Life Choreographed for Camera," *Aperture*, No. 195, Summer 2009, p. 42.

15. John S. Titford, "Object–Subject Relationships in German Expressionist Cinema," *Cinema Journal*, Vol. 13, Autumn 1973, pp 17–24, quoted p. 18.
16. Peter J. Dellolio, "Expressionist Themes in *Strangers on a Train*," *Literature/Film Quarterly*, Vol. 31, No. 4, January 2003, pp. 260–9, quoted p. 261.
17. Theresa L. Geller, "The Personal Cinema," p. 142.
18. Rachel Palfreyman, "Life and Death in the Shadows," p. 17.
19. Bill Nichols (ed.), *Maya Deren and the American Avant-Garde* (Berkeley, CA: University of California Press, 2001), p. 4.
20. Robin Wood, *Hitchcock's Films*, p. 261.
21. Robert Scholes, "The Monstrous Personal Chronicles of the Thirties," *NOVEL: A Forum on Fiction*, Vol. 31, No. 3, Summer 1998, pp. 414–29, quoted p. 419.
22. Robert Scholes, "The Monstrous Personal Chronicles of the Thirties," p. 427.
23. Alison Flood, "New Bloomsbury Archive Casts Revealing Light on Virginia Woolf's Death," *The Guardian*, 18 March 2010. Available at <http://www.guardian.co.uk/books/2010/mar/19/bloomsbury-archive-virginia-woolf-death> (last accessed 23 January 2015).
24. Robert Scholes, "The Monstrous Personal Chronicles of the Thirties," p. 416.
25. Available at <http://www.websters-online-dictionary.org/definitions/Maya+Deren> (last accessed 20 February 2013).
26. My adaptation of a passage from Roland Barthes, "The Death of the Author," in his *Image Music Text* (trans. and ed. Stephen Heath) (New York: Hill & Wang 1977), pp. 142–8, see p. 148.
27. Maya Deren, *An Anagram of Ideas on Art, Form and Film* (New York: Alicat Book Shop Press, 1946), p. 49.
28. Maya Deren, "From the Notebook of Maya Deren, 1947," *October*, Vol. 14, Autumn 1980, pp. 21–46.
29. Maya Deren, *An Anagram of Ideas on Art, Form and Film*, p. 49.
30. Ibid. p. 43.
31. Ibid. p. 17.

INDEX OF NAMES

Italic denotes figure

Abbott, Stacey, 94, 95
Abel, Alfred, 227
Abel, Richard, 223
Abraham, Karl, 43, 50–3, 60
Adorno, T. W., 32
Alfredson, Tomas, 183
Allen, Woody, 250, 255, 257
Alzheimer, Alois, 44–5, 50
Andra, Fern, 77, *80, 81,* 81, *82, 85,* 85, *88,* 230
Anger, Kenneth, 187–8
Anthony, Joseph, 117
Antonioni, Michelangelo, 188
Arce, Manuel Maples, 283
Arnheim, Rudolf, 21
Aronofsky, Darren, 188
Askonas, Paul, 191–3, *193,* 195, *196,* 197, *201*
Athie, Francisco, 188

Baigent, Michael, 187
Balázs, Béla, 2, 231
Barbusse, Henri, 152, 160, 162
Barlow, John, 128
Barney, Matthew, 188
Barry, Iris, 20
Barthes, Roland, 299

Bassols, Narciso, 271
Baum, L. Frank, 171
Beard, George M., 43, 250, 257
Beckmann, Max, 285
Bender, Paul, 45
Benjamin, Walter, 32
Berger, Ludwig, 16
Bergman, Ingmar, 186
Bergson, Henri, 60–1
Besant, Annie, 180–1
Binding, Karl, 110, 112
Binswanger, Otto Ludwig, 50
Bismarck, Otto von, 61
Blake, William, 171
Blavatsky, Helena, 172, 174, 175–8
Bloch, Ernst, 31
Bloch, Noë, 222
Böcklin, August, 25
Boese, Carl, 183
Bordwell, David, 224–5, 227
Borger, Lenny, 222
Borgström, Hilda, 178
Borré, Lia, 45
Bowie, David, 33
Boytler, Arcady, 282
Bradbury, Malcolm, 163
Brecht, Bertolt, 31, 271

INDEX OF NAMES

Breton, André, 284
Bridat, Don Juan Bustillo, 269
Brody, Richard, 289
Browning, Tod, 184
Bruss, Elizabeth, 291
Buñuel, Luis, 22, 188
Burel, Léonce-Henri, 147
Burroughs, Edgar Rice, 171
Burroughs, William, 171

Canby, Vincent, 257
Cantinflas, 284
Canudo, Ricciotto, 163
Cárdenas, Lázaro, 269, 271
Cardona, René, 282
Carroll, Lewis, 171
Cartwright, Lisa, 251
Catelain, Jaque, 222
Cegavske, Christiane, 188
Cendrars, Blaise, 153
Cervantes, Miguel de, 171
Chaplin, Charlie, 186
Chesterton, Gilbert K., 248
Chmara, Grigori, 127, *127*, 129
Christensen, Benjamin, 188
Clement of Alexandria, 175
Cocteau, Jean, 164, 187–8
Corneille, Pierre, 152
Cowan, Michael, 44
Creed, Barbara, 296–7
Cronenberg, David, 188
Cueto, Germán, 283
Curtiz, Michael *see* Kertész, Mihály
Czinner, Paul, 7, 133, 135–7

Dagover, Lil, *28*, 77, 85
D'Annunzio, Gabriele, 152
Darwin, Charles, 100, 175, 176–8, 238
Dauvray, Maryse, 147
Delaroche, Paul, 151
Dellolio, Peter J., 256, 294
Delluc, Louis, 22, 221
DeMille, Cecil B., 147
Dennert, Eberhard, 110
Deren, Maya, 10, 287–301, *295*, *297*
Derenkowsky, Eleanora *see* Deren, Maya
Dermoz, Germaine, 226
Dernburg, Ernst, 74
Descartes, 44, 107
Diaz, Porfirio, 267–8
Dick, Philip K., 171
Dickens, Charles, 174

Dieudonné, Albert, 155
Dijkstra, Bram, 260
Disney, Walt, 188
Dix, Otto, 285
Dostoevsky, Fyodor, 7, 117–18, 124–7, 129–30
Dreyer, Carl, 188
Dulac, Germaine, 221, 222, 226, 227
Dupont, E. A., 22, 29
Durant, Mark, 293

Ebert, Friedrich, 113
Edschmid, Kasimir, 2, 231
Ehrenfels, Christian von, 49
Einstein, Albert, 238
Eisenstein, Sergei, 22, 57, 278
Eisner, Lotte, 2, 4–5, 16, 19–20, 22, 24–5, 27, 28–9, 31, 35, 82, 221
Ellbon, Rio, 45
Elsaesser, Thomas, 2–6, 133
Epstein, Jean, 221
Erb, Wilhelm Heinrich, 50
Ermolieff, Joseph N., 222
Ewers, Hanns Heinz, 30

Faure, Élie, 163
Fehér, Friedrich, *28*, 135
Fejös, Pál, 191
Fellini, Federico, 188
Feyder, Jacques, 221
Fischer-Dieskau, Dietrich, 240
Fisher, Terence, 188
Flechsig, Paul Emil, 53–5
Fleck, Jacob and Luise, 191
Fleming, Ian, 171
Fleming, Victor, 188
Florey, Robert, 4
Frank, Paul, 136
Frederik, L. K., 81
Freisler, Fritz, 7, 133, 136, 192
French, R. W., 262
Freud, Sigmund, 43, 49–50, 53, 54–5, 59–60, 184, 238, 270
Freund, Karl, 16, 29, 136, 188
Friedrich, Caspar David, 16, 25
Fritz, Edmund, 191
Fritz, Walter, 136

Gale, Dorothy, 171
Gance, Abel, 8, 145–64, 221
Gardenour, Brenda, 109
Gasser, Lajos, 191

Geiser, Bruno, 53
Geller, Theresa L., 290–2, 294
Goebbels, Joseph, 32
Goethe, Johann Wolfgang von, 171, 240
Goetz, Carl, 137, 138–9, *139*, 142, 192, 197, *210*
Götz, Karl *see* Goetz, Carl
Greenaway, Peter, 188
Grelling, Richard, 160
Griffith, D. W., 145, 147, 148
Gronau, Ernst, *81*, *82*
Gurdjieff, Geogres I., 176
Guys, Angèle, 147

Haas, Willy, 21
Halbinger, Josefa, 57
Hales, Barbara, 42–3
Hall, Manly P., 187–8
Haller, Magda, 272, *275*
Hameister, Willy, 80, 81, 126
Hammid, Alexander, 292, 293
Harbou, Thea von, 16
Hardy, Robin, 188
Hatvani, Karoly, 197
Hausenstein, Wilhelm, 249
Heder, M. Beltran, 273
Heidegger, Martin, 100
Heim, Carlamaria, 57
Heine, Heinrich, 240
Heisenberg, Werner, 238
Helmetag, Charles H., 258
Herlth, Robert, 29
Hermann, Ludimar, 43
Herterich, Franz, *135*
Hesse, Hermann, 171
Hitchcock, Alfred, 22, 30, 250, 255–7
Hitler, Adolf, 42
Hobbes, Thomas, 110, 112
Hoeller, Stephan, 172, 176
Hoesch, Eduard, 191
Hoffmann, E. T. A., 184
Holm, Astrid, 179
Horak, Jan-Christopher, 42, 250
Horkheimer, Max, 32
Hughes Brothers, The, 188
Huntley, Raymond, 195
Huston, John, 188

Ihász, Aladár, 192, 197
Ihering, Herbert, 249
Illés, Eugen, 68

Ince, Ralph, 15
Ingram, Rex, 188

Jagger, Mick, 33
Janet, Pierre, 251
Jannings, Emil, 18
Janowitz, Hans, 20, 134–5
Jarmusch, Jim, 188
Jesus, Grovas, 284
Jiménez, Augustin, 282
Jodorowsky, Alejandro, 187–8
Joubé, Romuald, *146*, 147
Juarez, Benito, 267
Julian, Rupert, 184
Jung, Uli, 128–9

Kaes, Anton, 6, 42, 84, *95*
Kafka, Franz, 252, 256–7
Kahlo, Frida, 269
Kalbus, Oskar, 130
Kamenka, Alexandre, 222
Kandinsky, Vasily, 285
Kasten, Jürgen, 85–6
Kaufmann, Fritz, 51
Kelly, Richard, 188
Kende, Paula, 197
Kertész, Deszö, 191–2, 197
Kertész, Mihály, 191
Kettelhut, Fritz, 16, 29
Kipling, Rudyard, 152
Kirchner, Ernst Ludwig, *261*, 261, 285
Klein, César, 81
Klein, Charles, 8, 249, 250, 252–4
Klein-Rogge, Rudolf, 18, 227
Kokoschka, Oskar, 285
Koline, Nicolas, 223
Korda, Sándor, 191
Kracauer, Siegfried, 2, 4–5, 16, 18, 19–20, 22, 25, 28, 31–2, 35, 82, 230
Kraft-Ebbig, Richard von, 50
Krauß, Werner, *1*, *17*, 18, *23*, *34*, 143
Kryschanowskaja, Maria, 85
Kubrick, Stanley, 179, 188, 250, 255, 258–9, 261–2
Kühnberg, Leontine, 85
Kurtz, Rudolf, 20, 26, 82

Lagerlöf, Selma, 171–84, 186, 188
Lajthay, Károly, 8, 190–2, 194–6, *206*
Lamartine, Alphonse de, 152
Landry, Lionel, 153

INDEX OF NAMES

Lang, Fritz, 2, 4, 16, 21, 22, 24, 25, 27, 29, 35, 46, 99, 135, 153, 221, 227, 233, 249, 252
Langlois, Henri, 20
Leadbeater, C. W., 174, 177, 178–80
Lebius, Aenderly, 74
Lederle, Charles *see* Lajthay, Károly
Ledić, Franjo, 6, 8, 65–76, *66*, 67
Leffler, Robert, 69–70, 74
Lehmann, Rosamond, 297
Leigh, Richard, 187
Leiko, Marija, 85
Leni, Paul, 4, 22, 25–6, 27, 29, 184
Lenin, Vladimir, 41
L'Herbier, Marcel, 163, 221, 227
Liebknecht, Karl, 41
Liedtke, Harry, 16
Liguoro, Giuseppe de, 188
Lincoln, Henry, 187
Lissenko, Nathalie, 223
Lorre, Peter, 18, 118
Lovecraft, H. P., 171
Lubitsch, Ernst, 22, 65, 68
Lucas, George, 188
Ludendorff, Erich, 113
Lugosi, Bela, 191, 192, 195
Lukács, Georg, 31
Lundt, Grete, *135*
Lux, Margit, 191–3, *193*, 197
Luxemburg, Rosa, 41
Lynch, David, 188

McCormick, Richard, 83
McFarlane, James, 163
McGann, William C., 187
McGuire, Patricia, 297
Mack, Max, 16
Madero, Francisco I., 268
Madonna, 33
Magdeleno, Mauricio, 270
Martin, Karlheinz, *31*, 221
Marx, Karl, 238
Matheson, S. Richard, 171
May, Joe, 16
Mayer, Carl, 16, 20, 80, 126, 134–6, 143
Mayne, Judith, 104, 226
Megill, Allan, 246
Meinert, Rudolf, 134–5
Méliès, Georges, 141, 186, 270
Melville, Herman, 171
Mercury, Freddie, 33

Messter, Oskar, 65
Mierendorf, Kurt, 74
Milton, John, 171
Miyazaki, Hayao, 188
Monti, Maura, 282
Moore, Alan, 171
Morell, Sybill, 74
Morena, Erna, *31*, 45
Morris, Errol, 266
Mosjoukine, Ivan, 8, 220–3, *220*, 225–6, 230–3
Moussinac, Léon, 148
Munch, Edvard, 259, *260*
Murnau, F. W., 2, 7, 8, 16, 22, 24, 25, 29, 35, 70, 93–6, 104–6, 108, 110–12, 129, 136, 153, 163, 183, 190
Murphy, Richard, 86, 249, 254
Myl, Lene, 192, 195, 197

Negri, Pola, 65, 68
Neufeld, Max, 191
Nichols, Bill, 290
Nicholson, Jack, 179
Nicolella, Henry, 5, 118
Nielsen, Asta, 15–16
Nietzsche, Friedrich, 8, 43, 235–40, 243–6
Nin, Anaïs, 297
Nolan, Christopher, 188

Obersteiner, Heinrich, 44, 50
Obregón, Alvara, 268–9
Olcott, Henry Steel, 172
Oro, José, 282
Oro, Juan Bustillo, 8, 266, 269–71, 274–6, 278, 280–5
Oro, Manuel San Vicente, 282
Orozco, José Clemente, 268–9
Oswald, Richard, 16

Pabst, G. W., 16, 22, 27, 29
Palfreyman, Rachel, 288, 295
Pallme, Roberto, 137
Pánczél, Lajos, 192, 195, 196, *218*
Parikka, Jussi, 107
Pathé, Charles, 147, 148
Pavlovic, Miléne *see* Myl, Lene
Pechstein, Max, 285
Perczel, Oszkar, 197
Picasso, Pablo, 164
Piel, Harry, 15

306

INDEX OF NAMES

Piscator, Erwin, 271
Plato, 174, 178
Pocock, Judy, 261
Poe, Edgar Allan, 8, 130, 171, 250–1, 253–4, 259, 260, 263
Pommer, Erich, 20, 25, 26–7, 134, 143, 149
Pope, Alexander, 171
Porten, Henny, 15
Protazanov, Yakov, 222
Proyas, Alex, 188
Pynchon, Thomas, 171

Ramos, Samuel, 270
Reimann, Walter, 16
Reinert, Robert, 6, 41–3, 45, *46*, 51–2, 54, *56*–7
Reinhardt, Max, 2, 24, 25, 27
Reiniger, Lotte, 288
Rembrandt, 25
Renoir, Jean, 222
Réthey, Lajos, 192, 197
Rivera, Diego, 268–9
Röhrig, Walter, 16
Roldán, Emma, 272
Rowling, J. K., 171
Russell, Ken, 188
Rymer, James Malcolm, 171

Saint-Saëns, Camille, 155
Salt, Barry, 25, 26, 27
Salten, Lina, 68, 69, 74
Sarris, Andrew, 288–90, 298–9
Schadock, Hermann, 74
Schatzberg, Walter, 128–9
Scheunemann, Dietrich, 227
Schiele, Egon, 285
Schiller, Friedrich, 240
Schivelbusch, Wolfgang, 113
Schmedes, Erik, 135
Schnitzler, Arthur, 258, 261–2
Scholes, Robert, 296, 298
Schopenhauer, Arthur, 240
Schreber, Daniel Paul, 53–6, *59*, 60
Schreber, Moritz, 54
Schreck, Max, 18, 93
Schröter, Greta, 93
Schüfftan, Eugen, 16, 29
Schünzel, Reinhold, 16
Scott, Ridley, 188
Scott, Sir Walter, 171
Seeber, Guido, 16, 29, 30

Séverin-Mars, 147, 149, *152*
Shakespeare, William, 170–1, 181, 241, 245
Shelley, Mary, 171
Shklovsky, Victor, 262
Silberman, Marc, 287–9, 291, 292
Siodmak, Robert, 4
Siqueiros, David Alfaro, 268–9
Sjöström, Victor, 8, 169, 171–3, 178–9, 182–8, *186*
Soister, John, 5
Solo, Roberto, 270
Sonja, Magda, 135, *214*
Sophocles, 152
Spence, Lewis, 172
Spengler, Oswald, 42
Starevich, Ladislas, 222
Sternberg, Joseph von, 15
Stiasny, Philipp, 51
Stephen, Adeline Virginia *see* Woolf, Virginia
Sternberg, Josef von, 118
Stevenson, Robert, 188
Stevenson, Robert Louis, 270
Stoker, Bram, 8, 170–1, 190, 195
Stroheim, Erich von, 15
Svankmajer, Jan, 188
Svennberg, Tore, 173, *186*
Swift, Jonathan, 171
Szalkay, Lajos, 197
Szwarc, Jeannot, 188

Tarantino, Quentin, 170
Theimann, Paul, 222
Thoma, Hans, 25
Thompson, Kristin, 26, 224–5, 227
Thury, Elemér, 192, 197
Timar, Bela, 197
Titford, John, 294
Tolstoy, Leo, 117, *125*
Toomer, Jean, 177
Toro, Guillermo del, 173
Tourjansky, Viatcheslav, 222
Tourneur, Jacques, 188
Truffaut, François, 289–90, 298–9
t'Serstevens, Albert, 150
Tucholsky, Kurt, 21
Tuchten, Jenö, 194
Twardowski, Hans Heinrich von, *28*, *31*, 77, 80, *82*, *85*, *88*
Tybjerg, Casper, 172, 174, 185, *186*

307

INDEX OF NAMES

Uexküll, Jakob von, 93, 95, 100–12
Ulmer, Edgar G., 4
Urban, Max, 282
Urruchúa, Victor, 273–4, *275*

Vasconcelos, José, 268–9
Veidt, Conrad, 5, 7, 18, 129
Verne, Jules, 171
Vertov, Dziga, 107
Vidor, King, 15
Villa, Pancho, 268
Villatoro, Carlos, 272, 274
Volkoff, Alexandre, 222, 233
Vuillermoz, Émile, 153

Wachowskis, The, 188
Wagner, Fritz Arno, 16, 29
Wagner, Richard, 163
Walden, Harry, 136, 138, *139*, *140*, *142*
Wangenheim, Gustav von, 93
Warm, Hermann, 16, 20, 29
Watson, James, 8, 249–51

Webber, Melville, 8, 249–51
Wegener, Paul, 5, 7, 16, 30, 99, 183
Welles, Orson, 188, 255
Wells, H. G., 190, 192
West, Roland, 184
Whale, James, 4, 188
Whitman, Walt, 261–2
Wiene, Robert, 2, 5, 6, 7, 8, 15, 20, 77, 79, 80, 82, 99, 117–18, 124–30, 134–5, 145, 149, 183, 190, 191, 221, 230, 235, 257, 267
Wilde, Oscar, 171
Wilhelm II, 51
Winterstein, Eduard von, 45
Wong, Anna May, 187
Wood, Robin, 292–4, 296
Woolf, Virginia, 296–8
Worringer, Wilhelm, 20

Zapata, Emilio, 268
Zola, Émile, 160, 161
Zweig, Arnold, 95

INDEX OF FILM TITLES

Italic denotes figure

2001: A Space Odyssey, 188
8 ½, 188
99, 192

Ahí está el detalle, 284
Al son de la marimba, 284
Alice, 188
Alice in Wonderland, 188
Alraune, 16, 21, 191
Altered States, 188
Amapola del camino, 284
Angelo, das Mysterium des Schlosses see
    Angelo, Misterij Zmajgrada
Angelo, Misterij Zmajgrada, 6, 7, 68–75,
    68, 71, 73, 75
Ángel negro, El, 284
Angoissante aventure, L', 222
Asesino X, El, 284
Asi amaron nuestros padres, 284
Auberge rouge, L', 221

Backstairs, 16
Bat, The, 184
Beauty and the Beast, 187
Blackguard, The, 22
Blade Runner, 4, 188

Blood Tea and Red String, 188
Blow-up, 188
Blue Velvet, 188
Brasier ardent, Le, 8, 220–33, *223, 226,
    228, 231, 232*
Bride of Frankenstein, 188
Broken Blossoms, 145, 148–9
Brother, 187
Burning Soil, 70

Cabinet des Dr. Caligari, Das see
    Cabinet of Dr. Caligari, The
Cabinet of Dr. Caligari, The, 1, 2–5, 7,
    8, 15, 16, 17, *17*, 20, 21, 22, 23, 26,
    27, 28, 30, 33, 35, 36, 68, 76, 77,
    79, 80, 82, 86, 89, 99, 126, 128,
    129, 130, 133–6, 138, 141–3, 145,
    149, 150, 152, 153, 155, 159, 164,
    183–4, 190, 195, 221, 229, 232,
    250, 257, 267, 281
Cada loco con su tema, 284
Carmen, 68
Casablanca, 191
Cat and the Canary, The, 4, 184
Cheat, The, 147
Ciganska krv—Dobrotvorka Balkana, 76

INDEX OF FILM TITLES

Citizen Kane, 255
Clue, 117–18
Coeur fidèle, 221
Cornelie Aredt, 68
Crainquebille, 221
Cremaster Cycle, The, 188
Crow, The, 4

Dance of Reality, The, 188
Dark City, 4, 188
Dead Man, 188
Destiny, 16, 17, 22, 25, 26, 160
Devil Rides Out, The, 188
Dixième Symphonie, La, 149, 151, 158
Dr. Mabuse, der Spieler see Dr. Mabuse the Gambler
Dr. Mabuse the Gambler, 16, 17, 21, 22, 221, 227, 233
Dr. X, 191
Don Juan et Faust, 221
Don Porfirio times, 284
Donnie Darko, 188
Dos Monjes, 8, 266–7, 271–85, 272, 275, 279
Dracula, 195
Drakula halála, 8, 190–218, 193, 196, 201, 218

Ecce Homo, 150
EXistenZ, 188
Expulsion, The, 70
Exterminating Angel, The, 188
Eyes Wide Shut, 188, 250, 255, 258–9, 261

Fall of the House of Usher, The, 8, 9, 249–51
Fantasia, 18
Fantasma del convento, El, 283
Faust (1926), 18, 25, 35, 291
Faust (1994), 188
Fight Club, 35
Fountain, The, 188
Four Troublesome Heads, The, 186
Four Weddings and a Funeral, 299
Frankenstein, 4, 188
From Hell, 188
From Morning to Midnight, 16, 21, 31, 221, 229

Genuine, 5, 6, 7, 8, 77–89, 78, 80, 81, 82, 85, 88, 126, 129, 130, 221, 230

Golem, The 16, 17
Golem: How He Came Into the World, 99, 183
Gossette, 222

Hands of Orlac, The, 8, 16, 17, 191, 235–46, 236, 237, 239, 240, 242, 243, 245
Harry Potter films, 188
Haunted Castle, The, 70
Haus zum Mond, Das, 3, 3
Häxan, 188
Hoffmanns Erzählungen, 191
Holy Mountai, The, 188
Hombre sin rostro, El, 284
Homunculus, 42
Huapango, 284
Huella de unos labios, La, 284

I Walked with a Zombie, 188
Inauguration of the Pleasure Dome, The, 187
Inception, 35, 188
Inferno, 7, 133, 135, 135–7
Inferno, L', 188
Intolerance, 147
Invocation of My Demon, 187

J'accuse, 8, 145–64, 146, 152, 157
Jeune martyre, La, 151
Joyless Street, 16, 22
Júlisa kisasszony, 191

Kean, 222, 233
Klub samoubojica, 68
Königin Draga, 192

L. A. Confidential, 4
Last Laugh, The, 22, 25, 136
Let the Right One In, 183
Lidércnyomás, 191
Life and Death of 9413: A Hollywood Extra, The, 9
London After Midnight, 184
Lucifer Rising, 187

M, 18
Madame Dubarry, 22, 68
Magician, The, 188
Maison du mystère, La, 222
Man Who Would Be King, The, 188

INDEX OF FILM TITLES

Mandarin, The, 5, 7, 133, 136–43, 137, 138, 139, 140, 142, 192
Mania, Die Geschichte einer Zigarettenarbeiterin, 68
Marchand de Plaisir, Le, 221–2
Mary Poppins, 188
Mater Dolorosa, 153, 158
Matrix Trilogy, The, 188
Medallíon del crimen, El, 284
Meshes of the Afternoon, 288, 288, 290–5, 291, 293, 295, 297, 298, 300, 301
Metropolis, 5, 16, 17, 25, 33, 35, 46, 99, 249, 291
Mexico de mis recuerdes, 284
Misterio del rostro pálido, El, 284
Monja casada, virgen y mártir, 283
Mountain Cat, The, 22
Mountain Eagle, The, 22
Müde Tod, Der see Destiny
Mujer murciélago, La, 282
Mulholland Drive, 188
Mummy, The, 188
Murders in the Rue Morgue, 4
Mystery of the Wax Museum, 191

Naked Lunch, 188
Napoléon, 146, 147, 148, 155, 163, 164
Nászdal, 191
Nerven see Nerves
Nerves, 5, 6, 16, 41–3, 45–9, 46, 47, 49, 51–4, 56–61, 58, 60
Nibelungen, Die see Nibelungen, The
Nibelungen, The, 17, 27, 291
Night of the Demon, 188
Nosferatu, 2, 7, 8, 16, 17, 22, 33, 35, 93–100, 94, 96, 97, 98, 99, 103, 104–14, 109, 113, 129, 160, 183, 190, 231

Ombres qui passent, Les, 222
Orlac's Hände see Hands of Orlac, The
Orpheus, 187

Pandora's Box, 16, 27, 33, 192
Pan's Labyrinth, 173
Passion, 22
Peter Pan, 188
Phantom, 16
Phantom Carriage, The, 8, 169, 171–4, 179, 181–7, 182, 186

Phantom of the Opera, The, 184
Pi, 188
Pinocchio, 188
Pleasure Garden, The, 22
Ponyo, 188
Porco Rosso, 188
Propast svijeta, 68
Prospero's Books, 188

Raskolnikow, 7, 8, 21, 117–30, 119, 124, 127
Roman de renard,Le, 222
Roue, La, 146, 147, 152, 153, 154, 156, 157, 164

Santa Sangre, 188
Schreckensnacht auf Schloss Drachenegg see Angelo, Misterij Zmajgrada
Secrets of a Soul, 16
Sens de la mort, Le, 222
Seventh Seal, The, 187
Shadows and Fog, 250, 255, 257, 258
Shining, The, 179–80
Sixth Sense, The, 35
Skæbnesvangre Opfindelse, Den see Strange Case of Dr. Jekyll and Mr. Hyde, The
Sleeping Beauty, 188
Snow White and the Seven Dwarfs, 188
Somewhere in Time, 188
Souriante Madame Beudet, La, 221, 226, 227
Spies, 18, 25
Spione see Spies
Spirited Away, 188
Star Wars, 188
Strange Case of Dr. Jekyll and Mr. Hyde, The, 270, 274
Street, The, 16
Student of Prague, The, 17, 30

Tartuffe, 18, 25
Telltale Heart, The, 8, 249–50, 252, 253
Tesoro de Pancho Villa, El, 282
THX 1138, 188
Tláni, az elvarázsolt hercegasszony, 191
Topo, El, 188
Touch of Evil, 255
Trial, The, 188
Trilby, 191
Twin Peaks: Fire Walk with Me, 188

311

INDEX OF FILM TITLES

U borbi sa suncem, 68

Vampyr, 188
Varieté see *Variety*
Variety, 22, 291
Vera, 188
Von morgens bis Mitternacht see *From Morning to Midnight*
Vorrei morir, 206

Wachsfigurenkabinett, Das see *Waxworks*
Warning Shadows, 16
Waxworks, 4, 16, 17, 22, 26, 27, 34, 291
When Were You Born?, 187
Wicker Man, The, 188
Wild Strawberries, 187
Wizard of Oz, The, 188
Woman on the Moon, 25
Wrong Man, The, 250, 255–6, 256

Yo soy tu padre, 270

EU representative:
Easy Access System Europe
Mustamäe tee 50, 10621 Tallinn, Estonia
Gpsr.requests@easproject.com

www.ingramcontent.com/pod-product-compliance
Lightning Source LLC
Chambersburg PA
CBHW070749020526
44115CB00032B/1552